Governance
for Sustainable
Development

FIVE OECD CASE STUDIES

OECD

ORGANISATION FOR ECONOMIC CO-OPERATION AND DEVELOPMENT

ORGANISATION FOR ECONOMIC CO-OPERATION AND DEVELOPMENT

Pursuant to Article 1 of the Convention signed in Paris on 14th December 1960, and which came into force on 30th September 1961, the Organisation for Economic Co-operation and Development (OECD) shall promote policies designed:

- to achieve the highest sustainable economic growth and employment and a rising standard of living in Member countries, while maintaining financial stability, and thus to contribute to the development of the world economy;
- to contribute to sound economic expansion in Member as well as non-member countries in the process of economic development; and
- to contribute to the expansion of world trade on a multilateral, non-discriminatory basis in accordance with international obligations.

The original Member countries of the OECD are Austria, Belgium, Canada, Denmark, France, Germany, Greece, Iceland, Ireland, Italy, Luxembourg, the Netherlands, Norway, Portugal, Spain, Sweden, Switzerland, Turkey, the United Kingdom and the United States. The following countries became Members subsequently through accession at the dates indicated hereafter: Japan (28th April 1964), Finland (28th January 1969), Australia (7th June 1971), New Zealand (29th May 1973), Mexico (18th May 1994), the Czech Republic (21st December 1995), Hungary (7th May 1996), Poland (22nd November 1996), Korea (12th December 1996) and the Slovak Republic (14th December 2000). The Commission of the European Communities takes part in the work of the OECD (Article 13 of the OECD Convention).

Publié en français sous le titre :
La gouvernance pour le développement durable
ÉTUDE DE CINQ PAYS DE L'OCDE

Foreword

Faced with the growing challenge of implementing the sustainable development goal effectively, the OECD launched studies on governance for sustainable development in five OECD countries presenting efforts to develop truly integrated frameworks of effective institutions. The five selected countries, namely Canada, Japan, Germany, Netherlands, United Kingdom, while presenting many varied economic, environmental, social and cultural conditions, have all made efforts over the past decade to elaborate an approach to sustainable development. The studies have four main objectives: they present information on general aspects of the national system that matter for sustainable development; highlight specific institutional arrangements; describe decision-making mechanisms and main learning including successes and doubts as well as selective innovative initiatives. The first section of the book is an analysis which presents the main findings and conclusions of the studies.

The report was co-ordinated by Mr. Frédéric Bouder, OECD Public Management Service, who also prepared the overall analysis. The case studies were prepared by Mr. Frédéric Bouder (Canada); Professor Martin Jänicke, Mr. Helge Jörgens, Ms. Kirsten Jörgensen and Mr. Ralf Nordbeck (Germany); Mr. Mineo Kato and Ms. Emiko Ray (Japan); Mr. Frédéric Bouder and Mr. Philipp Fink (Netherlands); Mr. James Medhurst (United Kingdom). The report is published on the responsibility of the Secretary-General of the OECD.

Table of Contents

Improving Governance for Sustainable Development: Learning from Experience in Five OECD Countries

Overview

Introduction

OECD countries usually enjoy comparatively well-established and sophisticated public administration systems based on the rule of law, rational specialisation of tasks, transparency and accountability mechanisms, a professional and highly skilled civil service etc. It is generally accepted that these elements constitute building blocks of good governance. It could be deduced from this that OECD countries are well equipped to carry forward the complex challenge of sustainable development,[1] and that only minor adjustments would need to be put in place. In this context well functioning institutions would already be in place and achieving sustainable development would only require a political commitment to apply well-defined policy objectives.

The main question is, however, to consider to what extent these "well-functioning institutions" really do operate from a sustainable development point of view. As noted in the Brundtland report of 1987, institutions tend to be "independent, fragmented and working (…) with closed decision-making processes". (WCED, 1987, p. 310). Economic, environmental and social trends tend to show that sustainable development has not yet been achieved. Of course some "limits stem from the increased complexity of the challenges facing society, often characterised by small but non-eligible probabilities of catastrophic break-down in the longer-term" (OECD, 2001 p. 45). But are these complexities only "technical" or empirical or is there also a management issue that prevents progress towards sustainable development? Despite international and national commitments expressed on various occasions and at the highest level,[2] there has been a strong assumption that current governance models are not well suited to carry out the shifts that sustainable development implies. In order to identify what could be the main barriers to sustainable development stemming from governance practices, the OECD Public Management Service (PUMA) has undertaken case studies on "Governance of Sustainable Development" in five countries, which vary according to their location, size and political and administrative traditions. The case studies have examined the main challenges, trends, issues and practices in policies related to sustainable development of Canada, Germany, Japan, the Netherlands, and the United Kingdom.

Public sector institutions in OECD countries have proved to function in a certain context, for example to deliver efficient and effective services to citizens. But they may not be automatically suited to address new challenges with a high level of complexity. This difficulty is especially noticeable when issues require longer-term and sustained commitments. For example OECD countries have shown difficulties in grasping with the issue of ageing populations, which entails both a high degree of complexity and require making choices for the longer term. Among the main reasons for this is the pace of electoral cycles (about 5 years) which is an incentive to focus on short-term issues. Sustainable development is an intergenerational issue and as such solutions require strategic choices for the longer-term and a capacity to maintain commitments over time, as well as a capacity to provide decision-makers with adequate information and knowledge to support their decisions.

In addition, sustainable development is typically a cross-cutting issue. It implies creating a "triple bottom line", that is, to take into consideration all economic, environmental and social aspects before making decisions. This creates a new institutional difficulty, not only because it is challenging governments' capacity to act rapidly, but also mostly because it contradicts the way policies have traditionally been formulated and developed. The evolution of the modern state has been towards an increasing degree of sectoral specialisation, in order to respond more effectively to complex and differentiated problems. The inflation, until recently, in a number of specialised ministries and agencies provides a good illustration of this trend. For example, to cope with environmental matters most OECD countries have established specific environmental ministries since the 1970s. However the integrated nature of the sustainable development challenge calls for new capacities within the government machinery to achieve specific priorities and targets under a common "umbrella". In addition to this sustainable development may require some specific and new institutions to be established. One of the main challenges highlighted in the case studies presented below is to examine whether building new institutional frameworks, or whether the existing policy development and decision-making practices should be adapted in order to address sustainable development goals.

Sustainable development is of critical importance for all citizens, it engages choices that will affect essential aspects of our lifestyles, and, being typically cross-cutting, it should take into consideration various conflicting interests. Therefore it also requires efforts from society as a whole and the government commitments would become useless if they were not to be paralleled by similar commitments by the business sector and civil society. However the necessary broadly-based involvement of citizens is very challenging and requires well defined mechanisms and management practices to associate government and stakeholders in finding solutions, in particular given the conflicting nature of many economic, environmental and social issues among various groups, and the difficulty to find "win-win-win" solutions that would reconcile economic, environmental and social objectives.

Even though the countries covered by the case studies differ in their environmental, social and economic context, as well as in governance structures, traditions and political modus operandi, they face problems with similar issues when drawing up and implementing sustainable development strategies. Three common sets of issues have been identified by OECD work and were reinforced by the case studies: the challenge of policy integration, the need to improve interactions between government and society, and the need to create a longer-term view in government for dealing with the intergenerational challenges of sustainable development.

I.   The challenge of policy integration: Towards coherent government practice?

Sustainable development concerns essential human activities, and sustainable development goals are often expected to dramatically affect both individual and public choice to modify production and consumption patterns. One could expect strong interest from society as a whole for this ambitious and over-arching objective. In the countries surveyed it appeared quite clearly, on the contrary, that sustainable development is generally not very well known by the general public, even when economic, environmental and social concerns are high. In Germany for example, where environmental awareness has traditionally been high and has even been increasing in recent years,[3] the term sustainable development is known by only 13 per cent of the population (BMU 2000, p68).

Raising awareness and making commitments

The lack of public awareness of sustainable development issues, is not restricted to the general public, but is also apparent in members of the civil service. This can be attributed to an incorrect perception of sustainable development, considered to be a new name for "environmental management". Misconceptions and lack of communication are not only misleading for the general public, but could also impede the successful implementation of sustainable development policies. The lack of awareness in the civil service has been largely attributed to insufficient training. Improved mobility could also be beneficial. In the Netherlands the considerable degree of mobility of senior civil servants combined with a low degree of politicisation of the civil service is perceived as contributing to rising awareness. The recent establishment of central recruitment procedures for higher civil servants is reinforcing this trend. The Canadian and in the Netherlands case studies illustrate this in regard to certain policy areas concerned with greening government actions, such as the green procurement initiatives.

Another obstacle to developing sustainable development awareness is the fact that concern for the environment is often less steadfast among the general public than concern for economic and social development. Short-term considerations about levels of income and full employment are given priority. As a consequence the studies underlined the fact that during economic recessions, economic policies are preferred to sustainable development policies. This expresses itself not only in the choice of instruments, but also, as in the case of Canada and the Netherlands, in budget cut backs for those institutions dealing with sustainable development issues. Further, the issue of poor policy coherence can also be the result of a lack of overall co-ordination between policy sectors, actors and agencies, as in the Canadian case.

The lack of awareness, beyond specific environmental groups, has long been mirrored by an overall deficit of central high level political commitment and in the different policy sectors. Such was the case in Germany, where, until very recently, sustainable development lacked top-level government commitment by the Chancellery, and was only a concern of the lower chamber of the German federal parliament (Bundestag) through the reports of its Enquête Committees. A pivotal role was played by the two Enquête Commissions on "Protection of Mankind and the Environment" (1992-1994, 1995-1998) and resulted in the formulation of the triple bottom line definition of sustainable development and management principles. It was the pressure from the Bundestag that led the federal government to begin preparing the national sustainable development plan. As a result, the federal government set up the National Council on Sustainable Development to pursue the formulation of the national sustainable development plan and the "Green Cabinet" to support sustainable development policy integration. Canada explicitly stated that the need to restore economic prosperity was a major obstacle to a developing a commitment going beyond rhetoric until the end of the 1990s. Looking at the experiences presented in the case studies it is very likely that bottom-up initiatives would not be sufficient to balance a lack of high level commitment and that such a situation could hinder the long-term goals of sustainable development in favour of short-term economic goals.

Policy integration between the international and national level has usually been an important driving force for setting the agenda at the domestic level: policy priorities defined by each of the five countries are mainly related to the fulfilment of international obligations, the most pressing being the attainment of the CO_2 reduction goals outlined in the UNFCCC Kyoto Protocol. In countries with a well-established tradition of environmental management, like Germany and the Netherlands, there has been a two-way relationship between national and international priorities. Already in its initial phase in the 1970s, German environmental policy had to a surprising extent tried to incorporate aspects linked to environmentally sound economic development, which only two decades later were internationally established as key elements of the concept of sustainable development. In Canada, Japan and the United Kingdom the emergence of the concept of sustainable development has been partly driven by the international debate that led to the Montreal Protocol (1987) and the Rio Declaration (1992) and the Kyoto Protocol (1997).

The 1994 UK strategy for sustainable development was based on an earlier White Paper, *This Common Inheritance*. Since this publication, policies and institutions have undergone a considerable change. The recent policy changes have been caused by the devolution of central authority, which not only decentralised general policy-making but also sustainable development policies. A further factor influencing policy change not only in the UK, but also in the other European countries covered by the case studies, has been the European Union (EU). The initiation of environmental action plans and the environmental and social legislation has led to the inclusion of the social dimension in UK sustainable development policies. Similarly, the Rio Conference was the starting point for the Japanese move towards sustainable development policies. The Japanese Council of Ministers for Global Environment Conservation drew up the Japanese National Agenda 21 Action Plan in December 1993, which formulates the base for the integration of sustainable development in government policy-making. Further important steps are the reform of the Basic Environmental Law in 1993, which replaced two previous older laws on environmental regulation, and the introduction of the Basic Environment Plan in 1994 laying out goals to be achieved by all ministries. In Canada, federal government is the most influential figure in the process of formulation and integration of sustainable development issues. The first steps were taken relatively early as a result of the growing public awareness created by the signing of the Montreal Protocol in 1987 establishing measures controlling the production and emissions of ozone depleting substances. In the wake of the Brundtland Report and the preparations towards the Rio Conference, the Canadian government launched a national Green Plan defining policies and actions for sustainable development, in which it also committed itself to substantial rises in public environmental expenditure.

This commitment, driven by a mix of international and domestic concerns, or in some countries resulting primarily from implementation of international agreements, has influenced the nature of government strategic choices for managing the implementation of sustainable policies. Canada created a comprehensive framework to raise the issue of sustainable development within government and society. Following the Rio Summit the main government commitment was made in the "Guide to Green Government" (1995). This document presented the first government "corporate" view of the sustainable development challenge, established a framework for action and launched the process for all departments to elaborate sustainable development strategies, as well as "greening" the budget: that is, incorporating the environment and

13

sustainable development dimension into federal budgets. A slightly different path was followed by Germany, which has been active in promoting concrete environmental initiatives, for example in the field of climate policy, rather than laying the emphasis on general issues of sustainable development. Only in 2001 is a national strategy emerging on sustainable development.

Institutional responses

It has been said that government functions have been evolving towards more and more specialisation over time. In the countries surveyed, this evolution raised issues about the capacity to develop both coherent approaches and responses throughout the government machinery. This usually implied institutional arrangements of two sorts: attempts were made to develop new working practices within government in order to overcome traditional segmentation, and on the other hand new institutions were established to foster integration.

The individual policy responses to the challenges posed by sustainable development have been very different. This can be attributed to the different levels of commitment to the subject, but also is the result of differences in political systems and their respective cultures. Initial strategic choices have had significant consequences for the challenge of policy integration. The "comprehensive" approach followed by Canada and the United Kingdom implies a capacity to diffuse a coherent message to all public entities and to ensure their responsiveness. It also implies oversight through effective steering mechanisms. If not well managed, unfocussed efforts can indeed run the risk of being followed by little effective action and could promote a culture of "talking rather than acting". An approach focusing on environmentally sustainable economic development seems to facilitate concrete achievements. In Germany and in the Netherlands it has long been supported by a clear distribution of responsibilities as well as clear enforcement responsibilities within the environment ministry. This situation created a sense of leadership, but it also made the emergence of the notion of "sustainable development" more difficult. In Germany and in the Netherlands the notion of "sustainability" has long been restricted to environmental matters. This situation does not reflect the complexity of the issues at stake, which supposes a high level of awareness in society to build support among non-environmental interest groups.

The following table gives a non-exhaustive overview of the main recent institutional developments, which have taken place in the five countries covered by the case studies.

Moving to policy integration

Sustainable development can only be achieved if the challenges implied by this concept are clearly stated. In the Netherlands the government response has

Table I.   **Main incentive actors at national level**

	Main driving force within government
Netherlands	The Ministry for Housing, Spatial Planning and the Environment (VROM)
Germany	Federal Parliament Enquête Commission
United Kingdom	Cabinet Office
Japan	Prime Minister's office
Canada	"Corporate" commitment at federal and provincial level

for example been to consider sustainable development as the result of sound environmental management, which provided the basis for environmental policy plans. It is becoming clearer that sectoral policies are not sufficient and that a holistic approach must be chosen.

A truly holistic approach should encompass the various levels of government. This poses great strains on the governance systems and the government's organisation. As already underlined government's organisation in an industrial society is classified by specialisation, expertise and high autonomy. This can explain the heterogeneity of departmental responses to the same topic or, as in some cases, a lack of awareness towards sustainable development issues. Many OECD Member countries have also introduced wide reaching decentralisation measures to increase efficiency.

There is generally a sense that practices leading to more integration of objectives and action should take place both "vertically"– that is across international, national and sub-national levels of government – and "horizontally" – that is between the entities of a particular tier of government. The case studies focused mainly on horizontal integration at national level, with some less detailed developments concerning vertical integration across levels of government, and horizontal integration at the sub-national level. This focus on the national level must is linked to the nature of the available data but it should not be deduced that other aspects are irrelevant.

The different state of sustainable development policy integration and implementation can be attributed to the different driving forces in the concerned countries. The "incentive actors" in the countries studied differ. In some cases they are also the centres of responsibility, responsible for overall policy formulation and coherence.

Horizontal integration

Although different in their results, the countries studied have chosen similar paths to communicate sustainable development objectives throughout the government machinery, including some kind of strategic planning, usually developed

Table 2. Main institutional developments

	Institution building	Legislative changes	National sustainable development plans	Sector specific policies	International co-operation
Canada	National Round Table on Environment and the Economy (1993). Commissioner for the Environment and Sustainable Development (1995). Canadian Environmental Assessment Agency (1995). Federal Climate Secretariat (1998).	Canadian Environmental Assessment Act (1992). National Round Table on the Environment and the Economy Act (1993).	National strategies (in 1997 and 2001).	Toxic Emission Reduction Programme (ARET). Government *Greening* Programme.	Active contribution to the establishment of international agreements and initiatives. Code of Conduct for Responsible Fishing, various Arctic protection agreements.
Germany	National Council for Sustainable Development (2000). "Green Cabinet" (2000). Federal Energy Agency.	Amendment of the German Constitution to include sustainability goals (1994). Sector legislation on increased environmental protection (notably climate protection measures).	Pending.	Main emphasis has been purely environmental. almost all non-environmental policy sectors have been engaged in environmental activities. National Climate Protection Programme (2000) Programme for Sustainable Agriculture (2000).	Active participation in the preparation of UNCED (1992) and RIO+10 Summit in Johannesburg (2002) and strong co-operation with UNCSD. Strong emphasis on integration of environmental issues in development co-operation (technology transfer).
Japan	Ministry of the Environment (2001) Special Committee on Environment and Trade. Special Committee on UNCED Follow-up. Council of Ministers for Global Environment Conservation (1989). Council for Sustainable Development (1996).	Basic Environment Act (1993). Basic Environment Plan (1994). Action Plan for Greening Government Operations (1995). Conservation and Management of Marine Living Resources Law (1996). Environmental Impact Assessment Law (1997). Basic Law on Food, Agriculture and Rural Areas (1999). Law for Promotion of Introduction of Advanced Sustainable Farming System (1999). Law on the Rational Use of Energy (1999).	National Agenda 21 Action Plan (1993).	Main emphasis has been purely environmental; almost all non-environmental policy sectors have been engaged in environmental activities. Total Allowable Catch System for fishing industry (1997). Ecological Tax System (1998). Recycling Requirements for Building Wood (2000).	Development aid for developing countries to promote sustainable development. Japan also supports technology transfer and capacity building measures.

Table 2. **Main institutional developments** (*cont.*)

	Institution building	Legislative changes	National sustainable development plans	Sector specific policies	International co-operation
Netherlands	Reorganisation of the Ministry for Agriculture. Reorganisation of the Environment Ministry (1991). Environment Inspectorate (1991).	Environment Management Act (1993). Accessibility and Mobility Bill (2000). Pig Restriction Act (1997). See also NEPP.	National sustainable development policy setting in National Environmental Policy Plans (NEPP) since 1989 and continually revised every 5 years.	New Water Administrative Agreement (2001). Strategy on the Management of Substances Programme (2001). Ecological Tax Reform (2001) Implementation of Kyoto mechanisms. Mainly voluntary agreements for the implementation of NEPP.	Active support to international environment agreements and UNCED and Rio+10 Earth Summit in Johannesburg 2002. Environmental development co-operation projects with developing and transition countries.
United Kingdom	Environment Agency (1996). Sustainable Development Commission (2001). Reorganisation of the DETR to DEFRA including nutritional consumer affairs (2001). "Green Ministers" Committee. Cabinet Environment Committee. Environmental Audit Select Committee. Agriculture and Environment Biotechnology Commission (2000). Department for International Development (1997).	Environment Act (1995) Statutory instruments referring to devolution process, Government of Wales Act, Government of Scotland Act. Government of Northern-Ireland Act. Local Government Bill (2000).	Pending.	Introduction of ecological tax system: CCL (2001). Tax incentives for urban revitalisation.	Inclusion of sustainable development principles in development co-operation policies.

by the executive and vetted and controlled by the legislative. At the same time the Netherlands and Germany were finalising their own plans, although they have a well-developed practice of environmental plans. Canada and the United Kingdom have both introduced strategy papers formulated at the level of the Prime Minister and which are concerned primarily with government operations.

Instead of developing a body of detailed legislation, general guidelines form in most countries the basis for the overall public commitment. The Canadian report "A Guide to Green Government" and the United Kingdom strategy document "A Better Quality of Life – A Strategy for Sustainable Development for the UK" play similar roles towards improving inter-governmental coherence and integration of sustainable development in policy-making. The Canadian federal government report, which is a statutory requirement, also contains, next to procedures on how to "green" federal government operations, detailed departmental strategies and individual policy goals to reach sustainable development. Not only do the individual federal departmental goals have to be developed on a participatory basis and results oriented, but they also have to be comprehensive. This means that the individual departmental commitment towards attaining sustainable development should also be present in all their internal operations. It is interesting to note that these commitments are addressing the question of sustainable development policy integration primarily through enhanced sector responses, mainly choosing environmental policies as a driving force.

Usually, countries have given priority to progress in specific sectors, typically those where domestic tensions and international commitments require prompt action, like transport, agriculture, energy. Fully cross-sectoral oriented initiatives creating a"triple bottom line" commitment remain quite limited although they may address more adequately the peculiarities of the sustainable development challenge: the United Kingdom launched a programme of urban revitalisation, trying to combine social, environmental and economic aspects of urbanisation. The Canadian experience showed that rather optimistic attempts to make all policies sustainable within a limited time frame have proved to be unrealistic with regard to the complexity of the issues.

The countries covered in the case studies have tried to operationalise this overall commitment in various ways. The favoured answer is the establishment of inter-ministerial steering groups, such as the "Green" Cabinet in Germany, Council of Ministers for Global Environment Conservation in Japan or the "Green" Ministers Committee in the United Kingdom. These bodies try to guarantee sustainable development policy integration in central government as a crosscutting theme across all the departments. In the German and UK cases, departmental heads of the ministries concerned by sustainable development meet with high ranking political officials of the government. The Dutch Ministry for Housing, Spatial Planning and the Environment (VROM) is the leading government agency in matters concerning sustainable development. VROM is responsible for the co-ordination of the National Environment Policy Plans (NEPP) between the involved ministries and is considered to have the overall expertise in sustainable development issues.

In addition to the arrangements at Ministerial and Cabinet level other institutions have been established to improve horizontal integration. All countries have been very active in creating specialised institutions of either an independent or government nature to enforce integration and development of sustainable development strategies, while at the same time preferring not to introduce a new line ministry. The various new bodies also reflect the different conceptions of sustainable development challenges. These institutions can also fulfil specialised duties such as the Canadian Environmental Assessment Agency, which is charged with environmental impact studies and so advises the federal government. Independent bodies such as the various national councils on sustainable development are multi-stakeholder discussion forums designed to initiate public debates and advise the government on policy matters.

However, the creation of the Canadian Commissioner for the Environment and Sustainable Development is a novelty. This independent federal body is charged with a yearly "Green" report before the federal parliament on federal government performance on environment and sustainable development issues, especially the implementation and attainment of the government's sustainable development goals. It not only monitors the government, but can also recommend better practices. The United Kingdom established the Environmental Audit Select Committee of the House of Commons, which also plays a similar role in controlling, monitoring government's progress and recommending better practices, but the government is under no statutory obligation to follow these recommendations.

In the United Kingdom, next to the "Green" Ministers Committee, the Performance Innovation Unit is also responsible for sector specific administrative coherence. Even if not specifically concerned with sustainable development issues this Unit is charged with reviewing overall departmental policy coherence under the heading "Joined-Up Government".

Vertical integration

Although their degree of autonomy and discretion may vary, sub-national governments are responsible for tasks with a direct impact on sustainable development, including town planning, local transport, sewage systems, refuse collection and water supply. Therefore the implementation of international commitments like, for example, introducing "Agenda 21" requires a good interaction between levels of government including support from central government and commitment at the local level. In Japan, the Government supports Local "Agenda 21" initiatives, and there are at least 28 local "Agenda 21s" out of a total of 47 prefectures and

12 designated metropolitan cities involving about 73 per cent of the population. The Government provides assistance to the local authorities for their own voluntary and independent environmental activities – for instance, for the establishment of local "Agenda 21s", and for international co-operation at the local authorities level. Local authorities are directly involved in the implementation of laws, regulations and guidelines, and in the observation, measurement and control of pollution, etc. regarding conservation of the environment.

All countries have tried to improve vertical coherence in order to better manage the implementation of sustainable development goals across levels of government. According to the degree of constitutional autonomy enjoyed by sub-national government, the perception of the balance between the objective of policy consistency across levels of government (national, sub-national and local) and the need to protect sub-national autonomy has been quite uneven. In federal and decentralised countries there has been concern about strengthening coherence mechanisms, while in traditionally centralised systems like Japan or the United Kingdom the question of ensuring local ownership of sustainable development goals was essential.

Maintaining the right balance between the need to integrate policy goals throughout levels of government, the protection of sub-national autonomy to meet constitutional or legal requirements and the need to ensure local capacity to adapt to sustainable development, is a difficult challenge. Obviously these conflicting priorities affect to a greater extent federal political systems, where the share of responsibilities between levels of government is very rigid.

The relationship between national and sub-national governments on critical issues from the point of view of sustainable development is sometimes problematic, particularly in federal countries. In Canada, for example, jurisdictional disputes, especially over ownership and control of natural resources, exacerbate federal/provincial relations. As in other OECD countries, the five countries surveyed have been decentralising policy responsibilities and moving decision-making to the sub-national level in a number of critical areas in order improve efficiency. Although the main debates and driving forces behind devolution were political and related to sustainable development, the necessity to meet sustainable development policy goals better could also be a significant factor. The most recent initiative has been the devolution process in the United Kingdom (see Box 1).

But the main constraint to implementing sustainable development across levels of government remains the inadequacy of traditional co-ordination mechanisms in order to established truly integrated practices between levels of government. In Germany the responsibilities for sustainable development fall under environmental policies, which are divided between the federal and sub-national governments. One of the main instruments to induce policy coherence

20

Box 1. **Devolution and Sustainable Development in the United Kingdom**

Central government has delegated sustainable development responsibilities to the recently devolved sub-national assemblies of Northern Ireland, Wales and the Scottish Parliament and their regional development agencies as well as the Greater London Authority. The new assemblies will have to follow not only economic goals, but are also required to monitor sustainable development strategies at the sub-national level. The United Kingdom central government has widened the responsibilities of these bodies to promote their own respective economic, social and environmental well being. The Local Government Bill (2000) requires that all local authorities adopt local "Agenda 21" strategies. However, central government still has considerable influence on the drafting of regional and local sustainable development strategies through their regional representation offices (Government Offices). To facilitate the drafting of regional and local sustainable development strategies, the local authorities representative organisations have developed a checklist for local authority sustainable development policy-making, emphasising in particular budget policies.

---

is the Conference of Environmental Ministers of the federal and *Länder* governments. Due to the lack of an overall holistic approach to sustainable development and its low position on the political agendas, there is still no formal co-ordination instrument between central and sub-national levels of government explicitly related to sustainable development policies. The case is slightly different for the other federal state covered in the case studies, Canada. A thorough co-ordination of federal and sub-national levels is impaired due to the relatively large autonomy of the Canadian provinces. Co-ordination takes place in specific sector issues, such as fishing or climate change (creation of the Federal Climate Change Secretariat). Co-ordination instruments are the subjects of lengthy negotiations between the federal and provincial governments. Even though some Provinces have been very active in devising and implementing sustainable development strategies, not all Provinces show the same level of commitment, leading to an unequal state of affairs.

One of the main difficulties in implementing sustainable development goals is related to the existing barriers to concrete co-operation across levels of government. Countries with a federal political system, such as Germany and Canada, seem to be experiencing more problems than unitary states: Japan, the UK and the Netherlands. This is partly due to the larger circle of interests at political levels included in the political process of federal systems, which have to be accounted for in the decision-making process. This is also partly due to specific institutional rigidities. In Canada there are numerous initiatives and programmes run by federal departments to assist Canadians in making sustainable development decisions at the community level.

Key policy tools for integration

The case studies suggest the use of various policy tools that contribute to improving policy integration. These include:

- Greening of accounts and budget
- Greening of government operations
- Performance management systems
- Environmental impact analysis
- Evaluation and systematic cost benefits analysis
- Accountability mechanisms.

Most of these tools have been neither extensively used nor applied on a systematic basis, except specific regulatory tools, including alternative to regulations. Interestingly, the countries studied, with the exception of Japan, have introduced new regulatory instruments, favouring agreements with target groups, rather than direct regulations. Voluntary Environmental Agreements (VAEs) and Negotiated agreements (covenants) are particularly popular in countries with complex legislative and consultation systems, such as Germany and the Netherlands. Japan's exception could be explained by a traditionally strong degree of centralisation, which also extends to the integration and implementation of sustainable development. For example, the traditional attitude to pollution control is the "command and control system", based on a set of legislation and regulations providing administrative guidance. This system is sought to be still effective and necessary in many policy fields, for example air pollution standards. However, even in Japan, other types of policy and measures are sought to complement the weak points of this traditional system, for example subsidies or tax incentives.

In Germany, the Länder have chosen this approach. Bavaria has been the frontrunner in maintaining co-operative relations with the business groups, whereby the Bavarian government has preferred to create "environmental alliances" comprising environmental management schemes and other activities. At the same this measure has helped reduce direct regulation through the authorities.

The Netherlands has developed a system of negotiated agreements ("Covenants") between authorities and target groups to implement the NEPPs. In difference to the system of voluntary agreements used in Germany, these covenants do have a legal base outlined in the NEPP and their status is defined by Cabinet regulations. The negotiation level depends on the involved parties and the negotiated subject. Covenants can either be negotiated on an industry-wide, a sector-specific or a plant-specific basis, thus involving either the national government, provincial or local authorities. The agreements contain time frames and implementation strategies for pollution control. This degree of flexibility in legislative implementation allows a customised approach to environmental policy-making and has been an

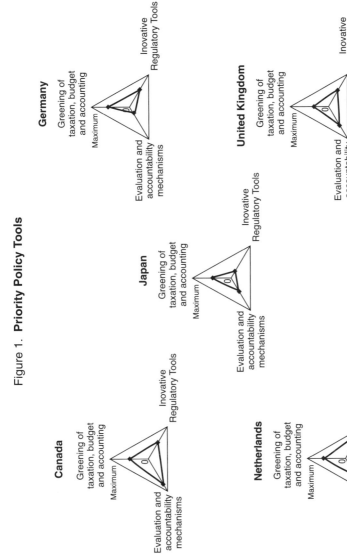

Figure 1. **Priority Policy Tools**

important instrument to gain support and acceptance for the NEPP from the private enterprise sector. There are concerns connected with the rising popularity of covenants for formulating and implementing environmental legislation. Even though strict cabinet regulations do define the legal basis, the participation of third parties and the transparency of the accords, there is general apprehension about the possible use of covenants to by-pass Parliament involvement and possible negative effects on industrial competition.

In addition to these innovations some efforts of various significance have been made to "green" taxation, budgets and accounting, as well as government operations (see Table 3).

Specific accountability mechanisms for sustainable development policies are still in their infancy, beyond institutionalisation of specific reporting and transparency tools. Interestingly, the broad nature of sustainable development has prevented many countries from introducing specific legislation and legal control. As a consequence sustainable development as such is no legal category in the countries surveyed, although social and environmental legislation are well developed. However some reporting mechanisms have been initiated. Among the most promising innovation the report of the Commissioner should be mentioned. This report, presented to parliament on a yearly basis is made public, which ensures scrutiny of the sustainable development management process. The case of the United Kingdom, which also introduced some reporting mechanisms, is slightly different. Although the government's strategy report is the basis for government policy-making in the area of sustainable development, there is no independent body, which can enforce policy changes, such as the Canadian Commissioner.

The capacity to develop reliable indicators for cost and benefits analysis and evaluation will constitute a key practical instrument to enhance accountability. All countries are making efforts in this direction. In Germany, for example, important steps have been taken in the development and operationalisation of environmental indicators, like Environmental Economic Account (*Umweltökonomische Gesamtrechnung*), which integrates into the economic data environmental burdens such as emissions, utilisation of materials and energy and pressures on soils.

II. The role of civil society: Engaging all citizens effectively

One key aspect of sustainable development is the capacity to make production and consumption patterns more sustainable. The exact role government should play to support more sustainable production and consumption is often subject to debate, but the policy mix suggested by the case studies include among other tools regulatory instruments and tax incentives. One useful but limited initiative followed by the countries surveyed has also been to "lead by example" through greening government operations (see Table 3).

Table 3. **Selected tools for greening of government**

	Canada	Germany	Japan	Netherlands	United Kingdom
Greening of taxation, budgets and accounting	Proposals made by NRTEE to green 2000 budgets were used as a basis for improving the sustainability of the federal budget.	Within the Ministry of Finance, the concept of sustainability was applied mainly to the long-term consolidation of the budget.	–	Green budgeting considered a key challenge for the future. New tax system (from 1 January 2001). The objectives of this revision include the promotion of sustainable economic development ("greening"). Also introduced an outcome and output focussed budgeting and management approach involving all government agencies.	The 2001 Budget announced a substantial wide-ranging package of fiscal measures aimed at bringing about an urban revival. The Budget measures are also complemented by local taxation measures included for consultation in the Local Government Finance Green Paper – including Town Improvement Schemes and a local tax reinvestment programme.
Greening government operations	Federal Greening of Government Initiative: all departments to integrate environmental considerations into their operations and put in place environmental management systems. Various efforts focussing on: – Energy consumption – Water consumption – Waste management – Fleet and transport – Government buildings and facilities.	"Climate Protection Programme" comprising over 150 measures including: – massive promotion of renewable energies; – "Green" targets (2001) "Energy Strategy for Transport" and "Integrated Transport Policy" proposed by the Ministry (2000); – integration of construction and physical planning laws (1997); – amendment of the Spatial Planning Act to include reference to sustainability; – comprehensive recycling of demolition waste.	– Action Plan for Greening Government Operations (June 1995). Requires use of recycled paper; energy-saving equipment; introduction of lower-emission vehicles; reduction of carbon dioxide emissions. – Law on the Promotion of Procurement of Eco-friendly Goods and Services by the State and other Entities (2000)	Key challenge for the future will be to: improve green procurement. Barriers to green procurement include: low awareness and motivation, lack of knowledge of possible options; budgetary constraints and technical barriers; deficits in decentralised purchasing.	The 1999 and 2000 reports of the Green Ministers Committee set out its achievements and future work programme including: – The agreement of a Model Policy Statement for Greening Operations accompanied by a Model Improvement Programme (almost all Departments now have their own green housekeeping strategies). – Targets for energy efficiency and waste recovery, as well as green transport plans for Executive Agencies and Government Officers for the Regions. – Provision of assistance to Departments on implementing Environmental Management Systems (EMSs), including issuing a guide, holding a major seminar, setting up a telephone helpdesk and establishing call-off contracts for consultancy advice. – Joint DETR (DEFRA) and HMT guidance to clarify the opportunities for Departments to take into account the environmental impacts of purchasing decisions through their procurement policies. – Advice to Departments on environmental appraisals of policies.

25

Changing consumption and production patterns effectively is particularly challenging, considering the need for balancing sustainable development priorities with the increasing demands of society for consumption goods and higher living standards, resulting from more individualistic lifestyles. How to combine, for example, social demands for more individual cars, and more individual houses with sustainable development goals? The difficulty in preventing further degradation of the environment has proved that these changes are difficult to put in place and suggest that this difficult objective would require a common understanding that "business as usual" is no longer possible as well as commitments and effort from the society as a whole.

This would require a minimum level of consensus on what should be the basic options available, although conflicting opinions often generate opposition between a multitude of economically, environmentally and socially driven interests. Most countries have experimented selected promising solutions presented in the case studies, mainly in the Agriculture and Fisheries sectors, partly due to sufficient pressure from government to agree on a minimum level of consensus. This could prove to be difficult to achieve in other sectors more central to the economy. In particular, the general difficulty of developing systematic conflict resolution methods between government, business and other categories remains a key feature of most systems. As underlined in the Japanese case study "One key obstacle to achieving sustainable development is the difficulty of replacing the rhetoric of win-win' solutions, which are unlikely to be found, by efforts to elaborate appropriate arbitrage techniques for conflict resolution".

Evolving relation between government and business

Partnerships between government and business are expected to play a critical role. In all countries there is a well established practice of formal relations between government and the private sector in order to support economic development, whereas sustainable development requires a great deal of adaptation of these mechanisms. This implies a new attitude from both the business community and the government side, in order to move from a logic of "lobbying" – which runs the risk of creating either "collusion" or conflicts between government and the private sector – to a logic of sound "partnerships" also open to other interests, *i.e.* social and environmental.

The renewal of the relationship between government, environmental and social organisations is therefore needed. In this respect some neutral organisations could play the role of "facilitator". In Canada, the International Institute for Sustainable Development (IISD) is playing a global role in advancing the sustainable development agenda. This organisation's aim is to contribute to sustainable development by advancing policy recommendations on international trade, economic instruments, climate change and natural resources management. It covers and reports on (using Internet communications) international negotiations and develops

North/South collaborative projects including recommendations with global partners. Its audiences are government, business and NGOs. An important achievement of the IISD has been to develop promising partnerships with business and government. Since 1995, the German *Länder* have also taken various initiatives to improve environmental management at company level. Bavaria was the front-runner, and most of the *Länder* followed the Bavarian example by creating different types of State-business co-operation. Generally, such co-operation aims to introduce environmental management activities and compliance audits according to the European Environmental Management and Audit Scheme (EMAS) at company level, while reducing direct control by environmental authorities.

One of the positive developments that most countries are witnessing is the integration of the sustainable development concept by business, independently of government incentives. Mainly driven by the necessity to look "cleaner" to citizens, traditionally polluting sectors like chemicals, energy, the pulp and paper industry etc. are engaged in greening their activities. Over the last few years, industry associations have usually been instrumental in developing an increasing number of industry-wide self-commitments or voluntary agreements. Voluntary activities by industries with environmental management systems such as ISO 14001, coupled with the growing "green consumer" citizens' movement, are therefore an important step towards the integration of economic activities and global environmental conservation through expanding international trade. However, the real effect of these measures is not yet always clear and there is a lack of evaluation.

A key element of the interface between government and business is the nature of the regulatory and control frameworks put in place by government. Controls should certainly not harm economic development, but at the same time, ensuring that environmental and social goals are given due attention by all private sector actors is a critical factor of success. In most countries there is a sense that traditional regulations, even when they are elaborated in consultation with the business community, are not fully adapted to the nature of some of the sustainable development challenges. Most initiatives focussed on "voluntary agreements". A condition of the success of these tools is usually linked to their binding nature. It also appeared, for example in the Netherlands, that licensing systems should be used in a flexible way according to the co-operative efforts made by the business themselves. For some companies, government should retain the option of issuing instructions; in other cases – *e.g.* when companies have developed efficient environmental management systems – more freedom could be granted.

Some examples of commitments by unions were also highlighted. In Germany, in 1999, the DGB introduced an initiative to integrate environmental concerns into the Alliance for Jobs (*Bündnis für Arbeit*), a "neo-corporatist" structured dialogue between government, trade unions and industry which was initiated in 1996 and re-launched in 1998, focusing on employment, education and training,

27

and competitiveness. The DGB listed almost eighty proposals for linking employment measures with environmental protection.

Widening participation to society at large

All studies also stressed the role of citizens and the need for change in the traditional relationship between government and various groups and individuals in order to achieve efficient policy integration of environmental, economic and social goals. Engaging citizens is a key concept in the implementation of sustainable development, and public participation can be divided into two forms. The first is the participation of representative groups, the so-called "stakeholders". These are normally engaged in the formulation of policies through counselling bodies, for example the Canadian National Round Table on the Environment, or National Councils for Sustainable Development, as in Germany, Japan or the United Kingdom. Certain government departments have also installed advisory bodies comprised of stakeholders, who advise the policy-makers on certain sector specific issues, as is the case in Germany and the United Kingdom. The case studies did not develop in detail the basis on which protagonists of consultation and participation are selected. However, a common trend is the tendency to open policy debate to wider communities at both national and sub-national levels. Sustainable development could even play the role of catalyst for broadening the scope of public consultation and participation in countries, which is not very surprising considering the pioneer role played by the environment sector since the 1970s.

The impact of participatory mechanisms may vary. In Canada and the Netherlands, for example, substantive influence was given to both "institutionalised" NGOs and less established groups at an early stage in the policy processes. In the Netherlands, for instance, consultation includes a large number of stakeholder groups in the formulation of the NEPP, and in Canada the formulation of ministerial strategies was largely open to groups of "stakeholders". This large degree of openness required developing sophisticated methodologies including reporting mechanisms. One key issue is the capacity to provide clear objectives as well as responsiveness and feedback to the people involved in the processes.

The second aspect is the engagement of the general public. In the United Kingdom, the Service First Unit (now the Modernising Public Services Group) in the Cabinet Office commissioned a market research company, and Birmingham University's School of Public Policy to set up a People's Panel (1998). The People's Panel consists of 5,000 randomly selected members of the public and serves as an assessment instrument of prevailing views on subjects concerning public services. It is planned to use the panel to assess issues on sustainable development. Japan has a similar method of receiving public views. The United Kingdom government has set up a public comment system to collect public opinions concerning policy-making, implementation and review processes. A further method is the possibility to influence policy-making through petitions; such is the case in Canada, where the Commissioner for the Environment and Sustainable Development receives public petitions. Some German *Länder* have also introduced direct democratic instruments, such as referenda and petition systems. Engaging the public also refers to widening the possibilities for public action, such as through legal complaints, public hearings or the support of local "Agenda 21" groups. These are all elements that are being pursued in the countries covered by the case study, even if with different intensity.

From empirical observation of the cases analysed, it seems more difficult to include all interests in federal systems where the amount of lobbying at different levels often makes the situation more complicated. Another type of problem that appears, for instance in the Dutch system of consensual politics, is the risk of impeding and distorting the implementation of sustainable development goals due to exhaustive consultation processes. On the other hand, to restrict consultation processes would have maybe even more important drawbacks. In the German case study, when it comes to energy or transport policy, government decision-makers see themselves criticised for including only economic interests. These tensions call for additional efforts to evaluate the cost and benefits of consultation and participation practices.

There has not yet been any evaluation of the exact influence of stakeholders in the policy processes. However, following the "inclusive" tendencies of Dutch "corporatism", the current trend is to accelerate the integration of NGOs in the policy process. Improving the quality of consultation and participation has been one of the major goals of NEPP4, and sophisticated consultative processes were put in place for developing NEPP3 and NEPP4. NGOs participate regularly in consultation processes. They have been invited to be official members of the scientific advisory councils of most ministries. But all NGOs cannot of course participate, which is clearly an issue in terms of equity. This is balanced by the fact that, increasingly, NGOs dealing with environment and nature are co-ordinating their efforts to come up with a single NGO position.

In addition to new participatory mechanisms, most countries have an ongoing debate on the extent to which the scope for judicial cases related to sustainable development should be widened. As sustainable development is in general not a legal category, there is an attempt to achieve this objective through judicial review of environmental law. In Germany practices already established at *Land* level have influenced further evolutions at national level. Some *Länder*, such as Lower Saxony or Brandenburg, already entitle NGOs to file legal actions (*Verbandsklage*). Federal government has taken up this issue recently in its proposal for the new Nature Protection Act.

III. Creating a longer-term view

The transgenerational and transnational nature of sustainable development requires not only a holistic approach regarding its implementation and integration in national decision-making processes, but also needs a long-term view entailing precautionary decision-making. This puts great strain on the traditional organisation of democratic systems: decision-making in democratic systems generally follows the electoral cycle (4 to 5 years) and so impairs a long-term decision-making perspective.

The sufficient policy relevant information on which to base a decision is more and more difficult to disseminate and to co-ordinate. As knowledge is becoming increasingly technical and specialised, this leads to an insufficient linkage between the knowledge system and decision-making levels. In addition, purely sector-specific responses to the rising technical content of problem solving can impair a coherent and efficient decision. One focus has been the broad research in the inter-related aspects of sustainable development. A second focus has been the enhancement of research in environmental problems and risks, as the policy access window to sustainable development in most countries is confined to environmental policy-making.

Responses have been relatively similar in the five countries. To date there have been only a few holistic approaches to strengthening longer-term capacities in government although there has been a series of pioneering initiatives. Some "sensitive" sectors have been subject to specific attention. The Netherlands has for example undertaken extensive research in agricultural aspects of sustainable development, with strong public sector involvement. Due to the content of the problems dealt with, the Ministry of Agriculture has a sophisticated organisation of highly specialised research institutes with over 3 200 employees.

However the five studies raised the more general issue of insufficient knowledge on which to base sound decision-making, and sectoral approaches seem to be too limited to handle this difficulty. Generally, a lack of sufficient knowledge has been found to impede an adequate long-term approach to policy making. Although countries such as Canada and the Netherlands have put in place different schemes to assess the environmental impact of certain investment projects, it is still felt that too little is known about the potential environmental risks caused by the implementation of certain policies. For this reason virtually all the case study governments are faced with the challenge of gathering sufficient policy-relevant information and of strengthening the links between decision-making and science.

The need to move to a comprehensive effort is noticeable, in particular the crucial need for reliable evaluation mechanisms. The Canadian federal government, for example, has increased federal funding for the development of sustainable development indicators by the National Round Table on the Environment

---

Box 2. **The National Initiative on Sustainable Development (NIDO) in the Netherlands**

The Netherlands has initiated an ambitious effort to improve the basis of knowledge of organisations. In order to address the issue, the National Initiative on Sustainable Development (NIDO) was launched at the end of 1999 and is one of the twelve initiatives taken by the Dutch government with the aim of investing in the Netherlands' knowledge infrastructure. NIDO's aim is to make a quantum leap forward in sustainable development. By acting as a spur to new development, NIDO can help organisations to fulfil their ambitions with regard to sustainable development. The Dutch government believes that major advances can be made if firms, government bodies, scientists and civil-society organisations are prepared to pool their resources and expertise. The job of NIDO, as an independent trailblazer, is to bring the various parties together and to enable each of them to find their own particular route towards sustainable development. To this end, NIDO initiates programmes such as that entitled "From financial to sustainable performance", which started in June 2000 and is due to run until the end of the year 2002. The Advisory Council on Nature and the Environment (RMNO) has launched for 2001 a programme directly connected to societal aspects of sustainable development.

---

and the Economy (NRTEE) and the Environment Ministry (Environment Canada). Federal funds have also been allocated to cross-sector research programmes on toxic substances in order to provide sufficient knowledge to decision-makers on the possible environmental effects related to their handling under the joint ministerial responsibility of Health Canada and Environment Canada. The UK Government has undertaken steps to include a full impact assessment of all policies through cost-benefit analyses. Traditionally, this has been a non-environmental approach with the aim to increase regulatory efficiency. The inclusion of environmental impact assessment in policy-making has led to the evaluation of non-market goods. The aim is to extend existing decision-making checklists to include a evaluation of non-monetised effects of Government regulations.

IV. Some common lessons

Despite various economic, environmental and social features, as well as heterogeneous experiences and government systems, the five countries must respond to a common difficulty of overcoming urgently numerous institutional and societal barriers in order to better respond to the imperative of sustainable development. It is significant that in none of the countries traditional decision-making mechanisms were considered to be adapted to overarching and longer-

Figure 2. **Traditional Decision Making**
Institutional set up

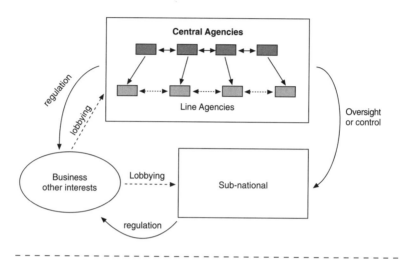

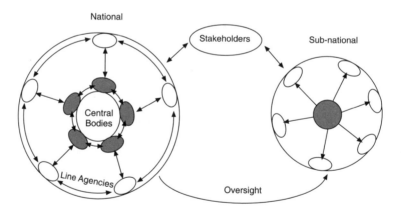

Decision Making for Sustainable Development
Institutional set up

term challenges such as sustainable development. In all countries sustainable development was considered a managerial challenge for government. In all countries there was a sense that implementing sustainable development goals would require an adaptation of decision-making models (see Figure 2).

32

Mainly driven by an agenda agreed at international level, the key issues of sustainable development generate relatively comparable challenges across countries. The main key points that emerged from the case studies include:

- Develop a clear, widely accepted and operational definition and goal structure for sustainable development and raise awareness within and outside government. The crucial question may be whether concepts of economic and social sustainability are adequately brought into the debate. This debate will be particularly challenging, considering the potential for conflicts between various interests.

- Develop a clear commitment within government at the highest level and communicate this commitment throughout the government machinery in order to support the development of a clear strategy. Relatively successful strategies (e.g. the climate-protection strategy in Germany) could serve as a model for the broader strategy for sustainable development. Key governance criteria against which strategies could be tested include: high-level political commitment for the formulation and implementation of ambitious goals; integration of policy objectives into other sectors; adapted policy tools including pioneer activities of local communities; and broad public participation.

- This strategy should be enforced by a "focal point" at the centre of government, and non-environmental policy sectors should be mandated to develop their own sectoral strategies in conformity with the overarching goals defined. For example the leading role of Cabinet – or the "Green Cabinet" – should be clear and accepted by all ministries. This should include a critical evaluation of both the formulation of sectoral strategies and their implementation, including from the point of view of the enforcement tools used (voluntary agreements etc.). Sectoral ministries should introduce pluralistic bodies and monitoring mechanisms for the early "internal" discussion of their sectoral sustainable development strategies, using the most appropriate policy tools. Environment agencies could play an important role, mainly supportive, in this process (so far these institutions have been rather cautious and have adopted a policy of "wait-and-see").

- Decentralisation is expected to prevent negative effects of lengthy consultation procedures and avoid too much politicisation of national debates. To be effective, decentralisation should be supported by specific attention to vertical integration in order to translate strategic policy directions into measures that can be implemented. Efforts should be aimed at avoiding fragmentation and overlap of responsibilities. They should also imply accountability for sustainable development as well as capacity building for translating national and international norms, support the implementation of environmental measures and improve technical knowledge where it is too weak. At the local level, general orientation

33 |

for "Agenda 21" processes, for example in the form of a competitive investment programme for local sustainable development initiatives, should be provided.

- Citizens should be encouraged to engage in decision-making, and it is the responsibility of government to ensure that the consultation process is linked effectively to the decision-making processes, so that it does not become an exercise in tokenism, but neither should it be used as an excuse for deferring decisions when faced with sensitive trade-offs in policy choices. Government "culture" has still to fully evolve to one that is more sympathetic to integrated and participative approaches, with the corollary of greater transparency in decision processes. There is evidence of the need for stronger political leadership in shaping the nature of the debate on how to take sustainable development forward. This leadership has, in turn, to address problems which result from maintaining "silo" thinking, from a reluctance to cede decision-making authority, and from "short-termism". Institutional development has to allow for iteration and to ensure transparency in decision making.

- Clear scientific input to problems that have to be solved is necessary, and results should be communicated to the general public as well as to relevant interest organisations to maintain a sufficient level of awareness and commitment. The methodological limits of approaches such as contingent evaluation, as well as the fact that scientific uncertainty is sometimes thought to be downplayed in the evaluation of effects (although this is a problem with whatever appraisal methodology is applied), call for the application of a precautionary approach and for intensive efforts in order to develop total evaluation of costs and benefits. Stakeholders should also be engaged in the appraisal and evaluation systems.

Notes

1. The "Brundtland Commission" defined sustainable development as development that "meets the needs of the present without compromising the ability of future generations to meet their own needs (WCED,1987).

2. The 1992 Rio Conference expressed a public commitment at the highest level.

3. The Environment Ministry reported for example studies from 2000, which showed a recent increase in environmental awareness (German case study p. 10).

Bibliography

BMU (2000),
   Umweltbewußtsein in Deutschland 2000. Ergebnisse einer repräsentativen Bevölkerungsumfrage, BMU: Berlin.

OECD (2001),
   Sustainable Development, Critical Issues, OECD Paris.

World Commission on Environment and Development (WCED) (1987),
   Our Common Future, Oxford University Press, Oxford, UK.

Canada

By
Frédéric Bouder[1]

Purpose

The study focuses on practices for improving institutions and decision-making for sustainable development in Canada.[2] It does not provide an exhaustive review of sustainable development governance in Canada, but rather highlights current trends as well as selected promising developments that could help achieve sustainable development. The paper focuses on the strategies that have been formulated and implemented but an overall review of policies and programmes was left outside the scope of the study. Similarly, it focuses primarily on developments within federal level government authorities and, therefore, does not cover the multiplicity of local and private initiatives, apart from selected illustrative examples. This paper was prepared following interviews with a range of officials and representatives from public, private and non-for-profit organisations (see appendix).

General introduction

Physical, economic and human features

Canada is the largest OECD country, with an area of about 10 million square kilometres. This entails a considerable variety of physical features, mainly a large interior basin centred on the Hudson Bay (covering four-fifths of the country) and highland regions rimming the basin. Canada is surrounded by three oceans: the Pacific, the Atlantic and the Arctic. It shares four of the Great Lakes with the United States. Natural conditions are characterised by wilderness compared to most OECD countries. Tundra and other forms of sparse vegetation along with wetlands and permanent ice or snowfields represent more that 40 per cent of the country. Forest and other wooded areas cover almost half of the Canada land area, while about 1 per cent of Canada is urban and industrial land. As a consequence, the diversity and richness of Canada's natural resources is very significant.

The Canadian population was 30 287 000 in 1997. The population density is low, about 3 inhabitants per square kilometre. It is concentrated in large urban

37

centres, separated by great distances along a strip of land of which 200 kilometres borders the United States. The region between Windsor and the city of Quebec, known as the Windsor-Quebec Corridor, is home to half of Canada's population. Within it the largest urban areas are Toronto (about 4 million inhabitants) and Montreal (about 3 million inhabitants). Population growth (about 1.1 per cent between 1996 and 1997) results mainly from immigration.

Canada's population is made up of two main linguistic groups, both of which have official status: about 75 per cent of the population speak English and about 25 per cent speak French. But in fact, English is the sole mother tongue of about 59 per cent of Canadians; and French, the first language of 23 per cent of the population. A full 18 per cent have either more than one mother tongue or a mother tongue other than English or French, such as Chinese, Italian, German, Polish, Spanish, Portuguese, Punjabi, Ukrainian, Arabic, Dutch, Tagalog, Greek, Vietnamese, Cree, Inuktitut, or other languages. Successive waves of immigration have created an increasingly varied population in terms of ethnic and religious background. In 1996, about 19 per cent of the population reported "Canadian" as their single ethnic origin, with 17 per cent reporting British Isles-only ancestry and 9 per cent French-only ancestry. About 10 per cent reported a combination of British Isles, French, or Canadian origins, with another 16 per cent reporting an ancestry of either British Isles, French or Canadian in combination with some other origin. Some 28 per cent reported origins other than the British Isles, French or Canadian. Religious affiliation is also diverse. According to the 1991 census, more than four-fifths of Canadians are Christian, with Catholics accounting for about 47 per cent of the population and Protestants about 36 per cent. Other religions include Judaism, Islam, Hinduism, Sikhism and Buddhism. Some 12.5 per cent, more than any single denomination except Roman Catholic, have no religious affiliation at all.

An important aspect of the diversity of the Canadian nation is the presence of the Aboriginal population: as of 1996 there were approximately 800 000 Aboriginals in Canada,[3] (the majority living in reservations or in the newly created territory of Nunavut. About 3 per cent of Canadians belonged to one or more of the three Aboriginal groups recognised by the Constitution Act, 1982: North American Indian, Métis, or Inuit. Of this percentage, about 69 per cent are North American Indian, 26 per cent Métis, and 5 per cent Inuit.

Economic conditions are linked with both these natural and demographic factors. Natural resources make an important contribution to the economy of Canada, with strong forestry, energy, fishing and agricultural activities. Canada relies heavily on exports of natural resources. Compared to other OECD countries per capita, Canada is a large consumer of natural resources and energy and, consequently, "a large generator of pollution and waste" (1997 report of the Commissioner of the Environment and Sustainable Development).

Canada's living standards are very high. Canada ranks sixth in the world in standard of living (measured according to gross domestic product per capita), behind only the United States, Switzerland, Luxembourg, Germany, and Japan.[4] Canada's rank among nations tends to rise even higher in assessments that consider GDP per capita along with other factors that contribute to "quality of life" (*e.g.* life expectancy, education). For example, social benefits are high. Basic health care, with the exception of dental services, is free at the point of delivery. Prescription drugs are in most cases dispensed without charge to people over 65 and to social aid recipients. Canada also has an extensive social security network, including an old-age pension, a family allowance, unemployment insurance and welfare.

These characteristics have various consequences in terms of setting the agenda for sustainable development. Over time, Canada's economic development has had an impact on the environment. This has called for thinking more carefully about the balance between economic growth and environmental preservation. For example, over the past 25 years agricultural land use has increased significantly as has permanent grassland, while wetlands have shrunk. This has a potentially major impact on ecosystems, from the point of view of protecting the habitat of natural species, disseminating substances used for agriculture, etc. In addition, identifying the best sustainable use of natural resources is somewhat challenging. One critical issue involves making strategic choices about Canada's development strategy. In the long term, if Canada were to continue to rely heavily on the use of natural resources, how, for example, could a balance be maintained between economic imperatives and the longer-term preservation of the Canadian natural heritage? The collapse of fish stocks in the 1990s, which severely affected Atlantic fisheries, clearly illustrates the existing tensions.

The interaction of these economic and environmental factors with human and social factors also raises crucial issues. One issue is the integration of significant numbers of immigrants. Economic growth has led to the concentration of the population in a few urban areas, which raises increasing concerns about the "liveability" of urban areas (*e.g.* in Toronto) and about the effects of this concentration on the environment. Another challenge is the need to develop the economy of the north of Canada in a way that preserves the environment and the social stability of First Nations communities.

Therefore, in Canada, sustainable development is perceived as a major challenge by various actors in the public, private and non-profit sectors. One aspect of this challenge is combining economic growth in a context of dynamic demographic evolution with the preservation of the country's natural assets. These assets constitute a significant share of the world's natural heritage (about 10 per cent of the world's renewable freshwater supply, 10 per cent of its forest and significant reserves of oil, gas and other minerals are located in Canada). Another issue is how to maintain a large degree of social cohesion. This means, in particular, addressing the demographic and diversity issues resulting mainly from the integration of substantial numbers of immigrants and the specific needs of aboriginal communities. In general, social issues are highly regional.

Governance patterns: Canada's constitutional base and practice

The patterns described above, linked to specific historical factors, have modelled the Canadian institutional and political culture, which is dominated by the sense of the need to overcome multiple conflicts through federalism. The colonial past of Canada (the Head of State is the British Monarch) motivated specific attention to relations with Aboriginal populations and the necessity to guarantee their rights (including their property rights) and prevent conflicts, in particular for the use of natural resources, often linked to the endangered sustainability of their communities: the politicisation of native movements is, for example, an important dimension of Canadian contemporary political culture. Canada was built by two constituent nations, the English and the French, with a long history of conflict. The strong separatist movement in the province of Quebec illustrates the deep roots of the conflict between the distinct French and English cultures of Canada. This is another issue requiring constant attention. Canada's diversity also generates different regional interests. Conflicts among regions and provinces continue to intrude on the political agenda. Jurisdictional disputes, especially over ownership and control of natural resources, exacerbate federal/provincial relations.[5]

Canada is a federal constitutional monarchy. The federal state was founded in the British North America Act, 1867. The Canadian Constitution was originally composed of a set of laws, to which practices and customs have been added. An act of British Parliament served as the constitution until the Constitutional Act was passed in 1982. Canada consists of ten provinces and three territories. The provinces are (from east to west): Newfoundland, Prince Edward Island, Nova Scotia, New Brunswick, Quebec, Ontario, Manitoba, Saskatchewan, Alberta, British Columbia. The three territories are the Northwest Territories, Yukon and the newly created territory of Nunavut. On April 1, 1999 the territory of Nunavut officially joined the federation of Canada, resulting from a division of the former Northwest Territories. It is unique as it incorporates Inuit values and beliefs – *e.g.* Inuktitut is its working language – into a contemporary system of government (see Annex IV). In a territory, the federal Parliament may enter into provincial-type affairs, such as school curriculum. The 1982 constitutional amendment formula provides no role for the territories in amending the Constitution.

A distribution of powers between the two orders of government, federal and provincial, is set out in the *Constitution Act*, 1982. Recognising the complexities of federal-provincial relations, it would be difficult to provide a sensible summary of the distribution of responsibilities between federal and provincial government.[6] It is, however, important to note that, although the Constitution sets out a distribution of powers, federal and provincial powers have occasionally intersected as the activities of governments became more complex. For example, the federal government controls the commercial fisheries (sea and freshwater), but the provincial governments control sports fishing for recreational purposes. Since concerns around sustainable development extend more generally beyond fishing activities, it is also important to note federal jurisdiction over the oceans. While grey areas have arisen in the distribution of powers between the federal and provincial levels, in such areas governments often develop pragmatic arrangements.

The spending power of the federal government covers some areas of overlap which have developed. The federal government can provide money to individuals,

---

Box 1. **Executive Federalism in Canada**

Two organisational facets of the Canadian system have a determining influence on the interdependency of the federal and provincial decision-making processes, which must be considered when dealing with horizontal issues such as sustainable development:

- *Functional federalism*: in which ministers and officials, usually from corresponding federal and provincial departments, meet to share views on specific undertakings negotiate. These meetings are sometimes multilateral, involving the federal government and all the provinces. At other times they are multilateral-regional, bringing a number of provinces with the federal government; and at other times still, they are bilateral – the federal government and one provincial government. There are more than 500 intergovernmental meetings a year involving federal provincial councils of ministers and committees of officials. Almost all of the meetings are "departmental", focusing on particular issues where co-ordination of policy positions or program delivery mechanisms is necessary. The meetings deal with diverse subjects ranging from law enforcement, through tourism, to budgetary policy.

- *Summit federalism*: this refers to the meetings of First Ministers (the term used to refer to the Prime Minister of Canada and to the ten Provincial Premiers and three territorial leaders). These summit meetings are always given a lot of publicity – they are sometimes televised – and they have at times been successful forums for the negotiation of difficult horizontal problems, namely problems that extend to more than one department of government. There have been more than 60 First Ministers' Conferences since Confederation.

Source: *Managing Across Levels of Government*, OECD 1997.

41

organisations of governments in areas of exclusive provincial jurisdiction as long as any conditions attached do not amount to regulation. In this way, the federal government has demonstrated national leadership by providing funds to the provinces to establish health care for all Canadians. Although there are ten provincial programmes that vary in detail, they respect certain broad principles, *e.g.*, universality, accessibility, comprehensiveness, public administration and portability.

A.   Main issues and tensions

The definition of "Sustainable Development" is similar to that given by the World Commission on Environment and Development in 1987, "development that meets the needs of the present without compromising the ability of future generations to meet their own needs" (1995 amendments to the *Auditor General Act*).

The emergence of the concept of sustainable development in Canada has been partly driven by the international debate that led to the Montreal Protocol (1987) and the Rio (1992) and Kyoto (1997) Summits. On September 16, 1987 the Montreal Protocol on Substances that Deplete the Ozone Layer was signed by twenty-four countries in Montreal, Quebec. It is considered the first effort at global co-operation to protect the environment. The Protocol established measures for controlling the production and consumption of ozone-depleting substances (ODS) that came into effect on January 1, 1989. At the Earth Summit in 1992, nations adopted a set of principles to guide future development. The Rio Declaration on Environment and Development defines the rights of people to development, and their responsibilities to safeguard the common environment. In December 1997, representatives from Canada and 160 other countries met in Kyoto, Japan and agreed to a Protocol that set targets for reductions in greenhouse gas emissions. Under what is called the Kyoto Protocol, the Government of Canada is committed to reducing its emissions to 6 per cent below 1990 levels between 2008 and 2012.

This ambitious agenda requires that economic development, social equity and environmental quality be reconciled in all aspects of domestic decision making – both nationally and locally, in business, government and community affairs.

International context

Traditionally, the Canadian Government has made noticeable efforts to remain active in the international arena. One of the objectives of the Speech from the Throne of February 2001 was to "enhance the Canadian voice in the world". In the field of sustainable development this active international role is shared by the government and civil society (see Box 2). This international concern is reflected in the need to implement international agreements, which have been a strong incentive to take action. Canada has a commitment to international action on climate change and biological diversity. For example, it has signed more than 30 international initiatives

---

> ### Box 2.   **Promoting Sustainable Development Globally:**
> ### **The Role of the IISD**
>
> The International Institute for Sustainable Development (IISD), which has its headquarters in Winnipeg, Manitoba, is playing a global role in advancing the sustainable development agenda. This organisation has offices in Calgary, Ottawa, New York and Geneva. Its aim is to contribute to sustainable development by advancing policy recommendations on international trade, economic instruments, climate change and natural resources management. It covers and reports on (using Internet communications) international negotiations and develops North/South collaborative projects including recommendations with global partners. Its audiences are government, business and NGOs. IISD receives financial support from the governments of Canada and Manitoba, among others; UN agencies; foundations; and the private sector. An annual report includes detailed information on the IISD activities and financing. An important achievement of the IISD has been to develop promising partnerships with business and government (see section below on *innovative decision-making*).

that affect environmental quality in the Arctic and contributes to international efforts to understand the Arctic's unique environment. Canada has recently engaged in the definition of a "Northern foreign policy", which will give a stronger voice to sustainability concerns in the international arena.

Canada's international commitments are also strong in some vital sectoral policies such as fishing. Canada played a key role in the elaboration and development of the United Nations Food and Agricultural Organisation (FAO) Code of Conduct for Responsible Fishing. The Canadian fishing industry is committed to the achievement of sustainability in marine and freshwater fisheries. For example, it has developed a Code of Conduct, consistent with the code of the FAO, for Responsible Fisheries Operations as an essential step in pursuit of this objective. The implementation process is currently under way and is expected to be ratified by fishing organisations across Canada.

This commitment to international standards calls for good implementation mechanisms at the domestic level. A sector, such as transport, that is heavily regulated by international agreements and monitored by international organisations will require a more coherent interface between international and national governance to implement sustainable development goals. Thus, globalisation relating to sustainable development can have concrete effects on national sovereignty.

In many cases the implementation of international agreements is problematic. One obvious reason for the difficulty is that meeting international agreements could

© OECD 2002

imply radical shifts in policy that may meet resistance from many sectors of society. For example, the Kyoto Protocol requires Canada to reduce greenhouse gas emissions[7] in the period 2008-2012 by about 25 per cent below the business-as-usual scenario (emission levels are among the highest in OECD countries). This target implies a great deal of adaptation from the business community; national, provincial and local governments; and the society as a whole (e.g. consumers). There is also a feeling that meeting Canadian commitments following the Earth Summit will be difficult given the jurisdictional complexity and governance challenges of the Canadian system. Canada has a federal structure with many decentralised actors. As most of the competencies concerning, for example, the use of natural resources are exercised at the provincial level, there is a certain degree of fragmentation and incoherence in the various sustainable development agendas. All provinces do not necessarily have the same priorities, given their particular natural and economic conditions as well as their different political commitments. A tendency to "talk" rather than to "act" is also being evoked in the Canadian context. After a long and comprehensive consultation process, ambitious strategies do not necessarily result in concrete action. A need for "moving talk into action" has been highlighted. Meeting international agreements will thus require well-functioning internal governance mechanisms.

Domestic challenges

It is difficult to isolate purely domestic concerns from the international context. At the national/international interface, Canada is bound by bilateral and multilateral agreements such as NAFTA and provisions concerning the Great Lakes area. The main domestic challenges that Canada is facing can be approached at two different levels, which reveal different perceptions, attitudes and priorities in Canadian society concerning the sustainable development debate.

At the level of "country-wide" issues, challenges relate mainly to the use of natural resources (mines, forests, fisheries), which represent a substantial part of GDP, affect most parts of the country, involve major economic actors and have international implications. Some specific issues also include: various aspects of urban and rural environment protection, liveability in urban areas (e.g. urban development), preservation of "first populations", stability and integration of immigrant populations.

Preserving the sustainability of the northern part of the country (the Arctic) is also a major challenge both for Canada and the rest of the world, and requires special attention (see Box 3).

Perception of issues and public awareness

In Canada, like elsewhere, sustainable development concerns first emerged from the environment community, and led to international agreements focussing

Box 3. **Preserving the Arctic Region:**
A Domestic and International Challenge

The Arctic represents about 40per cent of the Canadian landmass, but is sparsely populated and less developed than the rest of Canada. The natural condition of the North makes it disproportionately affected by global change. Environmental contaminants (*e.g.* pesticides, industrial chemicals and heavy metals), transported by air and water currents from industrialised and agricultural regions, present a major threat to its environment. On the social side, the damages have a direct and rapid impact on the sustainability of the communities living in the region, since contamination of fish and wildlife is a health concern for native Arctic peoples who rely on these foods as a significant part of their diet.

Changes in the Arctic environment and ecosystems have an effect on other parts of the world, and reciprocally. This awareness is reflected in an increasing number of environmental agreements and other arrangements to protect the Arctic, which Canada has signed or endorsed. It has also led Canada and the other circumpolar nations to collaborate in programmes of extensive scientific research and monitoring in the North.

on environmental sustainability. Therefore the primary focus of government in this area is the interface between environmental and economic issues – *i.e.* the need to enhance "environmentally sustainable development". It is reflected in the strategies initiated by departments at the federal and provincial levels and in Canada's international commitments (climate change, biological diversity, the Arctic). The emergence of social issues as a central part of the sustainable development paradigm is more recent.

The perception of sustainable development issues in the general public is somewhat fragmented: citizens usually see the link between environment and economy, but they are not necessarily aware of the "triple bottom-line" of sustainable development (economic/environmental/social). The relative weight of economic, social and environmental concerns in the public have also fluctuated. For example, the ecological concerns of the late 1980s and early 1990s that led to the Earth Summits declined during the recession of the mid-1990s when economic and social problems became critical. However, environmental concerns may be regaining prominence in Canada.[8]

Senior civil servants and private sector managers have been increasingly aware of the concept and implications of sustainable development, focusing on the relation between the economic and environment pillars. A 1999 survey conducted by the Commissioner's Office among senior managers showed that almost all senior managers are convinced that, given global trends in population growth, production and resource use, the environment will continue to be an important strategic consideration for organisations. According to this survey, managers do not talk only about challenges posed by sustainable development but also, increasingly, about the opportunities that it represents (*e.g.* in terms of comparative advantages for their organisation).

Political agenda

The growing presence of environmental concerns on the political agenda of the late 1980s and early 1990s has been the driving force for raising the issue of sustainable development. Fluctuations in the political agenda at both national and subnational levels took place, although not necessarily at the same time. Roughly speaking, three phases can to be observed from the early to the mid-1990s.

International negotiations were conducted and the main international agreements were concluded with related domestic measures. This can be characterised as an "action phase". Many new measures, including institution building, were initiated in federal and provincial government and significant efforts were made for the identification and formulation of strategies. In 1990, the federal government launched the Green Plan, a policy framework and action plan for sustainable development, in which it committed itself to substantial additional spending on the environment over the following five years (C$ 3 billion compared with annual federal environmental expenditure of about C$ 1.3 billion, which represented 1.2 per cent of overall budgetary expenditure at the time). The plan put emphasis on environmental research, national parks and monitoring and education programmes, but also included quantitative targets on specific environmental issues. All provinces also established sustainable development plans in the early 1990s, some with associated special funds. Important institutional developments included the creation of the Roundtable for Sustainable Development by an act of Parliament in 1993 and the Amendment to the Auditor General Act (1995) providing for the creation of the Commissioner of the Environment and Sustainable Development. The main government commitment was made in the "Guide to Green Government" (1995). This document presented the first government "corporate" view of the sustainable development challenge, established a framework for action and launched the process for the elaboration of sustainable development strategies of all departments as well as "greening" the budget: that is, incorporating the environment and sustainable development dimension into federal budgets.

In the 1990s, however, the political agenda was overshadowed by the need to maintain fiscal stability; cuts weighed heavily on environmental departments at both federal and provincial levels. Environment Canada's budgets stopped increasing in 1994/95 and had decreased by about 30 per cent by 1998/99 (compared to a

6 per cent reduction of overall federal budgetary expenditure). Given these budgetary constraints, the federal government reduced its budgets for the environment. The provinces, while receiving more competencies from the federal government for the implementation of their programmes, also substantially reduced their environmental budgets. For example, Ontario reduced its environmental budget by up to about 60 per cent between 1994/95 and 1998/99, while overall expenditure was almost stable over the same period. Budget cuts challenged the achievement of the sustainable development agenda, through affecting resource allocation. The fact that there were fewer resources to carry on environmental and social goals had a negative impact on the capacity to implement the ambitious strategies developed a few years earlier. Moreover, following a certain decline of interest from the public and the media, sustainable development went lower on the political agenda of most provinces and of some federal departments. Basic problems appeared, such as the difficulty in getting multiple actors to agree on a shared vision; the pre-eminence of short-term economic choices in a context of recession that gives less room for longer-term thinking; the fact that sustainable development is too sensitive when it comes to real decisions.

Finally, the recent situation is characterised by a growing awareness of the need to reinvigorate the debate and to design new approaches to achieve past commitments and set future directions. The environment and sustainable development were named as priorities in the Speech from the Throne in October 1999. Similarly, the most recent Speech from the Throne (February 2001) highlighted four important themes that are critical to sustainable development: building a world-leading economy driven by innovation, ideas and talent; creating a more inclusive society where children get the right start in life, where quality health services are available to all, and where Canadians enjoy strong and safe communities; ensuring a clean, healthy environment for Canadians and the preservation of natural spaces; and enhancing the Canadian voice in the world and its shared sense of citizenship. Another trend is a greater focus on the "social leg" of sustainable development.

B. Institutions and policies

Achieving sustainability implies that compatible sustainable development goals be brought into the decision-making processes of national, sub-national, private and not-for-profit organisations. In Canada, the institutional framework is highly complex, partly resulting from the country's geographical, human and economic diversity. This is reflected in the federal tradition and in the sectoral fragmentation between a great number of specialised departments at both federal and provincial levels. Sufficient communication and interaction between institutions are required, as well as specific processes for reaching decisions. The "circular nature" of Canadian federalism (see Box 1) has been the usual way of dealing with institutional complexity.

47

Federal involvement

The federal government has a central role in raising awareness and setting the agenda on sustainable development issues. It shares responsibility for the legal framework that affects the environment, social stability and economic development. As Canada's largest single employer, landlord and purchaser, the federal government can show leadership in taking due action. This central role implies high expectations concerning the leadership capacity of the federal government. This must of course be balanced against the importance of other levels of responsibility (sub-national, private, etc.), and against the political reality – other emerging issues and budget constraints, which limit government intervention.

The most visible illustration of federal commitment to sustainable development was the creation of two dedicated institutions, the National Round Table on the Environment and the Economy and the Commissioner of the Environment and Sustainable Development, the latter being an independent position that reports directly to Parliament. These have provided impetus and helped promote action and awareness for raising issues, finding new approaches, reaching agreements and fostering action.

The National Round Table on the Environment and the Economy

Canada created the National Round Table on the Environment and the Economy (NRTEE) in 1993 by an Act of Parliament although it had already existed for several years beforehand. It is an independent agency enjoying legal security. It arose following the success of a multi-stakeholder task force on economics and the environment, which published its concluding report in 1987. Its purpose is to serve as a catalyst in identifying, explaining and promoting the principles and practices of sustainable development.

One of the advantages of the NRTEE is that it offers an independent source of information. It is committed to providing decision makers and opinion leaders with reliable information and objective views on the current state of the debate on the environment and the economy. This reliability is reflected in the membership of the organisation: NRTEE's members are appointed by Governor-in-Council from different backgrounds, including business, labour, academia, environmental organisations and aboriginal people. Both its legal security and recognised neutrality have contributed to the credibility of the NRTEE expertise.

The NRTEE is more than a source of "reliable" information, however. It carries out national consultations, reports on areas of agreement and disagreement, and puts forward recommendations. The Reports of the NRTEE are made publicly available, which increases transparency, promotes understanding and increases public awareness through the creation of a broader audience. Therefore this institution is an essential source both of expertise and of clear incentives to take action.

The NRTEE focuses mainly on the economic and environmental aspects of sustainable development (*e.g.* climate change, greenhouse gas emissions trading; green budget reform). Some aspects of the "social dimension" of sustainable development are also being considered (links between health, environment and the economy; Aboriginal communities and non-renewable resources development), although the NRTEE, like other organisations, is facing conceptual and practical difficulties in dealing with the vast set of social issues associated with sustainable development.

Numerous round tables[9] similar to the NRTEE were established at provincial level in the late 1980s/early 1990s. They usually did not enjoy the same degree of legal stability, which often put them in an insecure position with regard to the sensitivity of the political debates. Most of them were eventually disbanded after a few years of existence, by the mid-1990s. Similar round tables have also been proposed at the local level.

The Commissioner of the Environment and Sustainable Development

The second institution that plays a central role is the Commissioner on the Environment and Sustainable Development. This is an institution which is very specific to Canada, and is a source of independent audit of the federal government in this field. Amendments to the *Auditor General Act* in 1995 created the position of Commissioner of the Environment and Sustainable Development, and at the same time required ministers to prepare sustainable development strategies that are subject to its oversight. The Commissioner is appointed by the Auditor General and reports directly to him; this provides him with authority and legal stability, although the office of the Commissioner enjoys a fair degree of autonomy.

One of the main functions of the Commissioner's office, whose role is to report on government performance on environment and sustainable development issues broadly, is to monitor and report on federal progress in implementing sustainable development strategies.[10] The Commissioner is responsible *inter alia* for:

- Review of departmental sustainable development strategies and their implementation.
- Audits of the federal government's management of environment and sustainable development issues.
- Studies aimed at improving understanding and strengthening management practices.
- Monitoring of petitions.

A yearly "green" report is presented to Parliament (see section below) and made publicly available on the Internet. Comprehensive information and databases are also available on the Commissioner's Internet site. A particular effort is made to assure sufficient visibility for this report. The Internet site includes evaluation of past achievements and promising practices, diagnoses of failures, explicit goals and recommendations to improve the elaboration or implementation of sustainable strategies, suggested future directions: all these provide clear incentives for government and a clear picture for citizens. The report also includes the Commissioner's observations on the number, nature and status of environmental petitions (see below for the amendment to the 1995 legislation).

It should be underlined that other audit groups in the Office of the Auditor General also carry out environmental audits, although the Commissioner's group conducts the largest amount of environmental audit work. Before the creation of the Commissioner's position, the Office of the Auditor General had already performed over 40 audits with a significant environmental or sustainable development dimension. Auditing in these areas has since increased, either as purely environmental audits or as part of wider audits, *e.g.* on fisheries.

a)   The role of Parliament

The Canadian Parliament, in which legislative authority is vested, has three components: the Queen (represented by the Governor General), the Senate and the House of Commons. Bills may originate in the Senate (except bills providing for the expenditure of public money or imposing taxes) or the House of Commons and must pass both houses and receive royal assent before becoming law. The main part of the Senate's work takes place in committees, where bills are reviewed and evidence heard. The Senate also carries out its own investigations into important public problems such as poverty, science policy or land use. The House of Commons, whose Members are elected by universal suffrage, is the major law-making body. It is responsible for bills providing for the expenditure of public money or imposing taxes, and the majority of Cabinet Ministers are appointed from among its Members. A vote of no confidence in the House of Commons means the defeat of the Government. A detailed description of budgeting processes in Canada is provided in *Budgeting in Canada.*[11]

Apart from giving assent to bills in the name of the Queen, one of the key functions of the Governor General is to officially open every new session of Parliament with the Speech from the Throne. This speech is an essential reference, as it sets out the broad goals and directions of the government and its strategy to accomplish those goals. The last two Speeches from the Throne of October 1999 and February 2001 certainly stressed Canadian concerns about environment and sustainable development issues.

Main parliamentary work is done in the Standing Committee on the Environment and Sustainable Development of the House of Commons Acts, which address sustainable development generally or under specific provisions including the *Canadian Environmental Assessment Act* (1992), the *National Round Table on the Environment and the*

Economy Act (1993), the *Auditor General Act* (1995 amendments), the *Oceans Act* (1996), and the recently updated *Canadian Environmental Protection Act, 1999*, as well as various statutes establishing departments. However, for the most part, sustainable development awareness did not lead to an in-depth review of Canadian legislation. This is not surprising, since sustainable development is not a separate policy area but rather a "goal" to be met. Part of the reason may also be that, traditionally, some of the concerns relating to sustainable development have been covered by specialised legislation, *e.g.* on environmental protection. On the other hand, in the context of the power sharing between levels of government, a number of areas crucial to sustainable development are legislated at the provincial level: for example, the use of natural resources.

As stated above, two important pieces of legislation established institutions to promote sustainable development and to ensure mechanisms for reporting to Parliament, namely the National Round Table on the Environment and the Economy and the Commissioner of the Environment and Sustainable Development. The 1995 amendments to the Auditor General Act established the request for Ministers to produce Sustainable Development Strategies and to report to Parliament. The Sustainable Development Strategies are being updated, as stipulated by the legal requirement for departments to update them every three years. The first Strategies were tabled in 1997, and their progress since then is reported annually to Parliament. The second set of updated Sustainable Development Strategies were developed and presented to the House of Commons on 14 February 2001.[12] The NRTEE also plays a role in informing Parliament and providing expertise. For example, in November 1999 NRTEE recommendations to incorporate a number of significant environmental initiatives into the 2000 Budget were presented to the House of Commons Standing Committee on Finance (see Annex I). Past NRTEE recommendations were considered by the Department of Finance in developing the 2000 budget bill.[13]

Perhaps one of the most important mechanisms of parliamentary oversight on sustainable development issues is the "green report" of the Commissioner for the Environment and Sustainable Development. The report is presented to the House of Commons on behalf of the Auditor General and covers the extent to which departments have implemented their strategies. The Commissioner of the Environment and Sustainable Development, as stated in his mandate, assists parliamentarians in their oversight of the federal government's efforts to protect the environment and foster sustainable development, by providing them with objective, independent analysis and recommendations.

b) The role of the Judiciary

In Canada, there is no specific legislation on sustainable development implementation. However, one of the purposes of the *Canadian Environmental Assessment*

51

Act is "to encourage responsible authorities to take actions that promote sustainable development and thereby achieve or maintain a healthy environment and a healthy economy". The courts' role is rather limited to legislation and regulations pertaining to the three pillars of sustainable development (*i.e.* environment, economic and social). NGOs have been increasingly active in using judicial review to question the proper application of environmental assessment law, particularly when major development projects could have significant environmental effects. One noticeable exception to the absence of legislation is the above-cited 1995 amendment to the Auditor General's Act.

Another interesting area is a recent change to the Canadian Environmental Protection Act: Law C.33, Section 209 1) states that the Governor in Council may, on the recommendation of the Minister, create regulations for the protection of the environment, including, but not limited to, regulations governing the establishment of environmental management systems. These are systems based on the ISO 14000 series of standards. Such provisions could result in more cases being taken before the courts. This amendment has already generated cases such as a recent court ruling that required a Canadian company to implement an environmental management system. It is likely that similar cases will develop in the future.

c)   The role of federal departments

In the Canadian government, line ministries are highly specialised along sectoral lines. This structural pattern could lead to policy fragmentation and inconsistencies in strategic choices with an impact on sustainable development. Therefore, efforts have been made to create a coherent framework out of potentially conflicting policy options. Since 1994, the federal government has re-focused its policies, programmes and operations in order to integrate sustainable development. As mentioned above, departments were requested by the 1995 amendments to the Auditor General Act to draw up sustainable development strategies, to further the "greening" of government (greening of budgets of government operations, etc.).

By December 1997, 28 departments and agencies had prepared their first Sustainable Development Strategies and tabled them in the House of Commons. Those Strategies provided a picture of how each government department viewed sustainable development and how they intended to promote it. Since then, departments have focused on implementing their Strategies and reporting their progress. A *Leaders' Forum on Sustainable Development* was organised on 4th April 2000 to help co-ordinate the strategies. The forum brought together federal government and non-government leaders to discuss the sustainable development challenges and opportunities facing Canada. It was held as a launch pad for updating departmental Sustainable Development Strategies and allowed federal government departments to seek advice on ways to better co-ordinate their approaches to advancing sustainable development across departments.

The 1995 legislation requires departments to draw up sustainable development strategies. Requirements for departmental strategies are detailed in a federal government publication entitled A *Guide to Green Government*. This Guide indicates that each strategy should be:

- **Comprehensive** – Dealing with both departmental policies and programmes, and the management of the department's internal operations.
- **Results-oriented** – Identifying the main results the department will achieve and how it will measure performance in terms of sustainable development.
- **Developed in consultation** with the department's client partners and other stakeholders.

Following these guidelines, departments have usually produced the following strategies:

1. The creation of an Advisory Committee composed of academics, civil servants, etc. These "experts in the field" met to define the issues and establish the first parameters of the strategy.

2. Broad and inclusive multi-stakeholder consultation (business, NGOs, etc.).

3. Planning, including objectives.

The Commissioner considers that the first round of sustainable development strategies provided a clear picture of how each department views sustainable development and plans to promote it. Preparing their strategies made departments – and also their clients and stakeholders – more aware of sustainable development issues.

However, the review conducted by the Commissioner and presented in his 1998 report (chapter 1) revealed some weaknesses in the strategies. Two of these are fundamental:

- Almost all departments failed to set clear enough targets that they, parliamentarians and the public could use to judge whether or not the strategy is being implemented successfully.
- Many of the strategies appeared to be more a restatement of the status quo than a commitment to change in order to protect better the environment and promote sustainable development.

The Commissioner underlined in particular the need to improve benchmarks. Departments felt that strategy setting is a complex process and that they were in a learning phase that would help them improve the next strategies.

Departments presented their second sustainable development strategies in February 2001. Although it is too early to evaluate the new strategies in this study, it is clear that they benefited from the experience gained from the first round of strategy preparation in order to achieve an improvement in strategy quality.

Consistent with the approach of continual improvement supported by the Commissioner of the Environment and Sustainable Development, ministries are already engaged in this exercise. For example, Industry Canada will make its strategy narrower but more focused on achievable targets. Transport Canada is trying to get more buy-in from the staff, not very involved in the former process, in order to facilitate the commitment to implement the strategy. One of the expectations of the Commissioner of the Environment and Sustainable Development is innovative thinking: departments are meant to focus more on *what they will do differently*.

It is too early to measure the impact of this evolution, which can be described as a step-by-step approach. Improvements should be highlighted, however. According to the 2000 report of the Commissioner of the Environment and Sustainable Development, departments reported that they had implemented 20 per cent of the commitments set out in their strategies, compared with 11 per cent in 1999. The fact that departments have been obliged to develop sustainable development strategies according to the Auditor General Act, 1995, that these strategies must be updated every three years, and that they are evaluated by the Commissioner, could help improve the coherence of departmental action in the longer term. Canada's f federal departments are now entering a second phase of their strategy development, and this is an opportunity for making noticeable progress to implement the strategies.

Responsibilities for the environment and sustainable development are shared across government. However, recognising the accountability arrangements inherent in Canadian parliamentary democracy, Canada has chosen a decentralised approach to advance the government's sustainable development agenda, with each minister accountable for progress under his or her mandate. Many of the participants in the first round of strategy preparation stressed the importance of developing a "Government of Canada" perspective on sustainable development. Therefore, effective co-ordination across these mandates and jurisdictions is also seen as a condition of success for future strategies, and this is what motivated the organisation of the *Leaders' Forum on Sustainable Development* of 4 April 2000. The approach developed aims to bring enhanced policy coherence to sustainable development at the federal level and to better co-ordinate the delivery of federal commitments. It has been undertaken in order to address the challenges of a decentralised approach to sustainable development across the federal family.

d) Government agencies

Following the 1995 *Guide to Green Government*, specific efforts have been made to integrate sustainable development concerns in the day-to-day management of government agencies. The most central example is the key role played by the Treasury Board Secretariat. The Treasury Board is one of four Cabinet Committees of the Queen's Privy Council of Canada. It was established constitutionally in 1867 and given statutory powers in 1869. The mission of the Secretariat of this committee (Treasury Board Secretariat – TBS) is to help the government of Canada manage its human, financial, information and technology resources. This includes planning and managing government-wide expenditure, managing the federal government's human resources, developing modern comptrollership systems for managing government resources, leading the use of information technology across government, and developing infrastructure programmes. As the federal government's employer, and the central agency responsible for the federal government's human resources management framework, TBS is a key agency for achieving sustainability. Therefore it has ensured that sustainable development principles be given due attention. TBS is involved in supporting the government's approach to establishing sustainable development strategies, and also provides a central incentive to green government operations. Selected illustrative examples include:

- Providing guidelines and support for implementation of strategies.

- Co-operating with the Department of Finance Canada to develop an Environmental Management System (EMS). The EMS provides a management framework for building on existing initiatives to incorporate environmental considerations into all facets of departmental operations.

- Developing partnerships with government departments and other levels of government. A good example includes the *Canada Infrastructure Works Programs.*

- Promoting, planning and integrating sustainable development principles into contract and asset management.

- Minimising negative effects of operations of government employees on the environment through integrating sustainable development principles into management practices.

- Developing a culture of change, which is fundamental to the government's ability to introduce its sustainable development strategies.

- Developing a comprehensive communications plan for increasing awareness of environmental issues.

In addition to the greening operations and planning of "traditional" agencies, some newly created agencies have been in charge of promoting sustainable development goals mainly for the purpose of environment protection. They have been driven by the need to carry out functions for achieving the implementation of both international agreements and domestic goals.

The Prime Minister established the Climate Change Secretariat in February 1998, following a December 1997 agreement among First Ministers (the Prime Minister and

Premiers of the provinces and territories) to establish a joint federal-provincial-territorial process for examining the consequences of the Kyoto Protocol, in advance of a federal decision on ratification. This 30-person secretariat has both national and federal responsibilities. The National Secretariat, staffed by federal and provincial officials seconded from their respective governments, supports the policy and programme development work of the National Air Issues Co-ordinating Committee on Climate Change (which is accountable to federal and provincial Deputy Ministers of Energy and Environment). The Federal Secretariat, also consisting of seconded staff, reports to the Deputy Ministers of Natural Resources Canada and Environment Canada and supplements, rather than replaces or duplicates, work done by federal departments.

- The Federal Secretariat supports the policy development work of federal departments for developing the federal government's domestic policy, as well as broad communications strategy development and programming climate change.

- The National Secretariat co-ordinates, in co-operation with federal, provincial and territorial officials, the implementation of the National Implementation Strategy on climate change. The strategy, publicly released in October 2000, sets out a framework for a co-ordinated Canadian response to climate change, involving both greenhouse gas emissions reduction and adaptation actions. The strategy's phased approach allows for progressive action through annual updates of a national climate change business plan and will position Canada to make major decisions, such as the ratification of the Kyoto Protocol and use of a major economic instrument.

- The Federal Secretariat manages the federal Climate Change Action Fund.

The First National Climate Change Business Plan was released in October 2000. This comprehensive set of federal-provincial-territorial actions draws extensively on the reports of 16 "issue tables", involving two years of work by 450 experts from government, industry, NGOs and academia. This business plan includes sectoral actions (*e.g.* transportation, industry and agriculture) and broader measures under four themes: enhancing awareness and understanding of climate change; promoting technology development and innovation; governments leading by example; and investing in knowledge/building the foundation for future actions.

The Climate Change Action Fund was established in order to build a foundation for policy and to initiate early action in addressing climate change. The Secretariat is responsible for developing the framework for assessment, decision-making and follow-up on project proposals to be funded. This $150 million fund was designed to operate over a three-year period. A three-year extension of this fund, effective 1 April 2001, was announced in the February 2000 federal budget.

The Canadian Environmental Assessment Agency (CEAA) was set up as an independent agency in 1995 with a mandate to better integrate environmental considerations into project planning. The 1995 *Canadian Environmental Assessment Act* (the Act) and the 1999 *Cabinet Directive on the Environmental Assessment of Policy, Plan and Program Proposals* (the Directive) were instituted as the basis for the federal environmental assessment (EA) process, at both the project and policy levels. The objective of the Act and the Directive is to provide an effective means of integrating environmental factors into federal planning and decision-making in a way that takes sustainable development into account. The CEAA is currently undergoing a five-year review, which will result in amendments to the Act.

The CEAA has six key roles:

- Administering the environmental assessment process established by the Act and its regulations.

- Promoting the uniformity and harmonisation of environmental assessment activities across Canada at all levels of government.

- Providing advice to the Minister of the Environment on the Minister's responsibilities under the Act.

- Promoting or conducting research on environmental assessment matters.

- Ensuring opportunities for public participation in the federal environmental assessment process.

- And promoting sound environmental assessment practices in a manner consistent with those established in the Act.

The CEAA assumes a leadership role at the federal level in promoting high-quality assessments. It also invests in research and development, especially in order to improve the quality of environmental assessment and its practicability. One of the benefits of its assessments is to contribute to informed decision making, which is a key element for sustainable development.

As regards the social side of sustainable development, the *Canadian Environmental Assessment Act* (Act) addresses the effect of environmental degradation on human health. Under this Act, the Office of Environmental Health Assessment (EHA) serves as a one-window access to Health Canada. The responsibilities of the EHA staff include:

- Co-ordinating and focusing the involvement of Health Canada in the environmental assessment process.

- Reviewing the health component of federal environmental assessment (EA) projects.

57

- Co-ordinating the preparation and presentation of the Department's scientific health information for another federal department, public review panel or mediator.

- Providing notice through public registry of any Health Canada project sent to the Minister of the Environment for referral to a mediator or panel.

- Sharing knowledge with representatives of other countries to develop environmental health assessment processes, regulations and scientific knowledge at the international level.

- Promoting health in environmental assessment.

The EHA was, for example, involved in the assessment of the environmental effects of the Pearson International airport of Toronto and in efforts to develop a concept on nuclear fuel waste management and disposal. It should be stressed that environmental assessment involves bodies reporting to different departments, which calls for good co-ordination mechanisms.

Working with sub-national government

a)   Provincial and local initiatives

Provincial governments have competencies – exclusive or shared– in several policy fields which directly affect sustainable development (natural resources, agriculture, immigration). Co-operative efforts are developing in the social area with a strong commitment from the centre. This is the case of the "social union" initiative, which is an umbrella under which federal-provincial and territorial governments are concentrating their efforts to renew and modernise pan-Canadian social policy. To date, they have reached a broad consensus on what should be the top priorities: poverty-stricken children and persons with disabilities. The National Climate Change Process also offers a good example of multi-level co-operation. An agreement was reached in October 2000 by the federal government and thirteen of the fourteen provinces and territories to release the National Implementation Strategy and First National Business Plan.

Provinces have developed policies accordingly. In the 1990s, several round tables on sustainable development were initiated at provincial level, as well as the requirement to develop sustainable development strategies within provincial governments. New initiatives also included passing specific legislation. Work is well under way under the Canadian Council of Ministers of the Environment Harmonisation Accord, including provincial and federal commitments to several Canada-wide standards. The developments in Manitoba and Ontario are reported below. They provide an illustration of sustainable development initiatives at provincial level, although these examples should not be considered as exhaustive or representative of the complex and varied experiences under way in Canada.

Box 4. **The Manitoba Sustainable Development and Consequential Amendments Act, 1997**

The Act established in section 2 the government obligation to consider sustainable development and the Principles and Guidelines set out in the Act in all of its activities. The 7 principles are:

- Integration of environmental and economic considerations.
- Stewardship.
- Shared responsibility.
- Prevention.
- Conservation and enhancements.
- Rehabilitation and reclamation.
- Global responsibility.

The guidelines are:

- Efficient use of resources.
- Public participation.
- Access to information.
- Integrated decision-making and planning.
- Waste minimisation and substitution.
- Research and innovation.

Source: *Government of Manitoba Internet site.*

Manitoba's Sustainable Development and Consequential Amendments Act (1997) created a framework through which sustainable development could be implemented in the provincial public sector and promoted in private industry and in society in general (see Box 4). For example, section 4 of the Manitoba Sustainable Development and Consequential Amendments Act established a Manitoba Round Table on Sustainable Development. The Round Table, which has at least 20 members from government and elsewhere, is responsible for promoting sustainable development and advising government. In Ontario, the *Ontario Transportation and Climate Change Collaborative* was set up by the former Ontario Round Table, which produced the report "A Strategy for Sustainable Transportation in Ontario" and ten research reports. The Ontario Ministry of the Environment also used the scenario-planning tool for long-term planning as part of its business planning efforts.

59

Of course, federal and provincial agendas do not necessarily match, but, generally speaking, some features of Canadian federalism (*i.e.* the importance of consultative processes) helped to maintain a certain commonality of talk between levels of government on major sustainable development orientations.

Municipal level innovative practices represent a variety of uneven experiences. Some local initiatives to collect and recycle paper or glass have had tremendous success all across the country,[14] *e.g.* blue box recycling programmes in Ontario or British Columbia. Currently there are attempts to unify practices and promote good management. This effort is partly driven by the Federation of Canadian Municipalities. For example, to help meet the targets of the Kyoto protocol, the Federation launched a "20 per cent club", with the objective of encouraging municipalities to undertake a sustained effort to reduce GHG emissions by 20 per cent. However, only thirty municipal governments are involved to date. A municipal sustainability charter is also being developed, which could become part of Canada's contribution to the final draft of the Earth Charter in 2002.

In Toronto, the new official plan that is being prepared for the amalgamated City of Toronto will include sustainability among its "core values". The city council set up the Environmental Task Force (ETF) in March 1998 to help the city respond to its environmental challenges. Part of the task force's mandate is to recommend a structure that will incorporate advanced environmental decision making into the political and administrative structure of the city. The content of the recommendation made by the task force is described in Annex II. This resulted from a consultation with over 200 people and was approved by the city in November 1999. One particular aspect of the task force's work was the recognition of the need for an integrated programme of sustainability education and outreach: ETF therefore formed a multi-stakeholder Education Working Group. The Group prepared recommendations for changes in the formal, informal and non-formal modes of instruction and learning. Local initiatives also include long-term planning and strategic thinking. *Hamilton-Wentworth Vision* 2020 describes the Hamilton-Wentworth community in the year 2020, if decisions affecting the community follow the principles of sustainable development.

b)   Improving collaboration between levels of government

The federal government has entered into environmental partnership agreements with the provinces in order to reduce overlap and duplication. Environment Canada and Fisheries and Oceans Canada initiated seven federal-provincial environmental agreements. These were made under the *Canadian Environmental Protection Act* (CEPA) and the *Fisheries Act* and cover activities such as inspection, enforcement, monitoring and reporting. Two of the agreements included environmental protection as a stated objective. The other five agreements mentioned environmental protection in their preambles. Another example of federal-provincial co-operation is the *Canadian Council of Fisheries and Aquaculture Ministers*. Sub-agreements on Environmental Assessment were also concluded on a bilateral basis with British Columbia, Alberta, Saskatchewan, and Manitoba, and negotiations are under way with Ontario and New Brunswick.

The agreements were audited by the Commissioner of the Environment and Sustainable Development, 1998, who highlighted some weaknesses in the process (*e.g.* lack of formal evaluation or documentation on the extent to which these agreements had been effective in avoiding duplication, lack of information to Parliament). Some improvements were suggested:

- The agreements should include specific reporting requirements that will be meaningful to Parliament, government, the public and industry.

- Better evaluation of existing bilateral agreements and incorporation of the "lessons learned" into any new agreements should be developed.

- Parliament should not be provided with incomplete or out-of-date information on how well the agreements are working.

Canada has established a mechanism for providing a multi-level framework on environmental issues, namely the Canadian Council of Ministers of the Environment (CCME). This plays a leading role in integrating views across levels of government and improving collaboration on environmental issues. It is composed of the 13 ministers of the environment for the federal, provincial and territorial governments in Canada. Working as equal partners in an area of shared jurisdiction, the ministers come together at the CCME table to meet the three objectives set out in 1991 in the CCME by-laws:

- To establish and maintain an intergovernmental forum for discussion and joint action on environmental issues of national, international and global concern.

- To harmonise environmental legislation, policies, procedures and programmes.

- To develop nationally consistent environmental objectives, standards and scientific databases and complementary strategies, accords and agreements.

One illustration of the positive impact of this mechanism is the *Canada-wide Accord on Environmental Harmonisation* that came into force on 29 January 1998. This is the framework agreement that establishes the common vision, objectives and principles that will govern the partnership between jurisdictions, and the development and implementation of sub-agreements (Canada-wide Environmental Inspections Sub-agreement, Canada-wide Environmental Standards Sub-agreement, Sub-agreement on Environmental Assessment).

Box 5. Selected Local Initiatives

GeoConnections is an initiative to develop the Canadian Geospatial Data Infrastructure on the Internet. One of the seven programmes developed by this initiative is "sustainable communities". It is aiming to build and strengthen the capacity of Canadian communities to effectively plan and manage their economic, environmental and social development using geo-info and services delivered through the information highway. Through selected pilot projects this programme should deliver data and technologies to communities to build capacity to support local decision-making and value-added SMEs using geo-info.

The *EcoAction Community Funding Program* is an Environment Canada programme that provides financial support to community groups for projects that have measurable, positive impacts on the environment. Non-profit groups and organisations are eligible to apply to the programme. This includes, but is not limited to community groups, environmental groups, Aboriginal groups and First Nations councils, service clubs, associations and youth and seniors' organisations.

The *Sustainable Community Indicators Program* is a Windows-based software and a website to help communities measure and monitor: environmental health; resource consumption; settlement patterns; human wellbeing; employment and commerce.

The Community Animation Program (CAP) is a joint initiative of Health Canada and Environment Canada that aims to support community capacity to act on issues involving both human health and the environment. CAP enables individuals and communities to make their own decisions to promote good health and ensure a healthy environment.

The 1998 Federal Budget confirmed funding of Can$20 million over four years for the *Canadian Rural Partnership* (CRP). The CRP is designed to support rural community development by adopting new approaches and practices to respond to rural development issues and concerns. A key component of the CRP is the Rural Dialogue. The objective of the Rural Dialogue is to better understand local and regional issues and to identify the appropriate role for the federal government in addressing key rural issues. The Rural Dialogue allows the federal government to engage rural Canadians and listen to their needs. The Rural Dialogue has been designed to facilitate broad participation, while respecting the need for managing expectations. It builds on existing consultation networks and federal government regional infrastructures.

Ecosystem initiatives respond to the problems of targeted areas and communities in addressing sustainable development. They aim to achieve environmental results through partnerships, pooling resources, focusing science, co-ordinating efforts, sharing information and experiences, and generating a broad basis of support. Moreover, they help build the capacity of all the players involved to make better decisions and to effect change (for background on specific local initiatives see: *www.ec.gc.ca/ecosyst/backgrounder.html*).

Source: *Government of Canada Internet sites.*

The Accord seeks to address issues of interests across Canada, for example:

- All governments agree to a number of fundamental principles, including the "polluter pays" principle, the precautionary principle and a recognition that pollution prevention is the preferred approach to environmental protection.

- All governments retain their legislative authority.

- The features of sub-agreements to be developed under the Accord are defined, including a one-window approach; the notion of roles being assumed by the government best situated to take them on; accountability through regular public reporting of measurable obligations and results; and a commitment to develop alternative plans if obligations are not met.

Currently, there are also numerous initiatives and programmes run by federal departments to assist Canadians in making sustainable development decisions at the community level (see Box 5). These initiatives are being examined with a view to building stronger capacity for SD where many decisions are made (e.g. by improving access to information, tools and best practices). The 2000 budget also provided Can$ 125 million to municipalities for improving their energy and environmental infrastructures under "Community Initiatives".

A specific effort was also made to take better account of sustainable development issues in the North, where the ecological and social implications of economic development are particularly sensitive. This included institutional reform at the sub-national level, improving federal capacity to deal with the problems of the North and new partnerships across levels of government (see Annex III).

The role of the non-governmental sector

It would be difficult to compare the approaches of different organisations such as private sector organisations, universities, professional organisations and citizens' organisations. But they all have an impact on the country's governance framework. Private companies are also increasingly looking at how to build environmental and sustainable development considerations into the way they do business. In particular, the natural resources corporate sectors have had to face sustainable development issues in their operations and policies. Like some of the first sustainable development strategies, initial corporate reports tended to focus narrowly on the positive aspects of environmental performance, but as they gained experience they developed specific management systems. The Commissioner of the Environment and Sustainable Development highlighted these positive development in his 1998 report and suggested that they be a source of learning for public organisations' management systems (see Box 6).

The general widely held idea is that the public and the private sectors should work together, primarily to ensure the competitiveness of the Canadian economy.

63

Box 6. **Corporate Reports Development in the Private Sector**

Commissioner's Observations, Report of the Commissioner of the Environment and Sustainable Development, 1998.

Like some of the first sustainable development strategies, initial corporate reports tended to focus narrowly on the positive aspects of organisations' environmental performance. But as organisations gained experience and worked with a management system that supported their strategies, the reports provided broader and deeper coverage of the issues facing the organisations and the way they were dealing with those issues.

International surveys of corporate environmental reporting carried out for the United Nations Environment Programme by Sustainability Ltd. show major improvements in the quality of reporting over time. According to Sustainability Ltd., today the best corporate reports:

- Cover all three dimensions of sustainable development – economic, social and environmental.
- Highlight the key issues directly linked to the company's core business, and priorities in dealing with them.
- Present performance indicators with targets that are specific, measurable, attainable and verified.

Those are the same characteristics the Commissioner of the Environment and Sustainable Development suggested for sustainable development strategies prepared by federal government departments in 2000.

Source: Commissioner of the Environment and Sustainable Development

---

When it comes to sustainable development, there is a clear perception in the Canadian government that the importance of the issue in terms of economic, as well as environmental and social, stability requires integrated efforts to provide a coherent public/private interface. The need for integration is shared to some extent by key sectors of the economy having a major impact on the environment, such as the mining industry, or pulp and paper, chemical or electricity producers. These have traditionally been the most polluting industries and were therefore subject to much criticism. In order to restore their image, these sectors are increasingly attempting to institute sustainable development strategies, and the concept of sustainable communities is growing.

Concerning co-operation with private companies, the main dilemmas from a democratic point of view would probably be two-fold: on the one hand, developing collaborative approaches without falling into "collusion between government and special interests", which would damage the credibility of public polices; on the other hand, determining which sector should be charged for the financial consequences of each particular arrangement.[15] Although this is not a guarantee *per se* against "collusion", collaboration with the private sector would take place in the framework of "multi-stakeholder" processes involving government, various economic interests and not-for-profit organisations. This would allow a dialogue and a degree of openness and transparency. This process results from both the public sector's initiative (*e.g.* consultation for the elaboration and follow-up of ministerial strategies) and from private sector initiatives. As an illustrative example, the approach followed by the Chemical Producers Association is described in Annex VII.

NGOs also started from specific sectoral perspectives (such as environment, health, and rights of indigenous people) and then moved toward looking at how the issues interrelated. NGOs, which indeed represent a number of interests and concerns, were increasingly involved in the policy process, particularly in the early stages of strategy setting or in the elaboration of specific legislation. In sectors such as health at the community level, or in giving advice (think tanks), NGOs have gained a role in the discussion of sustainability issues and the development of solutions. Roughly speaking, Canadian NGOs do not necessarily develop the same approaches, and retain various positions in the "governance framework". But they increasingly affect overall sustainable development governance. It is worth mentioning that there is a noticeable diversity of NGOs involved in the policy process in sectors as varied as health, community service, environment, youth, etc. An example of NGO involvement is provided in Box 7.

Several Canadian universities were active in developing expertise-related sustainable development issues (economics, environmental studies, work on social cohesion, etc.). Academics actively participated in the elaboration of the sustainable development strategies of the government (notably through the drafting of conceptual papers and participation in the consultation processes), which shows a potential for the integration of knowledge and policy making (see section below on *policy formulation*). A prominent university network for sustainability is the *Canadian Consortium of SD Research Institutes*. It includes well-known institutions such as the *York Center for Applied Sustainability*.

C.   Decision-making mechanisms

Reaching agreements

In Canada most of the major stakeholders (public organisations, major private companies and non-for-profit organisations) share a consensus on the broad definition of sustainable development that was developed by the World Commission

---

Box 7. **An Example of NGO Involvement in the Sustainable Development Debate: The Sierra Club of Canada**

The Sierra Club of Canada offers an example of a "campaigning" NGO. It is a national, non-profit, environmental research and advocacy organisation, membership based and volunteer driven. It is a thirty-year-old NGO affiliated to the Sierra Club in the US and chose to remain financially independent from the government. The means of intervention by the Sierra Club range from activism, such as lobbying, to organising demonstrations or supporting petitions. This illustrates that the Sierra Club is working as a "watchdog" organisation. However, the Sierra Club is open to participation in multi-stakeholder processes involving other NGOs, government organisations and industry. Its aim is to strengthen partnerships between NGOs and contribute to increasing the role of global NGOs. The Sierra Club has been very active in certain areas. One example is the protection of endangered species. Canada had no federal legislation for protecting endangered species. Both supporters and opponents discussed whether it should be a matter of debate, since most provinces have their own legislation. The Sierra Club has been a strong promoter of endangered species legislation, trying to convince other stakeholders (like industry) and parliamentarians to push this agenda before government and to bring a project to Parliament. The long co-operative process, partly driven by this NGO, helped raise awareness and arrive at a common understanding. The Accord for Protection of Species at Risk was signed in September 1999. A legislative proposal was introduced in April 2000.

---

on Environment and Development, that is, "meeting our needs without compromising future generations' needs". Beyond that commitment, different approaches are taken by the different stakeholders, reflecting their conflicting interests.

One basic issue for taking the right public decisions is how to arbitrate among opinions, which are often divided on issues (approach, appreciation of risk, proof, etc.). This may affect the perception of the issues among various parts of the public sector, which do not rely on several sources of expertise. This is the case of the management of toxic substances, for example . According to the 1999 report of the Commissioner of the Environment and Sustainable Development, even federal departments (*e.g.* environment, agriculture and industry) are deeply divided on many key issues and do not share a common vision on how toxic substances should be managed. The links between departments and various interest groups in the field, mainly businesses and lobbies, does not make decision taking easy. The process has to be managed in a way which at the same time does not compromise the core interest of these groups, and allows a sustainable solution to be found. A certain balance has to be struck.

This generates a complex coherence and co-ordination challenge in a potentially conflictual environment: how to integrate different concrete strategies with overall goals. Another central factor of complexity is the interaction between levels of government in reaching agreement, considering that implementation takes place regularly at the provincial and local levels. A concrete step has been initiated in the fisheries sector (see Annex IV), in order to improve decision-making mechanisms in the context of diverse interests leading to major management crisis.

More generally, an important factor for facilitating consensus building in the Canadian federal system has been informal mechanisms to reach agreement. Regular meetings are a good example (see Box 1).

Public participation and consultation

a) Public consultation and participation at the federal level

Since the 1990s, various federal initiatives have been taken, such as the development of a consultation policy and guidelines for public servants in 1992. A forum organised in 1997 to help design the reform of the health system deliberately engaged a variety of communities that might otherwise have been unable to participate, including homeless men, street children, immigrants, low-income mothers, senior citizens and First Nations (Aboriginal populations). This process involved working with community leaders and band members, as well as the translation of the consultation document into Inuktituk. The Canadian government has recently launched an initiative to update and enhance the 1992 consultation guidelines for public servants and to prepare a federal policy statement as well as new guidelines for consultation and engagement (see Box 8).

The elaboration of departmental strategies for sustainable development followed the general 1992 guidelines. Almost all federal departments (28) and agencies have consulted with citizens in drawing up their first sustainable development strategies. More than 1600 organisations and Aboriginal communities were involved in helping departments identify priorities for sustainable development and how to achieve them.

According to the 1999 report of the Commissioner of the Environment and Sustainable Development, the level of satisfaction with the consultations that departments used to prepare their first sustainable development strategies was high. Participants generally felt that departments had listened; in turn, departments believed that the consultations had broadened their own perspectives. However, the Commissioner of the Environment and Sustainable Development identified some weaknesses in the consultation process of some departments, i.e. limited co-ordination among departments, limited involvement of senior management (with, as a consequence, a lack of leadership and negative effects on staff buy-in), and limited feedback to participants. Attempts to address these problems have been dealt with in the consultation round leading to the strategy revisions.

67

Box 8.   **Towards a Federal Commitment to Engage Citizens**

The Privy Council Office, in collaboration with the Treasury Board Secretariat and all federal departments and agencies, is currently developing a *Federal Policy Statement and Guidelines on Engaging Canadians* to replace the existing federal consultation guidelines (1992). The purpose of the policy is to affirm the government's commitment to public consultation, to define general guiding principles and practices for the effective engagement of citizens in government decision making, and to outline roles and responsibilities in supporting a consultative culture in the federal government. The federal government commitment is intended to result in:

- Policies and programmes that are responsive to public priorities, needs and concerns.
- Well-informed, sound and broadly accepted decisions.
- Accountability to decision makers and the public.
- Ongoing improvement of federal consultation processes.
- Increased confidence in federal institutions.

Source: OECD/PUMA *Case Study on Strengthening Government-Citizens Connections in Canada* (see PUMA Website).

One particular aspect of public involvement is the petition process, which contributes to improving direct communication channels between government and citizens in a system that usually gives more space to "established" stakeholders, and to foster "active transparency" mechanisms. The amendments to the Auditor General Act created a formal vehicle for channelling public input and concern about environment and sustainable development issues to federal departments. They provided a statutory public petition process. Under this new process, residents of Canada can forward a petition in writing to the Auditor General. These petitions must relate to matters that are the responsibility of the specific departments and agencies required to prepare and implement sustainable development strategies. The Commissioner forwards these written petitions to the appropriate minister on behalf of the Auditor General. Ministers are required to respond to these petitions within a set time period. The Commissioner monitors the status of these petitions and reports his findings to the House of Commons in his annual report.

These petitions have been used several times (usually by organisations rather than individual citizens). Considering the active role of NGOs, their role is likely to increase in the future. For example, during the year ended 31 March 1999, nine new

---

Box 9.   **Involvement Through Agencies: The Role of the CEAA**

Public involvement should be included in all aspects of sustainable develop-ment and not only at the stage of designing strategies for future action; it is also a key objective of the Environment Assessment process. The CEAA, for example, encourages public involvement by:

- Ensuring that the public has an opportunity to review and comment on proposed class screening reports and comprehensive study reports before any decisions are taken.
- Providing guidance to federal departments and project proponents on effectively involving the public.
- Maintaining a public registry for all projects undergoing an environmental assessment.
- Providing guidance to federal departments in establishing and maintaining a public registry for projects, so that the public can conveniently access environmental assessment reports and supporting documents.
- Providing funding to interested groups so that they can participate in mediation sessions and panel reviews.
- Providing administrative and technical support for independent panel reviews that involve extensive public hearings.
- Maintaining the Federal Environmental Assessment Index (FEIA) (an electronic database of all federal assessments), and encouraging federal departments to keep the FEIA up to date.

---

petitions were received and sent to ministers for response. Seven of those petitions dealt with issues under the Minister of Fisheries and Oceans' mandate. Five of the petitions concerned environmental assessments.

Another aspect of direct citizen involvement that may play a crucial role is the use of new technologies, especially the Internet. The number of people being con-nected to the Internet is increasing rapidly in Canada. Considering the size of the country and the number of geographically isolated communities, the generalisation of access to computer technologies has changed the nature of the relationship between government and citizens. Citizens can express more direct demands, which need to be considered effectively. In the field of sustainable development, most of the information on ministerial strategies, work of sectoral agencies, etc. is now accessible to the citizens through the Internet. Public organisations are increasingly using an interactive mode (question and answer, feedback, etc.), which offers a potential aid for designing future policies. It is also very challenging,

---

since public bodies must develop a capacity to manage new flows of communication and respond to potentially conflicting demands. The success or failure of these processes could have a significant impact on sustainable development.

b) Public consultation at the sub-national level

At sub-national level, consultation and participation is also essential to move decisions closer to the citizens. Several processes have been developed relating to sustainable development. For example, the City of Toronto has recently set up a fairly sophisticated consultation process in defining its *Governance Model for Advanced Environmental Decision Making* (see Annex II). Similarly, in Hamilton-Wentworth, the *Vision* 2020 document was prepared after a two-and-a-half-year consultation process involving over 1000 citizens. However, these appear to be pioneering and exemplary initiatives rather than usual practice.

Turning talk into action

a) Improving federal capacities for implementation

At the federal level, sustainable development often represents a new way of thinking, and its implementation poses many challenges. The government is striving in particular to deliver on its international commitments, *e.g.* made at the Earth Summit in Rio de Janeiro in 1992 on biological diversity and at Kyoto in 1997 on climate change. Domestically, the federal government is mainly facing challenges for co-ordinating the work of departments that cross jurisdictions. Such co-ordination is essential, since some of the most pressing issues cut across mandates and political jurisdictions – and it is also necessary for assessing strategy implementation.

Therefore, some departments have established various mechanisms for measuring the implementation of their sustainable development strategies (see Annex V). The comprehensiveness of implementation assessment varied from one department to another. The Commissioner of the Environment and Sustainable Development suggested two main areas where it was felt departments should pay particular attention:

- Improving co-ordination and policy coherence within and beyond the public sector, including across levels of government.
- Making more efforts on "greening" of government activities. An initiative was launched for measuring the environmental effects of their operations and making better policy and programme decisions (see Box 10).

As a consequence of these efforts, departments seem to be progressing with strategy implementation. Based on the Commissioner's assessment of the information reported by departments in 1999, they met about 20 per cent of the commitments set

Box 10.   **Progress on the Greening of the Federal Government**

As this country's single largest enterprise, the way the federal government operates its facilities, manages its fleets, disposes of wastes, and purchases goods and services can make a significant contribution to Canada's sustainable development goals. Therefore, through the federal Greening of Government Initiative, all departments are required to integrate environmental considerations into their operations and put in place environmental management systems to manage their operations in line with sustainable development principles. Progress is subject to evaluation by the Commissioner of the Environment and Sustainable Development and regularly reported to Parliament. Various efforts are under way to improve environment management systems:

Energy consumption

The Government of Canada has committed to reducing greenhouse gas (GHG) emissions from federal operations by at least 20 per cent of 1990 levels by the year 2005. At the departmental level, Environment Canada has set its own quantitative targets to purchase 15-20 per cent of its energy from renewable resources by the year 2010. A number of programmes are in place to support departments and agencies, including the Federal Buildings Initiative (FBI), which helps managers achieve long-term cost savings without up-front capital investments or risk, through the intermediary of an external contractor. By October 1997, 4 000 federal buildings were involved in the FBI, with an estimated total potential energy savings of CAN$160 million per annum (nearly 25 per cent of the total annual federal energy bill).

Water consumption

In the 1995 Directions on Greening Government Operations, water efficiency was identified as a greening government best practice. However, it is difficult to evaluate achievements, as water consumption reduction strategies lie with individual departments. As a consequence, no data on results is being gathered on a government-wide basis.

Waste management

Industry Canada, Environment Canada, the Department of Defence, and Public Works and Government Services Canada are working with the Canadian Construction Industry and Industry leaders to develop better ways to manage non-hazardous solid waste from construction, renovation and demolition, which constitutes 25-30 per cent of all material sent to landfill. A survey of the public and private sector was completed across the country in Spring 1998 to identify obstacles to and opportunities for reducing the waste stream going to landfills. A joint project to research and analyse best practices in the area is under way and will be followed by recommendations to association members and federal departments on construction, renovation and demolition waste management.

71

Box 10.   **Progress on the Greening of the Federal Government** (*cont.*)

Fleet and transport

Canada reports the most detailed programme to reduce the environmental impacts of fleet and travel. The Alternative Fuel Act (1995) requires all Canadian Departments to ensure that 60 per cent of the vehicles which they acquired in 1998-1999 and 75 per cent of those acquired in 1999-2000 and thereafter operate using alternative fuels (subject to cost and operational considerations). In 1995/1996, only 2 per cent of the federal fleet was using alternative fuels. In addition, the Canadian government has set a 30 per cent reduction goal for GHG emissions from the federal fleet by 2000, based on 1995 levels. The Alternative Fuels Act requires annual compliance reporting, which has heightened the responsibilities of department fleet managers. Natural Resource Canada also has a federal fleet initiative, FleetWise, to encourage sound fleet management practices and to reduce the costs and environmental impact of vehicle operations. It is forecasted that FleetWise will reduce energy use by 11.1 per cent and GHG emissions by 12.1 per cent by 2010, principally through the reduction of the number of vehicles in the fleet.

Government buildings and facilities

Canada provides a number of specific tools to all departments to encourage more environmentally friendly building design and use. The National Master Specification, for use by building designers and architects, is currently under revision to include environmental considerations, including Federal Standards related to hazardous and solid waste reduction and energy and water conservation. The Green Office Plan is another federal tool that incorporates measures to maximise energy and water conservation, improve indoor air and lighting, and implement sound waste management principles. The Green Office Plan was piloted in Environment Canada by specifying environmental criteria in all facets of office floor renovation. Canada is also updating a 1995 handbook on "Environmentally Responsible Construction and Renovation", destined for non-technical asset and property managers, and a 1996 guide for architects on the "Sustainable Design of Office Buildings". Work is also under way to promote greener infrastructure and buildings both nationally and internationally (in partnership with 13 countries) through the two-year international project, Green Building Challenge "98. Finally, Environment Canada is proposing Federal Halocarbon Regulation under the Canadian Environmental Protection Act to promote pollution prevention approaches to ozone-depleting substances and other substances contributing to the greenhouse effect.

Source: OECD, 1999.

out in the Sustainable Development Strategies, compared with 11 per cent in 1998. They are also improving their management practices for implementing the strategies. In 1999 the Commissioner reported that, on average, departments had established about one-third of the management practices reflected in the ISO 14001 management standard, which is a benchmark of good practice. This year, on average, the six departments that were examined were applying about half of those practices.

In many departments one ambition for the updated sustainable development strategies has been to draw on past experience to focus on improving coherence and implementation. For example, to enhance its accountability and transparency as the strategy unfolds, NRCan has developed a Sustainable Development Action Items Management System. The system – which will be an interactive, web-based tracking and reporting tool – will expedite the reporting of progress to senior management, staff and stakeholders. The programme, called *Safeguarding our Assets, Securing our Future*, is just the first phase of an ongoing process that NRCan will pursue as it advances its sustainable development goals. Prior to the update of NRCan's Sustainable Development Strategy in December 2000, an independent advisory panel made up of interested stakeholders was invited to review NRCan's progress in sustainable development against the existing strategy and to advise the Department on priorities for the year 2000 and beyond.

b)   Improving coherence across levels of government

At the sub-national level, one major implementation concern is maintaining a sufficient degree of cohesion and a capacity for assuring some coherence among diverse policies (federal, provincial and local) that have an impact on one another. One of the factors presented as critical to success is improving "holistic multilateral" co-operative relationships between the federal government and the territorial governments, Aboriginal peoples, the private sector, voluntary and community-based organisations, and with individual Canadians. However, there is a feeling that this goal is far from being achieved, considering both the complexity of institutional and inter-sectoral relations and the existence of major conflicting interests. Where formal partnerships exist, they should require that all partners be held accountable for their part in the action items. According to the 2000 report of the Commissioner of the Environment and Sustainable Development, successful co-operation agreements depend on a "mix of subjective and objective considerations". Based on five case studies,[16] the report underlines the importance of relationships where partners build and maintain trust between themselves. Leadership and commitment from all parties involved are essential, as are public and political support. Partners also need the discipline to follow all the necessary steps during the life cycle of an agreement. According to the Commissioner, the key to a successful co-operation agreement is to meet all or most of these conditions.

73

Improving coherence of environmental management is an ongoing objective of the *Canada-wide Accord on Environmental Harmonisation*. Whereas the focus of CCME work had been on individual areas of environmental protection – such as water quality guidelines, codes of practice for underground storage tanks, or principles for cleaning up contaminated sites – the harmonisation initiative would aim to build a more effective and efficient system of environmental management in which the actions of all governments would be complementary and appropriate to their jurisdictions. The task of implementing sub-agreements to the accord – currently on inspections, standards and environmental assessment – offers governments an opportunity to put into practice this co-operative approach to environmental management. It will also allow governments to evaluate the effectiveness of this approach and, if necessary, make adjustments based on what has been achieved. Most importantly, the work under these sub-agreements, such as that on Canada-wide environmental standards, could provide concrete solutions to issues identified as having Canada-wide significance.

The *Canada-wide Accord on Environmental Harmonisation* reflects the willingness of governments to come together as partners and their commitment to meet their legal obligations for environmental protection. Governments are free to introduce more stringent environmental measures if circumstances call for them. If a consensus is not achieved in any given area, governments are free to act within their existing authorities, and all governments may continue to take action consistent with existing emergency response agreements. In this way, the Accord seeks to maintain a useful balance, allowing governments to take advantage of the potential for co-operation, efficiency and consistency without undermining their legitimate authority to protect and manage the environment.

The dissemination of good practice is essential. For example, the 1994 Ontario initiative, *Learning for Sustainability Partnership*, played a pilot role in the creation of the national initiative, *Learning for a Sustainable Future*, which seeks to introduce sustainability education.

D. Learning from the Canadian experience

Success and doubts

In short, the main lessons learned[17] from the Canadian experience of developing sustainable development strategies in federal departments resulted mainly from efforts to:

- **Evaluate** what has been done.
- Develop **consultation** and **participation** with stakeholders.
- Improve policy formulation.

- Improve **horizontal co-ordination** of both policy and process.

- Develop **partnerships** with the private and not-for-profit sector.

Developing the ministerial sustainable development strategies generated both success and uncertainty. One of the most obvious successes came from the wide consultation processes, which contributed to raising the issues and providing a platform for public debate with positive consequences for the potential resolution of conflicting interests. However, some doubts have been expressed concerning:

- The compatibility of the different strategies.

- Implementation issues.

- The difficulty to establish clear and measurable targets.

- The obstacles to review and evaluation.

- The need to improve co-ordination (across departments, sectors and levels of government).

One key obstacle to achieving sustainable development is the difficulty of replacing the rhetoric of "win-win" solutions, which are unlikely to be found, by efforts to elaborate appropriate arbitrage techniques for conflict resolution.

a)   Impediments to federal government's implementation of departmental sustainable development strategies

The Commissioner of the Environment and Sustainable Development, through regular evaluation of federal government strategies, provides a unique independent picture of the strengths and weaknesses of the implementation of federal policies. The Commissioner diagnosed an "implementation gap" in many cases between the federal government's expressed intentions and its domestic actions, although his 2000 report remarked on improvements at departmental level. The phenomenon was described as follows in his 1999 report: "departmental practices are most developed at the planning stage of the management cycle. They become weaker as the departments move from the planning stage to the implementation and operation stage, and weakest at the monitoring and corrective action stage". The Commissioner highlighted some of the main factors contributing to this implementation gap:

- Corporate responsibility for strategy implementation has been assigned but no clear targets have been established.

- The sustainable development aspects of specific departmental policies, programmes and activities have not been itemised or prioritised.

- Regulatory and other potentially applicable environmental and sustainable development obligations have not been itemised or prioritised.

- Key issues to be managed by lower levels in the departments have not been clearly identified or prioritised.

- The contribution and accountability of lower levels in the departments are largely undefined.

- Training requirements have not been assessed.

- Practices, procedures and work instructions for strategy implementation, monitoring and control are lacking.

The Commissioner also underlined that departments would need to determine better what they should do differently. This assessment (an effort for "moving up the learning curve") is a critical part of managing the sustainable development strategy process. Senior management needs to be involved in assessing the first strategy as the basis for improvement.

According to the Commissioner, the assessment should include a review of the following:

- The goals, objectives and targets set in the first strategy, and performance against them.

- Findings from our audits and departmental internal audits or self-assessments of sustainable development management processes.

- Changing circumstances, including policy direction, legislation, activities, advances in science and technology and stakeholder interests.

These questions – what has the department achieved with its first strategy, what has changed, and what needs to be done differently – are consistent with what participants in the first consultations said they would like the consultations to address in the next round of strategies. The Commissioner expressed his expectations about including a description of the assessment process and its outcome in the updated ministerial strategies. Several departments and government bodies, including the Privy Council, are reporting significant efforts to improve consultation and co-ordination. A good example is the *Leaders' Forum on Sustainable Development* on 4 April 2000.

There has not been any similar systematic evaluation of provincial and local initiatives. Any generalisation would be difficult to make. However, some NGOs, such as the Sierra Club, provide a record of these experiences. Their view suggests that the degree of implementation of sustainable development policies at sub-national level is very uneven and much more subject to radical shifts following political turnover.

b) *Promising initiatives*

1. Developing a central co-ordinating point for innovation dissemination

Various promising initiatives have been experimented at the federal and sub-national levels and in the non-governmental sector. For example, the NRTEE is prac-tising innovative ways of involving stakeholders and reaching agreements. As a cata-lyst in the process, the NRTEE brings a round table format, seeking progress on diverse issues with an environmental/economic interface. The social leg of sustain-able development has been less directly dealt with, although efforts to implement sustainable development goals in the North may enhance efforts to take better account of the social dimension (particularly with respect to "First Nations"). The process itself can help to overcome entrenched differences. Apparently there has still been no in-depth evaluation of this process and it is hard to see its limits. But, together with the evaluation provided by the Commissioner of the Environment and Sustainable Development, the NRTEE's guidance may contribute in the longer term to a "virtuous circle" characterised by incremental efforts to review past failures and achievements and improve future policies on the basis of these lessons.

2. Improving implementation through better policy formulation

Strong commitments and clear guidance and evaluation are necessary to improve the sustainability of management practices. Departments and agencies have a central role to play in this respect since they are responsible for the imple-mentation of the Commissioner's recommendation. But commitment, guidance and evaluation imply the ability to make the right decisions. It is particularly chal-lenging since many issues are the subject of much debate. Therefore, improving the quality of policy formulation on the basis of reliable information is crucial. The forum organised on 4 April, 2000 (*Leaders' Forum on Sustainable Development*) was structured around eight theme areas (Sustainable Development in Government Operations, Sus-tainable Development Indicators and Reporting, Knowledge and Information, a Sus-tainable Development Strategy for the North, Sustainable Communities, Enhanced Productivity through Eco-Efficiency, International Aspects of Sustainable Develop-ment, Social and Cultural Aspects of Sustainable Development, and Sustainable Development and Healthy Canadians). Using the Sustainable Development Strate-gies as the primary delivery vehicle, it also aimed to make a concrete contribution to strengthening links between information and decisions.

Access to reliable information for taking the right decisions generated an increasing awareness that better connections between this knowledge and deci-sions were needed. It is significant that one of the commitments made in the Speech from the Throne of October 1999 is to strengthen the government's capacity for environmental research and to place greater emphasis on sustainable development in government decision making. Budget 2000 committed the government to provide Can$9 million over the next three years to NRTEE and Environment Canada to develop environmental and sustainable development indicators in collaboration with Statistics Canada. Additional sources of expertise and information should also encourage debate and sound choices. Government agencies also provide a source of information to decision makers (see Annex VI), as do universities and citizens' organisations – whose views are mainly expressed in the context of public consultations.

In sectors where federal policies were the most criticised from a sustainability point of view, particular efforts were made to improve access to reliable information. This is for example the case of the management of toxic substances, an area where weaknesses in implementation were identified. A Toxic Substances Research Initiative (TSRI) has been established, with the key objective of helping to reach sustainable development goals through improving the knowledge base needed to define and reduce the risk of adverse effects of toxic substances. The TSRI will fund research on specific health and environmental issues: endocrine-disrupting chemicals, persistent organic pollutants, toxic forms of metals, cumulative effects of toxics and air pollutants. The initiative also meets a government commitment in the renewed Canadian Environmental Protection Act (CEPA) to conduct research on endocrine-disrupting substances. The knowledge generated as a result of this applied research is meant to provide government policy makers with the information needed to develop, modify or refine environment protection policies. The Initiative is overseen by a Science Management Committee, composed of approximately 20 scientific experts in the field of toxic substances from both governmental and non-governmental sectors. The Committee oversees the competitive, science-based process of technical peer review for research proposals from government, universities and non-governmental organisations, and makes final funding decisions. The renewed CEPA also contains new provisions for addressing past weakness in dealing with toxic substances, in particular through deadlines for federal action when a substance is declared toxic.

Cross-departmental co-operation and collaborative decision making is also encouraged through this process: the Ministers of Health and Environment will retain joint lead responsibility for overseeing the implementation of this new research initiative.

A similar initiative with a cross-sectoral perspective is under way, that is the Interdepartmental Sustainability Project. The project's goal is to improve capacity, through disseminating policy research in areas of priority concern, to address the implementation gap as it relates to sustainable development. This relates to the growing awareness of the importance of ensuring that policy development related to achieving sustainability is based on a strong foundation of horizontal policy research with a medium- to long-term focus. The Sustainability Project is the latest addition to the government-wide Policy Research Initiative. Six departments contribute to this project (Agriculture and Agro-Food Canada, Fisheries and Oceans, Health Canada, Natural Resources Canada, Transport Canada, Environment Canada). The main thrusts of this project include a review of indicators for sustainable development and their adaptability to the Canadian context; use of eco-efficiency; capacity building in communities, nationally and globally; improvement of the implementation of sustainable development; linkages between ethical investment practice and sustainable development.

3.   Building capacities

Capacities must be improved at both staff and community levels. As indicated in the 2000 *Report of the Commissioner of the Environment and Sustainable Development*, important roles exist at the departmental and central agencies levels to improve capacity for a coherent corporate approach to managing and reporting on sustainable development. In 1999 the OECD's Environmental Policy Committee reported that training and capacity building have been identified in many departmental sustainable development strategies as priority areas. Individual departments are responsible for developing the department-specific Awareness Training Working Group (EATWG), which develops common training and awareness materials and tools to improve environmental performance across the federal government. Environment Canada has developed an environmental compliance guide to help employees comply with federal environmental statements and regulations. In addition, Public Works and Government Services Canada has held a number of theme-specific workshops for operational, design and management staff, for example on Environmental Responsibilities and Liabilities. Another important capacity-building initiative is the efforts of Statistics Canada to assess the value of natural capital. At the community level, Human Resource Development Canada attempted to maximise the use of human capital in a sustainable way. Projects were encouraged, for example, at the local level, particularly to help community building of Aboriginal populations (see Box 11).

In search of win-win solutions

Traditional decision-making mechanisms – vertical, segmented and involving only limited consultation – seem to have reached their limits for engaging in such multi-stakeholder processes. In fact, it seems that neither "old-style" bureaucratic decision making nor consensual decision making deal successfully with several conflicting interests, while recognising the need to agree on shared goals. Some questions remain under discussion: how should decisions be made? Are "win-win" solutions a realistic approach when talking about conflicting interests? If not well designed, non-adapted "co-operative" decision making could jeopardise

79

Box 11. A Local Example. The Ouje-Bougoumou Cree, Québec

Between 1927 and 1986, the Ouje-Bougoumou Cree were forced from their traditional lands and left to live in shacks beside logging roads on the extreme margins of Canadian social, economic, and political life. They were the "forgotten Cree", facing complete social disintegration and living conditions almost incomprehensible in a developed and affluent society.

In 1975 the Ouje-Bougoumou Cree began building on the assets within their community: the foundation laid by the James Bay and Northern Quebec Agreement and their own commitment to self-determination. By 1995, the United Nations identified them as one of only fifty communities around the world best representing the ideals and objectives of that international organisation. During this twenty-year period, the community:

- Rebuilt its village using community labour and a design developed by the community itself in consultation with a leading Aboriginal architect.
- Assumed responsibility for delivering its own health services and built a new healing centre.
- Built its own youth centre, using the skills and commitment of its teenagers and young adults.
- Developed an elders' residence, day-care centre, school and cultural centre.
- Developed a unique, centralised method for heating all the community's homes using local resources.
- Began developing a sustainable local economy that incorporates not only wage labour but also more traditional land-based activities.

The community-building process in Ouje-Bougoumou incorporated all the lessons which have been identified in this report and can itself serve as a lesson for other communities about what needs to be done and what can be accomplished.

First and foremost, residents refused to see themselves as victims and instead focused on their assets, strengths, and goals. With that foundation:

- Community residents have planned all initiatives and regularly host workshops to discuss the roles and responsibilities of community living, how they wish to organise their own affairs and by what values they wish to live. During one workshop, residents discussed how traditional approaches for solving conflict could be integrated into a local law enforcement system. During another, they decided to include hunting breaks in the community's school and construction schedules so as to sustain their traditional ways.
- The community developed training programmes to give people the specific skills they required for building their own homes. The community also developed an innovative home-ownership programme, which tied payments to income. The community gradually built a community housing fund to sustain further development.
- The community made its school a centre of village life, serving as both a place of learning and of recreation. The community acknowledges every achievement with a formal ceremony and holds frequent celebrations to allow people to get to know each other and to help bring them together.

Source: Human Resource Development Canada.

democratic processes and lead to collusion. Developing future governmental strategies may require even more attention to the neutrality and openness of the processes followed.

a)   New partnerships

Although win-win solutions are not always possible for everyone, partnerships between business, NGOs and the government constitute a promising practice, at least for dialogue and shared views on issues.

As already mentioned above (see Box 6), the private sector improved its processes for advancing the sustainable development agenda, particularly in those industries that had been traditionally most criticised for damaging the environment, such as the pulp and paper, mining or chemical industries. The chemical industry sector, through the "Responsive Care Initiative", offers a good example of joint efforts to elaborate innovative decision-making mechanisms that associate the private and public sectors as well as NGOs. Similar initiatives were undertaken with the pulp and paper and the mining industries. The Chemical Producers Association (CCPA) launched this initiative to integrate environmental issues into business planning. This includes Member companies developing, integrating standards, guiding principles and codes of practice into their operations and activities. This objective is linked to the efforts of the rest of the society (see Annex VII). Similar partnerships were initiated at the provincial level. For example, *The Ontario Transportation and Climate Change Collaborative* brought together transportation sector stakeholders in Ontario.

Partnerships have also been fostered by the NGOs themselves. For example, the International Institute for Sustainable Development initiated a programme called *Solutions for Business* to incorporate sustainable development into business plans. An interactive website has been created, which is now visited by dozens of companies and which describes 15 methods for implementing sustainable development, ranging from "lifecycle assessment of materials" to "zero-emission processes", with case studies of each technique. The site also offers practical advice on new business opportunities. To attract businesses, this programme has developed key messages explaining why companies increasingly go beyond mere regulatory compliance to adopt sustainability as one business goal: on the one hand, consumers are now demanding environmentally friendly goods; on the other hand, environmental risks and environment market opportunities are becoming important to investors.

Selective achievements of the *Solutions for Business Programme* include partnerships with the public sector, *i.e.* Environment Canada. In 1998-99 it sought to help prepare both the business community and governments for the consequences of the Kyoto Protocol. The programme also prepared a policy paper for Environment

Canada, setting out compelling reasons for establishing policies that provide credit for early action so that the private sector can advance its plans and actions to reduce and capture greenhouse gas emissions. The programme also submitted a report to the Department of Foreign Affairs and International Trade to take into account the lessons of eight countries in planning offices to administer Joint Implementation and Clean Development Mechanisms projects with developing countries.

b)   Defining new modes of intervention

Both environmentalists and citizens' organisations often called in the past for more direct government intervention, including legislation and regulation. The opposite view has been expressed by businesses, which have been traditionally hostile to government burdens. In several areas there has been a perception, particularly among the business community, that traditional interventions, in particular regulations, were not adapted to the challenges of sustainable development.

Both sides have evolved somewhat. For example, campaigning NGOs are more keen to find solutions in consultation with other stakeholders, rather than to request systematic government intervention. On the other hand, the position of the chemical industry stated in the *Statement of Policy on Responsible Care* is now the following: "The chemical industry recognises that a degree of government regulation in combination with the self-initiated actions of industry is required to ensure a sufficiently comprehensive, timely and orderly advance towards the goal of protecting the health and wellbeing of Canadians and their environment." However, its strategy identifies the need for such regulation to be "based on scientifically supported data and/or expert opinion" and to be "realistic in terms of societal cost/benefit considerations". The seventh guiding principle of Responsible Care states the commitment of member companies to "work with and assist governments and selected organisations to foster and encourage equitable and attainable standards". These concepts, plus the intent to "work with government to develop voluntary actions which will accomplish desired objectives without regulation", are further addressed in CCPA's public policy development statement.

There is a growing sense that alternatives to traditional regulation should be explored to manage conflicts among major stakeholders differently. But this is challenging, considering the need to make various actors – often with conflicting interests – respect this "new deal". One way is to have stakeholders agree on "quasi-norms", which are less rigid and more easily adaptable than traditional regulations but still require action. This is a promising way of reconciling diverse approaches, although this could also be potentially problematic from a democratic point of view. On the one hand, these agreements should not jeopardise existing democratic rules, and the process should remain fair, transparent and open. In particular, all

Box 12. Selected Non-Regulatory Approaches

In Canada there is no long tradition of seeking alternatives to regulations. However, a number of recent initiatives have tested various mechanisms.

New mechanisms for implementing international norms

The Commissioner of the Environment and Sustainable Development, on the basis of federal government experience, suggested in his 1999 report the use of a systematic approach to continual improvement embodied in standards such as ISO 14001 to strengthen management practices. An example of the co-operative effort to apply norms is given in the field of air transportation. Transport Canada (TC) actively participated in a focus group of the Canadian Standards Association (CSA) to develop the June 1999 "Guide to the Implementation of ISO 14001 at Airports". The document is intended to provide guidance to airports for the development and implementation of an environmental management system (EMS). It was developed in consultation with Toronto and Montreal airport authorities, a major Canadian airline, an airport fuel consortium, Transport Canada, an ISO 14001 registrar, and a regional airport.

Reducing toxic emissions

The *Accelerated Reduction/Elimination of Toxics* (ARET) process was launched in March 1994 by a group representing different industries, health and academic associations, and federal and provincial governments. Companies representing 91 per cent of Canada's base metal production and all non-ferrous smelters have now joined ARET. Action plans were submitted to reduce emissions of 12 substances by 71 per cent from 1988 levels by the year 2000. Industry estimates it has surpassed this goal.

The example of GLYCOL management

Aircraft regulations stipulate that no aircraft may take-off with "contaminated wing surfaces"; aircraft must therefore be de-iced prior to take-off by spraying a heated glycol-based fluid on aircraft surfaces during inclement winter weather. The safety aspect of de-icing gained prominence due to three major aircraft accidents, including the 1989 Air Ontario accident in Dryden, Ontario. These accidents heightened public attention to the importance of de-icing and also resulted in the increased airline use of de-icing fluids.

Although glycol-based de-icers are necessary to ensure flight safety, these toxic chemicals have a detrimental affect on the environment. Up to 50 per cent of the de-icing fluid drains onto the apron surface, entering the drainage system, or percolates into subsurface soils. As an operator of airports, Transport Canada is responsible for its airport infrastructure (including storm water run-off) and as an owner/operator it must ensure compliance with applicable environmental regulations at its facilities.

83

Box 12.   **Selected Non-Regulatory Approaches** (*cont.*)

Transport Canada took a leadership role in sustainable development thinking by initiating discussions with Environment Canada to establish a regulatory mechanism which would address the environmental concerns of de-icing fluids.

1. A working group of the public and private sectors was established to assess technical, operational, policy, management control and operational control mechanisms. As a result of this consultative effort, CEPA Glycol Guidelines were established.

2. An "end-of-pipe" discharge level of 100 mg/L was established for total glycols at all airports on federal lands.

3. Air carriers must manage de-icing fluids to safeguard the environment, and bear the cost of clean-up in fulfilment of TC's "polluter pays' policy (TP1498).

4. Storm water monitoring (via water quality sampling) is carried out at airports operated by TC and airport authorities.

5. Detailed glycol management plans are required from airlines and/or ground-handling agents at TC-operated airports, and are encouraged from airport authorities before each de-icing season.

By incorporating safety, economic and environmental considerations into the issue of glycol management, TC achieved a win-win solution that helped to ensure public safety, minimise negative environmental impacts, and support the internalisation of environmental costs by the polluter.

Source: Transport Canada.

---

interests should have equal access to the development of these "quasi-norms". More practical issues also appear as to the degree of constraint that should exist for the implementation of the quasi-rules and the way to maintain consensus in a changing environment, which supposes that a due process is followed. There are examples of recent non-regulatory approaches (see Box 12).

E.   Concluding remarks: What consequences for public organisations?

At the federal level, Canada offers a number of arrangements and innovations aimed at overcoming sectoral and intergovernmental segmentation. The strategy followed to achieve these goals is characterised by:

- An approach generally based on partnerships and networks. This is reflected in the extensive use of consultation of stakeholders and citizens at the stage of policy elaboration (this appears less true at the level of policy delivery).

- The need to adapt to sustainable development issues is being affirmed through comprehensive plans and commitments, which include virtually all public organisations. This illustrates an affirmative attitude, even though this was not always followed until recently by equally significant progress in implementation.

In the longer term, the success of this strategic standpoint will have to be considered in the light of its capacity to respond to the current implementation gap, while tremendous challenges remain present.

Other levels of government seem to have developed very uneven initiatives, ranging from "best practices" to "unsustainable management". This results mainly from different and sometimes conflicting agendas and from financial and fiscal "imperatives". Similar differences exist in the private sector and in society as a whole. Canada is an immense country with vast expanses of wilderness, and, paradoxically, this could be a threat to achieving sustainability in sectors if there is still a feeling that resources are indefinitely renewable. Very often public awareness only grows when it is too late. This would imply that government should be "raising a red flag" on the dwindling of natural resources, for example through providing more information.

Thus, most interesting innovations include:

- The creation of a legal obligation to act, report and consult at the federal level and to some extent in the provinces.

- Strong public audit and reporting mechanisms through the Commissioner of the Environment and Sustainable Development, at relatively low cost (his office is part of the Auditor General Office's and it operates with a limited staff).

- The petitioner appeal mechanisms. This means that the Commissioner is giving a direct voice to citizens (in practice to citizens' organisations).

It also appears that implementing sustainable development goals poses a number of governance issues and requires significant management changes from government and non-government sectors. It represents both a challenge and an opportunity to adapt to longer-term and horizontal policies. In the case of Canada, much progress has been made in better designing, planning, co-ordinating, consulting and, more recently, assessing. Many lessons can be drawn which suggest possible future action:

- **Building a solid information base** through scientific research and monitoring. Attempts to develop policy research and increase channels between knowledge and policy decisions are critical.

85

- **Developing "inclusion" and co-operation** within Government and across levels of government. Although necessary, interdepartmental co-ordination is not sufficient. One critical factor is to speak the same language, particularly when conflicting views exist. Fora where issues of national concern are discussed and where, in the process, jurisdictions learn to speak and understand each other's language, are essential. This is the case, for example, of CCME (*Canadian Council of Ministers of the Environment*), JMM (*Joint Ministerial Meetings of Ministers of Energy and Environment*) and WMCC (*Wildlife Ministers Council of Canada*). But interdepartmental co-ordination should also be complemented by policy integration efforts. The positive role of the current Policy Research Initiative, which aims at creating a common basis of knowledge, should be emphasised.

- In a federal country like Canada, this also calls for maintaining and assessing current efforts (*e.g.* the *Harmonisation Accord*) to **manage jurisdictional complexity, better defining and integrating social aspects** of sustainable development into the current debate, which still relies mainly on environmental/economic tensions.

- **Keeping the debate and consultation open** to avoid capture by narrow perspectives.

- **Raising awareness** about the critical importance of sustainable development issues, both among staff and in society as a whole.

- **Developing a strong domestic regime for implementing** the agreements and contending with budget cuts, and **improving the allocation of resource and budgeting** to support sound sustainable development policies in a surplus environment. At the same time, there is a need to remain cost effective, since economic efficiency is one of the essential components of sustainable development.

- **Improving policy evaluation** in order to improve policies through developing benchmarks and disseminating good practices.

- Seeking mechanisms to **allow better arbitration between conflicting views**. Win-win solutions are difficult to achieve, at least on a short-term basis. One possible alternative is giving "losers" sufficient compensation, in order for them to agree to decisions against their own immediate interests.

One could underline the main ambiguity of the Canadian approach to sustainable development issues: ambitious processes but still significant implementation gaps. This calls for stronger political leadership in order for Canadians to adopt sustainable lifestyles more effectively. However, this relatively heavy process, which reflects some of the core characteristics of the Canadian political culture (the need to consult, the need to balance various interests in order to preserve cohesion, etc), may be crucial in itself to resolve implementation problems, provided that it remains at a relatively reasonable cost and that it be broadened. Past efforts to develop ambitious strategies, to institutionalise some key authorities such as the Commissioner of the Environment and Sustainable Development or the National Round Table of the Environment and the Economy, to consult better with citizens, as well as current efforts to recast the system in order to improve implementation may ultimately contribute to raising awareness and to drawing attention to the real issues.

Notes

1. The views expressed in this paper are those of the author, and do not necessarily reflect those of the OECD, or those of its Public Management Service.

2. It was prepared in 2000 and finalised in February 2001.

3. Statistics Canada, census data, 1996. See also Canadian Information Office online information at *www.cio-bic.gc.ca/facts/canadagen_e.html*

4. See *www.infocan.gc.ca*

5. *Politics in Canada: Culture, Institutions, Behavior and Public Policy*, Robert J. Jackson, Doreen Jackson, 4th edition, Scarborough: Prentice Hall Canada, 1998.

6. For more information on this topic see: OECD (1997), *Managing Across Levels of Government*, pp. 107-125; and *How Canadians Govern Themselves*, by Eugene Forsey, available on the Canadian Parliament Internet site at *www.parl.gc.ca/36/refmat/library/forsey/how-e.htm*

7. About carbon emission levels and intensity, see: OECD 2000, *Making Growth More Environmentally Sustainable, figure 32 and 33*.

8. Recent polling made by Ekos Research, May 2000, and released in *The Vancouver Sun*, June 19, 2000, p. A7, reveals an upswing in concern. The poll found that Canadians rank health care as their top issue, with the environment ahead of crime, unemployment and taxation. Moreover, air and water quality was identified as the leading factor affecting health, ahead of the health care system, individual lifestyles and income levels.

9. See also Doering, R.L. (1993). The IISD provides a description of Provincial round tables at: *http://iisd.ca/worldsd/canada/prov/prov.htm*

10. For a complete description of the areas of responsibilities of the Commissioner please see: *www.oag-bvg.gc.ca/domino/cesd_cedd.nsf/html/99mand_e.html*

11. Available at *www.oecd.org/puma/budget/index.htm*

12. The tabling of the strategies – required by 15 December 2000 – was delayed due to the federal elections which took place in November 2000.

13. See *www.fin.gc.ca/budget00/bpe/bpch5_1e.htm#Environmental*

14. The success of collecting and recycling waste was due to both political commitment and to the environmentally friendly attitudes of society. However, one should underline that these initiatives are complex to evaluate from a sustainable development perspective. On the one hand waste management is only a limited aspect of sustainable development, relatively easy to operationalise at the local level compared to longer-term strategic choices. On the other hand, the process of recycling is *not* uneconomical. A critical issue is who pays for the recycling. It was felt that what needed adjusting in the blue box programmes was precisely the cost factor. There was often a feeling that governments paid too much and industry – the main producers of waste – too little.

15. 2000 report of the Commissioner of the Environment and Sustainable Development, see *www.oag-bvg.gc.ca*

16. The reviewed agreements were the *Eastern Canada Acid Program*, the *National Forest strategy*, the *North American Waterfowl Management Plan*, the Statement of Commitment to complete the *Canada's Networks of Protected Areas*, the *Greenhouse Gas Emission Reducing Trading Pilot*.

17. 2000 report of the Commissioner of the Environment and Sustainable Development, see *www.oag-bvg.gc.ca*

Annex I

Summary of the National Round Table on the Environment and the Economy Proposed Measures for the 2000 Federal Budget

Federal Government Green Energy Procurement

To facilitate the commercialisation of "green" energy and energy efficiency technologies that do not produce the significant environmental impacts associated with conventional energy sources, the federal government would:

- Commit to have 20 per cent of its total electricity needs met by electricity produced from new "green" power sources by the year 2005 as part of an enhanced green power procurement strategy that would see more aggressive procurement targets adopted in future years, beginning with a 40 per cent commitment in 2010.

- And Commit to undertake energy efficiency retrofits in federal government buildings representing 50 per cent of the federal government's floor space by the year 2005, with more aggressive targets adopted in future years.

Budget Requirements – Federal Government Green Energy Procurement

Measure	Budget ($)	Type of Initiative	Purpose of Measure	Implementing Agency
Green Power Procurement	$3 million (2000) increasing to $18 million (2005 and 15 additional years)	Programme Spending	Expand existing programme by providing new funds to cover incremental costs of green power	Public Works and Government Services Canada
Energy Efficiency Procurement	$5 million (each year for 5 years)	Programme Spending	Increase funds available to the Federal Buildings Initiative	Natural Resources Canada

Accelerated Capital Cost Allowance Treatment for Investments in Highly Eco-Efficient Technologies

To facilitate the commercialisation and adoption of high energy efficient buildings and energy-using equipment, the federal government would create a new class of assets eligible for accelerated capital cost allowance depreciation. To be eligible, assets would need to:

- Either be subject to regulated energy efficiency standards (*e.g.*, the federal government's energy efficiency regulations for equipment) or voluntary federal energy efficiency guidelines (*e.g.*, the National Energy Code for Buildings).

- And be 30 per cent more energy efficient than the existing regulated energy efficiency standard or voluntary guideline.

The level of capital cost allowance deduction proposed for eligible assets are buildings (six percent) and energy-using equipment (40 percent). More analysis is required, however, to determine if these figures are appropriate. In time, this programme should be expanded to include other forms of eco-efficient technologies, equipment or process changes.

Budget Requirements – Accelerated Capital Cost Allowance Treatment for Investments in Highly Eco-Efficient Technologies

Measure	Budget ($)	Type of Initiative	Purpose of Measure	Implementing Agency
Accelerated Capital Cost Allowance Treatment	Further analysis required when measure more fully defined	Tax expenditure	To make investments in highly energy efficient buildings and equipment more attractive	Finance Canada

Canadian Programme for Applied Sustainable Economics

To facilitate the integration of environmental and social considerations into economic decision-making undertaken by Canadian governments, businesses and communities, the federal government would provide funding to support new research and the development and dissemination of practical tools that would build Canadian capacity in the area of applied sustainable economics.

The applied research work would be focused on four major areas:

- Improved measurement systems and indicators of human progress and well being (*e.g.*, genuine progress indicator, human development index and other alternative systems of national accounts).

- Improved valuation of environmental services, resource uses and losses (*e.g.*, pricing of waste outputs and traditionally "free" but scarce resource inputs).

- Full life-cycle inventory data, eco-profiling and eco-efficiency indicators.

- And new fiscal policy tools that support both quality of life and economic competitiveness.

Budget Requirements – Canadian Program for Applied Sustainable Economics

Measure	Budget ($)	Type of Initiative
Canadian Programme for Applied Sustainable Economics	$3.3 million a year for three years	Grants

Sustainable Solutions Network

The federal government would support the establishment of a network designed to compile and then provide information, tools and experience to decision-makers in municipalities and industry on credible, field-tested solutions that improve "eco-efficiency". It would address issues related to planning, procurement, capital investment and renovation, operations, and evaluation and assessment. Dissemination of information and tools would occur through speeches, training workshops, case studies and reports, and conferences.

Budget Requirements – Sustainable Solutions Network

Measure	Budget ($)	Type of initiative
Sustainable Solutions Network	$25 million over 5 years	Grant

Reducing Capital Gains Taxation on Ecological Land Gifts

To encourage increased donations of ecologically sensitive lands to conservation charities and agencies, the federal government would adjust the tax system in such a way that landowners who made such gifts would pay reduced capital gains taxes. Three options are proposed for consideration:

- Creating a roll-over provision whereby capital gains would not be assessed against qualified ecological gifts, but would become due in whole or in part should the property be disposed of to non-qualified entities.

- Allowing an enhanced points-based claim for adjusted cost base (under section 53 of the Income Tax Act), either immediately before the contribution or for determining the contribution pursuant to the ecological gifts provision, thereby reducing capital gains.

- Or making such gifts subject to only a 37.5 percent, rather than the ordinary 75 percent, rate of including capital gains into taxable income, thereby cutting the capital gains tax on such gifts in half.

The federal government would also implement a number of procedural measures that would streamline the land donation and valuation process for combined donation and sale of lands as well as for conservation easements to conservation charities and agencies.

Budget Requirements – Reducing Capital Gains Taxation on Ecological Land Gifts

Measure	Budget ($)	Type of initiative
Reducing Capital Gains Taxation on Ecological Land Gifts	$11 million (maximum annual loss of revenue)	Tax expenditures

A Stewardship Fund For Habitat Conservation

The federal government would make a commitment to provide seed funding for the establishment of a Habitat Conservation Stewardship Fund that would be supplemented by additional contributions from the public and private sectors, including the potential development of a voluntary direction into the fund from individuals' tax refunds.

Grants from the fund would carry out priority programmes for wildlife habitat conservation on private and public lands and would promote the building and maintenance of community organisations' capacity in this endeavour.

Income generated by the fund would be directed towards the recovery of endangered species and other species at risk and would support activities such as: recovery plan preparation, habitat conservation and planning, community partnerships and initiatives, research and monitoring, education, captive breeding, and species reintroduction. A small allotment of additional funds would support the establishment of co-operative agreements with respect to habitat around national parks, as well as innovative initiatives to promote ecological integrity and leading edge agency training programmes.

Budget Requirements – A Stewardship Fund for Habitat Conservation

Measure	Budget ($)	Type of initiative
Habitat Conservation Stewardship Fund	$100 million (2000 Budget)	Funding an Endowment
Partnerships and New Initiatives	$5 million a year for five years	Program Spending

Conditional Proposal: "Green" Canada Infrastructure Works Programme

This government has in the past used infrastructure works programmes to good effect and there is talk of such a programme for the year 2000. The following advice is offered by the National Round Table on the Environment and the Economy (NRTEE) on the assumption that the Government decides to proceed with an infrastructure programme proposal.

The NRTEE agrees with certain points made in the recent Federation of Canadian Municipalities proposal. The focus of that proposal on environmental conservation and pollution prevention is very positive and reflects the fact that the day-to-day costs of operating many Canadian communities remains substantially higher than they would be if the best available solutions were being used for:

- Community energy production, distribution and use.
- Water purification, distribution and consumption.
- Waste management and recycling.
- Wastewater collection and treatment.
- And community access and mobility systems, such as public transit.

NRTEE strongly believes there is a "conservation dividend" to be captured from investments to improve these community systems, which will typically pay for themselves within three to seven years. Wastage of resources by communities creates a wide range of ongoing negative impacts, including pollution of soil and groundwater, increased urban "smog," and contributions to greenhouse gas emissions and climate change. Should the government implement a new infrastructure programme, the NRTEE offers the following advice:

- Eligible items for federal infrastructure funding should not be widened much beyond those listed above. A focus on the environmental legacy for Canada's children and investment returns is required.

93

- The focus of the programme should be on the renewal of infrastructure (the infrastructure deficit) rather than expansion. Funding should support projects that bring existing municipal services to a basic level of environmental performance and also undertake repayable investments in projects that would increase the efficiency of municipal services provided (*e.g.* demand side management).

- Funding should also be provided for the National Research Council of Canada "National Technical Guide for Municipal Infrastructure", which will help disseminate best practices across Canada.

- Funding should be conditional on the creation of community-developed business plans that establish investment priorities and include provisions for preventing future pollution problems, and as appropriate, for recovering the costs of infrastructure developments through savings over time. These business plans could also be used by municipalities to leverage private sector capital and lend themselves naturally to increased use of Public-Private Partnerships for Infrastructure (PPI), as well as increased use of "Energy Performance Contractors" with private sector financing.

- Funded projects should be shown to produce the highest environmental and economic benefits for communities according to a standard ranking method and associated performance indicators developed in conjunction with provincial and municipal decision-makers.

- Any renewed infrastructure works program should also have a version accessible to Aboriginal communities, and to Indian reserves in particular, as many of these remain below the minimum standards for infrastructure services, despite the progress made in recent years.

There is also substantial discussion of a national highway renewal and expansion programme. The NRTEE notes that overall environmental impacts are bound to be higher than would a similar investment in rail transport. If the government nevertheless decides to proceed with such a programme, it should do so with firm environmental criteria for all projects, addressing a selection of rights of way in relation to land forms and habitats, provision for wildlife crossings, recycling of construction wastes, etc.

Source: NRTEEI *Internet Site.*

Annex II

The Governance Model for Advanced Environmental Decision Making for the City of Toronto

In Toronto, the Task Force in charge of responding to the City's environmental challenges set up a comprehensive consultation process to help develop its recommendations. In February 1999, after 10 months of discussion amongst Task Force members, informed by presentations from the Federal Environmental Commissioner and the Ontario Environment Commissioner, the Environmental Task Force released its consultation document "Towards Advanced Environmental Decision Making in the City of Toronto". It outlined what the Task Force means by governance, how environmental protection and sustainability affect our thinking about governance and the principles used in developing the governance options. Copies of the consultation document were circulated widely to community members, city staff, and city councillors and to those on the Task Force mailing list. In addition, the document was posted on both the City's official web page, and on two internal Intranet sites for City staff. Attached to each report was a feedback form to help gather consistent input from all participants.

A series of community workshops dedicated to examining the issues of environmental governance were also held in February and March 1999. Attended by 130 people, the workshops provided opportunities for participants to voice their opinions and hear the views of others on governance issues. Over 200 people and organisations have submitted responses to the document. The responses were compiled and analysed and became the basis of a report entitled *"Feedback from Community and Staff Consultation on: Towards Advance Environmental Decision-Making in the City of Toronto"* written by Task Force staff. In general the feedback suggested the following factors need to be consider ED for decision-making on the environment:

- One issue is whether we should take a formal or informal approach with broad, multi-sectoral involvement, or rely on more traditional mechanisms of representative democracy.
- Another issue is whether to take an "holistic" perspective (like a sustainable development approach) or address narrowly defined environmental issues. Linked to this point is a question about what takes precedence between local or regional issues.

The result of the consultation was also to underline the importance a set of principles for good governance. It was stated that decision-making should be transparent, understandable, involved and integrated, communicated and sufficiently resourced.

This consultation had a direct effect on the proposed governance structure. The most remarkable effects reported by the city were the following:

- It integrated best practices of draft models identified by respondents, in particular concerns regarding accountability, reporting, authority, leadership, community involvement, capacity building, duplication and gaps.

95

- It provided clear accountability mechanisms and clear mandates.
- It incorporated support from councillors across standing committees.
- It included suggestions for the creation of a round table which serves not as a "filter", but as a forum for strategic sustainability planning and policy development.
- It created a bridge between NGOs and the state sector.
- It included suggestions for the creation of an Environmental Auditor who has standing in both the political and the administrative worlds.

The Task Force recommended:

Leadership

1. That the Chief Administrative Officer (CAO), who is the head of the City of Toronto administrative machinery, become the "**Sustainability Lead**" and appoint a Sustainability Director to:

   - Prepare a plan, in consultation with the city staff and the round table (to be established under point 2), identifying how sustainability can best be promoted, facilitated and supported within the organisation of the City of Toronto. And that this plan be presented to Policy and Finance Committee by January 2001.

   - Work with other members of the Senior Management Team to incorporate sustainability into policies, programmes and decision-making processes within the City of Toronto.

   - Consider how Health and Safety Committees can be encouraged to bring matters of broad policy interests to the Sustainability Round table, where appropriate.

2. The task force proposed that a strategic, high level Sustainability Round Table be established to meet periodically. This round table, similar to the federal and provincial ones, would have various responsibilities such as:

   - Promoting sustainable development.

   - Helping the City Council facilitate consensus on contentious issues.

   - Monitoring progress and advising strategic and sectoral planning.

   - Encouraging public and grassroots in putting into operation sustainability planning of the city.

The round table will be composed of people with different backgrounds, like City Councillors of various standing committees of the City in the economic, environmental and social field, other senior staff (*e.g.* the Commissioner of Economic development, the Commissioner of Urban Planning and development services, the Medical Officer of Health etc.), organisations from the environment community as well as the social equity community, and the economic development community.

Advocacy

The governance model proposed that a sustainability advocate be appointed among the Council to co-Chair the Sustainability Round Table, to promote sustainability and to monitor the incorporation of sustainability into policies. Similarly, sustainability advocates would be appointed among the City Standing Committees to sit in the Round Table in order to ensure excellent communication between the Round Table and Committees.

Reporting

The City Auditor will write a report, in consultation with the Sustainability Round Table, as to how Audit Services can develop a Sustainability Audit and this report will be submitted to the Policy, Finance and Sustainability Committee within 2 years of the creation of the Sustainability Round Table.

It is also proposed to establish an Environmental Auditor Position, which parallels to the Commissioner of Environment and Sustainable development at the federal level. Standing Committees would also be requested to report annually on the environmental auditor's report, in order to close the loop between policy development, implementation and monitoring.

Source: Federation of Canadian Municipalities

Annex III

Better Governance for Improving Sustainability in the North

Two recent developments will certainly have an impact for improving the sustainability of the North and changing the nature of the relationship between the Federal Government and sub-national levels of government. One response has been mainly the "institutional" response to northern issues, that is the creation of the Territory of Nunavut, while the other initiative is more of a "procedural" nature, *i.e.* mechanisms for fostering the elaboration of an overall strategy for the North.

The creation of the Territory of Nunavut

The creation of Nunavut, an area which was formerly part of the Northwest Territories, returned to Inuit control over their own affairs in a context where their traditional and sustainable nomadic way of life had been threatened. Inuit negotiators recognised as early as the 1970s that while a land claim agreement with the Federal Government to restore their control over their resources could go a long way toward preserving the traditional Inuit way of life, political control of the central and eastern Arctic – and all the decisions that a territorial government makes which have an impact on education, economic development, and more – were equally important.

Therefore Inuit made the creation of the territory a prerequisite to the resolution of their land claim. After a long negotiation process with the Federal Government the territory known as Nunavut was established under the Statutes of Canada 1993, Bill C-132 – the *Nunavut Act*. It received royal assent on 10 June 1993. The *Nunavut Land Claims Agreement Act* came into law at the same time as the *Nunavut Act*. Implementation of the Nunavut Land Claims Agreement has been underway since 1993.

Although territories do not have as much power over their own affairs as provinces, the situation with Nunavut is a little different. The new territory permits territorial-level government to reflect the circumstances of the central and eastern Arctic, which are very different economically and culturally from those in the western Arctic. According to the Nunavut Land Claims Agreement (NLCA), the Nunavut government gained some decision-making capacity in areas of jurisdiction that the federal government normally keeps for itself in Canada's territories.

In particular, under the NLCA, both Inuit and the territorial and federal governments have guaranteed representation on institutions of public government responsible for issues that are left to the federal government alone in Canada's territories – these include agencies such as the Nunavut Water Board and Nunavut Wildlife Management Board, which make decisions affecting Crown (federal) lands and offshore areas. It is hoped that provisions in the NLCA intended to kick-start Nunavut's wage economy would eventually make Nunavut economically more sustainable and less dependent on federal government transfers.

The creation of the new Territory could contribute to finding local solutions to support the sustainability of threatened communities. It reflected the choice of devolving authority in a context of fragile economic, social and ecological sustainability. So far it seems that this contributed to raising the issue of sustainability in the new Territory, which itself established a sustainable development department.

Towards an overall strategy in the North

During the development of the first sustainable development strategies in 1996-1997, several federal departments jointly consulted with northerners. During those consultations, northerners expressed a strong desire for a single federal sustainable development strategy for the North, rather than several individual departmental strategies. In the 1999 Report of the Commissioner of the Environment and Sustainable Development, the Commissioner also underlined that an overall strategy for the North would help federal departments and agencies to carry out their scientific research, monitoring and other responsibilities in the Northern Area more effectively and efficiently.

The current consultation process

Northerners have been consulted in 2000 in the context of the recasting of ministerial strategies. The main objective of the consultations was for federal government departments to work together with northerners in the development of a Federal sustainable development strategy for the North as well as the revision of individual departmental sustainable development strategies. To a large extent the northern content of the sustainable development strategies will be based on the results of these consultations. The consultation meetings provided opportunities for:

- Participants to discuss their concerns with federal officials, suggestions on issues and other input regarding the Federal sustainable development strategy for the North, and individual departmental strategies.
- The federal government to present a co-ordinated approach for developing a federal sustainable development strategy for the North, and northern content of individual departmental sustainable development strategies.

Developing the strategy

The Federal sustainable development strategy for the North integrates northern objectives and actions to be implemented by departments having interests in the North. The broad goals that have been defined by the Federal government are the following:

1. Enhance capacity to participate effectively in northern consultations.
2. Respond effectively to complex northern issues and challenges in a sustainable manner (*e.g.* resource development, land claims, environmental protection).
3. Grasp opportunities to deliver and influence other international, national, and departmental agendas, and make direct linkages between the northern sustainable development agenda and other programmes.
4. Enhance capacity to participate in existing and emerging governance systems.
5. Increase awareness about sustainable development issues and federal programmes among all Canadians including northerners.

In particular, the federal government sees a Federal sustainable development strategy for the North as a more general opportunity to improve policy coherence (mainly through better integration of policies). One way in which we are trying to co-ordinate better within the federal government is by holding joint consultations.

The federal government has been following two different, but very closely tied processes: revising individual departmental sustainable development strategies, and developing the Federal sustainable development strategy for the North. The main steps in these processes have been:

1. Develop approaches to consultations.
2. Distribute materials to northerners (early fall 1999).
3. First round of consultation meetings (November 1999); set up web site consultation (starting fall 1999 and ongoing throughout the period).
4. Draft the first federal sustainable development strategy for the North and revise departmental sustainable development strategies (winter 1999-2000).
5. Distribute draft sustainable development strategies to northerners (spring 2000).
6. Second round of consultation meetings (late spring 2000); continue with web site consultation (ongoing).
7. Finalise departmental sustainable development strategies (late 2000).
8. Provide feedback and table departmental sustainable development strategies (December 2000).
9. Finalise the Federal sustainable development strategy for the North (early 2001) for review by the Deputy Ministers' Co-ordinating Committee for Sustainable Development, and distribute.

The role of the NRTEE in the North

Several bodies will have important sectoral responsibilities, including Environment Canada, Natural Resources Canada (see *www.nrcan.gc.ca/dmo/susdev/consult.htm*), and Indian and Northern Affairs Canada (see *www.inac.gc.ca/sds/index.html*). Support for developing a strategy for the North is also provided by the NRTEE efforts in raising sustainability issues. Its stipulates that it should "identify essential components of a process to guide non-renewable resource development over the next 10-15 years that balances the economic, environmental and social interests of Aboriginal communities, industries, ENGOs and governments located in Canada's North".

Annex IV

Improved Decision-making in the Fisheries Sector

Fisheries is a complex policy sector with major economic, environmental and social stakes. It contributes to a substantial share of the Canadian economy. But this development threatens the environment, as it is a renewable resource calling for specific management. For example a number of stocks are at risks and habitat damage continues to erode the productive potential of the resource. The environmental degradation is a threat, which could also lead to economic and social disasters. Taking the example of the commercial salmon industry, the economic viability of the salmon industry is declining partly due to excessive participation and lower abundance. On the other hand, fish (especially in the North and British Columbia) is a major source of food and cultural fulfilment for First Nations.

Improving decision-making has been perceived as one of the key factors for achieving sustainability. The fact that fisheries should be considered as an integrated ecosystem calls for an allocation of decision-making power and responsibility which vests all interests and internalises the sources of control, promotes long-term management, develop management skills among different interests, and, promotes adaptability to change. But the difficulty to make "consensual" decisions is a factor that could jeopardise the sustainability of the fisheries sector. Various initiatives have been taken to improve decision-making mechanisms.

Developing co-management

One initiative has been the development of *"co-management"* approaches in different areas of the fisheries sector. Co-management Fisheries will no longer be in the position of being ruled by government decisions and regulations but will share responsibilities for the management of this sector. This could involve specific management issues as well as contributing to data collection for science, reporting systems, sampling, supervising local initiatives etc.

Informal co-management arrangements have been experimented in the fisheries sector such as black cod, halibut and herring on the west coast as well as ground fish and lobster. Specific agreements have also been developed with Aboriginal groups (Aboriginal Fisheries Strategy) and for land claim settlements (co-management boards with legislated responsibilities).

A formal framework for co-management between government and commercial fisheries applicable largely to Atlantic and Pacific commercial fisheries has been in existence since 1997. It consists of fisheries for:

1. Providing input to *an Integrated Fisheries Management Plan*, which is an instrument (not legally binding) built on a transparent consultation process of the Fisheries. This ensures that conservation requirements and viability goals are achieved while forming the basis for a more ecological approach of fisheries management.

2. Working together with government on specific activities. This is called the *Joint Project Agreements* (JPAs). Entering JPA is voluntary and generally covers specific activities such as data collection, data analysis, science and/or fishery management activities.

In both cases, however, ministerial discretion is maintained over the co-management arrangements.

Improving conservation strategies implementation

The failure of the ground fish fishery system, especially in Atlantic Canada has been partly due to the difficulty of implementing conservation principles. Improving the effectiveness of conservation strategies is intrinsically interrelated with improving decision-making mechanisms. In particular current efforts to develop better conservation strategies focus on:

- **A proper communication and education system.** Both scientists and professionals (fishermen) have a key role to play to relate better to each other and encourage mutual learning. Workshops have been developed in some provinces to help fishermen provide accurate reliable data and also to help scientists better integrate knowledge gained from fishermen's experience into their own process.

- **Improving access to information and knowledge** should also be a central goal. It contributes to better understanding the resources available and improving the stock assessment. Access to reliable data could be achieved only through sound co-operation mechanisms between fishermen, science and the industry.

- **Improving planning and prosecution.** This could be achieved only through an active involvement of both managers (to avoid political interference, improve implementation and regulation, mechanisms, set up follow-up activities, use the precautionary approach, ensure proper consultation processes) and fishermen's group and associations to improve conservation awareness and develop Conservation Harvesting plans.

Source: Fisheries and Oceans Canada

Canada

Annex V

Measuring the Implementation:
The Example of Natural Resources in Canada

When Natural Resources Canada (NRCan) developed its Sustainable Development Strategy, it recognised that translating ideals into implementation would require both a concrete action plan and a consistent system to measure its performance. Consequently, the Department realigned its policy goals to match those in the Strategy and developed a single set of performance indicators to meet various reporting needs. This revised set of goals and objectives is now used in all corporate planning and reporting documents, ensuring sustainable development is integrated into the ongoing planning of Departmental business.

Measuring NRCan performance

Also in response to the May 1998 recommendation of the Commissioner of the Environment and Sustainable Development, the Department refined its draft performance indicators and established targets to measure progress against the strategy's objectives. This work benefited from the advice of stakeholders who were invited to review the appropriateness of NRCan's draft indicators. In total, 100 stakeholders were consulted on NRCan's draft indicators. Although comments were generally favourable, many suggested that the link between the indicators and the goals and objectives be strengthened, and that clear targets and benchmarks be established. Following this advice, NRCan developed assessment criteria to refine each indicator and establish targets where appropriate. Furthermore, the Department identified data sources to support each indicator to establish existing levels of performance for each target. Many of the targets included in the draft Performance Measurement Framework are directional. In this regard, NRCan will establish current performance, based on credible data sources, and subsequently strive to maintain or improve on current performance. Following an evaluation of the Department's performance against the directional targets, NRCan will be in a position to consider replacing directional targets with numerical targets. There are indicators included in the framework for which it would be too difficult to attribute NRCan's contributions (*e.g.*, the contribution of the natural resources sector to the Gross Domestic Product) with any degree of precision. As such, targets were not identified for these "macro" indicators. Nonetheless, the Department will track these indicators through trend analysis and monitoring because of their importance to NRCan and its client sectors. A framework for Performance Indicator reporting was also put in place.

Accountability at three levels

NRCan's work in promoting sustainable development can be assessed by stakeholders at three different levels.

- At the most basic level, through regular reporting on action commitments, stakeholders will have a clear indication of whether the Department is meeting its commitments.

103

© OECD 2002

- At the second level, through the refinement of indicators and establishment of targets, NRCan's performance can be measured against the Strategy's objectives.
- Finally, at a broader level, Canada's overall progress in the sustainable development of its natural resources can be assessed through indicators dealing with sustainable development practices in the areas of forest management, energy, and minerals and metals.

Source: Natural Resources Canada

Annex VI

The Role of the Canadian Environmental Assessment Agency (CEAA) in Providing Advice to Decision-makers

The CEAA serves as a source of information and advice on the federal environmental assessment process by:

- Providing training, information, guidance, and advice to federal departments and agencies on their obligations under the Act and under the *Cabinet Directive on the Environmental Assessment of Policy, Plan and Program Proposals*.

- Providing advice to project proponents and consultants conducting environmental assessments, to ensure compliance with the Act.

- Responding to requests from the public for both general information on environmental assessment procedures and specific information on the assessment of particular projects.

- Reviewing proposed class screening reports and comprehensive study reports to ensure compliance with the Act.

- Providing administrative and technical support for mediators and review panels.

- Providing funding for the public to participate in mediation and panel reviews.

- Working with provincial governments and other jurisdictions to ensure that environmental assessments of projects are co-ordinated and co-operative.

- And preparing a report on plans and priorities and a performance report on how the Act is being implemented across government departments and agencies.

Providing Advice to the Minister of the Environment

The Minister of the Environment has a critical review and decision-making role in the federal environmental assessment process. The CEAA provides legal, procedural, and policy advice to the Minister on meeting the Minister's responsibilities under the Act. For example, the Agency provides advice when the Minister:

- Reviews a comprehensive study report to ensure compliance with the Act.

- Determines, after reviewing a comprehensive study and public comments, whether a project can be referred back to the responsible authority for action, or whether further review is needed through mediation or a panel review.

- Decides whether mediation is an appropriate option, or whether a project should be referred to a panel review.

- Establishes terms of reference for a mediator or panel.

- Refer projects with potential significant trans-boundary impacts to panel review in the absence of a federal trigger.
- Appoints a mediator or panel members.
- And/or receives a report from a mediator or panel and makes it available to the public.

The CEAA also has a broader role in promoting and improving environmental assessment practices in Canada and abroad. Through its work with federal departments and agencies, project proponents, provincial, municipal, and territorial governments, interested public groups, aboriginal groups, and international organisations, the Agency:

- Promotes the principles of sustainable development and public involvement in environmental assessment.
- Works to ensure a consistent application of environmental assessment in all regions of the country.
- Supports research to improve environmental assessment methods.
- Promotes international co-operation on environmental assessment by sharing information with, and offering Canadian expertise to, other countries.

The CEAA also promotes greater public awareness of the important role environmental assessment plays in Canada through public information booklets, fact sheets, reports, speaking engagements, the Internet, training sessions and a variety of consultation mechanism.

Source: CEAA

Annex VII

The Chemical Industry "Responsible Care"

One fundamental objective of the policy initiated is for companies, in making decisions for the benefit of their shareholders to take into account and minimise the impact on the environment of their investments and actions. CCPA committees and staff work with governments and others to evaluate and modify the economic factors necessary for the competitiveness of Canadian industry and the development of sound management of products and processes. One way to make progress in support of environmentally sustainable economic growth is to develop codes and guidelines. This has been done in the "Responsible Care" programme, which was invented in Canada and has spread to other countries and influenced similar developments in non- chemicals sectors.

The "Responsible Care" commitment specifies that "... the codes do not contain static requirements which, once met, never change. Rather, they necessitate continuous performance improvement in an environment of changing knowledge and regulation". It goes on to clarify that "To meet only the letter of the law falls short of the intention of these codes" and that member companies must stay in touch with stakeholder concerns and adopt values that meet these evolving expectations.

This philosophy drives the involvement of CCPA and its member companies into such multi-stakeholder processes as ARET (*Accelerated Reduction/Elimination of Toxics*), MIACC (Major Industrial Accidents Council of Canada) and the waste minimisation task force. It underpins the sharing of expertise and experience through the CEO leadership groups, the implementation guidebooks, workshops and the compliance verification protocol.

Fresh input to the process of continuous improvement is also provided by the national advisory panel and community based advisory and involvement processes.

A multi-stakeholders approach

CCPA committees are currently evaluating full cost accounting with government and other stakeholders, and are guided by Responsible Care and its support of the principle of "polluter pays", as well as the need for a competitive environment for the industry in Canada.

CCPA is playing a key role for eliminating pollution at source. In this context CCPA members have also led in the development of a multi-stakeholder approach to reducing or eliminating emissions of persistent substances. CCPA the *National Emission Reduction Masterplan* (NERM) assist members in the reduction and public disclosure of emissions of all substances of environmental or health concern. This became a template for the *National Pollutants Release Inventory* (NPRI) of Environment Canada, and underpins CCPA's active involvement in the federal government's pollution prevention strategy. The *National Emissions Reduction Masterplan* (NERM) process lays out the approach for CCPA member companies to use in identifying, communicating and meeting public expectations for reductions in waste generation. CCPA

107|

supports the multi-stakeholder waste minimisation task force as a key vehicle for consolidating and extending this approach.

A multi-stakeholders approach has also been developed for the avoidance of accidents. CCPA was instrumental in the development and ongoing work of the Major Industrial Accidents Council of Canada (MIACC) to bring all stakeholders together to develop and implement consensus-based means to reduce the frequency and severity of, and respond effectively to, emergencies involving hazardous substances. Indeed, the internationally recognised CSA standard Z731 *"Emergency Planning for Industry"* was developed by MIACC based on the CCPA/CAER (community groups for Community Awareness/Emergency Response) code of practice.

Co-operation for environmental rehabilitation has manifested itself in CCPA's "polluter pays" philosophy as it participates in such multi-stakeholder as for that convened by the Canadian Council of Ministers of the Environment (CCME) to address the issues related to "orphan" waste sites. The waste management code of practice for member companies also provides for information sharing and co-operation with government agencies in any needed remediation.

A participatory approach

A participatory approach is increasingly developed through the consultation of the public. Involvement of all affected citizens in environmental decision-making is called for in most cases. Recognition of the need and right of the public and all stakeholders to understand, influence and reach acceptance of the risks to which they are subjected underpins the origins, development and implementation of "Responsible Care".

It is built into its policies, preamble, guiding principles and all codes of practice. The *Community Right To Know Policy* states that citizens around plants and along major transportation corridors are entitled to information concerning the health and environmental risks to which they are exposed and that "Accurate hazard information shall always be provided regardless of trade secrets". Management practices to ensure this is provided are described in the Community Awareness and Emergency Response, R&D, manufacturing and transportation codes of practice. Workshops have been held to assist members in community risk communications. Provision of hazard and risk information to employees and second parties such as contractors, customers, distributors, contract laboratories, waste contractors and carriers is also called for in the various codes of practice.

The Responsible Care compliance verification process, involving community and other public representatives, provides critical feedback. CCPA meets regularly with a panel of a national cross-section of advocates in areas related to Responsible Care to receive advice and feedback. All aspects of the initiative have incorporated and been influenced by this input.

Performance reporting

The Responsible Care compliance verification process evaluates each member company's management processes for, and effectiveness in, achieving publicly acceptable risk and performance communications.

Environmental performance reporting expectations of various publics have been researched through such means as CCPA's national advisory panel, interviews, national surveys and community dialogue processes. These have resulted in the development and implementation of CCPA's *National Emissions Reduction Masterplan* (NERM) and its use in the design of Environment Canada's *National Pollutant Release Inventory*. NERM calls for annual reporting by all CCPA member companies to their employees, communities and others of all current and projected 5-year emissions and wastes of environmental or health concern. Results are compiled into CCPA's annual *Reducing Emissions* report.

Similarly, member companies' experiences in the area of transportation incidents and spills are compiled in CCPA's *Transportation Incident Measurement* (TIM) programme and their occupational safety performance is compiled through the *Safety and Health Accident Reporting Experience* (SHARE) programme. A Responsible Care public "report card" on all these areas has recently been published.

Sharing knowledge

CCPA member companies and staff also share their environmental, health and safety expertise with industry people and others through such multi-stakeholder fora as CAER groups, TransCAER, the *Transportation Emergency Assistance Program* (TEAP), CSA technical committees, the Major Industrial Accidents Council of Canada (MIACC) and the waste minimisation task force. Company chemical expertise can also be accessed through the telephone. CCPA member companies have led the formation and management with universities of the Institute for Chemical Science and Technology for the development and sharing of research in non-competitive areas such as environmental improvement.

Environmental education at the high school level is enhanced through CCPA's support for the Knowledge of Environment for Youth (KEY) Foundation and the Foundation Riou Delorme and their work with teachers on curriculum development.

Source: Chemical Producers Association

109

People Interviewed for Study of Canadian Governance for Sustainable Development

John Arseneau, Director, Policy Analysis, Canadian Environment Assessment Agency.

Elisabeth Atkinson Senior Policy Advisor, National Round Table on the environment and the Economy.

Ronald Bergin, Director, in charge for relations between private and public secretariat and best practices and Wayne Kluskey, Principal, in charge of Environment Canada audits, Office of the Auditor General.

Diane Carroll, Director General, and Mark Hopkins, Strategic Direction and Policy Co-ordination, Environment Canada.

John Chibuk, Chief, Sustainable Development, Strategic Policy Branch Industry and Science Policy Sector, Industry Canada.

Louise Comeau, Senior Policy Analyst, Federation of Canadian Municipalities.

Philippe Crabbé, Director, Institute for research on the Environment and the Economy, University of Ottawa.

Bill Jarvis, Director General, Policy Research Branch, Environment Canada.

Gene Nyberg, Corporate Secretary and Director of Operations.

Mark Pearson, Director, Sustainable Development and Environment Division, Natural Resources Canada.

Norman Regelti (conference call) Regional Municipality of Hamilton-Wentworth.

Angela Rickman, Deputy Director, Sierra Club of Canada.

David Runnels, Interim President; International Institute for Sustainable Development.

Renetta Siemens, Manager, Sustainable Development, Environmental Affairs, Transport Canada.

Mark Ziegler, Senior Policy Advisor, Climate Change Secretariat.

Bibliography

Crabbé, P. (1997),
Sustainable Development: Concepts, Measures, Market and Policy Failures at the Open Economy, Industry and Firm Levels, Occasional Paper 16, Industry Canada, Ottawa.

Doering, R.L (1993),
Canadian Round Tables on the Environment and the Economy: their History, Form and Function, NRTEE March 1993 (revised September 1993).

Grafton, R.Q. and D. Lane (1998),
"Canadian Fisheries Policies: Challenges and Choices", Canadian Public Policy, Vol. XXIV, NO.2.

Harrison, K. (1996),
Passing the Buck – Federalism and Canadian Environmental Policy, UBC Press, Vancouver.

Hessing, M. and M. Howlett (1997),
Canadian Natural Resource and Environmental Policy – Political Economy and Public Policy, UCB Press, Vancouver.

OECD (2000),
Economic Surveys: *Canada*, OECD, Paris.

OECD (1997),
Managing Across Levels of Government, OECD, Paris.

OECD (1995),
Environmental Performance Reviews: *Canada*, OECD, Paris.

Van Kooten, G.C. and A. Scott (1995),
Constitutional Crisis, The Economics of Environment, and Resource Development in Western Canada, *Canadian Public Policy*, XXI:2:233-249.

Wyman, M. and D. Shulman and L. Ham (1999),
Learning to Engage: Experiences with Civic Engagement in Canada, report prepared for *Civil Society in the New Millennium*, A project of the Commonwealth Foundation, Canadian Policy Research Networks (CPRN), Inc., Ottawa.

Germany

By

Martin Jänicke, Helge Jörgens, Kirsten Jörgensen, Ralf Nordbeck
Environmental Policy Research Unit (FFU)
Free University of Berlin[1]

Purpose

The study focuses on practices for improving institutions and decision-making for sustainable development in Germany.[2] It does not provide an exhaustive review of sustainable development governance in Germany, but rather highlights current trends as well as selected promising developments that could help achieve sustainable development. The paper focuses on the strategies that have been formulated and implemented, but an overall review of policies and programmes was left outside the scope of the study. Similarly, it focuses primarily on developments within federal level government authorities and, therefore, does not cover the multiplicity of local and private initiatives, apart from selected illustrative examples. This paper was commissioned by the OECD and not extensively discussed with the German Government, respectively the Ministry of the Environment.

General introduction

Physical, economic and human patterns

The Federal Republic of Germany is located in Central Europe, bordering Poland and the Czech Republic to the east, Switzerland and Austria to the south, the Netherlands, Belgium, Luxembourg and France to the west, Denmark, the North Sea and the Baltic Sea to the north. Germany has a continental climate in the western regions with strong Atlantic influences in the northwest and a temperate climate in the eastern regions. Further inland, the winter temperatures are lower and the summers are warm, with slightly higher temperatures in the southwest. Germany is a country characterised by abundant rainfall and water. The major river systems of the Rhine, Elbe, and Danube as well as numerous lakes make up to 2 per cent of the territory. The North Sea and the Baltic Sea coastlines are more than 1 500 km in length.

As Western Europe's most populated country, Germany was estimated to have a population of 82 797 408 in 2000, living in a total area of around 357 000 square kilometres. The average population density of 228 inhabitants per square kilometre is one of the highest in Europe. 58 per cent of the population live in municipalities with more than 20 000 inhabitants. The major cities in Germany are Berlin (about 3.3 million inhabitants), Hamburg (1.7 million), Munich (1.2 million), and Cologne (960 000). Despite the high density of human settlement, some 55 per cent of the country's territory is used for agriculture and 30 per cent of Germany is covered by forests. Buildings and open areas account for 8 per cent of land use and transport for 4.7 per cent (Statistisches Bundesamt, 2000; SRU, 2000). Nevertheless, the main trend in land use is that the area used for settlement and transport is continually increasing, while that used for agriculture is decreasing (BMU, 1997).

Germany is one of the leading economies in the world. Its gross domestic product of $3,842 billion in 1999[3] ranks third behind the USA and Japan. The annual GDP growth was 2.1 per cent in 1998; it slowed down to 1.6 per cent in 1999, largely due to lower export demand and low business confidence. Fiscal consolidation and a recovering export demand boosted growth back to an estimated 3.1 per cent in 2000. German industry is highly integrated into the world market, with a high share of its wealth generated through exports (28 per cent) and also significant imports of raw materials and consumer goods. The integration of Eastern Germany remains a social and economic long-term problem with annual transfers of roughly $100 billion.

In terms of sustainable development, the above patterns have various consequences. Germany's high degree of industrialisation and its central location in Europe are factors generating high traffic volumes, which have increased considerably due to the German reunification, the economic opening of Eastern Europe and the creation of an internal European market. The competition between different types of land usage puts a particular burden on biodiversity, contributing to a generally declining pool of species, with 5 per cent of vertebrate species being registered as extinct and 50 per cent classified as endangered. A third of all plant species are considered to be threatened or extinct. High economic performance and high living standards among the German population involve high consumption of energy and raw materials. In 2000 the total primary energy consumption amounted to 14 173 petajoules resulting in 834.7 million tons of CO_2 emissions. The German economy's energy efficiency is below the OECD average (DIW, 2001).

The problem of pollutant emissions into the aquatic environment and the atmosphere was recognised early on in the 1960s, leading to a comparatively long tradition of environmental policy in Germany. The introduction of an ambitious preventive and precautionary environment policy from the beginning of the 1970s onward resulted in a relative decoupling of economic growth from energy and materials consumption as well as pollutant emissions since the 1980s. In contrast,

Eastern Germany was facing acute environmental problems. Article 34 of the accession treaty obliged the federal government to undertake significant efforts to increase environmental standards in the former GDR (Beuermann, 2000: 86).

Governance patterns[4]

The Federal Republic of Germany is a federal State characterised by a polycentric administrative structure, a co-operative system of federalism and the strong position of the Federal Chancellor as its head. Its administrative structure consists of three different levels: federal, Land (state), and local. Each level is legally autonomous and, in principle, independent in fulfilling its constitutionally defined tasks. The Basic Law distributes the competencies and tasks between the Federal Government and the Länder, while the local authorities form independent bodies of self-government which allows them to regulate all their local affairs under their own responsibility.

Germany is composed of 16 Länder with 13 territorial Länder (Baden-Wuerttemberg, Bavaria, Brandenburg, Hesse, Lower-Saxony, Mecklenburg-Western-Pomerania, North-Rhine-Westphalia, Rhineland-Palatinate, Saarland, Saxony, Saxony-Anhalt, Schleswig-Holstein, Thuringia) and 3 "city-states" (Berlin, Hamburg, Bremen) which are both a Land and a local authority.

The primary function of the federal government is to prepare political decisions and legislation. Legislative competencies are divided between federal authorities and the Länder. Where the Basic Law does not explicitly give legislative jurisdiction to the federal authorities, the Länder have such jurisdiction. Key areas where the Basic Law (Art. 73) gives jurisdiction to the federal authorities include foreign affairs, defence and monetary policy. In addition, the federal government can issue so-called "competing" legislation that override the Länder legislation in areas specified in Art. 74 of the Basic Law. This concerns, for example, the fields of waste management, air quality control, noise protection and nuclear energy. Finally, the federal authorities have the right to issue framework legislation (Art. 75 Basic Law) in areas such as nature conservation, landscape management and water resources management.

This division of jurisdiction makes the federal government largely responsible for environmental legislation, while the Länder and local authorities are responsible for implementation. Federal laws, ordinances, and administrative provisions are normally executed by the Länder under their own responsibility. In some areas, which are subject to federal supervision, the Länder execute federal laws on behalf of the federal authorities (e.g. laws on nuclear safety and radiation protection).

In decision making, the provisions of the Basic Law promote co-operation and policy co-ordination. On the federal level, proposed legislation (bills) can be introduced by members of the German parliament (Bundestag), by the Bundesrat

(*Länder* chamber) or by the federal government. After the B*undesrat* (in connection with initiatives of the government) or the federal government (in connection with initiatives of the B*undesrat*) has responded officially, the proposal for a bill is sent to the B*undestag*. Proposed legislation is treated in the B*undestag* in three "readings". If the B*undestag* passes the bill, it must then also be passed by the B*undesrat*, if it touches upon *Länder* interests.

Despite the strengths of this co-operative federalism, it poses some threats to the independence and relative political weight of the *Länder*, especially when joint financing is involved. This trend is further accelerated by the transfer of competencies to the European Union, and therefore the *Länder* are demanding greater involvement in EU decision-making processes.

With its high population density and its environmentally detrimental heavy industry, Germany is a country with a long tradition in air and water pollution control. Driven by a strong environmental movement (with more than five million members), the country was among the international front-runners in a number of areas such as regulating emissions from large combustion plants (*e.g.* coal power stations) or introducing car emission standards, and later in the fields of climate protection and waste management. At the beginning of the 1970s, Germany was already an early pioneer in strategic environmental planning. At that time, a number of innovative institutional arrangements and mechanisms were introduced for setting long-term environmental objectives, as well as concrete action goals (1971 Environmental Programme), and for integrating environmental considerations into the decision making of other sectors (notably a "Green Cabinet") (see Box 1). However, in spite of these early achievements and an altogether relatively successful environmental policy (see, for example, OECD, 2001), at present Germany seems to lag behind more pro-active European governments in its efforts to implement the more recent concept of sustainable development (Lafferty and Meadowcroft, 2000*b*: 419). The fact that Germany will be one of the last OECD countries to introduce a national strategy (Jänicke and Jörgens, 2000) for sustainable development illustrates this point. Similarly, at the international level, Germany has been active in promoting concrete environmental initiatives, for example in the field of climate policy, rather than with regard to general issues of sustainable development.[5]

A.   Main issues and tensions

Implementing sustainable development at the federal level: The former front-runner comes late

The rise of the concept of sustainable development challenges traditional policy making in a number of ways. Changes in the political decision-making process and the institutional framework required by this concept relate to three main issues: the coherent integration of policies in the environmental, social and economic spheres;

the wide-ranging participation of civil society in decision making; and a long-term view of problems and resulting strategies.

In its initial phase in the 1970s, German environmental policy had to a surprising extent tried to incorporate these aspects, which only two decades later were internationally established as key elements of the concept of sustainable development. The 1971 Environmental Programme, which gave the starting signal for modern environmental policy in Germany, set up the basic guiding principles of German environmental policy (precautionary principle, "polluter pays" principle, and principle of co-operation). It also formulated ambitious long-term targets for air pollution control and water protection, as well as a wide range of concrete policy actions. In retrospect, it can be seen as an early predecessor of modern "green" plans. One of its key objectives was to institute a process of long-term environmental planning (Bundesregierung, 1972; Wey, 1982). In addition, the programme not only developed the idea of environmental policy integration, but also translated this idea into new institutional arrangements (Müller, 1984: 127). The continuation of the Environmental Programme of 1976 furthered this idea by formally defining environmental policy as a "cross-sectoral task".

Box 1. **Environmental Policy Integration Mechanisms in Germany in the 1970s**

1971   Detailed Environmental Programme setting long-term targets for air and water pollution and formulating 148 concrete policy actions, evaluated and continued in 1976.

1972   Cabinet Committee for Environment and Health: 12 ministers, chaired by the Chancellor.

1972   Standing Committee of Director Generals from various ministries (StALA/Bund), chaired by the Minister for the Environment (at that time the Minister for the Interior).

1976   Environmental policy formally defined as a "cross-sectoral task" (Querschnittsaufgabe).

1970   Foundation of the Working Group on Environmental Issues (Arbeitsgemeinschaft für Umweltfragen), a pluralistic non-governmental policy transfer institution according to the "principle of co-operation" of the Federal Government.

1975   Principles for Environmental Impact Assessment of Public Activities of the Federal State.

Source: Jänicke, 1999, Bundesregierung, 1972, 1976.

Furthermore, the costs of most of the environmental laws and decrees foreseen for the following years were calculated in the 1971 Environmental Programme. Finally, participation of non-governmental actors in environmental rule making was to some extent formalised in the Federal Emissions Control Act of 1974 (§ 48).

In the late 1970s, however, the initial strategic planning approach and the attempt to treat environmental protection in an integrated manner lost much of its impetus and gave way to a medium-term command-and-control approach based mainly on permits and standard setting. Instead of setting qualitative medium- and long-term goals, environmental policy relied increasingly on emissions control at the source, based on highly detailed technical prescriptions (best available technology) (Jänicke and Weidner, 1997: 139). The Environmental Programme which had been formally evaluated and continued in 1976 (Bundesregierung, 1976), gradually lost impact and was finally dropped by the Christian-Liberal government in 1982. In this second phase, environmental policy had focussed mainly on air pollution control, water protection and waste management, and it was in these areas in particular that it had achieved remarkable success.

Against this background, the publication of the Brundtland Report in 1987 and the subsequent international rise of the concept of sustainable development received less attention in Germany than in other OECD countries (Lafferty and Meadowcroft, 2000a) and was mainly restricted to the preparation of the 1992 United Nations Conference on Environment and Development (UNCED) in Rio de Janeiro. While the UNCED stimulated some domestic changes – for example the creation of a rather weak National Committee for Sustainable Development or the amendment of a new Article 20a in the Constitution (Grundgesetz, see Section B) anchoring long-term environmental protection as a national objective – a more comprehensive reorientation of environmental policy towards a national strategy for sustainable development did not occur. In 1994, after the removal of the prominent Minister of the Environment, Klaus Töpfer, environmental planning in line with Agenda 21 was given low political priority in Germany.

Driven mainly by the commitments made at the Rio Conference, the work of NGOs (BUND/Misereor, 1996) and two successive parliamentary commissions of inquiry (Enquêtekommission 1994, 1998), the process of formulating a national strategy for sustainable development started – very slowly – in 1996 with discussions in special working groups, initiated and chaired by the Ministry for the Environment, Nature Conservation and Nuclear Safety (see Section C). The result was a strategy proposal published before the elections in 1998 by the Environment Ministry (BMU, 1998b). However, this strategy was never formally adopted by the cabinet. The scientific expertise gathered, particularly by the second parliamentary commission of inquiry, was used by the Social Democratic and the Green parties (both in opposition at that time) as a knowledge base for their claim for a German Environmental Policy Plan, which was part of the election campaign.

The current agenda

By March 2001, Germany had not yet fully developed a national sustainable development strategy, although it should be stressed that concrete initiatives have been taken in the last few years, one of the most significant being the October 2000 Programme on Climate Protection. In 1998, after the election and the victory of a "red-green" (Social Democratic/Green) party coalition the process of formulating a sustainable development strategy was taken up again, albeit very slowly. In January 2000, the German Parliament (*Bundestag*) asked the government to formulate a German sustainability strategy and to establish a Council for Sustainable Development (both actions having been agreed upon by the governing parties in their coalition treaty). In April 2000, the Conference of Environmental Ministers (UMK) of the federal states (*Länder*) supported this appeal, thereby emphasising the need for them to be included in the process. In July 2000, the Cabinet came up with a decision to elaborate a sustainability strategy and to create the institutional preconditions for this process: an Interministerial Committee on Sustainable Development (Green Cabinet) chaired by the chief of the chancellor's office, and a National Council for Sustainable Development. However, it was not until February 2001 that the members of the Council for Sustainable Development were formally appointed. The Green Cabinet is expected to begin its work in March 2001.

This slow start and the step-by-step approach in the formulation of a national strategy for sustainable development may to a certain degree be explained by a general scepticism resulting from the "planning euphoria" of the early seventies. The experience of that time has, indeed, made clear that green planning and environmental policy integration are not easy tasks. A key problem of the ambitious planning approach of the early seventies may have been the overestimation of horizontal co-operation between the environmental administration and those policy sectors which are closely linked to important target sectors such as energy or transport. This model was relatively effective when environmental policy was located within the more powerful Ministry of the Interior, and the responsible Minister of the Interior (Hans-Dietrich Genscher) was at the same time Vice-Chancellor of the Social Democratic/Liberal government and leader of the Liberal party. Later on, however, the horizontal approach often led only to "negative co-ordination" (Scharpf, 1993), in the sense that inter-sectoral co-operation was effective only in issue areas where sectoral interests were not strongly affected.

Another lesson to be drawn from the early German experience is that a low – or decreasing – level of environmental awareness is clearly a bad precondition for a demanding strategy such as sustainable development. One restriction to a comprehensive planning approach may also have been the federal structure of the political system, which restricts the scope of action of the federal government by

119|

allocating some legislative competencies to the *Länder*, thereby increasing the need for policy co-ordination between different levels of government.

Additionally, the ambitious start of environmental policy in 1970, and the subsequent successes especially during the 1980s and early 1990s, created a German policy tradition of its own in this policy field which restricted government's ability to strongly commit itself to the new policy approach brought forward by the concept of sustainable development. Following the publication of the Brundtland Report in 1987, the concept of sustainable development was to some extent perceived as a step back from what had already been achieved through the introduction of the precautionary principle and its implementation based on the systematic prescription of best available technology. "Therefore, an agreement on integrating economic, environmental and social concerns in decision-making (...) was judged to be a political "fudge' resulting from international negotiations that might weaken the German domestic commitment to environmental protection" (Beuermann, 2000: 88*f*). This

---

Box 2. Steps in the Formulation of a Sustainable Development (SD) Strategy in Germany

1991-94	Active participation in the UNCED process (1992); change of the Minister for the Environment (1994) led to a change of priorities; Commission of Inquiry of the *Bundestag* "Protection of Man and Environment" (1992-94) formulates four "Management Rules" of ecological SD.
1996-98	So-called "step process", organised by the Ministry for the Environment; "Sustainable Germany", published by the Federal Environment Agency (1997); 1998 draft programme "Sustainable Development in Germany", not formally endorsed by the Cabinet (quantitative targets for 2020); Commission of Inquiry of the *Bundestag* on SD (1995-98) formulates three-pillar approach to SD.
1998-2001	Renewed SD activity by the "red-green" government with concrete goals and measures, including a step-by-step process open to discussion with stakeholders and civil society organisations: • Strategy and Council for SD in the coalition treaty (1998). • Cabinet decision in July 2000: procedural and institutional regulation of the SD strategy formulation process, reintroduction of a "Green Cabinet".
2001	Formal appointment of the 17 members of the Council of Sustainable Development; first formal meeting of the "Green Cabinet". The three priorities for building a national strategy are "Climate Protection/Energy Policy", "Environmentally Compatible Transportation", "Environment, Nutrition and Health". The Council of Sustainable Development and the "Green Cabinet" are heavily involved in the preparation of a National Sustainable Development Strategy.

opinion was voiced several times in our interviews. When asked for an explanation of the slow Rio-plus-10 process in Germany, a leading official of the Federal Ministry for the Environment, Nature Conservation and Nuclear Safety answered: "Everything we do is a contribution to sustainable development".

Basic understanding of sustainable development

In the 1990s, two parliamentary Commissions of Inquiry on environment policy issues played an important role in creating the knowledge base for the German policy discourse on sustainable development. This included the basic understanding of the concept of sustainable development. The first Commission of Inquiry (1992-94) formulated four "management rules" of sustainability, which clearly focussed on the long-term protection of the environment and natural resources, at the same time emphasising the potential synergies for social and economic affairs. The second Commission of Inquiry, "Protection of Mankind and the Environment" (1995-98), established a broader definition of sustainability which gives equal weight to economic, social and environmental aspects. In our interviews we found that both concepts were prevalent in the actual debate. While, within the Ministry for the Environment (BMU, 1997a: 9) or the German Council of Environmental Advisors (SRU, 1994; SRU, 2000), the focus has clearly been on the ecological dimension, the other ministries and also the Green Party now prefer the "three-pillar approach" focusing equally on the environmental, social and economic dimensions of sustainable development. However, the opinions about this broader definition of sustainability ranged from "very useful" or "promoting learning across sectors" to "unclear" or "too complicated to handle". Within the Ministry of Finance, the concept of sustainability was applied mainly to the long-term consolidation of the budget. Within the Ministry of Labour and Social Affairs, sustainability was exemplified by the long-term security of the pension system, but also by the availability of "social capital". Social justice and participation have also been mentioned as criteria for defining sustainability.

According to a representative opinion poll carried out in 2000 by the Federal Environment Agency and the Federal Ministry for the Environment, the term "sustainable development" was known only to 13 per cent of the German population, representing a decrease compared to 1998, when 15 per cent of the population claimed to have heard of sustainable development. The study concludes that there is great uncertainty on the part of the citizens with regard to sustainable development (BMU, 2000: 68). Our interviews showed that sometimes even public servants who are professionally confronted with sustainability had no clear idea of how to operationalise this concept for concrete policy making. Although the term "sustainable development" has become an integral part of the standard vocabulary in almost all sectors of government, concrete sustainability objectives rarely exist and therefore have very limited impact on concrete policy making.

The fact that the most recent government initiatives with regard to sustainable development – the Cabinet decision of July 2000 to create a Council for Sustainable Development and a "Green Cabinet" and the appointment of the 17 members of the Council for Sustainable Development in February 2001 – went almost unnoticed by the media and the general public, tends to illustrate the low priority of sustainable development in Germany.[6]

In contrast, some aspects of environmental protection seem to have been much more successfully integrated into sectoral policies (see Table 1). This can be explained to a large extent by the strong tradition of the environmental policy field (see above). Contrary to the broader concept of sustainable development, which gives equal weight to social, economic and environmental aspects, the ecologically focused concept of sustainable development has developed a strong organisational and institutional basis in Germany.

The strength and influence of proponents of environmental protection such as the environmental movement, the German Green Party (at the State as well as at the federal level), as well as science and the media, could be another important explanatory factor for the strong and prevailing focus on environmental issues within the German approach to sustainable development (Jänicke and Weidner, 1997). Up to now, there have been no comparable pressure groups with regard to the broader concept of sustainable development. Instead, this concept has been interpreted and used by different societal actors (*e.g.* industry associations, trade unions, environmental organisations) in order to pursue their own interests and goals.

Selected sectoral issues

Sustainable development is internationally conceived as a general guiding principle for all government activities. While in most OECD countries the ministries for the environment have taken the lead in the preparation of UNCED and the implementation of Agenda 21 (see for example Lafferty and Meadowcroft, 2000*a*; Jänicke and Jörgens, 2000), it is essential that other sectoral ministries equally commit themselves to this goal. In this section, we therefore look at the non-environmental ministries and their contribution to sustainable development, while sustainable development activities of the Federal Ministry for the Environment – such as the development of the draft programme "Sustainable Development in Germany" (BMU, 1998*b*, 1998*c*) or the recent "Foreign Direct Investment Initiative" of the Ministry for the Environment and the Federation of German Industries – are described in other sections. A comprehensive account of the specific environmental activities of the German federal environmental institutions can be found in the recent OECD Environmental Performance Review of Germany (OECD, 2001).

In the following sub-sections, three policy sectors – climate and energy policies, transport and agricultural policy – will be described briefly. These are not only the priority sectors in the present debate within the European Union, but also sectors of high environmental relevance where significant policy change can be observed. Additional policy sectors are briefly characterised in Table 1. Policy sectors here are understood as responsible government institutions, together with the societal stakeholders who interact with them.

Climate and energy policies

Climate policy in Germany provides the longest and best experience as regards sectoral strategies for sustainable development. In the late 1980s, a Parliamentary Commission of Inquiry on Climate Protection created the knowledge base for the ambitious CO_2 reduction programme of 1990/91. In June 1990, the Cabinet adopted a CO_2 reduction target of 25-30 per cent between 1987 and 2005 which, in order to be consistent with international targets, was later modified to a reduction of CO_2 emissions by 25 per cent by the year 2005, based on 1990 levels. Also in 1990, an Interministerial Committee (*Interministerielle Arbeitsgruppe* – IMA) on climate protection was established, chaired by the Ministry for the Environment. It was highly effective in allocating responsibilities for climate protection to a number of environmentally relevant ministries (economic affairs, transport, construction, technology, agriculture) and thus integrating climate protection into the decision making of government in general. The IMA initially developed a programme for climate protection, which included 30 concrete measures for reducing CO_2 emissions, and which was later extended to a total of 109 measures (Beuermann, 2000: 101). When recent prognoses showed that only a CO_2 reduction of 18 to 20 per cent could be expected by 2005, the Federal Government presented in 2000 a new National Climate Protection Programme, which has now come to comprise more than 150 individual measures and which follow the path adopted by the former government. In this programme, the remaining shortfall of 5-7 per cent was translated into sectoral targets for private households and buildings, energy and industry and transport. Key measures taken in the course of implementing the successive programmes for climate protection include the ecological tax reform, the promotion of renewable energies (see Box 3), energy saving and the energetic renovation of older buildings (see Box 4). An Energy Agency was also established to support climate protection.

In order to fulfil its obligations in the area of climate protection, industry has opted for a voluntary self-commitment. In the 1996 Declaration by German Industry on Global Warming Prevention, 19 leading industry associations promised to reduce specific CO_2 emissions by 20 per cent by the year 2005. As this target was already reached in 1999 (23 per cent reduction of specific CO_2 emissions), a new

123|

Box 3.   **The German Renewable Energy Act**

An example of best practice in German energy policy is the 1999 Renewable Energy Act (based on the 1990 Act on the Sale of Electricity to the Grid). The Act obliges network operators to purchase electricity from renewable energy sources and sets out fixed prices of DEM 0.99/kWh for photovoltaic power and of DEM 0.13/kWh to 0.18/kWh for other renewables. These minimum feed-in tariffs for electricity from renewable energy sources, which take into account real generation costs, stimulated a massive boom in renewable power production. Although the economic efficiency of this Act has been questioned, its environmental effectiveness has been clearly demonstrated. The explicit goal of the Renewable Energy Act to double the proportion of electric power from renewables up to 2010 is rather modest compared to the present growth rate triggered by the new regulation. The Act is particularly remarkable because of its strong support by a new and broad societal alliance consisting of environmental NGOs, and also business associatio ns like the powerful German Peasant Association, the Union of Metal Workers (IG Metall), or the German Machinery and Plant Manufacturing Association. The Act was initiated and adopted in Parliament, where its cross-cutting societal basis was reflected by a coalition across governing as well as opposition parties.

---

agreement was signed by industry and government in November 2000 aiming at a 28 per cent reduction of specific CO_2 emissions by 2005 and a 35 per cent reduction of the six greenhouse gases listed in the Kyoto Protocol. The targets may still be modest, but the activity of industrial associations connected with this agreement may stimulate innovations that lead to a larger potential for improvement. German industry now regards itself as a strong driving force of sustainable development.

Transport

The transport sector was for a long time resistant to sectoral policy changes beyond "end-of-pipe" measures. In order to overcome this resistance, the new government formulated in 2000 a specific CO_2 reduction target for the transport sector (15-20 million tonnes). It also increased its support for the railway system, with a view to doubling its capacity. An Energy Strategy for Transport was formulated with the car industry (in parallel to the same EU initiative). One of its objectives is CO_2 reduction through better fuels and motor technologies. A significant tax reduction for fuel-efficient cars had already been introduced in 1997. A new environmental assessment scheme has been introduced for the Federal Traffic Route Planning System. The government plans a special duty on heavy goods transport on highways (DEM 0.25 per tonne kilometre). A special working group on

Integrated Transport Policy, including all major societal groups such as environmental NGOs, was established within the Federal Ministry for Transport, Construction and Housing. "Integrated Transport Policy" is also the title of the present "Transport Report 2000" of the Ministry (BMVBW, 2000). In this report, improvement of the environment is mentioned as one of ten priority fields.

In more general terms, the closer integration of the formerly separate systems of traffic route planning and spatial planning in the new Federal Building and Spatial Planning Act of 1997, and the subsequent merging in 1998 of the Federal Ministry for Transport with the Ministry of Construction and Spatial Planning, have improved the general conditions for a more integrated approach to spatial planning.

Agriculture

In Germany, agricultural policy belongs mainly to the jurisdiction of the federal states (*Länder*). As in other countries, the German Ministry of Agriculture has long been closely linked to the farmers' lobby. As a result, it has – until recently – been opposed to claims for a more ecologically sustainable agriculture. In just two years these traditional structures have been broken up and rapid change has taken place.

The "red-green" coalition treaty of 1998 formulates goals such as the general expansion of the federal government's environmental measures in the field of agriculture: the promotion of organic farming, reduction of intensive cattle breeding and the generation of renewable resources. Financial measures promoting ecologically sound production methods have been significantly increased. In March 2000, the peasant organisation published a Greenbook for Sustainable Agriculture and Forestry (*Deutscher Bauernverband*, 2000), describing all relevant international environmental obligations and signalling some reorientation of this powerful actor. At the same time, the Ministry for Agriculture published a Draft Sustainability Strategy for Agriculture, Forestry and Fisheries in Germany. This was partly a response to the Cardiff Process, but mainly a position paper to influence the German Rio-plus-10 process, especially the development of a German sustainable development strategy.

The main "learning shock" in the direction of sustainability came, however, from the BSE crisis in December 2000, which led to the removal of the Minister for Agriculture (himself a peasant with close ties to the farmers' lobby) and the "green" Minister for Health Affairs. The crucial event was the publication of a joint "green" policy paper prepared by the Deputy Ministers of Agriculture and Environment, which was strongly opposed by the former Minister for Agriculture and also by the majority of federal states. The subsequent reorganisation of the former Federal Ministry for Agriculture into a new Ministry for Consumer Protection, Food and Agriculture led by a "green" Minister and the reorientation of this Ministry to reduce intensive cattle breeding, to promote organic farming and contracting for

Table 1. **Recent Environmental Activities of Non-Environmental Policy Sectors and their Main Driving Forces in Germany**

	Sectoral Activities	Main Driving Forces
Energy	Ambitious "Climate Protection Programme" comprising over 150 measures; Energy Agency established	Path-dependent development; new "red-green" coalition government; Kyoto mechanism
	Massive promotion of renewable energies	Strong support by a new societal alliance consisting of members of most parliamentary groups, environmental NGOs, business and peasant associations and trade unions
Agriculture	"Sustainable Development Strategy for Agriculture, Forestry and Fisheries" proposed by the Ministry (2000); promotion of organic farming	Coalition treaty of the new "red-green" government EU (Agenda 2000), "window of opportunity" for policy change created by the BSE crisis
	Restructuring of the Ministry for Agriculture, Forestry and Fisheries "Green" targets (2001)	
Transport	"Energy Strategy for Transport" and "Integrated Transport Policy" proposed by the Ministry (2000); levy on heavy goods vehicles (planned); strong support for the railway system	EU New "red-green" coalition government
Construction	Integration of construction and physical planning laws (1997); amendment of the Spatial Planning Act in order to include explicit reference to sustainability; comprehensive recycling of demolition waste	Change of former environmental minister Klaus Töpfer to Minister of Construction (1994)
Development	Active role in the UNCED (1992); bilateral environmental technology transfer together with industry	Rio Process
Economic Affairs	Rapid increase in voluntary agreements; "greening" of economic reporting	Path-dependent policy development; EU
Finance	Tax reduction for cleaner cars (1997); ecological tax reform (1998); "Programme for the Future"; several credit programmes	Social Democrat/"Green" coalition government plus path-dependent development
R&D	Research support for SD	Path-dependent; "red-green" coalition government
Health	Action programme "Environment and Health"	"Red-green" coalition government
Social Affairs	Activities within the corporatist "Alliance for Labour and Training" (thematic dialogue "Labour and Environment"); reform of the Works Constitution Act (Betriebsverfassungs-gesetz) to include environmental protection among the specific competencies of the works councils	"Red-green" coalition government

nature protection, was explicitly supported by the German Chancellor. This reorientation is illustrated by new government targets such as an increase in organic farming of 20 per cent within ten years (instead of 2.5 per cent), a limit of two cows per hectare of farmland, and a ban on the preventive use of antibiotics in animal food.

B. Institutions and policies

As shown in previous sections, Germany, contrary to most other OECD Member countries, has not yet developed an official national strategy for sustainable development. Similarly, Germany has been rather reluctant in creating new institutions or mechanisms to more strongly integrate sustainability objectives into national decision making. However, although a general institutional reorientation towards a coherent policy of sustainable development is still lacking, a number of – sometimes disjointed – initiatives and incremental changes in the institutional setting can be observed. This section summarises the main political driving forces and institutional arrangements which are relevant for sustainable development in Germany.

Federal involvement

Central government

The Federal Ministry for the Environment has been the single most important institutional driving force for integrating environmental concerns into other sectoral policies. The different kinds of cross-sectoral environmental policy integration mentioned in Table 1 cannot be explained without the strong activities of this Ministry. Until 1998 it was also the main actor responsible for elaborating a national strategy for sustainable development (see above). Although in the past two years formal responsibilities for developing a sustainable development strategy have been shifted to the Chancellor's Office, it can be expected that the Ministry for the Environment will continue to play a leading role in this process.

Following the 1998 elections, a detailed coalition agreement was set up by the Social Democratic and "Green" parties, including a number of sometimes ambitious institutional and policy measures to be adopted in the course of the four-year legislative period. Generally, it depicts a number of important short- and medium-term objectives for ecological modernisation and sustainable development. As the coalition agreement is widely regarded as an important measure for the success of the new "red-green" government and clearly has a higher relevance and visibility than previous government declarations, it can be seen as an important – albeit often underestimated – contribution to a policy of sustainable development in Germany.

Box 4. **Procedural and Institutional Provisions of the Federal Government for the Formulation of a Sustainable Development Strategy (July 2000)**

- Strategy formulation as a task of the "Green Cabinet" (10 Secretaries of State).
- Annual report.
- Leading role of the Chancellor's Office.
- "Instruction" to the policy sectors to develop their own strategy.
- Council for Sustainable Development (15 members); primarily communicative functions.
- Planned focus of the strategy: energy, mobility and agriculture.
- Concrete practical examples.

The main measures outlined in the coalition agreement include the elaboration of a national sustainable development strategy, and institutional innovations to promote and organise the drafting of this strategy. In July 2000, the National Council for Sustainable Development was created by Cabinet decision. It is an independent and pluralistic advisory body on sustainability issues, composed of 17 individual members representing all major societal groups and actors (*e.g.* industry, trade unions, NGOs, science) which were appointed in February 2001. Among its tasks are the promotion of societal debate on sustainable development at the national and international levels (stakeholder dialogue) and the development of concrete projects for implementing a national sustainability strategy. The federal government may assign further tasks to the Council and ask for statements on specific issues.

A "Green Cabinet" consisting of secretaries of state of 10 ministries and chaired by the Head of the Chancellor's Office was created in July 2000 by Cabinet decision. Its main task is to co-ordinate governmental work on the sustainable development strategy and secure a stronger consideration of environmental and sustainability aspects in the decision making of the whole of government. The Green Cabinet is scheduled to begin its work in March 2001.

As both the Council for Sustainable Development and the Green Cabinet have not yet begun their work, it is difficult to assess their potential impact on the German strategy for sustainable development. However, it is generally agreed that their influence will depend to a large degree on the existence and extent of high-level government commitment and support to the goal of sustainable development and to the specific initiatives brought forward by these institutions.

Apart from these newly created institutional arrangements, a number of previous initiatives for promoting environmental policy integration, long-term policy orientation, or participation of major societal groups are worth mention. Mechanisms for horizontal policy integration include the already-mentioned Cabinet Committee on Environment and Health (1972), the Standing Committee of Directors General (StALA Bund) and Interministerial Committees (IMAs) which work on specific policy issues such as climate protection or waste management (for a more detailed account see Section A).

Interministerial co-ordination of legislative proposals is regulated in the Joint Standing Orders of the Federal Ministers (*Gemeinsame Geschäftsordnung der Bundesministerien*), which have recently been revised in the course of a general initiative for public sector modernisation. It regulates in detail not only interministerial co-ordination in the development of legislative proposals, but also early participation of the *Länder*, local authorities and societal associations. A general impact assessment for legislative proposals (not only for environmental matters) has been made obligatory. The ministries are seen now in a more strategic, goal-oriented role, which includes general rules for cross-sectoral policy integration. The Ministry for the Environment sees its position improved by this administrative reform, although environmental matters are not explicitly mentioned in the Joint Standing Orders (BMI, 2000).

In addition to these horizontal policy co-ordination mechanisms, most ministries have created their own environmental departments. Although these departments regularly act as a sort of "buffer" in the negotiations between the Environment Ministry and other ministries, in the long term they can be found to trigger environmental learning processes within non-environmental ministries and act as important driving forces for the ecologisation of sectoral policies. Only recently, the Ministry for Economic Affairs has formally enlarged the scope of its Department for General Affairs to cover sustainability issues; the responsible official is a leading representative of *Greenpeace*.

In 1994, the German Constitution (*Grundgesetz*) was amended to include environmental protection and responsibility for future generations as a national goal (article 20a). This constitutional amendment formally anchored environmental protection as a general and cross-cutting policy objective to be addressed by all parts of government, but it has so far had little direct and measurable impact on German policy making.

The role of Parliament

The German Parliament (*Bundestag*) has played an important role in setting the agenda for the sustainability debate in Germany. In particular, the successive Parliamentary Commissions of Inquiry have to a great extent created the knowledge base for a German strategy for sustainable development (see above). A similar contribution was made by the German Council of Environmental Advisors (*Rat von Sachverständigen für Umweltfragen*). The Office of Technology Assessment (*Büro für Technikfolgenabschätzung*) and the Environmental Committee are other institutional mechanisms for the consideration of aspects of environmental protection and sustainable development at the parliamentary level. While all parliamentary groups of the six political parties represented in Parliament have their own environmental working groups, only the Social Democrat and the Green parties have created working groups on sustainable development. In recent years, Parliament has repeatedly taken initiatives to speed up the process of formulating a national sustainable development strategy. The elaboration of such a strategy was decided by Parliament in 1998. Additional pressure has been exerted by means of parliamentary questions and conferences organised by the different factions. However, following the Cabinet decision of July 2000, Members of Parliament will not be part of the National Council for Sustainable Development and therefore will not participate directly in the preparation of a German sustainable development strategy.

Challenges at sub-national level

In the German federal system, legislative competencies in relevant areas of environmental policy such as air pollution control, waste management, noise and soil protection are located at the federal level, while in the fields of water and nature protection the *Länder* have a stronger position. Responsibility for the implementation of environmental legislation lies primarily with the *Länder*. The *Bundesrat* (the upper chamber of the German Parliament) – as representative body of the federal states – has considerable influence on federal legislation. In policy sectors such as waste management, and particularly in regulative policies which imply a high burden of administrative enforcement, the *Länder* try to retain some scope for action.

The *Länder* pay particular attention to the well-defined responsibilities in the vertical relationship between the federal and the sub-national levels. The main environmental policy co-ordination body between the *Länder* and the federal government, as well as among the federal states, is the Conference of Environment Ministers (*Umweltministerkonferenz* – UMK), which meets twice a year. As formulated in UMK protocols, sustainable development was adopted as a guiding principle of environmental policy in June 1997. In October 2000, the Conference of Senior Officials of Environmental Ministries asked the federal government to develop a national sustainable development strategy. This national agenda strategy should formulate goals and measures in selected priority areas. It should also take a horizontal approach to the media and across sectors, apply to all policy sectors and be combined with an indicator-based monitoring system. The horizontal relationship between the states can be described as moderately competitive. This competition may result in diffusion from one state to another of successfully practised policy measures in the same or a different form.

Agenda 21 strategies, public consultation and agreements between business and state at the state level

In terms of institutional settings and policy measures, *Länder* governance for sustainable development began relatively late. It varies from one state to another. A number of states have recently started to develop Agenda 21 strategies while others, notably Bavaria and Lower Saxony, have already adopted such a programme. However, concrete approaches differ widely: Baden-Wuerttemberg and Rhineland-Palatinate have each developed an environmental policy plan, while Schleswig-Holstein has formulated a set of environmental goals. In addition, some *Länder* have developed interministerial mechanisms for the horizontal integration of environmental goals into other policy sectors.

Public consultation at the state level has taken place in nearly all *Länder*; however, a minority considers decentralised Local Agenda 21 processes to be sufficient. Hesse has bound public consultations at the state level to sectoral consultations, for example in the Alliance on Sports and Environment (*Sport- und Umweltallianz*).

Box 5.   **Environmental "Pacts" or "Alliances" at the *Länder* Level**

Since 1995, the German *Länder* have taken various initiatives to improve environmental management at company level. Bavaria was the front-runner, and most of the *Länder* followed the Bavarian example by creating different types of state-business co-operation. Generally, such co-operation aims to introduce environmental management activities and compliance audits according to the European Environmental Management and Audit Scheme (EMAS) at company level, while reducing direct control by environmental authorities. These reductions in direct environmental control include reporting duties and technical monitoring in the areas of waste, air and water regulations. The key aim of these initiatives is to reduce environmental compliance costs for those companies participating in environmental management systems, to make the cost of environmental regulations easier for companies to calculate, and to promote organisational improvements at company level. It is planned to monitor most of this co-operation at the *Länder* level after one year. The Bavarian Environmental Pact was revised and updated in 2000. It was evaluated positively in particular because of its provision for a broad participation of business associations including industry, handicrafts and especially small and medium-sized companies.

(*www.umweltministerium.bayern.de/agenda/wirtsch/pakt.pdf*)

Another approach concerns agreements between business associations and the state. These agreements, called "environmental alliances" (Umweltallianzen) or "environmental pacts" (Umweltpakte) aim at a new business-state partnership by changing the traditional command-and-control approach, which had long been characteristic of German environmental policy (Jänicke and Weidner, 1997), to a more consensus-oriented policy style. They comprise environmental management activities and compliance audits according to the European Environmental Management and Audit Scheme (EMAS) at company level, and direct control by environmental authorities is reduced.

Furthermore, some states have integrated sustainability principles and goals into spatial planning (e.g. Berlin, Brandenburg) or into state laws (Saxony-Anhalt). Nearly all federal states provide institutional capacities to support Agenda 21 processes at the municipal level. These newly instituted Agenda Offices are usually affiliated to state environmental ministries or other environmental authorities, for example the State Office for Environmental Protection (Landesanstalt für Umweltschutz) in Baden-Wuerttemberg. Financial support for local Agenda 21 activities is provided in Hesse and North Rhine-Westphalia (NRW). So far, Hesse has the greatest number of local Agenda 21 initiatives, while NRW has the most advanced Agenda 21 processes at the local level.

Driving forces

A number of factors have acted as driving forces for the approaches to sustainable development at the state level, including the European Environmental Management and Audit Scheme (EMAS) which gained importance in some states in the course of a more general reform of the public sector. This led to a number of business-state agreements at the state level, to locally and NGO-initiated bottom-up Agenda 21 processes, which gave impetus to sub-national levels, to the Rio-plus-10 deadline, and to ecological modernisation as the core of the "red-green" coalition agreement and government programme.

Local Agenda 21 processes in Germany

Compared to other European countries, Germany has been described as a relative latecomer with regard to Local Agenda 21 initiatives (Eckerberg, Coenen and Lafferty, 1999). In November 1996, the International Council on Local Environmental Initiatives (ICLEI) counted only thirty Local Agenda 21 initiatives across Germany (ICLEI, 1997), whereas municipalities in countries like Sweden, the UK or the Netherlands were significantly more active in this field. In Sweden, for example, more than 60 per cent of local governments had started Agenda 21 processes by 1994 (Lafferty and Coenen, 2000). As comparative analyses show, central government involvement is a key variable for the diffusion of local initiatives. Institutionalised or systematic co-ordination and information dissemination, elaboration of guidelines and direct funding are important mechanisms for promoting Local Agenda 21 initiatives (Lafferty and Coenen, 2000).

In Germany, early Local Agenda 21 processes originated by and large from non-governmental players such as environmental and development organisations, church and youth groups, and to a lesser degree from local politics. Only seldom were they initiated by business associations (Zimmermann, 1997). Since 1995, some Länder as well as national and international transfer organisations support local initiatives. Federal and sub-national governance activities for sustainable development processes at local level increased significantly only after the 1997 Rio-plus-five Summit UNGASS. Financial support was first provided in North-Rhine-Westphalia in 1996. It offered DEM 0.50 per citizen to each municipality for local initiatives (BMU and UBA, 1999). Up to now the states of Hesse, Bavaria, Saarland, Lower Saxony and Schleswig-Holstein have introduced similar programmes. Since 1997, nearly all Länder have institutionalised some form of co-ordination office for Local Agenda 21 initiatives. At the federal level, Local Agenda 21 activities were supported through conferences, handbooks, studies and reports. As a result of these increased efforts, the diffusion of Local Agenda 21 processes has considerably quickened. In December 1999, 1,315 or nearly 10 per cent of all German municipalities officially worked towards the ratification of Local Agenda 21 programmes. By September 2000, the number of Local Agenda 21 initiatives had increased to 1,650 or 11.6 per cent of all German municipalities (*www.agenda-transfer.de*; last accessed 5 March 2001).

Societal sustainability processes in the new Länder

Governance for sustainable development in the new Länder has to deal with numerous societal reservations against the Local Agenda 21 approach, resulting from the profound political, economic and social changes of the last decade. The number of Local Agenda 21 processes in the new Länder (former GDR) is quite low. In September 2000, between 0.8 and 5.7 per cent of local communities in the new Länder and 3.2 to 54.6 per cent of local communities in the old Länder had taken up Local Agenda 21 processes (see Tables 3 and 4 in Annex). However, the new Länder are lagging behind, and not only with regard to local Agenda 21 initiatives. A performance gap also exists in areas such as waste management, water protection, the treatment of contaminated sites, agriculture, land-use management and nature protection. Additionally, conflicts often arise between nature protection and economic projects. Thus public policy is challenged to enable societal sustainability processes and to integrate social, economic and environmental concerns at the same time (Flath, 2000: 23ff.). Emphasis needs to be placed on exploiting win-win situations and creating positive synergies between different environmental, social and economic objectives.

133|

Table 2. **Sustainable Development Processes at the State Level**

	Sustainable development programme	Agenda 21 consultation	Business-state agreement
Lower Saxony	1996 Cabinet decision on initiation of SD programme; 1997/1998 State programme "SD in Lower Saxony"; 1999 Report to the Parliament	1997 Round Table Agenda 21	1998 Agreement
Rhineland-Palatinate	1995 Cabinet decision on initiation of SD programme; 2001 Cabinet decision on Agenda Programme Rhineland-Palatinate	1996 Alliance for Sustainability	Co-operation contracts with e.g. chemical industry, handicrafts, etc.
Bavaria	1997 Cabinet decision on Bavaria Agenda 21	1996 Environment forum BAVARIA	1995 Environment Pact 1; 2000 Environment Pact 2
Schleswig-Holstein	2000 Cabinet decision on initiation of SD programme; 2001 Cabinet decision on prioritised sectors (planned); 2002 Cabinet decision on the SD programme (planned)	1995 Kiel Environment Declaration on Local Agenda 21; 2002 Debate on prioritised sectors (planned)	1997 Environment Summit Kiel; 1998 Agreement: state, industry and handicrafts
Hesse	1997 "Red-green" government initiates SD programme; 2000 Christian Liberal government stops SD programme		2000 Environment Alliance Hesse
Saxony-Anhalt	1997 Cabinet decision on initiation of SD programme; Commission of Inquiry "Sustainable Saxony-Anhalt"	1997 Public debate	1999 Environment Alliance
Saarland	2000 Cabinet decision on initiation of SD programme; 2001 Cabinet decision on government SD programme (planned)	Working Group Agenda 21	2001 Environment Alliance based on SD programme of government (planned)
Baden-Wuerttemberg	2000 Cabinet decision on Environmental Plan 2000	2000 Consultation on Environmental Plan 2000	1997-98 Environmental Dialogue Sustainable Baden-Wuerttemberg

Table 2. **Sustainable Development Processes at the State Level** (*cont.*)

	Sustainable development programme	Agenda 21 consultation	Business–state agreement
Berlin	1999 Parliament decision on initiation of SD programme 2000 Senate decision on initiation of SD programme	2000 Agenda Forum	1999 Environment Alliance Berlin
North-Rhine-Westphalia	2000 Parliament decision on initiation of SD programme	2001 consultation (planned)	Environment Initiative NRW (steel industry)
Hamburg	2001 Ressort programme for the Environment Agency (planned)	1996 Future Council	
Thuringia	2000 Cabinet decision "10 Principles for the Implementation of Agenda 21 in Thuringia"	1999 Consultation on "10 Principles ... Thuringia"	Environment Initiative of Thuringia (industry)
Brandenburg		Round Table Berlin-Brandenburg	1999 Environment Partnership Brandenburg
Bremen		1996 Round Table Bremen	
Mecklenburg-Western-Pomerania	Scientific Council for a Sustainable Development Strategy		2000 Rostock Declaration on initiation of co-operation
Saxony			1998 Environment Alliance

Box 6. **Sustainable Development Initiatives in Saxony-Anhalt**

Saxony-Anhalt regards environmentally friendly public procurement, public building management, ecological construction and measures targeting environmentally friendly mobility as appropriate approaches, in which the public sector acts as a model (Häußler, 2000: 70 ff.). Voluntary agreements between government and business organisations set the framework for economic sustainability. They are expected to stimulate producer responsibility as well as learning and communication processes towards ecological modernisation. Some municipalities implement local environmental management systems to reduce both costs and negative environmental impacts.

The role of the non-governmental sector

Business

The network of industry and commerce associations in Germany ranges from umbrella organisations to specific sector organisations and Länder sub-groupings. Many have environmental committees focusing on environmental management standards and sectoral best-practice guidelines. They provide environmental information to their members and advise on legislative requirements.

The attitude of industry and trade associations towards environmental protection has changed very much over the last few decades, from simply opposing environmental regulation to a trilateral co-operative approach between government, industry and environmental organisations. Today, the situation of enterprises and their respective associations towards environmental policy is generally considered as ambivalent, with "green" enterprises and their ecologically oriented industry organisations emerging as new actors (Jänicke and Weidner, 1997: 146). Additionally, the production of environmental protection technology has become a significant industrial sector and environmentally related employment has increased to an estimated 1 million jobs or almost 3 per cent of total employment (BMU, 1998a: 24f.).

Over the last few years, industry associations have been instrumental in developing an increasing number of industry-wide self-commitments or voluntary agreements. Currently, the Federation of German Industries estimates that a total of around 100 voluntary agreements in the environmental field exist in Germany (BDI, 2000). Within the European Union, only the Netherlands makes greater use of this co-operative approach to environmental protection.

The Federation of German Chambers of Industry and Commerce (*Deutscher Industrie- und Handelstag*) comprises 83 regional centres. The central organisation is mainly concerned with promotion of the Environmental Management Audit Scheme (EMAS). Its Chambers of Foreign Trade, some of which include special "environmental area managers", play an important role in the promotion of environmental technology transfer to Central and Eastern Europe, Asia and Latin America (BMU, 1997a: 44).

The Federation of German Industries (BDI), the central umbrella association of 35 industrial branch associations, plays an important role in the field of climate protection. Together with other organisations, it signed a voluntary declaration in 1995 to promote the German national goal of a 25 per cent CO_2 reduction by 2005, which was updated in 1996 and further developed in 2000. Generally, the BDI considers German industry to have taken a leading role in the Kyoto process.

In July 2000, the BDI founded a Forum on Sustainable Development, consisting of eighteen prominent companies represented by their CEOs. This forum will function as the German industry's think tank for sustainable development, develop strategies for key sustainability issues and engage in the general sustainability debate. Active participation in the elaboration of a German strategy for sustainable development is considered a "central task" by the BDI.

In November 2000, the Federation of German Industries, together with the Ministry for the Environment, Nature Conservation and Nuclear Safety, initiated a Foreign Direct Investment Initiative as an institutionalised dialogue process for preparing the Rio-plus-10 Summit. It aims at an ecologisation of foreign investment of German industry. The Ministries of Economic Affairs and Development will be included in the dialogue network as well as environmental and other organisations.

Trade Unions

The German Trade Union Association *Deutscher Gewerkschaftsbund* (DGB) is an umbrella organisation embracing 11 individual trade unions, including the Union of Metal Workers (IG *Metall*), the largest German workers' association and the Industrial Union for Construction, Agriculture and Environment (IG BAU). By the end of 1999, total membership of the trade unions organised in the DGB was over 8 million. The DGB adopted its first environment programme in 1974 and the second environment programme on "Environmental protection and qualitative growth" in 1985. Since 1981, environmental protection is part of the DGB's guiding principles (*Grundsatzprogramm*). The latest version of the *Grundsatzprogramm* (November 1996) argues for a social and ecological reform strategy to reach the goal of sustainable development. The question of how to deal with environmental issues is controversially discussed in the trade unions, but at least in parts of the unions there is a continuous effort to integrate

---

> ## Box 7. **Turning Talk into Action – Renovation of Buildings for Energy Efficiency**
>
> Within the Alliance for Jobs (*Bündnis für Arbeit*) – a structured dialogue between government, the unions, industry, as well as other societal associations – an ambitious programme for the renovation of buildings for energy efficiency was decided at the end of 2000. The programme, which was developed within a working group on the employment potentials of environmental protection measures, aims primarily at improving the heat insulation of old buildings and replacing inefficient heating systems. Starting in January 2001 with a total expenditure of DEM 2 billion, the programme will offer credits for the renovation of buildings for energy efficiency of up to DEM 10 billion at a favourable rate of interest over a period of 5 years. The programme is conducted by the German Reconstruction Loan Corporation (*Kreditanstalt für Wiederaufbau*) and is expected to reduce CO_2 emissions by 2 million tons per year and create around 90,000 new jobs (BMU press release of 8 December 2000).

---

social and environmental demands with regard to the demands of sustainability (Krüger, 2000).

In 1999, the DGB introduced an initiative to integrate environmental concerns into the Alliance for Jobs (*Bündnis für Arbeit*), a "neo-corporatist" structured dialogue between government, trade unions and industry which was initiated in 1996 and relaunched in 1998, focusing on employment, education and training, and competitiveness. In a position paper, the DGB listed almost eighty proposals for linking employment measures with environmental protection (DGB, 1999). Two of these initiatives, the energy efficiency renovation of buildings (see Box 4) and an initiative to promote export of German environmental protection technology, have already found their way into the Alliance for Jobs.

Finally, in February 2001, the Federal Minister for Labour and Social Affairs adopted a reform of the Works Constitution Act (*Betriebsverfassungsgesetz*) to include environmental protection among the specific competencies of the works councils. This can be seen as an important step in extending the institutional provisions for workers' participation in the environmentally relevant decisions taken at the company level.

The German Peasant Organisation (Deutscher Bauernverband)

The powerful German Peasant Organisation (*Deutscher Bauernverband* – DBV) has traditionally been a strong opponent of the comprehensive integration of environmental considerations into agricultural policy. In recent years, and due to a number of factors such as WTO obligations, new EU policy initiatives (Agenda 2000) and the Cardiff Process, this has somewhat changed. The "Greenbook for a Sustainable Agriculture and Forestry" published in 2000 by the DBV (see Section A) has the ambitious subtitle: "The German Agriculture and Forestry as a Model of Sustainable Development" (*Deutscher Bauernverband*, 2000). Among other factors, it has been elaborated in order to set the agenda for the forthcoming German strategy for sustainable development and for the activities of the German Council for Sustainable Development where the agricultural sector is represented.

In the wake of the BSE crisis, the organisation was partly criticised by its own members and seems to have lost much of its former power. The new "Green" Minister for Consumer Protection, Food and Agriculture was accepted by the DBV without much resistance and a new, more co-operative attitude towards environmental and sustainability issues seems possible. In our interviews the organisation stressed its constructive attitude. According to the concept of "multifunctionality", agricultural activities beyond food production were stressed, such as protection of nature, landscape, soil and groundwater. But such services should not be free of charge for society. Organic farming is not rejected, but seen as a marketing problem. The activity of the state of North-Rhine-Westphalia supporting the marketing of products from nature protection areas was welcomed as an example of best practice. At the same time, the "ecological side" was asked to consider the difficult economic situation of German peasants (problem of rural depopulation). Generally, the DBV favours voluntary agreements on nature protection measures rather than administrative interventions. The EU Natura 2000 process was mentioned as an example of a bureaucratic, non-participatory policy style; for that reason, it was not widely accepted in rural areas.

Environmental NGOs

Germany has a complex network of organised interest groups in the environment sector. Between 5 and 7 per cent of the population are organised in environmental NGOs. The number of environmental groups is estimated at a total of 400. Environmental organisations have been a strong driving force, both for environmental policy integration and for a German strategy for sustainable development. The BUND, the German section of Friends of the Earth (230,000 members), together with the umbrella organisation The German Nature Conservation Council (*Deutscher Naturschutzring* – DNR; 5.2 million members) supported the idea of a German Environmental Policy Plan in the 1998 election campaign. The DNR comprises 108 member organisations and is funded by membership fees, institutional support from the German Ministry for the Environment, Nature Conservation and Nuclear Safety, project funds, donations, and fines. As a member of the European Environment Bureau (EEB), DNR co-ordinates the German NGO activities at the EU level. The *Grüne Liga*, a network of local initiatives in the new *Länder*, is quite active in Local Agenda 21 processes. In 1996, two prominent NGOs, BUND and

139|

Misereor, published a study entitled "Sustainable Germany", which initiated a broader public debate on sustainable development (BUND/Misereor, 1996). The study had a significant impact in stimulating public debate on sustainable development in Germany (Beuermann, 2000: 90). In particular, the four largest organisations (BUND, Greenpeace, NABU, WWF) have been engaged in sustainable development initiatives at the federal level through representatives at conferences and workshops, and in the working groups during the planning process for the draft programme for sustainable development in 1998. By publishing background papers and press reports, these organisations promoted the idea of sustainable development and pushed strongly for the elaboration of a new sustainable development strategy. Three representatives of environmental organisations (DNR, NABU, BUND) have been invited to participate in the work of the newly established Council for Sustainable Development.

C. Decision-making mechanisms

Integration at federal level through environmental monitoring and reporting

An important precondition for policy making is the availability of comprehensive and reliable data (*e.g.* on the state of the environment), as well as the development of performance indicators and effective monitoring systems. In Germany, comprehensive environmental reporting dates back to 1984, when the Federal Environment Agency (*Umweltbundesamt*) first published its national environmental data report (*Daten zur Umwelt*). Periodic reports issued by the Federal Office for Nature Conservation (*Bundesamt für Naturschutz*) and the four-yearly Environmental Report of the Federal Ministry for the Environment are other central sources of environmental information at the federal level. Moreover, the statistical yearbook published by the Federal Statistical Office (*Statistisches Bundesamt*) includes a wide range of environmental data. Finally, the proposal for a new Nature Protection Act foresees the introduction of regular environmental observation (*Umweltbeobachtung*).

A conclusive set of indicators for sustainable development has not yet been developed in Germany. However, important steps have been taken in the development and operationalisation of environmental indicators. Since 1989, the Federal Statistical Office has been developing an Environmental Economic Account (*Umweltökonomische Gesamtrechnung*), which integrates into the economic data environmental burdens such as emissions, utilisation of materials and energy and pressures on soils. In 1990, the Federal Ministry for the Environment appointed a scientific advisory council to work on refining the Environmental Economic Account. In its 1998 draft programme "Sustainable Development in Germany", the Ministry for the Environment proposed the introduction of an Environmental Barometer (*Umweltbarometer*). Its aim is to create an environmental equivalent to the already-existing aggregate indicators in the economic and social spheres, such as gross national product, unemployment rate or rate of inflation. The environmental indicators included in the Environmental Barometer are intended to cover the most important issues of environmental protection and align them with key environmental medium- and long-term targets. Six indicators have been formulated for the fields of climate, air, soil, water, and use of energy and raw materials. Environmental developments can be described and the success or failure of environmental policy can be measured by means of a small set of well-known and easy-to-understand indicators (BMU, 1998c). Although the draft programme "Sustainable Development in Germany" has never been formally adopted by Cabinet or parliamentary decision, the Environmental Barometer and the underlying environmental goals have been published in the Federal Government's Economic Reports of 2000 and 2001 (see above). Based on the Environmental Barometer, the Federal Environment Agency has developed the German Environment Index (*Deutscher Umwelt Index* – DUX), which links the indicators of the Environment Barometer to the main goals of German environmental policy and calculates goal attainment in one single numeric value. The DUX, which is updated regularly and published on the Internet pages of the Federal Environment Agency, can reach a maximum of 6 000 points, indicating that all major environmental goals have been attained. In October 2000, the DUX was calculated at 1 505 points, with a maximum of 692 points in the field of air pollution control and a minimum of minus 11 points for soil protection (*www.umweltbundesamt.de/dux-e/dux.htm*).

Integration across levels of government

Besides the mechanisms for horizontal policy integration described above, effective vertical policy integration plays an important role in a federal system where legislative competencies are divided among central and state governments. Vertical co-ordination of environmental policies is carried out mainly by the Conference of Environmental Ministers (*Umweltministerkonferenz* – UMK) which brings together the environment ministers of the *Länder* and the Federal Minister for the Environment. The UMK is paralleled by Länder Working Parties (*Länderarbeitsgemeinschaften*), which co-ordinate state and federal policies in specific issue areas such as waste and water management, air pollution control or nature conservation. However, a significant handicap for better integration of environmental concerns into sectoral policies could be the fact that many of the non-environmental ministries are well co-ordinated among all *Länder* and with the Federal level – for example, by means of planning institutions for joint funding mechanisms (*Gemeinschaftsaufgaben*). In comparison, environmental administrations have a less formal consultation and co-ordination structure.

The federal states have developed their own, sometimes original, approaches to sustainable development. While most Länder have focused on developing state programmes for sustainable development, environmental pacts or environmental

141

alliances with industry and trade have surged in states such as Bavaria and Saxony-Anhalt. In addition, many states have introduced institutional mechanisms for promoting local Agenda 21 processes (see above). Finally, the upper chamber of Parliament (B*undestag*) plays an important role in developing legislative initiatives for sustainable development.

Improving participation of civil society

The elaboration process of a national sustainable development strategy

A Working Group on Environmental Protection (AGU) was created in 1970 as a dialogue forum between government and different societal actors on environmental matters. In 1991, a National Committee was created by the Federal Chancellor to ensure participation of all major societal groups in the preparation of UNCED. The Committee comprised thirty-five representatives from all major societal groups including Parliament, political parties, environment and development organisations, science and research institutes, industry and commerce, trade unions, agriculture, churches, *Länder* and local governments. In 1994, it was renamed National Committee for Sustainable Development (*Nationales Komitee für Nachhaltige Entwicklung*) and chaired by the Federal Minister for the Environment (BMU, 1997*a*). The Committee met two or three times a year; however, in practice, high-level representatives of the major groups often did not attend its meetings. Its actual significance, therefore, was rather limited (Beuermann, 2000). Despite various attempts to reanimate the Committee, it was finally dissolved in 1998.

In June 1996, the Federal Ministry for the Environment, Nature Protection, and Nuclear Safety launched the so-called "Step Process". This discussion process was intended to place the dialogue with business and societal actors on a new level of quality (BMU, 1998*a*). Initially, the Ministry for the Environment published a discussion paper entitled "Steps towards sustainable development: environmental objectives and action priorities for Germany" (BMU, 1996). The paper proposed six fields for priority action: protection of the climate and ozone layer; preserving the ecological balance; reducing the impact on resources; safeguarding human health; environmentally compatible forms of mobility; and promoting environmental ethics.

Accordingly, six working groups were set up to stimulate discussion in society on approaches to sustainable development and "to arrive at a consensus on the priorities for action by engaging in a constructive dialogue with all the parties responsible" (BMU, 1997*a*: 16). Representatives of all major groups participated in these working groups and attended regular meetings. In June 1997, the results were published in an interim report and presented at a public workshop (BMU, 1997*b*, 1997*c*). The workshop was attended by high-level officials from various industrial associations, trade unions, environmental NGOs, and other organisations. The reports of the working groups and the podium discussion showed clearly that the process of dialogue had not achieved its main objective, *i.e.* to transcend the old rigid antagonisms. The working group papers showed open dissension between industry and other groups on a number of environmental issues. The discussions in the working groups on mobility and on natural resources (BMU, 1997*c*) were particularly controversial.

As a follow-up, the Ministry for the Environment elaborated a draft programme "Sustainable Development in Germany" (BMU, 1998*a*), which formulated ambitious quantified objectives in five environmental priority areas and proposed a set of headline indicators (Environmental Barometer) to monitor progress. However, a major shortcoming of this process was the fact that the programme was neither co-ordinated with other ministries nor formally adopted by either the Cabinet or Parliament. Following its publication, it was harshly criticised by the Ministries of Agriculture, Transport, and Economic Affairs (Hustedt, 2000). Following the 1998 elections, the draft programme was not taken up by the new government. However, the Environmental Barometer and some of the main goals formulated in the programme have been published in the Federal Government's Economic Reports of 2000 and 2001 and have therefore been – at least indirectly – adopted by government.

In 1998, when the new Social Democrat/"Green" government announced the elaboration of a national strategy for sustainable development, it was welcomed by all major societal groups. Most NGOs, however, criticised the slow pace of the process. The newly created institutional structure (Green Cabinet, Council for Sustainable Development) is generally considered to be appropriate, and the leading role of the Chancellor's Office in the process is regarded as particularly positive. Some criticism was directed towards the planned focus on energy and mobility. Both topics are considered to be central for sustainable development, but some NGOs argue for a broader scope of the strategy (*e.g.* NABU, 2000). This argument was reiterated in the parliamentary decision on the sustainable development strategy of December 2000 (German Bundestag, BT-Drs. 14/4606). It called upon the government to include further topics as parts of the strategy for sustainable development, and mentioned the following additional themes: nature conservation and biodiversity; construction, housing and urban settlement; environment, health and nutrition; sustainable rural development; sustainable economy; international co-operation and development; sustainable patterns of consumption and lifestyle, especially water management.

Institutionalising civil society participation

Institutional provisions for improving public participation in environmental decision making and broader questions of sustainable development include the

143|

above-mentioned creation in 1970 of the Working Group on Environmental Issues (*Arbeitsgemeinschaft für Umweltfragen*), the establishment in 1991 of a National Committee (*Nationales Komitee*) for sustainable development, and in 2000 the Cabinet decision to set up a National Council for Sustainable Development (*Rat für Nachhaltige Entwicklung*). All these institutions serve (or have served) as pluralistic fora for societal debate on environmental and sustainable development issues.

Participation of non-governmental actors in environmental rule making was to some extent formalised through the Federal Emissions Control Act of 1974 (§ 48). However, during the 1990s, participation rights were somewhat restricted by a bundle of legal amendments (so-called "streamlining laws" – *Beschleunigungsgesetze*), aimed at accelerating the licensing of industrial plants and larger infrastructure projects (Jänicke and Weidner, 1997: 141, 149).

While some *Länder*, such as Lower Saxony or Brandenburg, already allow for NGO standing in court cases (*Verbandsklage*), federal government has taken up this issue only recently in its proposal for the new Nature Protection Act.

The Environmental Information Act of 1994 entitles all citizens to access environmental information kept by environmental authorities. In practice, however, authorities are often rather reluctant to grant access to environmental information.

In recent years, a number of public dialogues have been initiated, embracing more than one dimension of sustainable development. These include the Alliance for Jobs (*Bündnis für Arbeit*), with its thematic dialogue on Employment and Environment, and the Foreign Direct Investment Initiative, launched in November 2000 by the Ministry for the Environment and the Federation of German Industries (BDI). The latter is a dialogue process aimed at developing environmental guidelines for foreign direct investment and promoting the transfer of environmental best practice to developing countries.

D. Learning from the German experience

As described above, Germany has not yet formulated a national strategy for sustainable development. Policy outcomes of the strategy cannot be evaluated so far. Our report, therefore, is strongly focussed on the policy formulation process. However, apart from a sustainable development strategy, there are other policy mechanisms and traditions that often lead in the same direction. They cannot be ignored and are part of our evaluation.

Strengths

There is a clear contradiction in Germany between the late, slow – and probably weak – process of implementing the concept of sustainable development and a much stronger – path-dependent – environmental and climate policy. Also, a general tendency to integrate environmental concerns into different policy sectors can be observed – as shown above – in the majority of the policy sectors and ministries. This process of environmental policy integration has its own dynamic and tradition and is clearly more influential than the German sustainable development process.

In the field of energy and climate policy, Germany has become an international front-runner, with high and increasing motivation even within industry. A well-functioning model has been developed and put into practice, consisting of the following key elements:

- High-level political commitment for the formulation and implementation of ambitious goals (Cabinet, Chancellor).

- Integration of environmental policy objectives into other sectors (Interministerial Committee on Climate Protection; strong institutional role of the environmental ministry).

- Voluntary agreements.

- Pioneer activities of local communities; and

- Broad public participation.

The scientific demonstration of the problem of climate change and the knowledge base provided by a special Commission of Enquiry of the *Bundestag* was an indispensable condition of its success. Unlike the partly competing interpretations of sustainable development, the problems and the relevant goals in climate protection policy were very clear and led to the strong motivation of all actors involved.

Environmental policy in general has also at a relatively early stage been connected to social and economic aspects such as employment, technology and competitiveness. A link can be found between German environmental policy and the broader international debate on sustainable development. This could be the entry point to a broader definition of sustainable development. An important driving force of environmental policy integration can be seen in the Social Democrat/"Green" government coalition with its programme of ecological modernisation, an innovation-oriented concept aimed at integrating environmental considerations into a wide range of different policies. This can be illustrated by the recent and far-reaching changes in the agricultural sector which were triggered by the BSE crisis, and which would probably have been less radical under the previous government.

Weaknesses

The late and slow process of formulating a national sustainable development strategy must of course be seen as a weakness of the German approach to implementing the guiding principle of sustainable development. Also, the *Länder*

145|

started late in developing their own sustainable development strategies. So far, Germany has shown little motivation to implement the EU Cardiff process of policy integration. The capacity for strategic action seems to be lower in Germany than in many of the smaller EU member countries. This has partly to do with the federal structure of the political system, which creates multi-level co-ordination problems. The different party composition of the upper and lower houses of Parliament and the confrontational policy style between both ("left" and "right") party blocks creates additional difficulties. The structural conservatism of the "old economy" (*e.g.* coal mining), together with the parties' strong regional power, is another restrictive factor.

Furthermore, there is a clear lack of problem-oriented long-term environmental prognoses, comparable to existing prognoses in fields such as public expenditure or social policy. Planning institutions – comparable to the strong Planning Division of the German Chancellor's Office in the early seventies or the Central Planning Bureau (CPB) in the Netherlands – do not exist at the moment in Germany.

A major weakness of the German situation has to be seen in the general lack of a clear and widely supported goal structure for sustainable development and the subsequent lack of a clear and positive orientation for the relevant actors. The term sustainable development – and especially its concrete implications for political and societal action – is unknown to the large majority of the public and has so far failed to trigger any interest by the media. Unlike environmental issues, sustainable development – especially in its broad definition – clearly lacks institutional and organisational support. As argued above (Section A), no societal pressure groups exist regarding the broader concept of sustainable development. Instead, this concept is regularly used by different societal actors as a flexible catchword in order to pursue their own interests and goals.

Finally, there is a clear contradiction between the responsibility taken on by the Chancellor's Office and the actual lack of political leadership in this institution.

E. Concluding remarks

Main recommendations

The following lessons can be drawn from the German case study on governance for sustainable development:

- Provide clear scientific input to problems that have to be solved. Problems of unsustainable developments should be demonstrated in long-term business-as-usual prognoses for different policy sectors. Communicate the results to the general public as well as to relevant interest organisations to raise the necessary awareness.

- Develop a clear, widely accepted and operational definition and goal structure for sustainable development. The crucial question may be whether concepts of economic and social sustainability are brought into the debate in such a way as to restrict far-reaching environmental goals and measures (a tendency which has long been criticised), or whether synergies and win-win solutions are the central theme of the broader concept of sustainable development. This is mainly a question to be addressed to the environmental divisions of the non-environmental ministries which – even in our interviews – defined themselves in the role of "watch-dogs" in respect of the Ministry for the Environment, thus using the broad definition of sustainable development.

- The strength of the German approach so far is the path-dependent focus on ecological sustainability (as defined by the four management rules put forward by the first Parliamentary Commission of Inquiry, "Protection of Man and Environment"). This strength can also be observed with regard to environmental integration (see Table 1). The relatively successful environmental strategy should form the basis of a German strategy for sustainable development. The sustainable development strategy should be an extension and step-by-step enlargement of the environmental strategy, rather than replacing it, towards a broader understanding of sustainable development. As in other OECD countries (the Netherlands, Spain, Denmark), environmental integration should be at the core of the strategy, at least in the first phase of the process. This is also the proposal of the German Council of Environmental Advisors (SRU, 2000).

- The relatively successful German climate-protection strategy could serve as a model for the broader strategy for sustainable development. As shown above, the key elements of this climate-protection strategy are: high-level political commitment for the formulation and implementation of ambitious goals; integration of environmental policy objectives into other sectors; voluntary agreements; pioneer activities of local communities; and broad public participation.

- Non-environmental policy sectors should be mandated to develop their own sectoral strategies. The leading role of Cabinet – or the "Green Cabinet" – should be clear and accepted by all ministries. This should include a critical evaluation of both the formulation of sectoral strategies and their implementation. The Federal Environment Agency and the Ministry for the Environment should play an important, mainly supportive, role in this process (so far these institutions have been rather cautious and have adopted a policy of "wait-and-see").

- Sectoral strategies for sustainable development should rely as little as possible on cross-sectoral co-ordination. Instead, the sectoral ministries should

147|

introduce pluralistic bodies and monitoring mechanisms for the early "internal" discussion of their sectoral sustainable development strategies. In doing so, clear sectoral responsibilities for the results of the sectoral strategies should be established.

• At the local level, general orientation for Agenda 21 processes, for example in the form of a competitive investment programme for local sustainable development initiatives (as practised in Sweden), should be provided.

Notes

1. The views expressed in this paper are those of the authors, and do not necessarily reflect those of the OECD, or those of its Public Management Service.
2. This case study was finalised in March 2001.
3. USD at 1995 prices and PPP.
4. The description of the German governance structure is based on OECD (1992), OECD (1997), and BMU (1997d).
5. Here, Germany's involvement as a pilot country in testing a set of sustainability indicators developed by the United Nation's Commission for Sustainable Development (CSD) can be mentioned.
6. However, the Environment Ministry reported studies from 2000 which showed a recent increase in environmental awareness. If this evolution is confirmed, it could lead to a reinvigoration of the sustainable development debate.

Annex

Local Agenda 21 Processes in the Old and New Länder

Table 3.   **Local Agenda 21 Processes in the Old Länder[1]**

State	Percentage of municipalities with Local Agenda 21 process
Hesse	54.6
Saarland	53.4
North Rhine-Westphalia	50.8
Bavaria	24.9
Baden-Wuerttemberg	23.7
Lower Saxony	8.8
Schleswig-Holstein	3.2
Rhineland-Palatinate	3.0

1. Excluding the city-states of Hamburg, Bremen and Berlin.
Source: Homepage of the Clearing House for Applied Futures – CAF/Agenda-Transfer
(*www.agenda-transfer.de*; last accessed 5 March 2001).

Table 4.   **Local Agenda 21 Processes in the New Länder[1, 2]**

State	Percentage of municipalities with Local Agenda 21 process
Thuringia	5.7
Mecklenburg-Western Pomerania	2.7
Brandenburg	1.8
Saxony-Anhalt	0.8

>50% of municipalities with Local Agenda 21 processes
>20% of municipalities with Local Agenda 21 processes
<10% of municipalities with Local Agenda 21 processes

1. Excluding the city-states of Hamburg, Bremen and Berlin.
2. Data on Local Agenda 21 processes in Saxony not available.
Source: Homepage of the Clearing House for Applied Futures – CAF/Agenda-Transfer
(*www.agenda-transfer.de*; last accessed 5 March 2001).

Bibliography

BDI (Bundesverband der Deutschen Industrie e.V.) (2000),
Freiwillige Vereinbarungen und Selbstverpflichtungen. BDI: Berlin.

BEUERMANN, C. (2000),
Germany: Regulation and the Precautionary Principle, in: William M. Lafferty and James Meadowcroft (eds.), Implementing Sustainable Development. Strategies and Initiatives in High-Consumption Societies. Oxford: Oxford University Press, pp. 85-111.

BMI (Bundesministerium des Innern) (2000),
Moderner Staat – Moderne Verwaltung. Gemeinsame Geschäftsordnung der Bundesministerien. Berlin: BMI.

BMU (Bundesministerium für Umwelt, Naturschutz und Reaktorsicherheit) (1996),
Schritte zu einer nachhaltigen, umweltgerechten Entwicklung: Umweltziele und Handlungsschwerpunkte in Deutschland – Grundlage für eine Diskussion. Bonn: BMU.

BMU (1997a),
Towards Sustainable Development in Germany. Report of the Government of the Federal Republic of Germany on the occasion of the Special Session of the United Nations General Assembly on Environment and Development in 1997 in New York. Bonn: Federal Ministry for the Environment, Nature Conservation and Nuclear Safety.

BMU (1997b),
Schritte zu einer nachhaltigen, umweltgerechten Entwicklung. Berichte der Arbeitskreise anlässlich der Zwischenbilanzveranstaltung am 13. Juni 1997.

BMU (1997c),
Schritte zu einer nachhaltigen, umweltgerechten Entwicklung. Tagungsband zur Zwischenveranstaltung am 13. Juni 1997.

BMU (1997d),
Klimaschutz in Deutschland. Zweiter Bericht der Regierung der Bundesrepublik Deutschland nach dem Rahmenübereinkommen der Vereinten Nationen über Klimaveränderungen. Bonn.

BMU (1998a),
Umweltbericht (1998). Bonn: BMU.

BMU (1998b),
Nachhaltige Entwicklung in Deutschland. Entwurf eines umweltpolitischen Schwerpunktprogramms, Bundesministerium für Umwelt, Naturschutz und Reaktorsicherheit, Bonn.

BMU (1998c),
Sustainable Development in Germany. Draft Programme for Priority Areas in Environmental Policy. Summary. Bonn: BMU.

BMU (2000),
Umweltbewußtsein in Deutschland 2000. Ergebnisse einer repräsentativen Bevölkerungsumfrage, BMU: Berlin.

BMU and UBA (Umweltbundesamt) (eds.) (1999),
Lokale Agenda 21 im europäischen Vergleich. Endbericht an das Umweltministerium. Bonn: BMU.

BMVBW (Bundesministerium für Verkehr, Bau- und Wohnungswesen) (2000),
Verkehrsbericht 2000 – Integrierte Verkehrspolitik: Unser Konzept für eine mobile Zukunft, Berlin.

BUND and Misereor (eds.) (1996),
Zukunftsfähiges Deutschland. Ein Beitrag zu einer global nachhaltigen Entwicklung, Basel, Boston, Berlin: Birkhäuser.

Bundesregierung (1972),
Umweltpolitik. Das Umweltprogramm der Bundesregierung, Stuttgart, Berlin, Köln, Mainz.

Bundesregierung (1976),
Umweltbericht (1976). Fortschreibung des Umweltprogramms der Bundesregierung vom 14. Juli 1976, Stuttgart, Berlin, Köln, Mainz.

Deutscher Bauernverband (2000),
Nachhaltige Land – und Forstwirtschaft. Die deutsche Land – und Forstwirtschaft als Modell einer nachhaltigen Entwicklung, Bonn.

DGB (Deutscher Gewerkschaftsbund) (1999),
DGB-Positionspapier zum Themen – und Fachdialog "Umwelt" im Bündnis für Arbeit: Arbeit und Umwelt – Ein Beitrag zur ökologischen Modernisierung und zur Schaffung von Arbeitsplätzen.

ECKERBERG, K., Frans COENEN and William M. LAFFERTY (1999),
The Status of Local Agenda 21 in Europe: A Comparative Overview. In: Lafferty, William M. (ed.), Implementing Local Agenda 21 in Europe: New Initiatives for Sustainable Communities. Oslo. pp. 241-263.

FLATH, Steffen (2000),
Umweltpolitik – quo vadis? Ein Antwortversuch aus Sachsen, *Zeitschrift für angewandte Umweltforschung*, No. 1-2, pp. 23-27.

German Bundestag (2000),
Antrag zur Nationalen Nachhaltigkeitsstrategie von den Fraktionen der SPD und Bündnis 90/Die Grünen am 07.12.2000. Bundestags-Drucksache 14/4606.

HÄUßLER, I. (2000),
Umsetzung der Lokalen Agenda in den neuen Bundesländern – das Beispiel Sachsen-Anhalt, in: Winfried Hermann, Eva Proschek, Richard Reschl (eds.), Lokale Agenda – Anstöße zur Zukunftsfähigkeit. Stuttgart. pp. 70-79.

HUSTEDT, M. (2000),
Strategien nachhaltiger Entwicklung in der Bundesrepublik. In: Jänicke, Martin and Jörgens, Helge (Hrsg.): Umweltplanung im internationalen Vergleich. Strategien der Nachhaltigkeit. Berlin *et al.*: Springer, S. pp. 171-182.

ICLEI (International Council of Local Environmental Initiatives) (1997),
Local Agenda 21 Survey: A Study of Responses by Local Authorities and their National and International Associations to Agenda 21. Prepared by ICLEI in co-operation with DPCSD

151|

(United Nations Department for Policy Co-ordination and Sustainable Development
www.iclei.org/la21/la21rep.htm).

JÄNICKE, M. and H. JÖRGENS (eds.) (2000),
Umweltplanung im internationalen Vergleich. Strategien der Nachhaltigkeit. Berlin,
Heidelberg, New York: Springer.

JÄNICKE, M. and H. WEIDNER (1997),
Germany, in: Martin Jänicke and Helmut Weidner (eds.), National Environmental Policies: A Comparative Study of Capacity-Building. Berlin, Heidelberg, New York: Springer.

KRÜGER, S. (2000),
Arbeit und Umwelt verbinden. Probleme der Interaktion zwischen Gewerkschaften und
Nicht-Regierungsorganisationen. WZB-Paper P00-512.

LAFFERTY, W. M. and Frans COENEN (2000),
The Diffusion of Local Agenda 21 in Twelve European Countries. Paper presented at
the international workshop "Diffusion of Environmental Policy Innovations". Berlin,
8-9 December 2000.

LAFFERTY, W. M. and James MEADOWCROFT (2000*a*),
Implementing Sustainable Development. Strategies and Initiatives in High-Consumption
Societies. Oxford: Oxford University Press.

LAFFERTY, W. M. and James MEADOWCROFT (2000*b*),
Patterns of Governmental Engagement, in: William M. Lafferty and James Meadowcroft
(eds.), Implementing Sustainable Development. Strategies and Initiatives in High-
Consumption Societies. Oxford: Oxford University Press, pp. 337-421.

MÜLLER, E. (1984),
Umweltpolitik der sozial-liberalen Koalition, Zeitschrift für Umweltpolitik, No. 2,
pp. 115-141.

NABU (Naturschutzbund Deutschland) (2000),
Leitbild Nachhaltigkeit. NABU-Eckpunkte zur Nationalen Nachhaltigkeitsstrategie. Berlin:
NABU Pressedienst.

OECD (1992),
Public Management: Profile Germany. Paris: OECD.

OECD (1993),
Environmental Performance Reviews: Germany. Paris: OECD.

OECD (1997),
Managing Across Levels of Government. Paris: OECD.

OECD (2001),
Environmental Performance Review of Germany. Paris: OECD.

SCHARPF, F. W. (1993),
Positive und negative Koordination in Verhandlungssystemen, in: Adrienne Héritier
(ed.), Policy-Analyse. Kritik und Neuorientierung, Politische Vierteljahresschrift
Sonderheft 24. Opladen: Westdeutscher Verlag, pp. 57-83.

SRU (Rat von Sachverständigen für Umweltfragen) (1994),
Umweltgutachten (1994). Für eine dauerhaft-umweltgerechte Entwicklung. Stuttgart:
Metzler-Poeschel.

SRU (2000),
Umweltgutachten (2000). Schritte ins nächste Jahrtausend. Stuttgart: Metzler-Poeschel.

Statistisches Bundesamt (2000),
   Statistisches Jahrbuch für die Bundesrepublik Deutschland. Wiesbaden: Metzler-Poeschel.

WEY, K-G (1982),
   Umweltpolitik in Deutschland. Kurze Geschichte des Umweltschutzes in Deutschland
   seit 1990. Opladen: Westdeutscher Verlag.

ZIMMERMANN, M. (1997),
   Lokale Agenda 21 – Ein Aktionsplan für die zukunftsbeständige Entwicklung der Kommune
   im 21. Jahrhundert, *Aus Politik und Zeitgeschichte*, B 27/97, pp. 25-38.

Japan

By
Professor Mineo **KATO,**
Faculty of Economics, Yokohama National University
and **Ms. Emico Ray**[1]

Aknowledgements

The objective of this report is to present an outline of the current status and main agenda of public policies in Japan to promote the change in Japanese society towards sustainable development. This report was prepared by Professor Mineo Kato, Yokohama National University, and additional research has been completed by Mrs. Emiko Ray. It represents the views of the author and there may therefore be differences of opinion between the Japanese Government and the writer. The author thanks the following people for their suggestions and stimulating opinions: Mr. Hikaru Kobayashi, Director, Personnel Division, Minister's Secretariat, Ministry of the Environment, who has been one of the important leaders in policy making related to environment and sustainable development; Professor Takehisa Awaji, Professor in Law, Faculty of Law, Rikkyo (St. Paul's) University, who also very actively presents innovations for sustainable development policies, both domestically and internationally; and Dr. Akio Morishima, Nagoya University and Jyo-chi (Sophia) University, who committed and led Japan's environmental policy, and who now holds, as President of the Government's Central Environment Council and Chair of the Board of Directors of the Institute for Global Environmental Strategies (IGES), the key position in environmental policy in Japan.

The concept of sustainable development includes many aspects and problems of our society. However, in the history of policy and activities in Japan up to the present day, sustainable development has been seen as being almost identical to environmental problems. Therefore, this report focuses mainly on policies for environmental issues, and the sustainable development agenda in other fields is only briefly mentioned. There have been many other studies and reports on sustainable development policies and the situation of Japan. For example, "Sustainable Development: Information Japan" on the United Nations Internet home page on sustainable development (*www.un.org/esa/agenda21/natlinfo/countr/japan/index.htm*) is based on the information submitted by the Government of Japan to the 5th session of the Commission on

Sustainable Development in April 1997. It provides very wide information on sustainable development related policies, institutions and activities in many sectors. Therefore, this report focuses on some specific topics and movements in very recent years and attempts to analyse the issues in more depth.

The concept of "sustainable development" (*jizokukanou na kaihatsu*) was introduced in Japan relatively recently. In Japan, the concept of "sustainable development" is primarily associated with preparation for and follow-up after the 1992 United Nations Conference on Environment and Development (UNCED) in Rio de Janeiro. With over 50 other countries, Japan participates in the studies on national development of sustainable development lead by the Commission on Sustainable Development (Jizokukanou na kaihatsu iinkai), set up in 1993 in the United Nations Headquarters in New York.

General introduction

Physical, economic and human patterns

Japan is located in the monsoon zone of the eastern coast of the Asian continent. The total land area of the country is 377,836 km^2. Over two-thirds of Japan is covered by mountainous terrain, and alluvial plains occupy only 13 per cent. The notable features of the climate of Japan are the wide range of annual temperatures and the large amount of rainfall. However, because of the complexity of land configuration, there are numerous regional differences in climate throughout the seasons.

Japan's population is over 126 million, the seventh largest in the world. The population is ageing faster than in any other country in the world, a situation that is causing serious problems for Japanese society. The percentage of the population aged 65 or over was only 7 per cent in the 1970s, but it reached 14 per cent in 1995. With rapid economic growth during the post-war period, there was a strong tendency towards regional concentration. As a result, more than 40 per cent of the Japanese population lives in the three major city areas of Tokyo, Osaka and Nagoya.

The Japanese economy is the world's second largest market economy, with a gross domestic product (GDP) of over US$5 trillion in 1998. Per capita income is more than US$30 000. This high-income scale was achieved largely due to high economic growth from the mid-1950s to the late 1960s. Following the 1986-1991 boom period, known as the "bubble economy", economic growth slowed drastically and Japan fell into a recession.

The rapid economic growth resulted in significant changes to Japan's industrial structure. Production shifted from a heavy reliance on agriculture and light manufacturing to a focus on heavy industry and, increasingly, services. In the mid-1950s, the primary sector still accounted for 24 per cent of output and 37 per cent of the labour force; in contrast, manufacturing accounted for only 24 per cent of output and 19 per cent of employment. Then in 1995, 6 per cent of the labour force was in primary sector occupations, 33 per cent in secondary, and 61 per cent in tertiary.

From the mid-1960s to the early 1970s, rapid economic growth also led to an average 10 per cent annual increase in energy demand. During the same period, the energy source shifted from coal to oil. Japan's dependence on imports for its energy supply rose to over 90 per cent. Because Japanese corporations positively initiated the development of energy-saving technologies in the face of the 1970s' oil crisis, Japan has become the most energy-efficient country. In 1995, energy consumption per capita was 3,573 kgs, which was less than half of that of the USA.

As Japan has developed economically it has become increasingly dependent on overseas resources. Due to its heavy reliance on foreign resources, Japan views external and internal sustainable development as essential.[2] In addition to depending on oil, Japan is heavily reliant on the importation of timber in order to meet domestic demand. Japan's government has faced increasing pressure to take initiatives in order to help preserve the tropical forests in the areas from which tropical timber is imported.[3]

Governance patterns

Japan is a unitary State led symbolically by the Emperor, but governed democratically by a parliamentary cabinet system characterised by "flexible separation of powers" among the legislative, executive and judicial bodies. Constitutional provisions were established in the Constitution of Japan, which was promulgated in 1946 and came into effect on 3 May 1947. The Emperor is the Head of State. The legislative authority is exercised by the National Diet (Parliament), which is the highest organ of State power and the sole law-making organ of the State. It is composed of two houses: the House of Representatives and the House of Councillors. In the case of irreconcilable differences between the two houses, the House of Representatives has precedence over the House of Councillors. The Head of Government is the Prime Minister, who is designated by the Diet from amongst its own members and appointed by the Emperor. Given Japan's party government, the head of the political party which secures a majority in the Diet usually becomes the Prime Minister. He or she is the Head of the Cabinet, in which the executive power is vested, and appoints the Ministers of State.

In the past, Japan has used many different types of organisation (*e.g.* agencies, corporations) to develop and implement public policies. Recently, the Japanese government has been characterised by a major movement in the reorganisation of the governmental system. As a consequence, the setting and implementation of the policy for sustainable development could experience major changes.

157

Reorganisation of Japanese Ministries and Agencies

Old System (23 Ministries and Agencies)	New System (12 Ministries and Agencies with one Cabinet Office)
Prime Minister's Office Economic Planning Agency Okinawa Development Agency Financial Services Agency	Cabinet Office (Financial Services Agency)
National Public Safety Commission Defense Agency	National Public Safety Commission (National Police Agency) Defense Agency
Management and Co-ordination Agency Ministry of Home Affairs Ministry of Posts and Telecommunications	Ministry of Public Management, Home Affairs, Posts and Telecommunications
Ministry of Justice Ministry of Foreign Affairs	Ministry of Justice Ministry of Foreign Affairs
Ministry of Finance	Ministry of Finance
Ministry of Education Science and Technology Agency	Ministry of Education, Culture, Sports, Science and Technology
Ministry of Health and Welfare Ministry of Labour	Ministry of Health, Labour and Welfare
Ministry of Agriculture, Forestry and Fisheries	Ministry of Agriculture, Forestry and Fisheries
Ministry of International Trade and Industry	Ministry of Economy, Trade and Industry
Ministry of Transport Ministry of Construction Hokkaido Development Agency National Land Agency	Ministry of Land, Infrastructure and Transport
Environment Agency	Ministry of the Environment

Prior to 2001, Japan's central government consisted of 23 ministries and agencies, including the Prime Minister's Office. In January 2001, these 23 ministries and agencies were reorganised into 12, with a Cabinet Office as co-ordinator (additional information on the central government reform can be obtained at *www.mofa.go.jp/about/hq/central_gov/index.html*).

The main purposes of this drastic change in administration system are to:

- **Establish a system with more effective political leadership**. In order to strengthen the administrative leadership of the Cabinet and Prime Minister, the reform introduced new positions in the Cabinet Secretariat; established a new Cabinet Office; created ministers for special missions; set up councils on important policies, such as the Council on Economic and Fiscal Policy; placed new politically appointed positions of state secretary and parliamentary secretary within each ministry and agency.

- **Restructure national administrative organs**. The reorganisation of ministries and agencies is based on the realignment of the roles of the government. Policy co-ordination on issues that concern two or more ministries or agencies

---

Box 1.   **Key Events in Japan's Policy Regarding Sustainable Development**

1988   Law concerning the Protection of the Ozone Layer through the Control of Specified Substances (Ozone Layer Protection Law).

1991   Largest employers' association, Keidanren, adopts the Keidanren Global Environment Charter.

1992   Rio Conference on Environment and Development in Rio de Janeiro. Participating countries agree on general guidelines that are published as "Agenda 21".

1992   Law for the Conservation of Endangered Species of Wild Fauna and Flora.

1993   Japan formulates its National Agenda 21 Action Plan.

1993   Basic Environment Law replaces prior laws on pollution and environmental conservation.

1994   Basic Environment Plan is approved by Cabinet. The Plan establishes, among other things, a framework for co-operation between governmental organisations.

1995   The Action Plan for Greening Government Operations is adopted by the Cabinet.

1996   The Basic Plan for Forest Resources (for sustainable forest management).

1996   Law concerning Conservation and Management of Marine Living Resources.

1996   The Keidanren Employers' Association reaffirms its commitment to sustainable development in the Keidanren Environmental Appeal.

1996   Law concerning the Exercise of Sovereign Rights concerning Fisheries in the Exclusive Economic Zone.

1997   Environmental Impact Assessment Law.

1997   Total Allowable Catch (TAC) system based on the Law concerning Conservation and Management of Marine Living Resources.

1998   Law concerning the Promotion of Measures to Cope with Global Warming.

1998   Revision of the Forest Law.

1999   Basic Law on Food, Agriculture, and Rural Areas replaces Basic Agricultural Law.

1999   Fisheries Industry Basic Policy (is passed).

1999   The Revised Law concerning the Rational Use of Energy (is passed).

1999   Law for Promotion of Introduction of Advanced Sustainable Farming System.

2001   Environmental Agency elevated to Ministry of the Environment.

(See also Annex 3 on Laws for Marine Protection in Japan).

Sources: The United Nations Report on Natural Resource Aspects of Sustainable Development in Japan, Imura (1997), and Japanese Report for Rio + 5 Process.

159|

---

becomes more effective by the overall co-ordination by the Cabinet Office, which is given higher status than other ministries and agencies.

- **More transparent administration.** 89 government undertakings, such as the operation of national museums and research institutes, are now conducted by IAIs (Independent Administrative Institutions), which are organisationally independent from the government. The establishment of another 59 IAIs has been legislated, and most of them started operating on 1 April 2001. In this system, the performance of each IAI is evaluated by a third party; the general principles of the accounting system of private companies are incorporated; a wide range of information is disclosed; the salary of each employee reflects his/her performance, as well as the performance of each IAI.

- **Drastic streamlining of the central government.** With this reorganisation, an objective is to cut the number of national civil servants by 25 per cent over the next decade. The number of bureaux is reduced by 25 per cent, from 128 to 96, and the number of divisions by 20 per cent, from approximately 1 200 to 1 000.

A. Main issues and tensions

Currently, the representative issues generally recognised as of importance on the sustainable development agenda are climate change, waste management and recycling, and bio-diversity conservation, although there are other issues and problems in environment- or natural resources-related fields as well as in non-environmental fields. Other critical issues for Japan's sustainable development are energy use, international environmental co-operation, environmental education, and developing appropriate technology for environmental conservation.[4]

Energy[5]

Energy use in Japan is a particularly important issue as Japan enters the 21st century. As Japan's economy grew in the 1960s and early 1970s, Japan's energy consumption rose at the average rate of 10 per cent per year. As Japan's energy consumption increased, its primary energy source shifted from coal to oil. Without any domestic petroleum reserves, Japan became very dependent on imported petroleum.

As a result of this dependence, Japan was especially hard-hit by the oil-crisis of the 1970s. After the oil crisis Japan focused much energy on become more energy efficient. As a result, Japan's industries, which were the hardest-hit by the crisis, become among the most energy efficient in the world.

Nonetheless, Japan's industrial strides towards energy efficiency have not broadened into societal efficiency. Individual energy consumption remains a problem and must be addressed.[6]

The Basic Environment Plan demands that "things removed from the Earth, such as raw materials and energy must pass cleanly through our socio-economic system at every stage". The plan specifically calls for:

- Increasing energy and material efficiency in production processes.
- Promoting use of new and renewable sources of energy.
- Using environmentally sound technologies for sustainable production; and
- Increasing awareness for sustainable consumption.

The Revised Law concerning the Rational Use of Energy and the Law concerning the Promotion of Measures to Cope with Global Warming were passed in 1998. Through these laws, the Japanese government promotes the sound use of energy by citizens and companies by providing concrete incentives to do so. Those who use fuel-efficient automobiles, trains, and aeroplanes are rewarded through tax relief and, in some cases, through having access to governmental funds. The Law concerning the Promotion of Measures to Cope with Global Warming also aims to promote the development of clean, efficient energy for the country as a whole. Pilot projects have been conducted to study the viability of innovative energy solutions, such as the use of biomass and small hydroelectric power generation systems for rural irrigation.

In addition, Japan passed the Law concerning Special Measures for Promotion of Utilisation of New Energy in order to further encourage the use of alternative energy sources in order to achieve Japan's energy consumption goals for 2010. This law outlines basic policies for encouraging alternative energy use and for providing financial incentives to businesses that use such alternative energy.

While it is still early to evaluate the effectiveness of the recent energy legislation, the Japanese government has been disseminating information to the public in order to promote the recent measures that address global warming. In July 1999, the National Centre for the Promotion of Activities to Cope with Global Warming was designated by the Environment Agency; . . . this Centre services the information on environment-friendly products.

The challenge of reducing carbon dioxide emissions will likely prove very challenging for Japan.

"In [the] transport sector, the emission of carbon dioxide has been constantly increasing, in spite of the introduction of High Fuel Efficiency Vehicles into the market. The assessment method of policy and measures in this sector is not so well developed; . . . taking effective policies and measures are difficult.

In [the] residential sector, the problem . . . [of] household electrical appliances such as TV sets, refrigerators has become bigger . . . [during the] last decade. This phenomenon induces the further electricity consumption in the sector. Monitoring energy consumption by different appliances in detail is required in order to formulate and adopt more efficient policies.

In Japan, forests cover already two thirds of the total land area, and the remainders are already utilised so such as agricultural or residential areas. Therefore, given the limited space, it is difficult and hence implausible to increase the forest area. The scientific information and knowledge on the marine resources for increasing green house gas sinks are too limited to develop the resources as practical policies and measures at present stage and a study aiming at evaluating the capacity of marine resources as a sink is in progress."

Energy issue decisions for sustainable development are made as follows:

• Ministry of the Economy, Trade and Industry (METI) – energy issues in general;

• Ministry of the Environment (MEO) – protection of atmosphere; and

• Ministry of Land, Infrastructure and Transport (MLIT) – energy-related aspects of transportation

Regulation of automobile pollution is an example of co-ordination between agencies in order to prevent emissions of traditional air pollutants. ME establishes automobile fuel quality standards; METI regulates fuel standards and collects data used mainly to calculate the total national energy consumption. MLT collects its own data on transportation energy consumption and is authorised to collect data on pollution from various transportation modes.

In order to co-ordinate the efforts of the ministries, the Global Warming Prevention Headquarters was established in 1997.

Under the Basic Plan for Research and Development on Energy of 1995, the Japanese government has conducted extensive research and development in the area of alternative energy. Solar energy, wind energy, geothermal energy, and ocean energy are the primary alternative energies being researched by the Japanese government.

Climate change

Greenhouse gases (GHGs) emission in Japan is about 5 per cent of the total world emission. Japan ranks fourth after the USA, China and Russia, and takes second place among the OECD countries. The emission per capita is far lower than the OECD average but a little higher than the average of EU countries (15 states). Japan's per capita emission is also double the world average.

Carbon dioxide is the principal GHG emitted in Japan from fossil fuels (mainly oil). According to the 1996 (fiscal year) statistics, 40.2 per cent of these emissions were from the industrial sector. High economic activity in the country causes a high volume of emissions, even though industrial energy efficiency has greatly

Box 2. **The "Guideline of Measures to Prevent Global Warming"**

In addition to the recent legislation regarding global warming, the Japanese government established the Guideline of Measures to Prevent Global Warming' in 1998 in order to reduce green house gases through efficient energy use. Among other things, the Guideline requires carbon dioxide emissions from the transport sector to be reduced by 13 million tons by 2010. The Guideline also enumerates technologies that reduce green house gas emissions. By 2000, the following technologies had been developed in furtherance of the goals of the guidelines:

"In [the] energy sector, the adoption of air conditioning systems with heat storage [that] us[e] night time electricity and coolers which use gas fuelled heat pumps;

1. In [the] transport sector, development of compressed natural gas (CNG) vehicles, dimethylether (DME) vehicles; . . .fuel cell vehicles that use alternative fuels are also under way. Research and development is being made for low-emission and high-efficiency gas turbine cargo ships ("Super Eco Ships") that will improve the fuel efficiency by about 10% and reduce NOx emission by 1/10 in comparison with the present ships. The arrangement of new systems utilising information system such as Universal Traffic Management Systems (UTMS), Electronic Toll Collection System (ETC) started in order to optimise traffic control and to avoid traffic congestion.

2. In [the] industry sector, the performance of highly efficient industrial furnaces and boilers has been confirmed and is to be introduced in practice.

3. In [the] commercial / residential sector, the development of compound semiconductors which are material of light emitting diodes, liquid crystal displays of low electricity consumption and highly efficient solar battery is under way. As for household . . . appliances, technology for reducing electricity consumption is being explored with a view to reduc[ing] [the amount of] electricity consumed while not in active use.

4. The development of technologies concerning HFC, PFC and SF6 are also under way, such as alternative gases of SF6 and PFC and systems in cleaning and etching process of electric devices production as well as continual recovery and destruction of HFC-23 produced as [a] by-product in HCFC-22 production process.

5. In many sewage plants, electric power plants were introduced, utilising energy contained in digestion gas derived from waste water sludge."

Source: United Nations Report on Natural Resource Aspects of Sustainable Development in Japan: *www.un.org/esa/agenda21/natlinfo/countr/japan/natur.htm*

163

improved. Transportation caused 20.4 per cent, and 11.6 per cent was emitted by the commercial sector and 12.9 per cent by households. The emissions from transportation and households have recently increased.

Policy response

The target of climate change policy is set by international agreements. The 1992 UNFCCC (United Nations Framework Convention on Climate Change) required stabilising the emission of greenhouse gases (mostly carbon dioxide in Japan's case) at the 1990 level until the year 2000. The 1997 Kyoto Protocol of the UNFCCC set Japan's new target of a 6 per cent reduction on 1990 emission levels by the year 2008-2012. This is a very tough challenge for the Japanese government, industries and the daily life of citizens. Japan's Action Plan to Prevent Global Warming, agreed by Cabinet, announces a target of stabilising emissions at the 1990 level after the year 2000.

The 1998 Global Warming Policy Promotion Act set the national climate change policy, requiring the promotion of GHGs reduction in national and local governments and in the private sector by making a GHGs emission reduction plan. The act also supported citizens' activities in climate change. The Secretary of the Environment Agency was allowed to request that, if necessary, the heads of other ministries and agencies co-operate in policies and actions for climate change. This could lead to broader policy co-ordination and a more comprehensive approach to climate change.

The 1998 amendments to the Energy Conservation Act introduced the "front-runner method" to promote continuous improvement in energy efficiency. This method set energy standards at the level of the most energy-efficient goods on the market. Penalties for non-compliance with the energy standards were also reinforced. Energy-consuming factories were required to submit an Energy Savings Plan. Despite these amendments, the approach of the Energy Conservation Act did not necessarily lead to a more widespread reduction in GHGs.

A comprehensive approach and policy are necessary to make a climate change policy effective. The Global Warming Policy Promotion Act should play such a role, although its effectiveness is questionable. One reason is that, under the Global Warming Policy Promotion Act, setting up, implementing and publicising an emissions reduction plan is not obligatory but just a voluntary activity in the private sector because of the so-called "adjustment" with the administrative authority of the Energy Conservation Act. It is not clear how to secure the request from the Secretary of the Environment Agency to other ministers and secretaries. The system to introduce economic incentives such as an environment tax is also lacking. In order to effectively promote a comprehensive climate change policy, a legal basis is required to co-ordinate related acts and policies and introduce new measures.

International co-operation[7]

As the second largest economy in the world, after the USA, and one of the most heavily reliant on imports, Japan's economy naturally focuses attention on international co-operation. In order to assure reliable imports, it is in Japan's interest to work with countries from which it imports in order to assure a reliable supply of resources to Japan.

In addition, Japan is surrounded by countries whose environmental impacts are increasing. As other Asian countries develop, their environmental impacts will have drastic, direct effects on Japan. In particular, Japan's air quality and oceanic resources are heavily influenced by the actions of Japan's neighbours. Thus, while other countries may find international co-operation to be a secondary concern, Japan sees international co-operation as crucial.

Japan tries to influence international sustainable development in two ways: 1) by providing direct aid to developing nations in order to promote sustainable development; and 2) by trying to set a good example of economic success combined with sustainable development.

Box 3. **Japan's Environmental Research and Training Centre in Thailand**

As part of Japan's efforts to help developing countries balance economic success with environmental responsibility, Japan has aided Thailand in the establishment of an environmental management, conservation, and training centre. At the request of the Thai government, the Japanese government has helped establish and maintain the centre. From 1995 to 1996, the Japanese sent 21 environmental specialists to help train over 1 800 Thai trainees. The Japanese government supports similar centres in Indonesia, China, Mexico and Chile.

Source: The Japan Report for Rio+5 Process.
www.ecouncil.ac.cr/rio/national/re ports/asia/japan.htm

Developing pollution control technologies

An essential aspect of Japan's international sustainable development co-operation is developing and providing pollution control technologies. By developing technologies that allow industries to produce efficiently and citizens to

---

Box 4.   **The Midori Satellite – Monitoring Global Climate Change**

In order to monitor the earth's continuing global change, the Science and Technology Agency has used its Midori satellite to gather data regarding the earth's changing climate. The data gathered by Midori is integrated with data from oceanic observational research ships in order to better understand and predict global climate change in the 21st century.

Source: The Japan Report for Rio + 5 Process.
www.ecouncil.ac.cr/rio/national/re ports/asia/japan.htm

---

live comfortably with minimal impact on the environment, Japan hopes to be able to help other countries conserve the environment without having to sacrifice economic productivity and wealth. At the same time, Japan applies these technologies in its own industries in order to showcase successful businesses that are environmentally friendly.

Education[8]

Because sustainable development is a relatively new concept to Japanese society in general, environmental education will prove to be a crucial step towards long-term sustainable development in Japan. Individuals, through their personal consumption and lifestyle habits, have a tremendous impact on the environment. By educating Japanese citizens, Japan hopes to alter societal norms.

Environmental education in Japan is currently being done by many. The government, corporations, universities, and citizens' groups provide environmental education programmemes in schools, community centres and workplaces.

As part of its ongoing educational work, the Ministry of the Environment encourages the "Junior Eco Club" which promotes environmental education in communities throughout Japan. The Junior Eco Club was created to help educate primary and secondary school children. By 1995, over 2,500 such clubs had been formed throughout Japan.

The Ministry of Education, Culture, Sports, Science and Technology also actively promotes environmental awareness. The Ministry of Education provides incentives for environmental education by recognising communities that have promoted environmental awareness and by designating certain schools as Model Schools for their environmental programmes.

The Japanese Consumers' Co-operative Union promotes environmental education by sponsoring community environmental monitoring of air quality. Numerous other private organisations promote education, often by rewarding and recognising outstanding examples of environmentally sound programmes.

Co-ordination between Government Agencies and Ministries

One of the primary duties of the Ministry of the Environment is to co-ordinate the efforts and policies of all government agencies and ministries in sustainable development (Imura 1997). Co-ordination is one of the primary challenges Japan faces.

In 1994, the OECD concluded that many government agencies and ministries appeared to be acting independently of one another, at times promoting policies that conflict with one another. According to this, many government employees appeared to owe their loyalty primarily to their agency or ministry, without regard to the overall effectiveness of government policy (Imura 1997). While local governments often lacked well co-ordinated action between agencies, the national government appears to have much more severe problems in this area.

Waste management and recycling

Waste management is another serious problem. The space for landfills is running short, especially around big city areas. Careful measures have to be taken in the operation of incinerators to prevent the emission of toxic materials such as dioxin. These conditions make waste disposal very difficult. On the other hand, the volume of solid waste has been increasing. The fundamental measure in tackling the problem of waste is the reduction of waste itself. In order to reduce waste and encourage recycling, Japan recently introduced numerous recycling policies, such as recycling regulations for packaging, for construction waste, for specific electric household appliances, and for food waste, with a basic policy act for promoting a new society which effectively circulates energy and resources, although the implementation of these policies and regulations has not yet begun.

Japan's waste management policies are an example of Japan's efforts to incorporate provisions of Agenda 21 into its national policies. In the National Agenda 21 Action Plan, Chapters 19 and 20 of Agenda 21 have been incorporated by requiring Japan to co-operate internationally to (Hanaoka 1996).

- Work with other countries to promote and implement international chemical labelling, classification, and risk assessment.
- Exchange information regarding chemical toxins and their risks.
- Prevent the illegal international transport of chemical toxins. And
- Promote international co-operation concerning legal transportation of dangerous chemicals (Hanaoka 1996).

167|

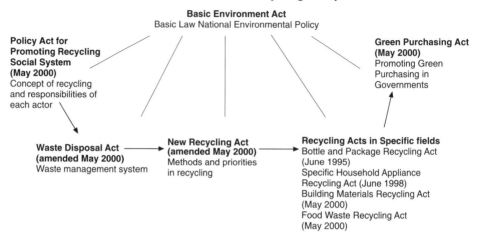

Present Framework for Recycling in Japan

In May 2000, the Japanese Diet enacted four new acts on recycling and amended two major acts on waste management and recycling. As a result, a considerably wider framework for recycling exists. However, many problems have been reported related to the already enforced recycling system. Some recycling systems, to be enforced in 2001, are expected to have many operating problems.

Bio-diversity conservation

As noted in many reports and studies, such as *Environmental Policies in Japan* (OECD, 1972), nature conservation has been the weakest point in Japan's environmental policy. Although bio-diversity conservation is on the international agenda, policy response and implementation in this field have not been so obvious. The management of natural areas such as national parks is still poor, and the number of species (both fauna and flora) on the "red list" is increasing. The National Strategy for Biological Diversity, established in 1995 in accordance with the United Nations Convention on Biological Diversity, has so far received little attention.

However, it is hoped that this situation will gradually change. With the Convention on Wetlands of International Importance Especially as Waterfowl Habitat (Ramsar Convention) hosted in 1988 at Kushiro, a northern town located near Kushiro Marshland National Park, and the registration in 1993 of two natural areas (Yakushima Islands and Shirakami-sanch mountains) in the "World Heritage" under the United Nations World Heritage Convention, the importance of the international and global dimensions of ecosystem management has been recognised.

Many systems can be seen to relate to nature conservation in Japan. For example, the Natural Parks System (under the Natural Parks Act) consists of 28 national parks, 55 quasi-national parks and 304 prefectural natural parks, and covers more than 14 per cent of Japan's land area. Wilderness Areas (currently five areas) and Nature Conservation Areas (currently ten areas) are designated under the Nature Conservation Act, along with Prefectural Nature Conservation Areas designated by the ordinance of each Prefecture. Wildlife Protection Areas are also set up under the Birds and Beasts Protection Act, and natural monuments are protected by the Cultural Heritage Protection Act. There are also other systems such as many kinds of protected forest or preserved forest, as well as rapidly increasing Forest Ecosystem Conservation Areas in national forests. The Endangered Species Preservation Act is the most recent of this kind.

However, the levels of management and conservation in these areas are insufficient. The main reason is that almost all of these systems are based on zoning and regulation, and not on land ownership by governmental authority (usually the Environment Agency). Without land ownership by governments, management of the area has to be a kind of compromise with the existing landowners and users, thus making it difficult to implement sufficient conservation management. As a result, many national parks in Japan do not reach the level of national parks by world standards and are classified merely as Protected Landscapes according to the United Nations List of Protected Areas by the IUCN – World Conservation Union.

Also lacking is the concern for bio-diversity and ecosystem conservation. Japan's natural parks are, according to the Natural Parks Act, established to protect beautiful natural landscapes, not to conserve important ecosystems. Therefore, many areas that are important for safeguarding bio-diversity, such as wetlands or countryside, are left unprotected. Wildlife protection has been considered mainly from the point of view of controlling hunting and regulating poaching, and the idea of safeguarding bio-diversity is lacking. In June 2000, the concept of more positive management was introduced by an amendment to the Birds and Beasts Protection Act, although actual management measures have not yet been developed.

Policy response

The 1995 National Strategy for Biological Diversity emphasises the importance of preservation of the diversity of existing species, as well as the conservation of protected areas to sustain diversity. Its long-term objectives are:

- To preserve and sustain the diversity of existing species.
- To seek the preservation of diverse interrelationships among species, as well as the conservation of protected areas for the reproduction of species.

Unfortunately, this strategy has so far received little attention. The National Strategy for Biological Diversity proposes appropriate objectives for the conservation of

169

ecological systems. But it is unclear about how to achieve these objectives and the necessary administrative and social actions. In fact, only a few specific actions have been taken so far towards the achievement of such objectives.

Sustainable forest management

Sustainable development issues in forestry are two-fold; how to support the national forestry sector with good nature conservation methods, and how to promote reasonable and non-wasteful use of imported forest materials at the international level. The public is very concerned about how to support domestic forestry. This may seem strange, as in many countries forestry is considered a kind of destructive activity to nature. In Japan, the perception of and concern for nature conservation is very high and continuously increasing. This situation can be explained by the fact that in Japan, forestry has traditionally been considered a nature-friendly and nature-conserving activity. The majority of Japan's forests are not wild but planted, and such planted forests have created their own unique ecosystems; they protect the land from natural disasters such as landslides and waterlogged land, and they provide beautiful landscapes. However, logging activities in Japan are decreasing, as domestic lumber has lost its market competitiveness because of its high cost, forested areas are ruined and forests are losing their nature conservation function. Many people in Japan therefore think that good forestry methods should be supported and maintained domestically.

National policy response

The policy for forestry is basically how to support the sector, either as a business or as an important nature-conservation activity. The important purpose of the national forest, which covers one third of Japan's forested area and is administered by the Forestry Agency, is changing from logging to nature conservation. The Forestry Agency is also considering a new subsidy to support the nature conservation function of private forests, as well as the private forestry sector in general. Many local governments have already financially supported forestry, and the Water Source Tax, which has been envisaged for a long time, is now beginning to look practicable.

Citizens and NGOs are also actively supporting forestry by helping to plant and maintain forests. Companies are also supporting forestry, either financially or through ownership of forests. One reason for companies' action in forestry could be that forest conservation is very popular in Japan.

International concerns and policy response

Compared to the popularity of domestic forestry, public awareness and concern for forestry in the international context is different and seemingly low. Japan is one of the biggest importers of lumber from tropical and temperate forests. Japan also hosts in Yokohama the Headquarters of the International Tropical Timber Organisation (ITTO), which plays an important role administering the International Tropical Timber Agreement (ITTA). Japan should therefore be in a position to have both interest and responsibility in the preservation of the world's forests, especially tropical forests. Ironically, however, people in Japan do not realise that a large number of trees are now being cut down overseas instead, and forests are disappearing globally. Since lumber is used mostly as plywood in the construction process or consumed as processed goods such as paper and wooden products and does not usually reach the general citizen, the end consumers do not take strong actions that are directly linked to tropical forest conservation, even if they are concerned. On the other hand, it should also be noted that comprehensive approaches including counter-measures within exporting countries along with international trade measures are very important, since the volume of lumber put on the international trade accounts for only 14 per cent of all the lumber production (3.3 billion m^3 annually) in the world.

However, the new recycling policy may force considerable change in the use of timber products, especially plywood used in construction. The Building Materials Recycling Act, introduced in May 2000 and enforced in April 2001, requires recycling of wood materials used and disposed of in the construction industry (see Section A – Waste management and recycling). Through this act, and positive action from the construction sector, the wasteful use of plywood is expected to decrease.

The Japanese government has also been trying to respond positively to the international aspects of forest conservation. Japan, Canada and the USA participate in meetings of non-European countries in respect of setting the standards and criteria for the management of sustainable forest, and Japan is engaged in technological co-operation in forestry with other countries in South East Asia, Oceania and South and Central America. In fact, of all the member countries of the ITTO, Japan makes the greatest financial contribution.

A positive response from the industrial sector can also be seen. Some trading companies are taking the environment into consideration when importing lumber. Construction companies and paper manufacturing companies are attempting to reduce the amount of lumber used and are concerned about the environmental situation of the lumber exporting countries. These companies pay special attention to the Forest Certification System and the recent trend in labelling on lumber and lumber products aimed at maintaining a Sustainable Forest through careful forest management. The Forest Certification System with labelling is expected to be an effective environmental measure with respect to lumber production (forestry) industries, since other environmental management systems such as the ISO 14001 have not been implemented or widely accepted in forestry on a global basis.

171|

Other issues

There are other issues on the agenda for sustainable development. Many of them are related to the concerns for environmental and/or natural resources, such as fisheries and agriculture, and for the prevention of and response to natural disasters.[9] However, other sustainable development problems have also been emerging recently (*e.g.* managing a rapidly ageing society and reforming economic structures).

The Japanese government sees sustainable management of agriculture, forestry, and fisheries as essential to the long-term prosperity of Japan. As Japan has developed, a lot of change has occurred in these areas. With increased exposure to the cultures of other countries, Japanese citizens have diversified their diet. Japanese increasingly consume foods imported from abroad, such as dairy and livestock products, while consuming less rice, the primary Japanese agricultural product. As Japan's dietary tastes have changed, its self-sufficiency ratios have dropped. In addition, few young Japanese are choosing to work in the agriculture, forestry, or fishery industries. To compound this problem, Japan's population continues to shift towards a smaller, older population.

Due to global population and environmental problems, the Japanese government feels that it is worthwhile to encourage and develop its own national agriculture, forestry, and fishing industries in the 21st century. In the realm of agriculture, the Japanese government sees its primary task as maintaining and improving national productivity by ensuring that adequate, clean soil and water is available for agriculture, forestry and fishing. The government promotes genetically diverse, multi-functional agriculture, forestry, and fishing industries.

To do this, the Japanese government has: established the Basic Law on Food, Agriculture, and Rural Areas in July 1999; established the Fisheries Industry Basic Policy in Dec. 1999; and undertaken Comprehensive Forestry Policy Reforms in December 2000. In order to effectively implement measures based on the Basic Law on Food, Agriculture and Rural Areas, the Ministry of Agriculture, Forestry and Fisheries (Norinsuisansho) was reorganised in January 2001. As part of the reorganisation, 17 independent administrative entities, including former operations and research facilities, were created in April 2001. While the government has restructured itself in order to better-manage the agricultural, forestry and fishing industries and to provide a stable food supply, it is actively encouraging citizens to provide creative suggestions.

Some important aspects of improving the agricultural, forestry, and fishing industry are: improving rural infrastructure; ensuring that waste water is treated properly; encouraging larger-scale rice, soybean, and wheat farming in order to benefit from economies of scale; and improving irrigation systems.

Agriculture

Unlike many other OECD countries, where agriculture is shown to be one of the most environmentally damaging activities, Japanese agriculture is generally considered to be a conservation activity. The main reason is that Japan's agriculture is based on rice cultivation in paddy fields and this activity is, at least in the traditional sense, a kind of sustainable agriculture, as proved by the history of some thousands of years. Rice cultivation in paddy fields also has many positive environmental functions, such as supporting a unique ecosystem and storing water. It acts as a reservoir for water resources and as a dam to prevent flood damage. However, because of the subsidy-based protective policies for agriculture over many years, Japan's agricultural sector has been losing its economic competitiveness as well as the capacity to adapt itself to the new style of agriculture where more consideration and action is required to promote sustainability.

In this situation, the present governmental policy for agriculture aims to:

• Strengthen the productivity and economic competitiveness of the agricultural sector.

• Support the environmental protection function of sustainable agriculture.

To achieve such aims, many changes have been made to the basic policy for agriculture and the sustainable development concept has been adopted as one of the main objectives.[10] In 1999, the Basic Agriculture Law, which was almost 40 years old, was revised to become the Basic Act for Food, Agriculture and Farming. One of the four important policies of this new basic act is sustainable agricultural development [Section 3 of the basic policies (Chapter II)].

In 1999, Japan enacted the Law for Promotion on Introduction of Advanced Sustainable Farming System. The Law requires farmers to improve soil quality by using composted animal manure or other organic materials. It also requires that farmers reduce their use of chemical fertilisers and pesticides. The initial cost of implementing these changes is covered by the national budget.

In 1994, the National Council for Sustainable Agriculture was formed by the national organisation of agricultural co-operatives. The Council's objective is to help achieve sustainable agriculture goals. On of the primary ways the Council encourages sustainable agriculture is by organising agricultural competitions. The Council is composed of farmers, consumers, distributors, researchers and scholars. Currently, approximately half of Japan's agricultural co-operatives provide technical support to member farmers in order to promote sustainable agriculture.

"The number of co-operatives committing to the promotion of sustainable agriculture is expected to increase. Since the Government and the Council have maintained a good relationship, the voice of farmers can be delivered to the government through the Council and political decisions can also be announced via the Council."

Fisheries[11]

Sustainable use of marine resources and the conservation of the marine environment are considered important matters for fisheries in Japan. In 1998, the total amount of marine products decreased by 10 per cent compared to 1997. The main factor in the decline in marine resources is attributed to the deterioration of the marine environment. In order to improve this situation, the following policies have been initiated or are under consideration:

- Making new fishing agreements with China and South Korea in the Japan Sea.
- Utilising the TAC (Total Allowable Catch) system efficiently.
- Promoting resources for the management of fisheries.
- Improving fish farming.
- Controlling recreational fishing.
- Promoting research and development.
- Enhancing public awareness of the conservation of the marine environment.

As a highly industrialised country with much reliance on marine resources, Japan has contributed much to the conservation of the marine environment, especially in the area of improving sewage treatment.

The total value of the fish caught by Japanese fishing vessels is approximately 2.2 trillion yen per year – approximately 0.5% of Japan's GNP, 0.43% of GDP. The Japanese government has implemented strict total-allowable-catch restrictions on the fishing industry in accordance with related laws and regulations. Japan has implemented licensing systems for commercial fisherman and has restrictions on fishing-gear and fishing methods.

Commercial shipping has impacted the environment of coastal zones in the following ways:

- Pollution caused by illegal dumping of oil, wastes, etc. from ships.
- Pollution of and influence on coastal ecology caused by oil spill incident, solution of harmful anti-fouling paints in to the sea.
- Air pollution by emission of exhaust gas from ships. And
- Competitive use of coastal zones by fisheries (fishing operation, aquaculture, etc.) and ship navigation.

Other industries (including tourism) have negatively affected coastal areas in the following ways:

- Disappearance of natural coastline: As a result of reclamation along the coast of the Seto Inland Sea.

Box 5. **Total Allowable Catch System**

Japan introduced its Total Allowable Catch (TAC) system in 1997, in further-ance of the Law concerning Conservation and Management of Marine Living Resources. Upon introduction of its TAC system, the Japanese government acknowledged the following challenges:

- Providing accurate scientific research in order to determine the total allowable catch of various fish species.
- Determining how to distribute the total allowable catch among Japan's fishermen, especially since fisherman do not all use the same fishing techniques.
- Constructing of a system to monitor catch information.

Source: The United Nations' report on Natural Resource Aspects of Sustainable Development in Japan.
www.un.org/esa/agenda 21/natlinfo/countr/japan/natur.htm

- Disappearance of habitat of marine organisms: Coastal reclamation results in the loss of habitat of marine organisms, which may cause adverse effect on marine living resources.

The primary land-based sources of marine pollution are liquid and solid wastes from individual households and industries. Illegal dumping, accidental chemical spills, and natural disasters are also causes of water pollution in Japan's coastal areas.

The Japanese government organises meetings to raise awareness among pub-lic officials, fishermen, and concerned citizens regarding the sustainable use and conservation of marine living resources. The government and fishery organisations also make efforts to educate the public at large. June is officially recognised as the "Seto Inland Sea Environmental Conservation Month"; during this month the Japanese government and fishery organisations focus their efforts to educate Japanese citizens about the environmental issues of the Seto Inland Sea.

Given the fact that Japan accounts for more than 30 per cent of the world fish import value, Japan must be sensitive to the conservation of world fish stocks. There have been several cases in the past where import of a certain fish product into the Japanese market contributed to depletion of that fish stock. Japan should import fish in a sustainable manner.

175

Box 6. Japan and the Management of Whales

Japan's primary whaling concern is that conservation of whales should be done in order to establish responsible, sustainable, whaling. Japan sees no reason to exempt whales from the concept of sustainable development. Japan, therefore, strongly supports the affirmations of the UN Conference on Environment and Development in 1992 in which whales were treated as another resource that can be harvested in a sustainable manner.

Japan sees whaling as natural. Japan, in fact, has a long tradition of using whales for food. Whales are one of Japan's most important cultural foods.

The International Whaling Commission (IWC) was established under the International Convention for the Regulation of Whaling (ICRW). The ICRW was established to conserve whale stocks and to ensure the sustainable development of whaling. Japan feels that the 12-year moratorium that the IWC has imposed on commercial whaling runs counter to the idea of sustainable whaling and counter to the purpose of ICRW. In an attempt to normalise relations with the IWC, Japan has undertaken to:

1. "Provide High Quality Scientific Information to ensure advanced whale resource management. Japanese scientific surveys include sighting surveys for estimation of whale population and comprehensive biological studies using a limited research take of minke whales as provided for under the ICRW. Sighting surveys are appropriate means to grasp the general number and geographical distribution of whales, but are not sufficient. Sampling surveys are essential for a) estimation of such biological parameters as age composition, sexual maturity and pregnancy rate required for stock assessment of whales, and b) elucidation of the roles of whales, prey-predator relationship between whales and their food sources etc., in various marine ecosystems. These research efforts need to be continued to answer questions raised by the IWC scientists.

2. Introducing Opinions of International Legal Experts to correct questionable decisions of the IWC. Particularly, strong opinion that the Southern Ocean Sanctuary contradicted the letter and spirit of the ICRW exists among the international lawyers.

3. Presenting Views of International Anthropologists on the cultural and socio-economic significance of whaling in some Japanese small coastal communities. An Interim quota of minke whales for these communities is necessary to alleviate the current serious hardships resulting from the moratorium by the IWC.

4. Enforcing Current Regulations of the IWC as a responsible contracting party, although some of the past IWC decisions are still legally questionable."

Source: Ministry of Foreign Affairs of Japan.
www.mofa.go.jp/policy/economy/fishery/whales/index.html

Managing a rapidly ageing society

In October 1999, the population of Japan over the age of 65 reached 21 186 000, representing 16.7 per cent of the total population of 126 686 000. This percentage is rapidly increasing. In 1998, the elderly represented 16.2 per cent of the total population. The growth ratio between 1998 and 1999 was 3.31 per cent. An official estimate by the Ministry of Public Management, Home Affairs, Posts and Telecommunications shows that in about 2000, Japan was the most rapidly ageing society (in terms of percentage of the elderly over 65), and that in 2040, the elderly will number 33 726 000, representing 31 per cent of the total population, which will have declined to 108 964 000. This is the most rapidly ageing society in the world. In Japan, it took only 24 years (1970-1994) for the percentage of the elderly population to double, from 7 to 14 per cent, while in France it took 115 years (1864-1979) and it is estimated that in the USA it will take 71 years (1942-2013).

This rapid ageing causes many problems for society. Pensions is considered the major issue, although this is only part of a wider problem: how to maintain the social welfare system. For example, in order to respond to the increasing demand for social welfare, the revenue-raising system must be reformed, taking intergenerational balance into account. Labour policy, including foreign labour, needs to be examined in order to adapt it to the ageing or already-aged society. These situations are becoming widespread and are discussed as important policy issues, although no noteworthy steps have been taken so far.

The following issues on Japan's policy agenda, which are usually unrelated to the sustainable development debate, should also be considered important factors in the achievement of sustainable development goals:

- Economic structural reform.

- Education reform.

- Modernisation of the political system.

- National security discussion (including the possibility of and necessity for amending the Constitution).

- Establishing emergency systems for managing risks (resulting from human activities or from natural disasters).

B. Institutions and policies

Japan's institutional and legislative efforts to better integrate sustainable development have been led at both national and sub-national levels. Business and non-profit organisations are also playing an increasing and evolving role.

Involvement at national level

Policy setting and decision making for sustainable development at national level has involved, on the one hand, the establishment of co-ordinating bodies and, on the other, the elaboration and promulgation of nation-wide environmental laws and further implementation of them through the administrative systems. In this respect, the 1993 Basic Environment Act states fundamental principles in environmental policy.

Co-ordinating bodies

The *ad hoc Group on Global Environmental Problems* was established in 1980 by the Japanese Prime minister. This group was to serve as a private, independent advisory body for the director of the Environmental Agency. The group was created to evaluate Japan's environmental policies with regards to current and future global environmental issues. Since its formation, the group has evolved into two committees – the Special Committee on Environment and Trade and the Special Committee on UNCED Follow-up. This group has written numerous influential reports and often takes the lead in addressing environmental issues in Japan. One of its earliest reports from 1982 entitled *International Activities for Global Environmental Problems* led to the creation of the United Nations World Commission on Environment and Development (Hanaoka 1996).

The *Council of Ministers for Global Environment Conservation* was formed in 1989. It was created to co-facilitate communication and co-operation between governmental bodies in order to effectively implement policies to address global environmental problems. All Cabinet Ministers and concerned members of the ruling parties participated in this Council. In 1990 the Council published the *Action Plan on Prevention of Global Warming*. In this report, the Council detailed a national plan to reduce carbon dioxide emissions in order to stabilise carbon dioxide emissions at 1990 levels. The plan included changes in urban planning, industrial activities, and transportation systems (Hanaoka 1996).

The Japanese Council for Sustainable Development was established in June 1996. It is composed of representatives from government, industry and NGOs, and aims to facilitate dialogue among its members concerning sustainable development issues. As an advisory body to the Government, it is mandated to follow up on the progress of measures taken each year under the Environment Plan. The Council undertook a first review in June 1996, and identified areas requiring further improvement. In the area of global warming, it called for further effective measures to meet the targets set. In the field of waste management and recycling, the activities of the line ministries and other entities should be effectively linked to a socio-economic system. Concerning nature conservation, comprehensive measures and detailed programmes are necessary, which take into account the value of the natural environment.

The Council works to promote sustainable development by encouraging and facilitating co-operation and communication between government, NGO, and business organisations.[12]

Regarding disputes on pollution, the Environmental Disputes Co-ordination Commission conducts mediation, arbitration and adjudication, and also rules on such matters, based on the Environmental Disputes Settlement Law. Based on the Law concerning Compensation and Prevention of Pollution-related Health Damage, Japan is taking measures, including compensation for damage to human health, in illnesses such as Minamata disease and asthma.

Legislation and policy on domestic and global environmental problems

Japan has policies, programmemes, and/or legislation consistent with Agenda 21 in the following areas: changing consumption and production patterns; atmosphere; land use planning; forest and deforestation; sustainable mountain development; sustainable agriculture; biological diversity; biotechnology; oceans and coastal areas; fresh water management; toxic chemicals; hazardous wastes; solid wastes; radioactive wastes; energy; and transportation.[13]

Japan's policies and legislation in sustainable development have combined regulation and control technology. The government has gradually raised environmental targets and regulations, after initially allowing industries some time to develop their own control technologies. The government simultaneously promotes the development of control technology to help companies that have difficulties meeting new environmental regulations (Imura, 1997).

Agenda 21

At the 1992 United Nations Conference on Environment and Development in Rio de Janeiro, Japan and other participant governments formulated overarching commitments and guidelines for sustainable development. These commitments and guidelines were detailed in Agenda 21. (Hanaoka, 1996).

Japan's National Agenda 21 Action Plan was formulated in December 1993 by the Council of Ministers for Global Environment Conservation. In formulating the Plan, the Council consulted Japanese employers' groups and labour unions as well as other non-governmental organisations. The Council is responsible for overseeing implementation of the Action Plan. In Japan, as in many other countries, Agenda 21 has served as a guiding principle for raising national awareness of environmental issues. In order to effectively implement Agenda 21 at the national and local level, various government ministries have jointly participated in activities co-ordinated

Box 7.   Changing Consumption Patterns – The Eco-Life Pledge

In preparation for the Kyoto Conference on Global Warming, the Ministry of the Environment sponsored a national Eco-Life campaign, the purpose of which is to encourage Japanese citizens to dedicate themselves to leading environmentally-friendly lives. Citizens are encouraged to dedicate themselves by taking the Eco-Life Pledge:

Eco-Life Pledge:

1. I will refuse the bags offered at the cash register and use my own bags when shopping.
2. I will separate garbage and recycle everything possible, including my empty cans, bottles, magazines and newspapers.
3. I will keep my heater below 20C in the winter and my cooler above 28C in the summer.
4. I will turn off my fluorescent lights and pull the plugs out of appliances when not using them.
5. I will walk or ride my bike when going a short distance for things like shopping; I will take public transportation when out on the weekend.
6. I will use as little water as possible when doing things like washing my face and brushing my teeth.
7. I will turn the temperature down slightly on my water heater.
8. I will buy goods that display the Eco-Mark whenever possible.
9. I will not waste food, and I will try to cook in an eco-friendly way, conserving energy when possible.
10. I will use the "Kankyo-Kakebo" (an environmental household bookkeeping system developed by the Ministry of the Environment) to make sure that I am living an environmentally friendly lifestyle.
11. I will turn off the engine of my car when waiting for someone or when picking up or dropping off loads.
12. I will use the stairs instead of the elevator when going three floors or less. The Ministry of the Environment sponsored the Eco-Mark (see n° 8 above) as a method of labelling products for consumers in order to help consumers to choose products that are environmentally friendly.

Source: Ministry of the Environment Internet Site, pages on climate change. *www.env.go.jp/en/topic/cc.html*

by the Ministry of the Environment (Hanaoka, 1996). The goals of the Action Plan are to promote sustainable development by:

- Promoting public awareness of the need to alter lifestyles in order to lessen personal environmental harm.
- Contributing to and participating in international systems in order to conserve the global environment.
- Helping to establish an international framework for the financing of projects to preserve the global environment.
- Helping developing countries develop the means to address environmental problems by assisting with the transfer of relevant technologies.
- Promoting and assisting international environmental co-operation and monitoring; and
- Co-ordinating the Japanese central government, local governments, business community, NGOs efforts in sustainable development.

The National Agenda 21 Action Plan will likely continue to provide the core structure for future sustainable development activities in Japan (Hanaoka, 1996).

Basic Environment Law

Prior to 1993, Japanese environmental policy was governed by two laws: the Basic Law on Pollution Control (1967) and the Nature Conservation Law (1972). These laws focused primarily on restricting pollution and by the late 1980s were proving to be insufficient as bases for innovative environmental policies. In November 1993, these laws were abolished and superseded by the Basic Environment Law. This new law provides a new framework was designed to respond to the growing challenges of conserving the environment on a global level (Hanaoka, 1996).

Basic Environment Plan

Pursuant to the Basic Law, the Japanese government created the Basic Environment Plan, a national plan to help agencies within the government better co-operate with one another. The Japanese Cabinet approved the Basic Environment Plan in 1994. This Plan's main purpose was to help different government agencies co-operate in order to achieve environmental goals. The primary themes of the Plan are:

- recycling;
- living in harmony with the environment;
- promoting voluntary participation in environmental programmes; and
- supporting environmental programmes in developing countries.

181

All Japanese ministries and agencies are required to participate in and contribute financially to the Plan.[14] Each year, the Central Council for the Environment reviews Japan's progress towards the goals of the Plan.[15]

Basic Law on Food, Agriculture and Rural Areas

In July 1999 the Basic Law on Food, Agriculture, and Rural Areas replaced the Basic Agricultural Law. An important difference between the old and new law is the new law's recognition of the multiple functions that agriculture serves. The new Basic Law's provisions recognise not only that agriculture provides food and resources for Japan's population, but that agriculture also helps preserve water resources and the environment.

Japan has implemented several acts in order to deal with typical pollution problems (*e.g.* the Air Pollution Prevention Law, the Water Pollution Control Law, the Vibration Regulation Act, the Noise Regulation Act, the Odour Prevention Law and the Agricultural Land Soil Pollution Prevention Law. The 1967 Basic Pollution Policy Act laid the foundation for anti-pollution measures and was in effect until it was replaced by the Basic Environment Law in 1993.

Box 8. The Maintenance and Promotion of Natural Fertilisers

Article 32 of the new Basic Law and the 1999 Law concerning the Appropriate Treatment and Promotion of Utilisation of Livestock Manure concern promotion of natural livestock manure in order to maintain and promote the natural agricultural cycles. These laws direct the Japanese government to facilitate the use of livestock manure as soil fertilisers in order to promote a natural return of nutrients back to the soil from which they came. Article 32 also directs the government to help farmers use artificial chemical fertilisers properly in order to maintain the environment.

The 1999 Law concerning the Appropriate Treatment and Promotion of Utilisation of Livestock Manure addresses the technical side of using livestock manure. This law ensures the appropriate processing and treatment of livestock manure prior to its use as fertiliser. By mandating appropriate processing of livestock manure, the Japanese government ensures that agricultural products remain safe for human consumption and that the environment of farms where natural fertilisers are used will not be negatively impacted.

Source: The United Nations' Report on Natural Resource Aspects of Sustainable Development in Japan.
www.un.org/esa/agenda21/natlinfo/c ountr/japan/natur.htm

The major anti-pollution measures that have been enacted are the setting of environmental standards, regulations on pollutant emissions and noise levels, and financial assistance – such as subsidies and tax reductions – for achieving standards. Such actions are generally the responsibility of the national level, but air and water pollution management is delegated to local government. This delegation system, however, has come under fire and is one of the important issues to be discussed, as government authority has recently become more decentralised.

The establishment and operation of the Pollution-Related Health Damage Compensation System, which provides pollution victims with adequate medical treatment and compensation for other financial losses caused by pollution-related issues, was also one of the significant actions at national level against environmental pollution problems. Although it seems that such a compensation system is no longer in great demand with the decrease in severe environmental pollution, it is still essential to develop appropriate compensation measures to safeguard the public from any further pollution problem, should it arise.

The management and handling of various chemicals harmful for humans and the environment is a recent environmental problem that requires urgent countermeasures. The OECD has already suggested the implementation of the Pollutant Release and Transfer Register (PRTR) system to deal with such problems. Japan promulgated the "Law concerning Reporting etc. of Releases to the Environment of Specific Chemical Substances and Promoting Improvements in their Management" to implement PRTR in 1999, and Japanese PRTR started in April 2001.

The Japanese government has been actively participating in and promoting many global environmental policies, such as global warming prevention, ozone layer protection and the preservation of worldwide biological diversity. Japan has enthusiastically entered into international treaties such as the Ozone Layer Protection Treaty (1985) and its Montreal Protocol (1987), the UN Framework Convention on Climate Change (1992), the Biological Diversity Convention (1992) and the Environmental Protection Protocol to the Antarctic Convention (1997), and is further developing international measures (*e.g.* hosting COP3 of the UNFCCC, in which the Kyoto Protocol was adopted).

Relevant domestic laws have been amended in order to comply with the purposes of the above-mentioned treaties. For instance, manufacture and use of specific freon gases (CFC) is now regulated, based on the Ozone Layer Protection Act and some amendments were made to the Energy Conservation Act in order to deal with the global warming problem and to reach the standard of carbon dioxide emissions reduction enforced by the Kyoto Protocol (6 per cent less than the 1990 standard). In 1998, the Global Warming Policy Promotion Act was enacted and the basic national policy to address the problem was formulated, although concrete actions have not yet been taken.

183

Authority and commitment in central government

The Environment Agency

Environmental administration at the national level is the responsibility of the Environment Agency (which became the Ministry of the Environment in January 2001). As stated in Article 3 of the Environment Agency Establishment Act, the duties of the Environment Agency are to prevent pollution, to conserve the natural environment, and to promote the broad administration of environmental conservation in order to contribute to and ensure that citizens lead healthy lives. The main role of the Environment Agency is to act as an administrative liaison for other ministries and agencies that deal with the environment. Since the Environment Agency does not always have absolute authority over other ministries, there are cases where it cannot act in the most effective way in order to ensure the conservation of the environment.

The Ministry of the Environment (*Kankyosho*) is in charge of the implementation of the National Agenda 21 Action Plan. As part of its ongoing oversight, the Ministry of the Environment publishes an annual report that evaluates the ongoing environmental situation in Japan, specifying areas that need attention (Hanaoka, 1996).

Ministry of Labour

In 1992 the Ministry of Labour established a labelling system for all dangerous and toxic chemicals in accordance with the National Agenda 21 Action Plan. The Ministry identified 91 specific chemical substances which industries will have to label at every stage of processing. By ensuring consistent, accurate labelling, the Ministry expects the system to assist employees as they handle chemicals (Hanaoka, 1996).

Greening of Government

In June 1995, the Cabinet adopted the Action Plan for Greening Government Operations. The Plan requires the greening of Government operations, by such means as use of recycled paper or energy-saving equipment, introduction of lower-emission vehicles, and reduction of carbon dioxide emissions.

The role of the Judiciary

The Judiciary was an important actor in sustainable development when pollution control was the main concern and policy target. In the absence of appropriate acts, law courts tried to help victims of severe pollution by using general tort rules.

Box 9. **Greening of Government**

In July 1995, the Japanese government passed the "Action Plan for Initiative Action on Environmental Conservation by Government as Operator and Consumer (the Action Plan for Greening Government Operations)". The Plan called for government agencies to:

- take environmental considerations into account when purchasing and using goods and services;
- take environmental considerations into account when constructing and maintaining government facilities;
- conduct government administration in an environmentally friendly manner;
- educate government employees regarding environmental conservation; and
- establish a system to promote green government and to evaluate governmental environmental performance.*

In order to further promote environmentally friendly government, the Ministry of the Environment has recently released guidelines for government purchasing.

---

* *Ibid.*

Source: OECD Environment: Increasing Resource Efficiency.
www.oecd.org/env/efficiency/gog/facil.htm

However, after Japan's success in controlling severe pollution, the Judiciary has not been very aware of or concerned about other wider environmental problems and the sustainable development movement.

In the absence of a specific clause giving citizens the right to sue for their concern in environment and sustainable development, the strictly limited legal interpretation of standing to sue has prevented citizens' access to court. An attempt to change this situation by widening the standing to sue has been continued by some lawyers and citizens' NGOs, and this movement is becoming increasingly popular. Some argue that this movement is becoming increasingly popular, although this view is not shared by the Japanese government.

Initiatives at sub-national level

Although central government has strong legal authority in environmental management (especially in pollution control), local governments have played an important role in preventing pollution, especially at a time when the state government had not come up with sufficient anti-pollution measures to deal with serious air and water pollution. Many anti-pollution measures initiated by local governments are remarkable in their resourcefulness and ingenuity. For example, regulating the total amount of emissions as a countermeasure to air and water pollution was initiated by local governments in Yokkaichi, Osaka and Kanagawa, where such problems were of an urgent nature.

Despite the strong authority of the central government in Japan's government, local governments actually took some the first environmental initiatives during the 1960s, prior to environmental control by Japan's central government. Because many environmental problems – notably pollution of air and water – occur at the local level, many local governments passed their own environmental regulations during the 1960s. These regulations not only paved the way for national environmental reform, but also probably prompted Japanese businesses to become environmentally conscious prior to strong national-level regulation (Imura 1997).

The local governments of the Kumamoto and Osaka prefectures and the cities of Kawasaki and Kobe have established their own environmental regulations. Tokyo is currently developing plans for the establishment of sustainable development regulationsMany other local governments have created local Agenda 21 action plans and are in the process of implementing regulations to carry out their plans. Most of these plans regard the integration of environmental considerations in industrial development.[16]

The Global Environment Department of the Environmental Ministry has organised conferences to assist local governments in successful implementation of their plans (Hanaoka 1996)

"The Government supports Local Agenda 21 initiatives, and there are at least 28 Local Agenda 21s out of a total of 47 prefectures and 12 designated metropolitan cities involving about 73 per cent of the population. The Government provides assistance to the local authorities for their own voluntary and independent environmental activities – for instance, for the establishment of Local Agenda 21s, and for international co-operation at the local authorities level. Local authorities are directly involved in the implementation of laws, regulations and guidelines, and in the observation, measurement and control of pollution, etc. regarding conservation of the environment."[17]

One of the most interesting aspects of local governments' anti-pollution actions is the pollution prevention agreement between a company and each local government. The agreement prescribes the responsibilities of companies and regulations on their industrial activities such as on pollutants including soot, smoke, drainage, noise, vibration and offensive odour. It also includes administrative inspection and operation shutdown as a punitive measure in the event of contract violation.

Box 10. **Agenda 21 Kanagawa**

The Kanagawa prefecture is one example of Japanese local governments implementing local regulations and policies in order to effect Agenda 21. Agenda 21 Kanagawa implements the broad goals of Agenda 21 with an emphasis on acting locally in Kanagawa while thinking globally. Kanagawa's plan is aimed at providing guidance to citizens, businesses, and government agencies in the Kanagawa prefecture. Kanagawa's plan emphasises four primary goals:

- Developing personal lifestyles that are compatible with environmental conservation.
- Planning urban development that is environmentally sound.
- Forming a social system in which environmental considerations are central; and
- Promoting international environmental co-operation.

Each of these goals was followed by concrete quantifiable action principles and specific programmes for implementation. 21 action principles and 77 specific programmes were announced.

Source: Japan Report for Rio+5 Process.
www.ecouncil.ac.cr/rio/national/re ports/asia/japan.htm

Local governments took such measures because they – particularly municipalities – had inadequate authority over pollution control. Since the harmful influence of pollution on residents had to be urgently dealt with, instead of using their administrative powers to impose regulations on companies, local governments had no other choice but to make agreements with them. Another reason was that, as opposed to imposing regulations by law, making agreements allowed local governments to be flexible in dealing with each company on an individual basis, and this was therefore considered to be a more effective anti-pollution measure at the local level.

Local governments are also under tight constraints in introducing regulations by ordinance. When a local government tries to set up new regulations, it must be very careful not to deviate from the national laws in related fields. Local governments are allowed to establish new regulations only in cases where their authority to enact an ordinance is either not regulated by national laws, or these new regulations are different from the existing regulations prescribed by national laws. (This is often referred to as "*yokodashi*", or supplemental). It has been widely argued whether local governments should be allowed to establish new regulations

187

that are stricter than the existing regulations set by the national government (often referred to as "*uwanose*", or add-over).

Although the 1970 amendments to the Air Pollution Prevention Act and the Water Pollution Prevention Act allowed prefectural governments to add stricter regulations to the existing ones set by national laws on air and water pollution, it is still necessary to develop rational guidelines regarding national and local government authority in environmental issues. Regulations with national standards are not necessarily adequate in all circumstances; stricter and wider-ranging pollution regulations by local governments are therefore required, depending on the social and environmental circumstances of each area.

Similar problems can be seen in the implementation of Environmental Impact Assessments (EIA). Prior to the national government's enactment of the Environmental Impact Assessment Act in 1997, many local governments already implemented their own assessment programmemes by ordinance or guideline. Some of the assessment schemes developed by local governments are more advanced than the requirements set out in the National Assessment Act, in terms of the range of target projects, items to be evaluated and residential participation, but the newly introduced national assessment scheme may not allow stricter (and thus more "progressive") requirements in the local assessment process.

Some prudent adjustments should be made to local and national governments' assessment schemes, in order to balance them out. For example, some local assessment processes require public hearings, but the national system only requires an information meeting for citizens. The public hearing is considered to be a stricter requirement than the provisions of the national assessment scheme. Consequently, public hearings are not part of the national scheme. In this connection, some local governments – such as Kawasaki City in Kanagawa Prefecture – have made a unique innovation: opening public hearings to form a mayor's opinion, which he/she is then allowed to give in the national assessment scheme.

The role of the non-governmental sector

Businesses

Chapter 30 of the National Agenda 21 Action Plan emphasises industries' role in sustainable development. Enterprises, especially small ones, are seen as essential participants in sustainable energy planning. As many industries are taking their operations overseas, the Plan emphasises the promotion of technology transfer to developing nations (Hanaoka, 1996).

Japanese companies have experience with industrial pollution because they have had problems in the past. Now that these same companies have overcome many of the challenges of making profit without damaging the environment, they are helping to promote and provide pollution control devices and expertise in Southeast Asia and other developing countries. There is also increasing pressure from Japanese citizens for Japanese companies to be environmentally responsible in their operations abroad. In 1995, the Global Environmental Forum, under the direction of the Ministry of the Environment, conducted a survey of Japanese companies' environmental practices in Thailand, Indonesia, the Philippines, and Malaysia. Most of the companies expressed their hope that the Japanese government would aid them by providing information about the environmental issues of the specific foreign regions in which they operate. Many companies also expressed the desire to establish a system for sharing best practices amongst themselves. In response to this survey, the Ministry of the Environment researched Japanese environmental practices abroad. The purpose of the research was to provide concrete information and examples in order to help Japanese companies operate in an environmentally friendly manner in their foreign operations.[18]

Box 11. Keidanren's Sustainable Development Efforts

Industries in Japan have often taken environmental initiative without government prodding, seeing environmental friendliness as a corporate duty. In 1991, prior to the Rio Convention, the Keidanren, the largest employers' association in Japan, voluntarily adopted a Global Environmental Charter. This charter serves as a guide for member enterprises and includes guidelines for overseas operations, specifying that members should, among other things, obey all local environmental regulations, promote the transfer of appropriate control technologies to developing nations when possible, and evaluate the environmental impact of overseas operations.

In 1992, Keidanren established the Keidanren Nature Conservation Fund. This fund supports the sustainable development efforts of NGOs in developing countries. The fund also finances an international environmental task force. The fund first focused its international aid assistance on China and other Asian countries.

In 1996, the Keidanren association reconfirmed its commitment to environmental responsibility by announcing the Keidanren Environmental Appeal. In addition to reconfirming the aspirations of the Keidanren Global Environment Charter, the Appeal called for businesses to voluntarily: take concrete measures to combat global warming; conduct environmental audits; and take into account environmental considerations when conducting overseas projects.

Source: Japan Report for Rio+5 Process.
www.ecouncil.ac.cr/rio/national/re ports/asia/japan.htm

The Industry Structure Council in the Ministry of International Trade and Industry has provided ongoing direction to industries in their efforts to conduct business in an environmental friendly manner.[19]

The Japanese Federation of Employers' Associations (JFEA) and the Keidanren employers' organisation have worked to promote environmental protection as a social responsibility of for-profit business. These industrial groups have encouraged businesses to see environmental responsibility as a corporate duty. As a result, many businesses have voluntarily entered into pollution control agreements with local communities.[20]

When the first serious pollution problems arose in Japan, companies and industries were not very co-operative. As defendants in civil trials for compensation of pollution-related damages, they strongly denied charges. Companies also opposed new regulations for pollution control. On the other hand, individual citizens and communities strongly criticised the companies that were causing pollution. The Polluter Pays Principle (PPP), proposed by the OECD, fostered the idea that a polluter is responsible for all the expenses incurred in cleaning up polluted areas. In Japan, this principle was interpreted as the "Polluter Punishment Principle"; *i.e.* a polluter should be punished.

This situation gradually changed and the private sector became willing to negotiate with governments and citizens regarding pollution prevention. For instance, companies responded positively to making agreements with local governments on pollution prevention. Today, as the severe pollution problems of the 1960s and 1970s are almost resolved and public awareness of the environment is increasing, companies are very careful not to be pointed out as polluters. They also readily agree to settle pollution-related problems out of court in order to avoid being labelled publicly as polluters. As well as this change in attitude, there has been another noteworthy trend in the private sector. Some large companies are integrating pollution-prevention activities into their corporate projects, using a new PPP principle, Pollution Prevention Pays.

Positive action from companies also results from the generalisation of the use of norms like ISO 14001 in both the private and public sectors. Many Japanese companies are trying to promote their environmental sustainable development policies. Examples are provided in Annex I.

The Federation of Economic Organisations (FEO or "*keidanren*" in Japanese), an organisation of leading industries in Japan, developed the FEO Global Environment Charter in 1991 and formulated their own global environmental principles. This is probably the first of such declarations by industries that address environmental concerns. The charter requires industries to consider environmental issues in all their activities, as well as their active participation in environmental protection, applying the latest information and appropriate technologies to both domestic and overseas operations, especially in developing countries.

One of the most noteworthy actions by the private sector in respect of global environmental problems is its effort to deal with the global warming problem. The FEO identified objectives for each industry in its Voluntary Action Programmeme, and it is working towards their achievement. A manufacturer of automobiles, which are the primary source of carbon dioxide emissions, recently set up a large-scale afforestation project in Australia in co-operation with some trading companies, aimed at offsetting the carbon dioxide emissions of the company and the cars it produces and preparing for future negotiations concerning carbon dioxide emission rights. This type of overseas afforestation project is becoming popular among industries.

Another trend is that companies are developing new competitive business plans directly linked to the solution of the global warming problem (see also second paragraph of ISO14001 heading).

Labour Unions

Chapter 28 of the National Agenda 21 Action Plan emphasises the need for labour unions to be involved in planning for sustainable development. Labour unions are seen as key to raising awareness among workers by implementing training programmes. Unions are also seen as essential participants in planning sustainable development activities, especially in co-operation with industries. Japanese Labour Unions are actively involved in seeking long-term solutions to environmental challenges. RENGO, one of the largest labour unions, includes environmental policies in their annual "Demands and Proposals for Governmental Policies and Institutions". In 1994, RENGO published a separate report on environmental challenges in Japan entitled *Guidelines of Activities for Environmental Problems in Workers' Unions* (*Japanese Trade Union Confederation*, 1994a). This report included case studies, guidelines, and recommendations for sustainable development. RENGO participates in most government sponsored sustainable development meetings (Hanaoka, 1996)

NGOs

As Japan's main objective in environmental management was to control pollution from industrial activities which required strict legislation, broader sustainable development concerns by NGOs are not yet very popular in Japan. The only area in which many citizens have participated and many NGOs have been established is the conservation of wildlife and of the natural historical environment, in the context of a relatively limited number of influential NGOs in Japan.

However, with the shift of environmental concerns from pollution control to the broader aspects of nature conservation, global environmental problems and sustainable development have emerged as an issue among NGOs. NGO activities

191

now cover more areas. Some of these NGOs have had considerable influence on policy making in governments and companies.

In order to campaign effectively, NGOs in Japan must be well organised. Acquiring a corporate status is a critical factor. The recent Non-Profit Activity Promotion Act (the NPO Act, 1998) is expected to help NGOs to acquire corporate status.

Sustainable development in Japan appears to be seen by the government as primarily an environmental issue. Because sustainable development within Japan is centred on environmental concerns, NGOs that focus on sustainable development in a broad sense are primarily involved in international efforts in developing countries.

Many NGOs in Japan face challenges of limited "financing, human resources, and information". In order to assist and encourage NGO sustainable development work in Japan and developing nations, the Japanese government and private-sector donors created the Japan Fund for Global Environment in 1993. Furthermore, "Japan attaches importance to providing assistance for activities in developing countries, through the Subsidy System for NGO projects, small-scale grants assistance, the Voluntary Deposit for International Aid System, and the NGOs International Construction Development Assistance Programme. In addition, based on regional environmental protection funds established by prefectural governments, Japan will continue to provide assistance for environmental conservation activities at the grass-roots level in different regions in Japan."[21]

As Japanese concern for the environment has grown in recent years, so has the number of local and national NGOs in sustainable development. Many of these NGOs strongly advocate and support policies that place all environmental costs on the polluter – "polluter-pays policies". These NGOs are also at the forefront in advocating regulation of polluting vehicles and environmental controls over polluting industries. Due to the newness of many of the NGOs in Japan, they often work quite independently of one another without co-operating or systematically communicating with one another.[22]

C.   Decision-making mechanisms

Japan's commitment to sustainable development should be evaluated against its efforts to implement Agenda 21. These are based principally on two action plans, the National Agenda 21 Action Plan and the Basic Environment Plan, which were drawn up in 1993 and 1994 respectively. Japan has been promoting and will further develop various measures in accordance with the provisions of these plans. The National Agenda 21 Action Plan was completed in December 1993. The Plan lists various policy measures that need to be taken, consistent with the programmeme areas provided in Agenda 21.

Through the process of restructuring described above (see section on governance patterns) in which ministries and agencies are reorganised according to the nature of their roles, not according to their authority, new governments are expected to set and implement more effective policies. This change is expected to facilitate the incorporation of developmental and environmental concerns, thus leading to more efficient sustainable development policies. However, this has not been the case so far. Within a merged ministry, policy making has sometimes needed much more time than before because of the negotiation process between or among the divisions originating from different ministries and agencies. A clear, strong national policy needs to be set by the Cabinet Office, but up to now no such decision has been taken.

Dispute resolution and new competition among Ministries and Agencies

The Japanese government has used "pollution control agreements" for dispute resolution between communities and companies/industries. These agreements serve not only as a basis for resolving environmental problems, but also help prevent the occurrence of environmental problems. These agreements are credited with helping to achieve drastic reductions in industrial air and water pollution (Imura 1997). For example, Canon has entered into a voluntary pollution control agreement with the city of Akimachi.[23] This voluntary agreement provides an understanding between Canon and the community of Akimachi, thus making disputes over pollution less likely.

Under the Basic Environment Plan of 1994, all Japanese ministries and agencies are required to co-operate in order to achieve the sustainable development goals of the Basic Environment Law. In concrete terms, each ministry and agency must contribute financially to the Plan (Hanaoka, 1996).

A noteworthy trend at the national level in the field of sustainable development is a kind of competitive situation in which a ministry or agency plays an important role in setting and implementing policy. Previously the Environment Agency gave advice on environmental protection to other ministries and agencies that handled affairs in the development field and in industry, such as the Ministry of Construction, the Ministry of International Trade and Industry (MITI) and the Ministry of Agriculture, Forestry and Fisheries. Although this scenario still applies to the current relationship among those ministries, there are some changes in the handling of specific environmental problems.

The Environment Agency, which became the Ministry of the Environment, is asked to strengthen its function as follows:

- To strengthen functions and structure on international efforts in environmental administration, for example, global warming issues, etc.

193

- To promote environmental administration comprehensively by co-ordinating and strengthening co-operation with related administrative organisations, etc.
- Unification of waste/recycling administration to the Ministry of the Environment, etc.

The Ministry of the Environment works together with other ministries to determine standards, guidelines, policies, plans and regulations, etc.

Ministry of International Trade and Industry

The Ministry of International Trade and Industry (MITI) has been very active in environment-related policy setting and implementation. Industry-related environmental policies such as recycling and the reasonable use of energy are basically under the responsibility of MITI.

Thus, when the COP3 (Third Conference on Environmental Protection) of the UNFCCC in Kyoto ended successfully and the amendments to laws and regulations dealing with global warming were considered, there was an apparent conflict between the MITI, which favours a more energy-related approach, and the Environment Agency, which seeks more comprehensive measures.

The afore-mentioned Voluntary Action Programmeme by the Federation of Economic Organisations (FEO or "*keidanren*") to reduce greenhouse gas emissions from the industrial sector is actually the result of negotiations between FEO and MITI, not the Environment Agency.

Ministry of Agriculture, Forestry and Fisheries

Among other issues on the agenda for sustainable development, the newly revised Basic Law on Food, Agriculture and Farming incorporates the idea of sustainable development as one of the key concepts for agriculture. Under this new policy, many mayors are granted considerable subsidies to support a more sustainable agriculture.

Forestry Agency

Historically, the Forestry Agency, which has been committed to cutting trees for commercial profit, and the Environment Agency, which has historically advocated environmental protection, would often find themselves on opposite sides of a philosophical fence, as most areas of public land within the Natural Parks System (national parks, quasi-national parks and prefectural natural parks) and other nature reserves (mainly under the authority of Environment Agency) are located in national forests.

However, the Forestry Agency has changed its stance recently and is becoming very active and positive in the environmental movement. Sustainable forest management is the key concept for the new policy. Under the policy, consideration is being given to direct subsidies to support environmentally sound management of privately owned forests. National forest management has also been changing from logging to conservation. For example, the Forest Ecosystem Protection Area system was introduced recently by the Forestry Agency. It is probably the most advanced nature conservation system in the national assessment scheme, with the strong authority of the agency based on ownership of national forests. The Forestry Agency is also very active in encouraging good relations between forestry and citizens' NGOs.

Ministry of Construction

The Ministry of Construction (reorganised to Ministry of Land, Infrastructure and Transport) was once perceived as having a major destructive impact on nature through its activities such as building dams and reservoirs, road construction, river improvement and shore protection works, and so on.

However, new policies stipulating concern for the ecosystem and some activities of the Ministry are very environment friendly. For example, following the recent amendment to the Rivers Act, which incorporates some environmental concerns, the Ministry of Construction, which administers major rivers, has been handling related conservation issues. The Ministry is currently carrying out river environment recovery works.

Ministry of Transport

Transport, especially car transport, is a major concern for environmental conservation and sustainable development. The Ministry of Transport has been active in this field, by setting energy-efficiency and emission standards. The first "green tax" at national level (although tax reduction proceeds and heavy taxation on "dirty" cars do not yet exist) has been introduced for a car taxation system, in which the Ministry of Transport has had a strong influence.

This competition among ministries and agencies may be considered as only another example of their traditional struggle for authority. But the attention to environmental problems can have positive effects on overall environmental governance. It is seen as a step towards more positive policy integration in environmental administration.

The competition itself may have an effect on improving the quality and standards of environmental administration. However, there is a fear that in such a situation the administration of environmental affairs could become so decentralised and powerless as to render it completely ineffective. In either case, it is worth noting that environmental issues and sustainable development concerns have become so important that ministries and agencies compete for their management.

195|

The impact of the decentralisation of decision making

The decentralisation of governmental powers, which is taking place now, could also have considerable influence on the setting and implementation of a sustainable development policy. More power at the local government level will help to improve the formulation of sustainable development policies, according to the specific circumstances of each area. On the other hand, some sustainable development issues, such as bio-diversity conservation, require adequate policies and actions at the national level. In order to efficiently promote sustainable development, the allocation of power and authority must be prudent.

One of the most difficult problems is probably the financing system. Greater authority and sufficient funding are needed in support of local government initiatives. Up to now, however, decentralisation in Japan has meant only the transfer of some authority, but no financing or revenue-raising functions.

Faced with the need to prepare their own financing mechanisms, many local governments are studying the possibility of introducing new taxes within the present legal framework. The Tokyo Metropolitan Area is the best example. It has already introduced a new tax system for commercial banks operating within Tokyo, and has made preparations for other taxes. Other local governments are very interested in this trend and are seeking to introduce their own taxes. Many of these taxes are related to the environment, such as the Local Environment Tax, which is under consideration in many areas, and the Recreational Fishing Tax, which is to be introduced soon by local governments near Mt. Fujiyama.

The impact of new environmental management systems

The environmental management system "ISO14001" (or the "ISO 14000 series") of the International Organisation for Standardisation (ISO) has had a great influence on environmental projects undertaken by the private sector. The system is used by individual companies to evaluate the negative environmental impacts of their corporate activities, in an effort to reduce such impacts. Acquiring the ISO 14001 certification is optional, but many leading Japanese companies are hurrying to get one, since in the past they were late in acquiring the ISO 9000 Quality Management System and were very adversely affected in the international market.

By December 2000, there were 21 449 ISO 14001 certifications in more than 50 countries and regions. Japan held 5 222, ahead of Germany (2 400) and the United Kingdom (1 400). Japan had acquired only 1 530 certificates by December 1998; the number has increased more than threefold within two years, and various kinds of industries are eager to acquire this certification. Non-business sectors such as public services, government offices – both central and local – and universities are also seeking to be certified. By 31 January 2001, for example, 144 local governments and authorities had received ISO 14001 certificates. Farmers have joined this movement very recently, and eight agricultural activities and one forestry activity are now certified to ISO 14001.

The reason for the popularity of ISO 14001 in Japan is that a company with ISO 14001 has a better corporate image; without it, a company can be ostracised in business transactions. The number of companies acquiring ISO 14001 is rapidly increasing because large companies that already have ISO 14001 are also asking their business partners to acquire it.

Such initiatives, where companies take voluntary action against environmental problems, are desirable. However, the current environmental management system by ISO does not require companies to disclose the environmental impact of their corporate activities. Since the disclosure of companies' environmental performance is not mandatory, it is difficult to compare the environmental impact caused by their activities with their efforts to improve environmental performance. In this respect, the acquisition of ISO 14001 by companies may simply be a way of improving their corporate image, although some companies are going to try to share the result of their environmental performance with the public by means of an environmental report. In March 2001 a survey by the Ministry of the Environment found that about 430 companies prepared environmental reports, and the number of companies preparing environmental reports is increasing every year. They are also seeking to be rated on the basis of their environmental efforts.

Accountability and evaluation of sustainable development policies and activities

How to evaluate policies and activities for sustainable development is also an important matter, as is accountability for such policies and activities in order to effectively promote sustainable development. Generally speaking, Japan's political and administrative systems have been unable to carry out policy evaluation, although, faced by citizens' increasing concerns and NGO activities, there is a growing demand for improved accountability.

Japan plans to continue to develop indicators of sustainable development. These indicators take into account environmental factors and are used to help co-ordinate sustainable development across different sectors and agencies. Japan has a System of National Accounts (SNA) that is based upon the SNA Handbook on Integrated Environmental and Economic Accounting of the United Nations. This system of national accounts integrates economic and environmental costs and benefits.[24]

There is no established system for the evaluation of government policies and activities. The introduction of a new Administrative Policy and Action Evaluation Act is under discussion in the Diet. With the radical transformation of ministries and agencies in national government, such an act is expected to improve the efficiency of government policy setting, implementation and accountability.

197|

The government of Hokkaido has developed an interesting activity in the field of policy evaluation. The idea is to review policies and decisions made several decades ago in the light of present-day needs. Following this "Assessment over time", some projects have been cancelled (*e.g.* construction of dams, reservoirs and roads.

Environmental planning

Proper planning in environmental management is essential to the promotion of any comprehensive environmental policy. Some local governments have implemented area plans focusing on environmental conservation. In 1993, when the Basic Environment Act was enacted, it became mandatory for the national government to establish its basic environment plan. A national Basic Environment Plan was therefore developed in 1994. Local governments are currently working on environment plans for their respective areas. The four fundamental principles of the national Basic Environment Plan are:

- Conserving the natural ecocycles and promoting recycling in society.
- The need for the co-existence of different constituencies.
- Full participation by all sectors and citizens; and
- Promoting a global environmental policy.

The Basic Environment Plan is currently in the process of performance evaluation and revision for the 2nd Plan.

Environmental Impact Assessment

The implementation of Environmental Impact Assessment (EIA) at the national level had been delayed since 1983, when the proposed Environmental Impact Assessment bill was scrapped. Assessment at the national level was therefore guided by an agreement made by the Cabinet on some large-scale projects (the Cabinet Assessment). However, many local governments had already implemented their own assessment systems by establishing ordinances or guidelines. In this respect, Environmental Impact Assessment as a preventive measure had already taken root in the country.

The Environmental Impact Assessment Act was passed in 1997, and the basic concepts and procedures of EIA were finally standardised at the national level. Some important measures, such as alternative plans that lacked Cabinet Assessment, were announced, examined and incorporated into the Act. Implementation of EIA based on this new act began in 1999.

One of the important problems at present is how to ensure consistency between EIA procedures at the local level and the newly introduced national EIA procedure. The purpose is to maintain local EIA systems, some of which are more advanced than the national one, while ensuring that they are in line with the new national EIA scheme.

Public involvement

The provision of adequate information and involving the public in policy formulation are important for raising awareness in society and thus more widely promoting sustainable development. Public involvement in policy planning and implementation is essential for good environmental governance, and access to information should be the basis for such participation. Recent policies and measures addressing environmental problems reflect these ideas.

Environmental hazards and public access to information

Information is critical for managing many risks that exist in today's world. It is necessary to provide reliable information on the environment or sustainable development and to provide extensive public access to it, although Japan has not always been able to achieve this.

Recently, however, many changes are apparent in the government agenda. The EIA is one of the tools for providing information to the public. The Pollutant Release and Transfer Register (PRTR) system was introduced by the "Law concerning Reporting, etc. of Releases to the Environment of Specific Chemical Substances and Promoting Improvements in their Management" (so-called PRTR law). A public comment system has also been introduced, which requires ministries and agencies to consult citizens before policy setting.

The Law concerning Access to Information Held by Administrative Organs was passed in 1999. This law guarantees public access to most information collected and written by the government. This law went into effect in April 2001. This freedom of access to government information helps ensure government accountability and transparency in the realm of sustainable development. The Global Environment Information Centre was established in 1996 by the Environment Agency and the United Nations University. It provides a forum through which NGOs and private organisations can share experiences and information.[25]

The public comment system is a system for collecting public opinions before government policy setting, decision making and implementation. It was decided by the Cabinet in March 1999, in connection with the government policy for deregulation, and was introduced in ministries and agencies.

Information is obtained through Internet homepages and by the distribution of newspapers and magazines, news releases, government newsletters, etc. to each administrative office concerned. Opinions can be sent by mail, facsimile and e-mail. The consultation lasts about a month. Ministries and agencies make their

Box 12.   Japan Council for Sustainable Development –
Dialogue for Development

In order to evaluate Japan's progress in sustainable development and to maintain dialogue, the Japan Council for Sustainable Development (JCSD) was established in 1996. The primary goal of the JCSD is simply to establish and maintain communication between the diverse parties who are involved and have a stake in sustainable development. In 1997 the Council met to evaluate Japan's sustainable development efforts of the previous five years, the first five years after the Rio Conference of 1992.

At the time the Council wrote its *Japan Report for Rio+5 Process*, it was composed of officials and leaders from:

The Government

The Research and Development Bureau, Science and Technology Agency
The Ministry of the Environment
The Ministry of Foreign Affairs
The Ministry of Education
The Ministry of Health and Welfare
The Ministry of Agriculture, Forestry and Fisheries
The Ministry of International Trade and Industry
The Ministry of Construction

Industries and Non-Governmental Organisations

Kobe Steel, Ltd.   Nissan Motor Co., Ltd.
T.O. Ogasawara Co. Ltd.   Tokyo Electric Power, Inc.
Suntory Ltd.   ITOCHU Corp.
Yasuda Fire and Marine Insurance Co. Ltd.

KEIDANREN (Japan Federation of Economic Organisations)
Central Union of Agricultural Co-operation   People's Forum 2001
Japan NGO Centre for International Co-operation
Japan bar Association Union   Environmental Journalists Association of Japan
Japanese Trade Union Confederation   Consumers Co-operative Union

A SEED JAPAN   World Wildlife Foundation – Japan
Environmental Information Promotion Centre
University of Tokyo, Graduate School of Art and Sciences
City of Kita-Kyushu

In order to structure and limit their dialogue, members of the Council limited the report to two topics – Critical Issues and Priorities, and Successful Practices. Within this structure, members of the JCSD debated Japan's sustainable development.

Due to diversity and, at times, disagreement within the Council, the Council was unable to reach consensus on many issues. The Council, therefore, wrote a collaborative report that included the primary opinions of all. The Council sees the dialogue behind the report and the necessary co-operation in producing the report as an essential first step in sustainable development – establishing dialogue between all concerned.

Source: Japan Report for Rio+5 Process.
www.ecouncil.ac.cr/rio/national/re ports/asia/japan.htm

decisions after due consideration of the opinions collected, and they are obliged to make their response to the opinions more transparent.

This public consultation system can be evaluated positively from the point of view of improving the transparency of government decision making. With the increase in the number of Internet users, the system is becoming more popular, although there may not always be a large number of citizens' responses.

Involvement of women

Chapter 24 of the National Agenda 21 Action Plan emphasises the need for women to be involved in sustainable development. The Plan promotes women's involvement in creating training programmemes and making plans for environmental conservation; it also calls for women to be appointed as members in public meetings arranged by the government, and it directs the Japanese government to help promote the participation of women in sustainable development internationally (Hanaoka, 1996).

D. Learning from the Japanese experience

In the past, the traditional attitude to pollution control in Japan was the "command and control system", based on a set of legislation and regulation providing administrative guidance. This system is still effective and necessary in many policy fields. However, other types of policy and measures are sought to complement the weak points of this traditional system.

From specific "command and control" to a wider framework for sustainable development

Traditional "command and control" with financial subsidies

The core measures taken against environmental pollution problems such as air and water pollution were regulations on emissions and financial support in the form of subsidies or tax reduction to companies committed to reducing pollution.

As an anti-air pollution measure, a set of Emission Standards for individual pollutants was set (density regulations) along with the Air Quality Standard, a standard for ideal air quality. Regular inspections were conducted and compliance with the regulations was enforced according to this emission standard. In industrial areas where there were many facilities causing pollution, special standards were determined according to the total amount of emissions in the area, since it would be nearly impossible to achieve the environmental air quality standard in such areas even if each facility complied with normal regulations. In each of these areas, the pollution reduction target was determined by the total amount of pollution in the

201

area, and Total Amount Regulations, different emission standards stricter than those used in other areas, were then enforced.

While establishing such regulations, most laws, such as the Basic Pollution Policy Act, the Air Pollution Control Law and the Water Pollution Control Law, had financial support provisions such as subsidies and tax incentives to companies for pollution reduction so that they could readily comply with the regulations. This type of financial support measure has been incorporated into the Basic Environment Law.

Wider economic incentives

Preparing subsidies and/or tax reduction for industries has been very popular already in pollution control policies. Although providing companies with financial assistance for pollution reduction may be considered a sound industrial policy, it may not ring so clear when it is tied to the Polluter Pays Principle. Some say that, instead of giving financial aid to companies, they should be charged special environmental taxes as long as they are polluting the environment. The Japanese government has not yet seen fit to implement such measures. Recently, the possibility of introducing taxes and charges, such as a carbon tax, was widely discussed.

Developing mechanisms to implement the Basic Environment Plan

Citizens, businesses and governments in Japan are realising the need for a broader framework for sustainable development. The concept of sustainable development and the basic policy for sustainable development have already been made known by the 1993 Basic Environment Act and the 1994 Basic Environment Plan. As mentioned in the section on Information and Public Involvement – Environmental Planning, the Plan has set four fundamental principles: conserving the natural ecocycles and promoting recycling in society; the need for the co-existence of different constituencies; full participation by all sectors and citizens; and promoting a global environment policy.

The Basic Environment Plan is one of the important national plans based on the Basic Environment Act, which is itself one of the most important basic acts after the Constitution. Considering the status of the Basic Environment Plan, it should be respected in policy setting, decision making and implementation, although integrating the new concepts and systems in the Plan into traditional economic and social activities is not so easy. However, some recent actions such as the climate change policy and the recycling scheme, and the enactment of a series of related laws, are examples of the effort made to achieve this?

Probably one of the most important and realistic issues on Japan's current agenda is the development of mechanisms to integrate the concept and policies of the Basic Environment Plan into many activities in society. In this respect, it is worth noting that the Basic Environment Plan is being harmonised with other policy setting and decision-making systems. In 1999, for example, a clause was introduced into the Forestry Act, which is under the authority of the Forestry Agency, stating that "the National Forest Plan should be harmonised with the Basic Environment Plan". Such efforts are expected to be effective for implementing the concept and policy of the Basic Environment Plan.

Voluntary activities by industries with environmental management systems such as ISO14001, coupled with the growing "green consumer" citizens' movement, are an important step towards the integration of economic activities and global environmental conservation through expanding international trade. However, the real effect of the ISO environmental management system is not yet clear.

ISO 14001 *as a tool for sustainable development*

The influence of ISO 14001 cannot be ignored in examining Japan's new movement in environmental governance for sustainable development. Acquiring the certification of ISO 14001 for "Environmental Management" is almost considered a "business licence". The eco-business boom is another important trend. "Environmental ranking" has appeared in the business world and "green funds" are drawing considerable money from investors. Some industries are enthusiastically reporting their environmental performance to consumers and their business partners.

Besides such a change in attitude, there has been another remarkable trend in the private sector. Companies (especially large ones) are beginning to realise that the international environmental movement can be a new business opportunity. Pollution control and energy conservation are already important areas of new business (*e.g.* automobiles and appliances, new energy-generation systems such as solar or wind power, recycling businesses and the manufacture of new types of vehicles in view of future demands for improved fuel efficiency. Even nature conservation is sought after as a possible business opportunity, through recreation and tourism.

However, as already mentioned, the ISO 14001 environmental management system does not necessarily provide the public with sufficient information on companies' activities. Systems are required which encourage a wider disclosure of companies' environmental performance.[26]

Citizens as "green consumers"

Consumers' awareness of environmental conservation is also an important factor in making the market "green", and gives industries a signal and an incentive to be environmentally concerned. Consumer action is an ongoing pressure, and therefore the market itself becomes more environmentally concerned. As the market becomes "green", companies are forced to check the environmental performance of

203|

their products and activities. This means that citizens, as "green consumers", can take very strong initiatives in the environmental movement, both at the national and international levels.

Slowly but surely, Japanese citizens are becoming environmentally concerned in their daily lives. When they select goods and services, they think about their environmental impact. "Green consumer" citizens are expected to play a very important role in promoting environmental conservation, in both local and international aspects. Many companies in Japan are already aware of such a trend. Active environmental communications strategies via television, radio, newspapers and other media, are their response to this green consumer movement.

However, problems do exist. When individual citizens try to take concrete action to contribute to solving environmental problems in their everyday lives, information is limited and few options are available to them. Even if they want to buy products that have a less harmful impact on the environment, they do not have access to information on the impact of every product. It is hard to find products without waste, such as heavy packaging. Governments must provide more information, and industries and new systems must be created which support environmentally sound consumer decisions. The Law concerning the Promotion of Procurement of Eco-Friendly Goods and Services by the State and other Entities was published in May 2000. The Government has been taking leadership to encourage a shift in demand toward eco-friendly goods by greening its procurement based on the law. The law also establishes the necessary provision to encourage appropriate information providing on eco-friendly goods.

Notes

1. The views expressed in this paper are those of the author, and do not necessarily reflect those of the OECD, or of its Public Management Service.

2. See the Japan Report for Rio+5 Process on the Internet site of the Japan Council for Sustainable Development: *www.ecouncil.ac.cr/rio/national/reports/asia/japan.htm*

3. See *Forests.org* news release and comments: *http://forests.org/recent/2001/jaeminti.htm*

4. See the Japan Report for Rio+5 Process: *www.ecouncil.ac.cr/rio/national/reports/asia/japan.htm*

5. Detailed information on the legal framework in the energy sector is provided in the United Nations' report on Natural Resource Aspects of Sustainable Development in Japan: *http://www.un.org/esa/agenda21/natlinfo/countr/japan/natur.htm*

6. See the Japan Report for Rio+5 Process: *www.ecouncil.ac.cr/rio/national/reports/asia/japan.htm*

7. *Ibid.*

8. *Ibid.*

9. Further information can be accessed through the Internet site of the Ministry of Agriculture, Forestry and Fisheries at *www.maff.go.jp/e_guide/e_guide.html*

10. Further information on specific developments are provided in The United Nations' Report on Natural Resource Aspects of Sustainable Development in Japan at *www.un.org/esa/agenda21/natlinfo/countr/japan/natur.htm*

11. Further information about fisheries is also provided in United Nations' Report on Natural Resource Aspects of Sustainable Development in Japan at *www.un.org/esa/agenda21/natlinfo/countr/japan/natur.htm*

12. See National Level Co-ordination Structure of Agenda 21 Actions at *www.un.org/esa/earthsummit/japan.htm*

13. See United Nations' report on Natural Resource Aspects of Sustainable Development in Japan at *www.un.org/esa/agenda21/natlinfo/countr/japan/inst.htm*

14. *Ibid.*

15. See Japan Report for Rio+5 Process at *www.ecouncil.ac.cr/rio/national/reports/asia/japan.htm*

16. See Cornell University Internet pages on Work and Environment Initiative: *www.cfe.cornell.edu/wei/japan.htm*

17. See United Nations' report on Natural Resource Aspects of Sustainable Development in Japan at *www.un.org/esa/agenda21/natlinfo/countr/japan/inst.htm*

18. See Overseas Environmental Measures of Japanese Companies: *www.env.go.jp/earth/oemjc/index.html*

19. See Japan Report for Rio+5 Process at *www.ecouncil.ac.cr/rio/national/reports/asia/japan.htm*

205

20. See Cornell University Internet pages on Work and Environment Initiative: *www.cfe.cornell.edu/wei/japan.htm*

21. See United Nations' report on Natural Resource Aspects of Sustainable Development in Japan: *www.un.org/esa/agenda21/natlinfo/countr/japan/inst.htm*

22. See Cornell University Internet pages on Work and Environment Initiative: *www.cfe.cornell.edu/wei/japan.htm*

23. See Information provided on Canon Internet site at *www.canon.com/environment/report/sub2000/33.htm*

24. See United Nations' report on Natural Resource Aspects of Sustainable Development in Japan: *www.un.org/esa/agenda21/natlinfo/countr/japan/inst.htm*

25. *Ibid.*

26. For encouraging voluntary environmental conservation activities in corporations, the Ministry of the Environment published "Environmental Reporting Guidelines" in February 2001 (URL:*www.env.go.jp/en/eco/erg2000.pdf*), "Environmental Performance Indicators" in February 2001 (URL: *www.env.go.jp/en/eco/epi2000.pdf*), and "Environmental Accounting Guidelines" in May 2000 (URL:*www.env.go.jp/policy/kaikei/report00e.pdf*).

Annex I

Selected Private Sector Initiatives

Toyota Automobile Manufacturer

In January 1992, Toyota established its own global environmental policy, the Toyota Global Environment Charter, and in February 1993 set up the Toyota Environmental Action Plan (revised in April 1996), based on the charter. The Charter was revised in April 2000 to promote more integration of activities in view of an environmentally friendly society. The 3rd Toyota Environmental Action Plan for 2001-2005 was also decided upon. The key policies of the Charter and Action Plan are the following:

Basic Principles

- To contribute to a wealthy society in the 21st Century.
- To develop environmental technology.
- To promote voluntary activity.
- To co-operate with other parts of society.

Guidelines

- Always take the environment into consideration.
- Company employees contribute to making good environment.
- Work of the company is part of overall society objectives.
- Promote better understanding of the issues.

Honda Automobile Manufacturer

Honda is trying to reduce the burden on the environment in each step of the lifecycle of goods, *i.e.* in research and development, purchasing, manufacture, distribution, sales and service and waste disposal. Under this principle, the following targets have been set:

- To improve energy efficiency and to "green" gas emissions.
- To increase the recyclable percentage of new cars.
- To reduce the use of lead in new cars.
- To reduce energy use and waste in the production process.

Nissan Automobile Manufacturer

Nissan's basic principle for environmental policy is "Symbiosis of the Human Being, Automobile and Nature". Under this principle, the following three targets have been set:

- To develop environmentally low-burden goods.
- To adapt to an environment-respecting society.
- To promote environmental concerns in corporate activities.

Nissan's policy is to manufacture environmentally friendly cars and to achieve a high level of "Environmental Friendliness" and "Joy for Run". Under this policy, the following targets have been set:

- To develop a low-emission vehicle.
- To create a lightweight structure.
- To improve energy efficiency.

Making recyclable cars is also Nissan's policy. The aim is to achieve 90 per cent recyclability (75 per cent at present). Actions for achieving this target are:

- Use of recycled materials.
- Change to easy-to-recycle materials.

Finally, in order to promote an environmentally friendly corporation, Nissan's present target is to acquire ISO 14001 certification for all factories in Japan within the next two years. To achieve this target, Nissan has set the following requirements:

- Set up a Nissan environmental management system.
- Improve environmental conservation in the manufacturing process.
- Employees should also take positive environmental action in the office.

Sony (Electrical Appliances Manufacturer)

Sony has the following vision for corporate environmental activity:

- Realising that the conservation of the global environment is the most important issue for humanity in the 21st century.
- Sony contributes positively to the conservation of the global environment and to the achievement of sustainable development through continuing technological improvement and creative business development.
- Sony understands the importance of the global environment for every form of life, and sustainable economic development is the first priority for the Sony Group. Sony also promotes the careful use of the earth's limited resources, so that future generations can enjoy healthy, wealthy, equitable and happy lives.
- Sony provides its customers with goods of high quality and high performance, at the same time continuously reducing the environmental burden through the efficient use of energy and resources. Sony tries to find new ways of harmonising relations between man and nature by generating high economic value from a small amount of resources.
- All members of the Sony Group continue to study complex and expanding environmental problems and, through good co-operation with its stakeholders, will make an effort to greatly improve the environment for Japanese society.

Nestle Japan (food manufacturer)

Nestle Japan has its own environmental policy, organisation and activities. The Nestle Environmental Management System (NEMS) consists of environmental activities as well as management activities.

Environmental activity is based on "3R" concept (Re-use, Reduce and Recycle). Management activities are based on the concept "Plan-Do-Check-Act", which has been introduced for BECA (Business Excellence and Common Application) and *Kaizen* ("improving") activities. NEMS aims to systematically consolidate environmental awareness.

3R activities are implemented in Nestle factories. For example, "returnable boxes to buy caps' is "Re-use", energy saving and waste reduction is "Reduce", and energy recovery using coffee grounds is "Recycle".

Annex II

Sustainable Development for Fisheries and other Marine Activities

The management of sustainable fisheries and other coastal and marine activities involves a myriad of Japanese agencies, each with unique responsibilities.

The overall responsibility for managing the sustainable development of the coastal zone is the duty of:

The Environment Agency (now Ministry of the Environment)

• The Science and Technology Agency.

• The National Land Agency.

• The Ministry of Agriculture, Forestry and Fisheries.

• The Ministry of Transport; and

• The Ministry of Construction.

For marine environmental protection, coastal sewage is managed by:

• The Ministry of the Environment.

• Ministry of Health and Welfare.

• Ministry of Agriculture, Forestry, and Fisheries; and

• Ministry of Construction.

For marine environmental protection, agricultural waste and industrial effluents are the responsibility of:

• The Ministry of the Environment.

• The Ministry of Health and Welfare.

• The Ministry of Agriculture, Forestry, and Fisheries.

• The Ministry of International Trade and Industry.

• The Ministry of Construction.

For marine environmental protection, discharges of ballast from ships are the responsibility of:

• The Environment Agency.

• The Ministry of Agriculture, Forestry and Fisheries.

• The Ministry of Transport.

For marine environmental protection, oil spills are managed by:

• The Environment Agency.

• The Science and Technology Agency.

- The Ministry of Agriculture, Forestry, and Fisheries.
- The Ministry of International Trade and Industry.
- The Ministry of Transport.
- The Maritime Safety Agency.
- The Ministry of Construction.

For sustainable use and conservation of marine living resources, the following are responsible for decision-making:

- The Environment Agency.
- The Ministry of Foreign Affairs.
- The Ministry of Agriculture, Forestry and Fisheries.
- The Ministry of Construction.

Overall co-ordination of all these sustainable development responsibilities is provided by the Council of Ministers for Global Environment Conservation and the Conference on Environmental Pollution Control. Both of these groups are chaired by the Prime Minister and have been established specifically to help the government make co-ordinated decisions regarding sustainable development.

This sector (oceans and seas) is financed by the national budget, fiscal investment and loans from various government-affiliated financial institutions.

Source: The United Nations' report on "Natural Resource Aspects of Sustainable Development in Japan".

Annex III

Laws for Marine Protection in Japan

For the sustainable development of coastal zones, Japan has enacted numerous laws:

- The Basic Environment Law (1993).
- The Law Concerning Special Measures for Conservation of the Environment of the Seto Inland Sea (1983).
- The Natural Parks Law (1957).
- The Nature Conservation Law (1972).
- The Seacoast Law (1956).
- The Environmental Quality Standards related to the conservation of the living environment on coastal waters (1971) under the provisions of the Basic Environment Law; and
- The Tentative Guideline (1990) under the provisions of the 4th Comprehensive National Development Plan (1987).

For marine environmental protection, both from land-based activities and from sea-based activities:

- The Basic Environment Law (1993).
- The Law Relating to the Prevention of Marine Pollution and Maritime Disaster (1970).[1]
- The Water Pollution Control Law (1970).
- The Environmental Impact Assessment Law (1997).
- The Law Concerning the Examination and Regulation of Manufacture, etc. of Chemical Substances (1968).
- The Agricultural Chemicals Regulation Law (1948).
- The Sewerage Law (1958).
- The "Johkasou" Law (1983).
- The Waste Management and Public Cleansing Law (1970).
- The Nature Conservation Law (1972).
- The Natural Parks Law (1957).
- The Law for the Conservation of Endangered Species of Wild Fauna and Flora (1992).
- The River Law (1964).
- The Law Concerning Special Measures for Conservation of the Environment of the Seto Inland Sea (1983).
- The Fishery Resources Protection Law (1951); and

- The Mine Safety Law (1949).
- The International Convention for the Prevention of Pollution from Ships, 1973 as modified by the Protocol of 1978 relating thereto.
- The Convention on the Prevention of Marine Pollution by Dumping of Wastes and Other Matter; and
- The United Nations Convention on the Law of the Sea.

For sustainable use and conservation of marine living resources the following laws have been passed:

- The Nature Conservation Law (1972).
- The Natural Parks Law (1957).
- The Wildlife Protection and Hunting Law (1918).
- The Law for the Conservation of Endangered Species of Wild Fauna and Flora (1992).
- The Fisheries Law (1949).
- The Fishery Resources Protection Law (1951).
- The Law concerning Conservation and Management of Marine Living Resources (1996).
- The Law concerning the Exercise of Sovereign Rights concerning Fisheries in the Exclusive Economic Zone (1996).[2]
- The Law for Regulation of Fishing Operations by Foreign National (1967).[2]
- The Coastal Fisheries Grounds Enhancement and Development Programme Law.
- The Marine Fisheries Development Promotion Law (1971). And
- The Tentative guidelines for development of prefectural comprehensive seashore-utilisation plan (1990).

Environmental standards for coastal waters are established by the government. Various measures including regulations have been taken to achieve these standards. With respect to marine living resources, many local fishermen's organisations have also adopted their own sustainable-fishery guidelines to accompany official government regulations.

International sustainable fisheries and marine management agreements to which Japan is a party are:

- Protocol of 1978 Relating to the International Convention for the Prevention of Pollution from Ships, 1973.
- International Convention Relating to Intervention on the High Seas in Cases of Oil Pollution Casualties.
- Protocol of 1992 to Amend the International Convention on Civil Liability for Oil Pollution Damage, 1969.
- Protocol of 1992 to Amend the International Convention on the Establishment of an International Fund for Compensation for Oil Pollution Damage, 1971.
- Convention on Limitation of Liability for Maritime Claims, 1976.
- Convention on the Prevention of Marine Pollution by Dumping of Wastes and Other Matter.
- Convention on International Trade in Endangered Species of Wild Fauna and Flora.
- United Nations Convention on the Law of the Sea.
- Convention on Wetlands of International Importance Especially as Waterfowl Habitat.

213|

- Protocol to Amend the Convention on Wetlands of International Importance Especially as Waterfowl Habitat.
- Convention for the Protection of the World Cultural and Natural Heritage.
- International Convention on Oil Pollution Preparedness, Response and Co-operation, 1990.
- Convention on Biological Diversity.
- International Convention for the Regulation of Whaling.
- International Convention for the Conservation of Atlantic Tunas.
- Convention for the Conservation of Southern Bluefin Tuna.
- Convention on the Conservation of Antarctic Marine Living Resources.
- Convention for the Conservation of Antarctic Seals.
- Convention on Future Multilateral co-operation in the Northwest Atlantic Fisheries.
- Convention between the United States of America and the Republic of Costa Rica for the Establishment of an Inter-American Tropical Tuna Commission.
- Convention on the Conservation and Management of Pollock Resources in the Central Bering Sea.
- Agreement for the Establishment of the Indian Ocean Tuna Commission. And
- Code of Conduct for Responsible Fisheries.

In addition to international agreements, Japan is also a party to numerous bi and multilateral agreements regarding sustainable fisheries and marine management. Some private fishery agreements have also been concluded between the Japanese fishermen's organisations and the governments of other countries.

Notes

1. One of the purposes of this law is to implement the following international conventions.

2. The measures based on these laws aim to ensure the obligations stipulated by the UNCLOS, to avoid deterioration of marine living resources and to avoid detrimental effects on Japan's maritime fishermen under the circumstances that depreciation of marine living resources is widely observed in Japan's coastal fishing areas.

Source: The United Nations' report on "Natural Resource Aspects of Sustainable Development in Japan"
based on Japan's submission to the 5th and 7th Sessions of the Commission on Sustainable Development. Last update: November 1998.

Annex IV

List of Websites

The 1993 *Basic Environment Act* and the 1994 *Basic Environment Plan* are available at:
www.eic.or.jp/eanet/en/index.html

"Sustainable Development: Information Japan", based on the information submitted by the Government of Japan to the 5th Session of the Commission on Sustainable Development, April 1997, is available on the United Nations Internet home page on sustainable development at: *www.un.org/esa/agenda21/natlinfo/countr/japan/index.htm*

Information on the Central Government Reform can be obtained at:
www.mofa.go.jp/about/hq/central_gov/index.html

The United Nations' Report on Natural Resource Aspects of Sustainable Development in Japan:
www.un.org/esa/agenda21/natlinfo/co untr/japan/natur.htm

The Japan Report for the Rio+5 Process:
www.ecouncil.ac.cr/rio/national/rep orts/asia/japan.htm

Ministry of Agriculture, Forestry and Fisheries home page (in English):
www.maff.go.jp/eindex.html

Cabinet Office home page (in English):
www.cao.go.jp/index-e.html

Cornell Work and Environment Initiative
www.cfe.cornell.edu/wei/

Ministry of Economy, Trade and Industry home page (in English):
www.meti.go.jp/english/index.html

Ministry of the Environment home page (in English):
www.env.go.jp/en/index.html

Ministry of Health, Labour and Welfare home page (in English):
www.mhlw.go.jp/english/index.html

Ministry of Land, Infrastructure and Transport home page (in English)
www.mlit.go.jp/english/index.html

Global Environment Information Centre:
www.geic.or.jp

EIC Environmental Information and Communication Network:
www.eic.or.jp/newlist/total71.html

Overseas Environmental Measures of Japanese Companies:
www.env.go.jp/earth/oemjc/index.html

Canon:
www.canon.com/environment/report/su b2000/33.htm

215

Bibliography

ABE, T. and T. Awaji (ed.),

"*Environmental Law* (2nd *edition*)", Yuhikaku Publisher, 1998.

BROADBEAT, J.,

"*Environmental Politics in Japan*", Cambridge University Press, 1998.

GRESSER, J., K. Fujikura and A. Morishima,

"*Environmental Law in Japan*", MIT Press, 1981.

HARADA, N.,

"*Environmental Law*", Ko-bundo Publisher, 1981.

HANAOKA, T 1996.,

"ILO National Review on Environment and World of Work", Internet site of Cornell Work and Environment Initiative, 1996.

HARASHIMA, Y.,

"Effects of Economic Growth on Environmental Policies in Northeast Asia", Environment, Vol.42, No.6, pp. 28-40, 2000

IGES Environmental Governance Project Report,

"*Business and Environmental Governance*", IGES, 1999.

IMURA, H. in Martin Jänicke and Helmut Weidner,

"*National Environmental Policies*", Springer, p 73-88, 1997.

Industrial Structure Council Global Environment Committee,

"*The Environmental Vision of Industries*", 1994.

Japan Environment Agency,

"*The White Paper on Environment* 2000", Gyo-sei Publisher, 2000.

KITAMURA, Y.

"Environmental Administration in Local Governments", Ryo-shyo Fukyukai Publisher, 1997.

Japan Forestry Agency,

"*Forestry White Paper* 1997", Japan Forestry Association, 1999.

MATSUMURA, Y.,

"*Environmental Law*", Seibundo Publisher, 1995.

The Pollution-Related Health Damage Compensation and Prevention Association,

"*Japan's Experience in the Battle against Air Pollution – Working towards Sustainable Development*", Tokyo Publisher, 1997.

YAMAMURA, T.

"Law and Strategies for the Conservation of Nature (2nd edition)", Yuhikaku Publisher, 1994.

The Netherlands

By
Frédéric Bouder and Philipp Fink[1]

Purpose

The study focuses on practices for improving institutions and decision-making for sustainable development in the Netherlands. The paper focuses on the selected strategies that have been formulated and implemented, but an overall review of policies and programmes would have been too ambitious and was left outside the scope of this study. Similarly, it focuses primarily on developments within the national level government authorities and, therefore, does not cover the multiplicity of local and private initiatives, apart from selected illustrative examples. This paper was prepared following interviews with a range of officials and representatives from public, private and non-for-profit organisations.

General introduction

The size of the Netherlands is relatively small (41 864 square kilometres). The country lies on the northwestern edge of the European continent on the North Sea coast and is situated on the estuaries of four Western European rivers (the Rhine, the Meuse, the Scheldt and the Eems) and is bordered by Belgium to the south and Germany to the east. As its name indicates, it is a flat country. The highest point is 321 meters high and nearly half of the country is below sea level. The lower Netherlands consists largely of flat "polders" surrounded by dikes, where the water table is regulated artificially. This explains why the history of the Netherlands from the Middle Ages onwards is characterised by an attempt to gain land over sea in order to fight against flood and extend arable land.

This comparatively small area is extremely densely populated. With a population of 15.8 million inhabitants, the Netherlands has over 400 inhabitants per square kilometre. The population is also concentrated. About two-thirds of the Dutch people live in the western part of the country, the so-called *Randstad*, which is a highly urbanised area.

The Dutch economy could be described as a middle-size economy, very open and internationalised which means a strong emphasis on competitiveness. Key economic sectors still include activities with potentially polluting risks such as agriculture (including dairy farming, pig raising and the flower industry), chemical refining, freight transport, electronics, food processing, and some parts of the service industry. The Dutch economy has taken advantage of the country's strategic location. Rotterdam, which is the main outlet of continental Europe, has become one of the largest port in the world. What is more, the Netherlands has one of the largest transport network systems, including one of the biggest airports in Europe and the most up-to-date communications technology systems. In short, the high population density and the geographical position result in major urbanisation, one of the major European industrial areas, intensive agricultural activities and a prominent transport industry.

The above-described patterns explain the particular features of the environment in the Netherlands. The landscape has been deeply transformed and "humanised", more than in most countries, by centuries of economic development. The main characteristic of the Dutch environment is that a significant part of the land, *i.e.* the "polders", is man-made. "Cows in the pastures" are a major feature of the Netherlands. There are only limited natural areas in the Netherlands: 11 per cent (1997) is protected as natural areas. Nature in the Netherlands is largely a "culture-nature landscape" and the link between nature and environment management is more obvious than in other countries.

Despite its relatively small size the Dutch society has traditionally had noticeable social contrasts, the most prominent being the Catholic/ Protestant split which led (until the 1960s) to distinct socio-cultural organisations. There is also a traditional east/ west economic split. However, compared to other societies, the modern Dutch society retains a relatively high degree of social cohesion, mainly due to relatively homogeneous income levels. One key feature is also its sophisticated and efficient welfare system. The Netherlands has an extensive social welfare system, widely regarded as an important national asset. In recent years the system has been reformed to introduce tighter controls, tackle such problems as long-term sickness, and create employment. The underlying goal of the welfare system is to ensure that everyone can play an equal part in society. This is characterised by specific attention to people, who need help to participate: The old and disabled, families on low incomes, young people without qualifications, ethnic and other minorities, the homeless, and addicts. In the context of major societal debates (for example, for the management of urbanisation or the creation of new infrastructures) the relatively high levels of cohesion may well have been a positive factor for reaching consensus among strongly conflicting interests.

Governance patterns

The Netherlands is a constitutional monarchy. The Dutch Democracy is based on a parliamentary system. The Cabinet is nominated by H.M. the Queen, her decision being based on the outcome of elections. Cabinets are usually coalitions of two or three parties. In May 1998, the Christian Democrats, who had been in government for over 70 years (in different coalitions with the Liberals and Social Democrats), gave way to a coalition of Liberals, Social Democrats and Democrats.

The Netherlands is a unitarian state, though with a strong tradition of self-government. It consists of three levels of government (*bestuurlagen*): Central government, provinces and, municipalities. The concept of *bestuurlagen* involves entities directly elected by the citizens. Through this concept a "general purpose government" is implied, and these bodies are considered to be in charge of their own affairs in that they are basically independent in deciding the scope and size of the tasks deemed necessary for performing their role and function (OECD 1997, p. 281). In addition to this there are also complementary governmental structures with functional tasks.

There are at present 12 provinces which vary in size and population (for example, population varies from about 4000 000 inhabitants in Zuid-Holland to about 300 000 inhabitants in the new province of Flevoland created in 1982). The role of provincial government has been presented as a "mediating role between central government and the municipalities" (OECD 1997: p. 286). There are about 500 municipalities,[2] The smallest being Schiermonnikoog (about 1000 inhabitants) and the largest Amsterdam (about 715 000 inhabitants). In addition to provinces and municipalities, the Netherlands has an original system of special purpose governments. The "water boards" (*waterschappen*), which track their existence back to the Middle Ages, are authorities responsible (in co-operation with the provinces) for the maintenance and the quality control of surface water in their respective areas. There are to date about 60 water boards in the Netherlands. The representational structure of the water boards involves a combination of direct and indirect elections and differs according to the task area.

A. Main issues and tensions

The small size and high population density combined with high living standards and a fast growing economy create considerable pressure on the environment, which has raised concerns about the ability of the country to reach sustainable development. These pressures are similar to those of most OECD countries, though amplified. Considering the main physical, economic and social patterns of the Netherlands, the need for concrete action to ensure sustainability has been somewhat more pressing and tangible than in many other countries. Major obvious tensions include, for example, the need to secure the existence and stability of "natural areas", which have been put under pressure by both farming and urbanisation.

219|

The necessary trade-offs resulting from this situation provide a context full of tensions and potential conflicts. They illustrate the constant need for strategic choices in order to integrate all aspects of sustainable development to guarantee both economic and environmental sustainability and to maintain a sound "living environment". The highest standards of environmental protection and nature conservation are crucial, including nature protection and sometimes recreation, preserving and restoring bio-diversity in a modified environment, minimising the negative impact of the economy on the environment, ensuring the most efficient level of transport and housing development, etc. One key challenge is to balance these priorities with the increasing demands of the Dutch society for consumption goods and higher living standards resulting from more individualistic lifestyles. Social demands for more individual cars, and more individual houses must be combined with the sustainable development goals. It has been underlined that "the severe and visually apparent environmental degradation eliminated the need for prolonged discussions about the necessity of immediate action" (De Jong, 1996: p. 10).

International context

The commitment of the Netherlands at European and international level can be briefly characterised as follows:

- A strong commitment in international arenas. For example, the Netherlands has been an active supporter of measures to preserve bio-diversity. The Netherlands is also committed to implementation of several international agreements. For example national plans for environmental policies are developed in the framework of the UNDP policies. Also the mechanisms of OECD country reviews and the United Nations Common Supply Database (UNCSD) country reports promote the integration of environmental policies to help better institutionalise environmental policies in overall government policies.

- Within the European Union, the Netherlands often appears as a "pioneering" country, for example to move to more sustainable fisheries in the North Sea.

- The Netherlands is a country with active economic interactions with its neighbours involving many environmental issues, in particular for the management of the Rhine valley and the North Sea coast. This includes a commitment to sustainable practices, which have led to actions against polluters from Belgium and Germany. Since 1974, local authorities, water companies and Dutch NGOs have brought to trial a number of individual polluters for polluting Dutch waters. These trials, which have taken place in Dutch and foreign courts, greatly increased public awareness of pollution risks and have forced polluters to change their habits. The success of the first court cases against polluters has led to numerous international accords

---

Box 1.   **Climate Policy Co-operation**

The Dutch Government has launched activities in the area of international climate policy co-operation to help cut back greenhouse emissions in foreign countries as part of its international obligations under the Climate Convention and the Kyoto Protocol. These activities are designed to achieve 50 per cent of the target to which the government has committed itself (a 6 per cent reduction of 1990 levels between 2008-2012). The remaining 50 per cent are to be achieved by national measures outlined in the National CO_2 Reduction Plan. The Dutch government has envisaged the implementation of the three Kyoto mechanisms (Joint Implementation Programme, Clean Development Mechanism and Emissions Trading) each focusing on different world regions. The programme is carried out under the joint responsibility of the Ministry of Economic Affairs, the Ministry for Development co-operation and the Ministry for the Environment (which co-ordinates the individual efforts and has the overall responsibility). Under the coalition agreement, 500 000 000 Guilders (€ 226 800 000) of Official Development Assistance have been reserved from the Homogeneous Budget for International co-operation for the implementation of the Clean Development Mechanism in Third World countries during the current election period. The Homogeneous Budget also includes 300 000 000 Guilders (€ 136 130 000) which are reserved for the carrying out of the Joint Implementation Programme in Central and Eastern European Countries.

Source: Ministry for Housing, Spatial Planning and the Environment (VROM) internet site *www.minvrom.nl/minvrom/pagina.html?id=*1572).

---

on pollution control and reductions of toxic effluents in the main rivers flowing on Dutch territory (the Rhine, Meuse and Scheldt). The city of Rotterdam, for example, has negotiated a series of accords between Dutch and foreign companies in Belgium, Switzerland and Germany, which are situated along the Rhine (OCDE 1995: p. 198).

Observers have characterised the Dutch attitude on the international scene as "a mixture of self-interest and a sense of being co-responsible" (Bressers/Plettenburg 1997: p. 123), focusing on what the Netherlands could do to promote environmental policy rather than how international agreements should be translated into domestic legislation.

There are generally three main challenges for successful formulation and implementation of sustainable development strategies, namely: the need to improve policy integration, overcoming knowledge gaps, and ensuring adequate transparency and public participation.

- Policy Integration: The Netherlands has a comparatively long tradition of formulating National Environment Policy Plans (NEPP). The first plan was adopted in 1989 (NEPP I) and currently the government is working on NEPP IV. This long tradition of environmental policy planning has led to the precise formulation of cross-sector aims and targets as well as problem identification by the responsible ministry, the Ministry for Housing, Spatial Planning and the Environment (VROM). Still, there is a lack of overall sector co-ordination in the implementation of the devised policies. This can be attributed to a lack of resources for ensuring effective implementation, as well as a lack of sector specific commitment to integrate sustainable development policies in their decision-making. This has also led observers to describe the Dutch performance as being "tough on goals, light on action" (Van Muijen 2000).

- Knowledge Gaps: The second identified challenge to effective sustainable development policy-making is a lack of scientific knowledge which can impede a long-term perspective on sustainable development issues and a sufficient sector integration of sustainable development policies. This situation has led to uncertainties in the concise formulation and implementation of sector policies. In the transport sector, large progress has been made in the reduction of poisonous gases, but the rise of traffic volume has increased CO_2 and NOx pollution. For instance, precise environmental impact studies could increase sustainable development awareness in the construction of transportation infrastructure. Similarly, although waste pollution in agriculture has been curbed in recent years, effluents do remain superior to the levels prescribed in the National Environment Policy Plans. This can be the result of a lack of knowledge in the area of long-term soil contamination and accumulation of pollutants, which further contaminate the environment. Further, this lack of knowledge can also account for the low activity in soil decontamination of phosphates and nitrates.

- Transparency and participation: The Dutch approach to sustainable development can be characterised as being consensual, as it tries to attain a broad social consent to environmental policies. There is a large involvement of social stakeholders in all areas of decision-making. Also, the quality and number of official documents are superior to those of many OECD member countries. Still, there is room for progress. Increased transparency in decision-making may reduce opposition to the further implementation of sustainable development policies. For example, a further transparent reform of the tax system to include further ecological taxes on transportation and carbon fuel consumption without raising the overall tax burden could potentially reduce individual uncertainty and opposition.

Domestic context

- The Dutch society has to face a number of "mega issues", which affect sustainable development. A major societal shift is taking place similarly to many other OECD countries: The move from an industrial and agricultural economy to a service-driven economy. In the case of the Netherlands, the consequences are particularly important and thus the very nature of public debate is affected. These shifts provide specific opportunities for more sustainable options, *e.g.* the opportunity to diminish the overexploitation of land by agriculture and to convert some areas back to nature. But this also involves challenges, for example, satisfying increasing demands of the citizens for housing. Some of this "free land" taken from agriculture and industry installations is converted to residential neighbourhoods. These topics pose new sustainable development issues, such as transport and liveability questions, in a context of major constraints linked to the density of population (particularly in the western part of the country).

- The biggest and most typical environmental problem of the Netherlands is manure coming from massive livestock production (mainly pigs and poultry), which generates massive manure surpluses. In 1986 manure production reached its peak, with excretion levels of 713 million kg of nitrogen and 273 million kg of phosphate. This has placed manure management at the centre of Dutch environmental policies, and since then there much progress has been achieved. Other serious problems in the Netherlands are soil pollution, noise (partly coming from the population density), solid waste processing, water quality, acidification and desiccation of natural areas.

- Construction of infrastructure and urban development are also certainly among the most important issues of the country. In addition to demands for new infrastructure resulting from new lifestyles, the majority of citizens do not want to live in the traditional "agri-landscape". Their preference is to live in open space and enjoy natural areas. Therefore the government must take into account the balance between developing suburban areas (with related infrastructure) and converting a significant part of land to natural areas. For example, the Ministry of Agriculture, Nature Management and Fisheries is engaged in freeing land from agriculture by converting arable land into nature areas, while other government departments would prefer to use land to build new houses.

- Dematerialisation and management of substances are also receiving increased attention in the Netherlands in the form of packaging legislation, recycling and ecodesign programmes. This is one of the new challenges since dematerialisation is often less clear than initial expectations. In 2000 a study

223|

Box 2.   **Main Pollution Problems in the Netherlands**

Climate change

Progress has been made on the reduction of greenhouse gas emissions, notably CO_2 emissions, but the recent economic expansion could well have impaired a further reduction of emissions similar to the reduction during the recession years of the early 1990s.

Due to more stringent international agreements on CFC use and stricter national legislation, Dutch CFC emissions have been reduced, but many CFCs still remain in the production and consumption chains.

Acidification

The increased use of natural gas (instead of oil or coal), low-sulphur coal and desulphurisation filters in the power generation sector have led to substantial reductions in SO_2 emissions.

The introduction of obligatory catalytic converters and the phasing out of older car models have only slightly decreased the discharges of NO_x.

Ammonium emissions (NH_3) in the agricultural sector have been successfully reduced through the introduction of new fertilisers and the covered storage of manure.

Manure production

Improved legislation restricting the size of poultry and pig stocks, the use of manure for fertilisation purposes (previewing its eventual phasing out) and enforcing new storage methods have successfully reduced nitrogen and phosphor pollution. Still, pollution arising from manure production is one of the most pressing environmental issues, as it affects all environmental media (water, air and soil). Also, in the area of soil contamination there is a large knowledge gap.

Toxins

The dispersion of toxins has been greatly reduced, due to the introduction of environmentally friendlier surrogates and restrictions on their use. Still, and especially in the area of heavy metal pollution of surface waters, there remains much room for improvement.

Waste

In the area of waste management, the government has made progress in reducing the amount of waste that is produced, stored and incinerated. The recycling rates are higher than the OECD average and a successful system of waste separation has been put in place. Still, the overall tonnage remains very high and there do remain the problems remain, regarding efficient recycling, rapidly increasing bio-waste amounts and hazardous waste disposal.

Box 2.   **Main Pollution Problems in the Netherlands** (*cont.*)

Disturbances

Disturbance pollution, meaning disturbances in the immediate environment of people (such as noise, odours, vibrations, lighting, etc.) has not been considered in depth. Although new provisions have been put in place, for instance noise pollution control at Schipol Airport, the problem of disturbance will most probably increase due to the recent economic growth and a rise in public awareness causing an increase in the filling of complaints.

Dessiccation

This poses a very serious problem for the Netherlands, as it leads to the erosion of coastlines and the loss of arable land and grasslands. Desiccation is mainly caused by the extraction of drinkable ground water for domestic and agricultural use. The counter-measures that have been introduced in the form of a water extraction tax are too recent to predict any changes as yet.

Dissipation

Efforts to halt the loss of natural flora and fauna have not been efficient enough. Despite specific achievements in selected provinces (*e.g.* Friesland), National and regional bio-diversity are on the decline and suffer further depletion every year.

Source: Bressers/Plettenburg 1997: 111-113; OCDE 1995.

---

commissioned by VROM, presented several new ideas and policy suggestions. This study tried to define the problem of increasing material flows in developed societies as an obstacle to sustainable development. Dematerialisation is a policy requirement, which includes the change of consumption patterns and the adaptation of national innovation systems towards increased resource efficiency. Decision-making on dematerialisation calls for basic research in the cause-effect mechanisms lying behind increasing material flows and in the failure of past policies, and requires the initiation of macro and micro-level monitoring systems in order to develop sufficient indicators and to assess the environmental impact of consumption patterns. This requires acceptance that increased resource inefficiency is an endemic result of highly developed societies and thus necessitates state action through the adaptation of consumption patterns and the innovation system via price controls and negotiation between various societal actors. Dematerialisation policy also

---

requires international co-operation with other countries to share knowledge and experiences (Te Riele *et al.* 2001:p. 8-9).

Perception of issues and public awareness

The awareness of sustainable development as a concept is not very developed in the Netherlands. The term "sustainability" (*Duurzaamheid*) is more widely used, although its definition has been a matter of debate. It was once defined by the government in terms of "ecological user space", but this definition was criticised by the scientific community and in particular the Netherlands Scientific Council for Government Policy (WRR) in a study of 1994 (Bressers/Plettenburg 1997, p. 126). However, some "sustainable development talk" was used in the late 1980s in the context of the elaboration of the first National Environment Policy Plan (NEPP), and sustainable development was designated as a general guideline for the government policy. But discussions have usually focussed on "environmental sustainability" rather than on the triple-bottom-line of environmental, economic and social development. There is generally no extensive thinking on the specific implications of the concept of "social sustainability", due perhaps to the high level of social cohesion and welfare of Dutch society.

In contrast to the constantly high concern of Dutch society about growth and unemployment, interest in the environmental component of sustainability and the attention paid by the political institutions varied over time, with a tendency for greater interest in times of economic prosperity. The cyclic concerns on global environmental issues are quite similar to other OECD countries, as shown by the other country studies presented in this report. The environment has been declining since the end of the 1980s, but like many other countries new concerns came to fore in the 1990s following the 1992 Earth Summit in Rio de Janeiro. As environmental and social problems became less visible in the late 1990s, public concern dropped, to rise again at the turn of the new millennium. Studies tend to show that once awareness has reached a certain level, it tends to remain steady for a while before decreasing, even after the economy is slowing down again. Awareness is also being sustained by the active role of the media, although depth and quality of the information can vary over time (Gutteling/Caljé 1993: p. 14-19).

Past initiatives described in the section above show that, although no extensive sustainable development strategies were issued, increasingly integrated approaches to environmental policies were developed. The need for more integrated policies is partly supported by societal consensus on the need to maintain a high degree of social cohesion when developing the economy as well as ensuring that a clean environment and more natural space be preserved or recreated (Bressers/Plettenburg 1997, p. 124). The need to evaluate the consequences of environmental policies on social stability is less obvious. It is also important to underline that the attitude of the general public towards the environment has evolved since the end of the 1980s from protecting nature to caring for tomorrow, which moves it closer to the concept of sustainable development (Gijswijt/Van der Vliet 1993).

Individuals and companies are now more accustomed to integrating environmental concerns in their day-to-day operations and business. People have become more familiar with the most "immediate" aspects of sustainable development (such as recycling, etc.), but there is difficulty in going a step further and expecting the average citizen to develop concerns in the middle term. One obvious reason is that it is very difficult to see the immediate implication of policies on sustainable development: What will be the effects on nature of building new residential areas? On a more general level, will post-industrial development really contribute to reducing the level of pollution? All these questions remain uncertain and therefore the public often refrains from taking a stand.

Within government, one factor that contributes to rising awareness is the considerable degree of staff mobility of senior civil servants combined with a low degree of politicisation of the civil service. The recent establishment of central recruitment procedures for higher civil servants is reinforcing this trend. The consequence is that a civil servant from the Ministry of Finance or the Ministry of Economic Affairs, for example, may then move to VROM or another ministry. This mobility is a crucial factor of cross-fertilisation and mutual understanding between different ministries. A related factor is the effort to sustain "professionalisation" and to advance training of government personnel on the integration of responsibility for environmental protection.

Political agenda

There has been only limited experience in developing fully integrated sustainable development policies in the Netherlands. The first national environmental policy plan (NEPP I) called for an ambitious target of reaching sustainable development by 2010, which seemed rather unrealistic. However, the Netherlands has usually been presented as a leader in developing an innovative environmental policy, although for some observers the policy results have often been quite limited until recently (Bressers/Plettenburg 1997, p. 109).

As early as 1810, when the Netherlands was under Napoleonic rule, a decree was issued introducing a licensing system aimed at controlling the hazards, damage and nuisance caused by industry (De Koning 1994). However, it was only in 1962 that the term "environment" was used for the first time in the government, when the Minister of Social Affairs and Public Health of that time set up a Public Health Inspectorate responsible for environmental protection; and it was in 1971 that environmental protection became formalised, through the creation of the

227|

Directorate General for Environment Protection (DGEP) within the Ministry of Public Health, that became the Ministry of Public Health and Environment Protection.

In the 1980s, the Dutch government recognised that only dramatic change in its operating procedures, industry operations and consumption patterns could accomplish the significant pollution reduction necessary to contribute to a more sustainable future. Between 1972 and 1982, the resources of DGEP, once very limited, increased significantly and the perception of the issues evolved: although the concept of sustainable development was not yet fully developed, it became clear that environmental issues had wide implications in terms of strategic spatial choices (including economic choices). In response, a restructuring took place to better reflect this in the government structure. In 1982, the Ministry for Housing, Spatial Planning and the Environment was established (the Ministry of Public Health and Environment Protection was dismantled and its tasks relative to environment protection were transferred to the new ministry. In 1989, the first environment plan was developed, at a time when the environment took a prominent place on the agenda.

In the 1990s, there was an effort to improve rationalisation and harmonisation of the legal framework (including a degree of deregulation). This included better definitions, improving policy planning, using tools such as quality standards and licences, developing voluntary agreements ("covenants"). Main achievements are described below.

The Environment Management Act of 1993 provided a general framework supplemented by three separate Acts in specific Acts on water management (under the responsibility of the Ministry of Water and Transport), soil protection and chemical substances (under the responsibility of the Ministry for Housing, Spatial Planning and the Environment). Water permits and building permits were also modified in order to include co-ordinating provisions between the different Acts. Efforts currently concentrate on improving integration of general environmental protection provisions contained in the Environment Management Act, with specific legislation on water, mining and nature protection.

VROM is of course the central vehicle for environmental protection in the Netherlands, in particular for the implementation of the Environment Management Act. Its budget has been subject to a moderate increase. For example, the expenditure of the Environment Directorate increased from 289 million guilders in 1972, to 608 million in 1985, 1 269 million in 1990 and 1 583 million in 1993. The total environmental expenditure of all sectors in the Netherlands amounted to 1.1 per cent of GDP in 1980, 1.3 per cent in 1985, 1.9 per cent in 1990 and 2.7 per cent in 1995. Environmental expenditure is predominantly aimed at water pollution (37 per cent), waste management (23 per cent) and air pollution (17 per cent) (OCDE 1995, p. 114-116). However, it is hard to evaluate precisely the exact impact

---

Box 3.   **New Policy Processes in the 1980s and 1990s**

From 1985 on, VROM officials began to implement the "twin track" policy process and to develop integrated environmental legislation and licensing procedures. This process required time as it involved a considerable culture change and policy makers needed to gain confidence in handling the new concepts of themes, target groups, etc.

Information

A great deal of knowledge and expertise already existed in sector areas, which was relevant to environmental quality monitoring and technical problem-solving. As officials began to focus more on setting objectives and influencing sources of pollution, there was a need for new information. The report *Concern for Tomorrow*, produced by the National Institute for Public Health and Environmental Protection (RIVM) in 1988, provided a scientific basis for establishing quality objectives and emission reduction targets required by each of the major economic sectors. In addition to environmental information, more use was made of data on economic sector activity, supplied by the Central Planning Bureau, the Central Bureau of Statistics and other organisations.

Institutional change

In 1991, the Environment Directorate of the Ministry was restructured to reflect the policy approach, which had now become established. Reorganisation did not occur entirely along theme and target group lines but broadly reflected the two policy "blocks" of environmental effects (policies relating to quality and factors directly affecting quality: substances, waste, noise) and sources (policies relating to target group activities and products).

An unexpected benefit of these changes was the emergence of a common vocabulary to serve the integrated policy approach. Many specialist terms that had no meaning (or different meanings) in certain departments have been replaced and communication was improved.

Legislation

The Environment Management Act of 1 March 1993 superseded numerous laws relating to sector quality and nature protection and introduced an integrated system of issuing permits. With the exception of activities covered by the Surface Waters Pollution Act, industries could now obtain a single licence to cover all operations. An early step involved the appointment of Target Group Managers. These were high-level appointments. It was the task of the new managers to ensure co-ordination throughout the Ministry of all work relating to each of the themes (quality, standards) and target groups (instruments directed at economic activities).

Source: Royal Netherlands Embassy (*www.netherlands-embassy.org/c_envalg.html*).

229

---

of these additional resources. It should also be emphasised that more burden was put on provinces and municipalities, with the consequence that VROM is now committed to help build capacities in some disadvantaged provinces. The Budgets for 2001 put emphasis on issues of importance for sustainable development (see Annex II).

Main current challenges include the development of sound infrastructure and the strategic choices that this implies. The Ministry of Transport, Public Works and Water Management has envisaged an ambitious plan, the Urban Accessibility Offensive, for improving accessibility in the densely populated *Randstad* in the western part of the country. The government has reserved a sum of approximately NLG 10 billion (€ 4.54 billion) to finance this infrastructure development programme until 2010. The core of the plan is to decentralise transport policy in the area, by allowing the four major cities to develop and implement their own transport policies financed by a regional mobility fund. Furthermore, the Urban Accessibility Offensive aims to increase capacity efficiency of the main motorways (A1/A9 and A12 motorways) and trunk roads in the *Randstad* through the introduction of "intelligent" motorways equipped with state-of-the-art traffic surveillance and guidance systems developed in close co-operation with private enterprise. These technologies will not only be used to increase efficiency, but also to enforce road tolls and pay lanes. The Accessibility and Mobility Bill previews the introduction of a system of variable road charges around 2010, which will be based on the "polluter pays" principle. Charges will be levied on a per-kilometre basis. Another main aspect will be the further development of the public transport system, notably by introducing high-speed trains, increasing existing services in the *Randstad* and connecting the area to other provinces. In addition, the government plans to introduce new environmental and safety standards at the Amsterdam Airport, Schipol. After 2003, air traffic at Schipol will no longer be regulated by aircraft numbers, but the actual noise pollution will determine the number of flights (Ministry of Transport 2000).

The main social issue in a context of low unemployment rates and high social cohesion is to better integrate immigrants. It seems that foreigners in the Netherlands have not profited to the same extent as Dutch nationals from the recent Dutch economic expansion. Their participation rate in 1998 was 66.5per cent for men and 40.8 per cent for women, substantially lower than for Dutch men (83.2 per cent) and women (63.5 per cent). Furthermore, foreigners experienced a much higher level of unemployment. Only 3.1 per cent of Dutch men and 5.6 per cent of Dutch women were registered as unemployed, whereas 11.6 per cent of male foreigners and 14.1 per cent of female foreigners were unemployed (OECD 2001a, p. 171). This inequality also applies to higher rates of long-term unemployment for foreigners compared to Dutch nationals. The government is therefore trying to improve the position of immigrants with extra training and employment incentives for companies. In 1998,

Box 4. **National Environment Policy Plans (NEPP)**

The Netherlands has a comparatively long tradition of institutionalised environmental policy planning. The environmental plans are the joint responsibility of the Economics, Transport, Agriculture and Environment Ministries, whereas the Environment Ministry is the lead ministry. This allows a cross-sectoral approach to environmental policy planning. The first National Environment Policy Plan (NEPP I) was brought into effect in 1989, as a response to the study of the National Institute of Public Health and Environment Protection (RIVM) on future environmental issues based on the conclusions of the Brundtlandt-Report on sustainable development published in 1987.

NEPP I (1989)

The first national environmental policy plan included a detailed statistical description of the global and Dutch environmental situation and its foreseeable development in a business-as-usual projection. This compiled the scientific basis for the setting of goals to attain the main aim of Dutch sustainable development within a generation (25 years). The plan set out a wide scope of environmental goals, objectives and time frames. It also identified the target groups and to a certain extent incorporated stakeholder participation. Largely it restricted itself to using traditional instruments, which concentrated on output regulation.

NEPP II (1993)

NEPP I preliminary results were evaluated by the environmental evaluation report prepared by the RIVM and incorporated in the following NEPP II. The evaluation led to a revision of the goals and also to the creation of a legal basis outlined in the Environment Management Act 1993 for the implementation and the formulation of future NEPPs every four years. The Act also empowered subnational entities to formulate respective local environmental policy plans. Contrary to the NEPP I, the discussion base for the agenda setting was very much enlarged to include 600 participants from the scientific community, NGOs and target groups. In all, NEPP II included 50 strategic objectives, 200 specific goals and time frames concerning eight policy sectors and directed at nine target groups. In general, the NEPP II can be classified as a refinement of NEPP I, setting out a strategic framework designed as an action plan. The consensual nature of the agenda-setting period was also included in the implementation stage by the introducti on of decentralised voluntary agreements between target groups, and between national and subnational public authorities in the form of negotiated agreements (covenants).

NEPP III (1998)

The next NEPP was presented to the public in 1998. Whereas the earlier plans contained concrete strategies, goals, objectives and implementation periods, NEPP III could be considered to be more of a policy document surveying progress and posing questions on further issues, thus focusing on the quality of the objectives. NEPP II takes a more international view on sustainable development, stressing the international context of national environmental policies, calling for increased action on EU level and underlining Dutch international obligations.

NEPP IV (2001/2)

The NEPP IV, whose implementation is previewed to be in 2002, is dedicated to the very long-term perspective of attaining sustainable development in the Netherlands. A re-evaluation of the past 30 years of Dutch environmental politics will take place. The results will define the future shape of environmental politics until 2030. In particular, the global dimension will be further outlined and the role of the Netherlands in international environmental policy-making will be analysed.

Source: (Van Muijen 2000: 146-148, 153-157; Jänicke/Jörgens 1998: 32-34).

231

the government set up the Taskforce on Minorities and the Labour Market for senior businesspeople, trade unionists, and policymakers. The government also uses compulsion: shortly after arriving in the Netherlands, new immigrants now have to attend courses in the Dutch language and social institutions, and they receive help finding jobs. It is still too early too evaluate the results of these efforts, while past policies have not always been very successful.[3]

Within government, the debate on sustainable development remains a significant concern of three ministries: VROM, the Ministry of Agriculture, Nature Management and Fisheries, and the Transport, Public Works and Water Management. The Ministry of Housing, Spatial Planning and the Environment has been responsible for developing National Environment Policy Plans (currently the fourth National Environment Policy Plan is being developed, see Box 4). To date the Netherlands have no sustainable development strategy. However, in 2001, the Dutch government has launched started the preparation of the Dutch National Sustainable Development Strategy (NSSD). The document will be finished by the end of 2001. It will be send to the United Nations as input for the World Summit on Sustainable Development which will take place in 2002 in Johannesburg. The document will be used as a starting point for a discussion in Dutch society about the next steps to be taken to achieve a more sustainable development in the Netherlands. Sustainable development is understood as a development path in which the social, the economical and the ecological dimensions are taken equally into account and in which future generations and people in other countries must be able to satisfy their needs as well. The strategy therefore has a clear focus on policy integration and the development of a longer-term view. The themes the NSSD specifically adresses are: Demografic developments; Water; Climate, energy and mobility; Biodiversity, natural resources and agriculture; Life long learning and the Knowledge based society. The Dutch NSSD will be drawn on the EU strategy and the OECD strategies for sustainable development.

At subnational level, an incentive to take action is the fact that, although provinces exercise relatively limited powers compared to other OECD countries, their main field of competence is local planning and environmental protection. This feature is an incentive to take action.

B. Institutions and policy-making

There is often a tendency to believe that sustainable development equals environmental management and, consequently, that it should be a prerogative of VROM. There has been a traditional feeling that "VROM is responsible for environ-ment matters" (and, by extension, sustainable development) and that the Ministry of Finance, for example, is responsible for economic development issues. There-fore introducing an integrated "triple bottom line" approach has not been high on the central government agenda, and expertise is mostly solicited from VROM for sustainable development matters. This specialised approach based on traditional boundaries between sector competencies calls for efforts to improve policy coherence and to enforce sound regulatory monitoring. It is slowly evolving, however, mainly because of pressures resulting both from concerns of the Dutch society and from the highly sophisticated context that calls for better integration of environmental aspects in sector policies.

Legislation and the role of Parliament

The Netherlands legal system and bureaucracy are organised along the lines of a traditional continental European system. This means that there is a tendency on the one hand to address societal demands by introducing new legislation when issues emerge, but on the other hand there is some conservatism against the creation of new legal categories. In the case of sustainable development, no specific legislation has been developed, and sustainable development *per se* has no legal existence. However one should not conclude from this that no progress is being made to integrate sustainable development goals. This integration is taking place in the framework of more traditional fields of legislation, like environmental protection, agriculture, water management, etc., reflecting the view that sustainability goals should be achieved within the traditional legal framework.

There is no specific legislation on sustainable development. However a comprehensive body of legislation covering many aspects of environmental protection on the one hand and social protection on the other has been developed in the last century. Concerning environmental management one major step forward was made through unification of the legislation on nuisance, pollution, noise, waste material and chemical waste under the Environment Management Act (EMA) of 1993. This Act provided the opportunity to partly address those concerns, making the environmental legislation far more transparent and easier to enforce. The EMA incorporated most of the Netherlands environmental laws into one statute and established one regulatory scheme for all levels of government. The major objective of this integration effort was to provide consistent guidance and interpretation of regulations and to stabilise the body of environmental law. Key elements of the Act include uniform environmental quality standards, consistent enforcement procedures, multimedia issuing of permits, required evaluation of progress and possible refinement of the National Environmental Policy Plan every four years (De Jong 1996, p. 5). The main legislative provisions are summarised in the table below.

In the 1970s political will in the lower Chamber of Parliament played a key role for raising government awareness on environmental issues and providing the DGEP with sufficient resources and powers.

Table 1.   **Key Environmental Provisions**

1896	– Nuisance Act that governed hazard, damage and nuisance caused by specific installations.
1970s	– Some restrictions of the Nuisance Act were tightened up and incorporated into separate laws and regulations. Sectoral laws on: water pollution (1970), air pollution (1971), chemical waste (1976), waste materials (1977), and noise nuisance (1979).
1 March 1993	– Unification of the environmental legislation on nuisance, pollution, noise, waste material and chemical waste under the Environment Management Act (EMA).

When draft laws come to Parliament, they have already been preceded by efficient mechanisms to ensure the quality and consistency of the draft with government objectives and with the legal framework. Following inter-departmental mechanisms (see below), traditional procedures for law-making include advice from the State Council (*Raad van State*).

The role of the judiciary

The concept of sustainable development is not yet a legal concept as such with legal binding effects. However, since 1974, municipalities, water companies and NGOs have initiated numerous judicial reviews against individual polluters (OCDE 1995, p. 198). The risk of "losing the public" due to extra legal action or to court actions seems to create pressure to improve consultation and participation methods. For example, extra-legal methods including citizen initiatives are now being tried. (OECD 2001*b*).

The role of the executive

The number of ministries is limited to 13 (there is no seniority rank between the various ministries). Each ministry covers various portfolios under the responsibility of separate State Secretaries. For example, there is one single ministry covering housing, spatial planning and the environment. Under this system, various portfolios enjoy various degrees of autonomy, and their integration may vary according to the specificity of each ministry and to political will.

As in other OECD countries, there is no ministry in charge of sustainable development; nor is this wished. However, the strict repartition of tasks goes along with a capacity to integrate both economic and environmental concerns into the policy frameworks of various ministries, while the integration of social concerns does not take place to the same extent.[4] A particularly significant feature of the Dutch system is that many environment-related tasks have been entrusted to other ministries than VROM.

The Ministry deals with issues including nature conservation and recreation, or the use of pesticides nature management, for Agriculture, Nature Management and Fisheries. The Ministry of Economic Affairs is in charge of the integration of the effect and consequences of its policies on the environment. The Ministry of Transport and Water is responsible for water quality aspects and is expected to develop sustainable transport schemes; for example, the Directorate-General for Passenger Transport has established an Innovation Department responsible for the development of new, innovative projects for passenger transport over land and water: and the Traffic Safety and Infrastructure Department was is responsible for policy on construction and maintenance of the national infrastructure, taking care of measures which enable optimal use of the infrastructure and contributing financially to large regional infrastructure projects. The department also contributes to the realisation of a sustainable safe traffic and transport system. Recently, the Ministry of Finance has been active in developing environmentally friendly tax incentives (e.g. to stimulate investments made by industry). The new tax policy introduced in 2001 addresses environmental concerns in addition to the traditional economic and social concerns. It includes for example environmental taxes (see Annex I).

Box 5. **The Evolving Mission of the Ministry of Agriculture,
Nature Management and Fisheries.**

One key factor for sustainable development in a context of relative segmentation is how each ministry perceives its own "mission", and role as an organisation. In this respect, the evolution of the attitude of the Ministry of Agriculture, Nature Management and Fisheries vis-à-vis environmental issues is remarkable. Being responsible for nature management, it has increasingly integrated nature preservation into its key objectives (see also the departmental organisation of the Ministry in Annex IV).

This Ministry went through a major cultural change. It has long had a "privileged relationship" with farmers. In the past, farmers unions had a dramatic influence on the Ministry's strategic orientation and mission. Basically the Ministry was meant to "protect the farmers' interests". This situation has evolved greatly, resulting from both political reasons and institutional change (the new structure of the Ministry described above). In the past 5-10 years the idea, that the Ministry's mission should take into account more diverse views and respond to the overall needs of the Dutch Society has emerged. The consequence is improved coherence of views between strategic orientations of the Ministry of Agriculture, Nature Management and Fisheries and VROM.

235|

Some joint research programmes balance policy segmentation. The Ministry of Economic Affairs is, for example, funding research on economic instruments for environmental protection. The tendency towards segmentation is also balanced in the Dutch context by the existence of significant formal and informal co-ordination and consultation mechanisms between different ministries. In addition to this there are strong mechanisms that ensure policy coherence within government. For example, when drafting new legislation, inter-departmental groups review the content of the new Act. Considering the consensus-driven system of the Netherlands, these mechanisms – supplemented by informal inter-ministerial co-operation – contribute to policy integration. These mechanisms are enforced in cases where environment concerns must be integrated using specific guidelines developed by VROM in the 1990s. The Ministry of Economic Affairs together with the VROM and the Ministry of Justice have also established a "cell" to check on the environmental impact of economic legislation. This unit, which operates within the Ministry of Economic Affairs, is staffed in fact by people from VROM.

Another positive factor for policy coherence is the increasing mobility of civil servants and the low degree of politicisation of the Dutch civil service. These contribute to the reinforcement of impartial judgement and the sharing of knowledge and competencies.

Management innovations taking place at agency level could also provide opportunities for sustainable development. For example, the Netherlands has introduced an outcome and output focussed budgeting and management approach involving all government agencies. As part of that reform, agencies will be evaluated every 3-4 years on a recurring basis in addition to the annual performance reporting. These evaluations – used to integrate sustainable development criteria – could expand the scope of sustainable practices in government.

Working with subnational governments

Box 6 provides a brief summary of the distribution of power across levels of government. Although economic policy and the main aspects of social policy are determined nationally, environmental regulations have been traditionally an exclusive competence of the local level, and the municipalities long remained the only government body responsible for the issuing and monitoring of licences. This situation, characterised by a strict separation in the distribution of power, could have been a threat to developing sustainable development policies. In 1970s, licence-issuing powers were transferred to the regional tier of government (the provinces) in cases involving detailed and technical issues of major polluting companies, and national government expanded its steering role through the development of new legislation and regulations, as well as national policy planning in the

---

Box 6.   **Distribution of Power Across Levels of Government**

Objectives and standards are mainly determined by national government (similarly to other EU countries with an increasing role played by the European Union), although in some areas subnational authorities may play a critical role. Policy implementation is shared across levels of government. About 90 per cent of the budgets of provinces and municipalities come from central government, and only the remaining 10 per cent come from provincial and local taxes. The share of competencies could be summarised as follows:

- *Legislation* is primarily made on a national level.
- *Permits* are almost always granted by provinces and municipalities.
- *Enforcement* is a duty of the authority that is entitled to grant the permit, as well as of the police and the Public Prosecutor.

However, the role of provinces and municipalities is not only to grant and enforce. Subnational governments exercise critical responsibilities for sustainable development through:

- Entering into dialogue with citizens, organisations and industry in order to produce local agenda for sustainable development.
- Stimulation of energy conservation.
- Stimulation of prevention, separate collection and recycling of waste.
- Ensuring the cleaning-up of the soil.
- Reducing the burdening of the environment by passenger cars and freight transport.
- Preparing and carrying out regional projects for restoring nature and good environmental conditions.

Source: VROM, April 2000.

---

field of the environment. This led to national targets and norms applicable to lower levels of government.

The situation resulting from this evolution is characterised on the one hand by national prescriptions to be implemented or taken into account by lower levels of government, and on the other hand by autonomous and specific municipal and provincial policies, since provinces and most municipalities conduct their own policy planning. In the present system, responsibility for environmental regulation, for example, is found at the three levels of government: national, provincial and municipal. The national government is responsible for establishing national goals and creating basic statutory requirements. Provincial and/or municipal governments are

---

Box 7. **The Dutch Policy Planning System: Developing Efficient Planning Systems at the Three Levels of Government**

The Dutch policy planning system presents some original features. These are not only features of the central planning system but are also common to most provincial and local planning systems. The Dutch system distinguishes itself from similar systems (that often borrowed some aspects from the Netherlands) in three main ways:

- It is an attempt to operationalise ideas from the "strategic choice approach".
- Its main goal is not to stipulate future action but to improve coherence and to focus on the future quality of motivation and openness in external participation in subsequent decision-making.
- It contains precise and quantitative goals, for instance on emissions reduction.

These features are common to most national, provincial and local plans.

Source: Bressers/Pletteburg 1997, p. 117.

---

responsible for setting standards and emission levels of facilities within their jurisdictions. They are also responsible for the routine inspection and evaluation of plant operation and compliance with regulatory conditions. This situation calls for specific vertical co-ordination and consultation in order to achieve a sufficient degree of policy coherence.

VROM, in charge of spatial planning, is the main ministry responsible for co-operation with provinces and municipalities in key sectors relating to sustainable development. A co-ordinating board including representatives from the central and local levels meets five times a year. Generally speaking, provincial and municipal governments rely heavily on central Government transfers; about 90 per cent of the budgets of municipalities and provinces come from central government. When the first environment plan was developed (1989), decentralised authorities had no sufficient financial capacity. Central government transfers have aimed since then at improving local financial capacities. For example, additional budgets are provided for intensifying the execution of environmental laws (permit granting and enforcement) and for other duties in the execution of the NEPP. However there are still some issues related to the capacity of local government, in particular concerning small municipalities. In the smallest municipalities, one or two people only are dealing with environmental related issues, which means that, to develop and implement effective policies, they must co-operate with their neighbour authorities.

Transfers to local authorities in the environment field initially came directly from VROM, which then applied a rather tight control of the use of the funds. When the system became well established, most of the transfers then came from the general budget with less detailed inspection. A system of monitoring rather than control is now being developed in order to achieve empowerment of local levels. Mechanisms exist to ensure value for money. Decentralised authorities must report yearly on the use of transfer funds. Since the transfer of the grants for the municipalities from the VROM budget to the General Municipalities Fund (Gemeentefonds) in 1998, there is no longer a need for the municipalities to prepare plans for the spending of the grants. The Gemeentefonds is considered to be the own money of the municipalities. An agreement of the central government is not necessary anymore, and there is no longer co-ordination by the Ministry of the Interior like it used to be under the previous system.

One major issue about improving channels between levels of government is to ensure effective implementation, in particular when policies have not been formulated by VROM. A good illustration of the existing tensions is provided by the policy on nitrates. A position statement was signed between the Ministry of Agriculture, Nature Management and Fisheries and the National Board of the Farmers Union. However, mainly due to a constituency problem of the Farmers Union, the message did not get through the subnational level. This kind of example illustrates the difficulty of interpreting priorities at the local level. The need to implement the objectives of Agenda 21 is also a clear incentive to enhance co-operation between levels of government. The central level (mainly VROM) funded the creation of "Eco teams" at the local level to contribute to implementing local Agenda 21.

Non-governmental organisations and others

Citizen engagement has deep roots in Dutch history. From the Middle Ages onwards, the fight against floods from the sea promoted a tradition of active citizen involvement. Organisations such as water boards offer a good example of these tendencies. As a consequence, there is a strong tradition of a lively civil society in the Netherlands and an impressive number of organisations, unions, and associations. This is also true in the environmental and social sectors. In the Dutch context, environmental NGOs are those most likely to interfere with the development of sustainable policies. In particular, nature conservation organisations – the nature conservation movement dates back to the end of the 19th century – have a well-established internal structure and are staffed by people with good levels of expertise. They represent an increasing number of members: for example, the number of Greenpeace members grew from 90 000 in 1975 to 600 000 in 1995 (Bressers/Plettenburg 1997, p. 119). The participation of these NGOs in the formulation of policies has also undergone a dramatic change in the past 30 years.

239|

Until the late 1970s, NGOs often did not concern themselves in the formulation of political objectives but preferred lobby and exercise pressure (mainly through "extra-parliamentary" action). On the other hand, the consultation processes also remained rather closed from the government side, and only "institutionalised partners"(unions, etc.) were involved in public policy formation. This had the following negative consequences: the 1970s laws on the environment (see section on Public Consultation) attracted criticism from various sections of society because of the lack of openness of policy-making. At that time, citizens alleged that the public participation and appeal procedures were biased against them (De Koning 1994, p. 68-169).

Since then, the move towards integrated environmental management systems has fostered collaborative efforts between government, business and other stakeholders, for instance: Green Polder Deliberations. This is particularly true for land use planning at the municipal level.

Some non-governmental organisations play a key role for sustainable development. This is the case of the Society for Nature and Environment (*Stichting natuur en Milieu*), for example. It acts as a think tank and puts forward many of its representatives on committees and other consultative structures both inside and outside government. It also plays a co-ordinating role with regard to the other NGOs, and is subsidised by VROM.

Companies (in particular major Dutch groups like Philips), are increasingly integrating sustainable development into their concerns and have initiated multi-stakeholder processes. Their effort is encouraged by the powerful Confederation

---

Box 8.   The Centre for Agriculture and Environment

The work of the Centre for Agriculture and Environment (CLM) provides an example of the integration and institutionalisation of NGOS in the Netherlands, now reaching out to sustainable development issues. This NGO provides research and advisory work to public and private organisations: it develops about 50-60 per cent of its projects for the government, working mainly for the Ministry of Agriculture, Nature Management and Fisheries, VROM, the Ministry of Transport and Water, and the Ministry of Economic Affairs. Its board is composed of four people from the environment community, four people from the farming community, and an independent person. In addition to carrying our research projects, it is regularly associated with working groups and consultation processes. It is also a member of the Advisory Board on Nature Conservation.

Source: CLM Internet site: *www.clm.nl*).

---

of Netherlands Industry and Employers (VNO-NCW) which has traditionally been closely associated with the formulation of economic policy, mainly through lobbying and influencing government policies. In the 1980s, as environment policy was developed, this organisation was confronted with a dilemma: the new environmental policy set up targets which on the one hand, were in clear contradiction to the interests that the organisation were promoting (at least in the short-term), but on the other hand, the formulation of environment policy guaranteed a degree of predictability and provided business with longer-term perspectives. Instead of opposing the process, the VNO-NCW continued to try to influence policies rather than opposing them. This option was, at that time, very challenging for the organisation. Another powerful organisation is the Farmers' Union. It remains the key interface between the government and farmers. Although it participates actively in participatory consultation processes involving stakeholders, it has lost its former influence over formulation of agricultural policy.

Among other sectors of society, there is still limited debate on sustainable development. It is even true of universities where debates concern very specific aspects of sustainability without mentioning overall commitments to achieve sustainable development. For example, a specific university initiative was organised in 1999, the National Initiative on Sustainable Development (NIDO). It took place in Leeuwarden (Friesland) but operated with only limited resources.

C.   Decision-making mechanisms

Reaching agreement

Considering the small size of the country and the unitary nature of the State, it might have been possible in the short term for government to dictate reform through legislation and regulation. However, at the end of the 1980s when the issue emerged, there was a clear perception that the long-term nature of the sustainable development goals required a participatory process in which each actor accepts personal and corporate responsibility for the solution (De Jong 1996: p. 34). The focus of decision-making has therefore been on developing shared visions and mechanisms for co-operative implementation. This has implied moving from compliance to co-operative management, with a substantial commitment from industry, the public, and the government.

Four main criteria have been identified for the success of consultative processes for national environmental policies (De Jong 1996, p. 34):

- Economic stakeholders and the public need to believe in the benefits of the process and the strategy, which implies that the Government provide a solid credible argument for change based on solid scientific consensus.

241|

Box 9. Moving from Compliance with the Rules
to Co-operative Management

The environment sector

Since the formulation of the first National Environment Policy Plan, new instruments have emerged for developing environmental policy. These could lead to a new, more open "policy style" contributing to sustainable development goals. These instruments contribute to a review of the relation between government and stakeholders and between stakeholders themselves. The main instruments include:

- Target group consultation.
- Covenants.
- Emissions trading.

Environmental policy focuses on improving a sense of responsibility rather than compliance (*e.g.*, company and personal liability, research and information obligations) and on creating a framework for improving knowledge-based and impartial decisions, mainly through:

- Regulations requiring companies to employ staff with adequate expertise.
- Environmental impact assessments.
- Company environmental management systems.

The agriculture sector

Historically the agriculture sector was a highly regulated sector, and farmers had to comply with numerous rules. In the beginning of the 1990s this management model came increasingly under question on the basis of three major government failures. Firstly, for about ten years regulations were not sufficient to solve the manure problem (phosphates). Secondly, one Minister had to resign, because of the failure of the quota system in the fisheries, and thirdly, the use of hormones in the calf industry could not be controlled by regulations, while the activism of consumer organisation had more tangible effects than government intervention. These failures called for new modes of government intervention in the sector and in particular for more adapted steering:

- The reform of the decision-making system implied a new methodology for developing regulations. Traditionally these regulations were elaborated on the basis of agreements between the Ministry of Agriculture, Nature Management and Fisheries and the farmers. Wider consultation bringing together farmers' organisations, environmental organisations and central and local officials has been introduced, to come to a shared view on the magnitude of the problems.
- On the basis of these discussions it remained a government responsibility to set clear goals. However, consultation with the various stakeholders has also been developed for implementing the goals, and decentralised implementation by the stakeholders themselves has been introduced.

Increasingly farmers and environment groups sit and discuss issues together. The decentralisation process has taken the form of more provincial intervention in rural policies and transfers of budgets from central government to provinces. One of the *rationale* behind this shift is the emerging idea that government should not make things so much "its" problem when in fact it requires the participation of society to be handled. One of the *benefits* of the process is that it allowed the evolution of the traditional position of the Farmers Unions. The main *challenge* that is related to this new approach is, how to keep steering and oversight functions, whilst giving more responsibilities to stakeholders in the policy process. *Lessons for government* include the need to formulate clear goals, the focus on sound processes, and the need to keep government pressure in order to maintain a balance between ambition and feasibility.

- Government recognises that industry involvement in the creation of policies and solutions would encourage its complete participation in the success of the strategy. Long-term success requires each participant to accept personal and corporate responsibility for the solution.

- The success of the process rest on continuity. This is the ability of industry to sustain its operations while reducing its emissions and the ability of municipalities to monitor and organise its efforts.

- Each sector needs to secure benefits and recognise concessions of the other parties.

The covenant system, *i.e.* negotiated agreements, constitutes a central policy tool of new co-operative management practices (mainly taking the form of "covenants"). The covenants are not purely voluntary agreements between industry and the government. Their legitimacy is defined by legislation outlined in the NEPP and their legal status is defined by Cabinet regulations. The covenants are key elements in the implementation of the NEPPs for the private sector. The negotiation level depends on the involved parties and the negotiated subject. Covenants can either be negotiated on an industry-wide, a sector-specific or a plant-specific basis, thus involving either the national government, provincial or local authorities. The agreements contain time frames and implementation strategies for pollution control. Trade-offs may occur depending on the structure of the involved industry (such as between large and small businesses), the degree of technical sophistication and capital requirements. This degree of flexibility in legislative implementation allows a customised approach to environmental policy-making and has been a main reason to gain support and acceptance for the NEPP from the private enterprise sector. There are concerns connected with the rising popularity of covenants for formulating and implementing environmental legislation. Even though strict cabinet regulations do define the legal basis, the participation of third parties and the transparency of the accords, there is general apprehension about the possible use of covenants to by-pass Parliament involvement and possible negative effects on industrial competition (OECD 1999, p. 131; De Jong 1996, p. 8-9).

The use of these "voluntary approaches" can be relatively successful when they include sufficiently binding provisions. However there are a number of limits to their use the field of sustainable development, as described below.

In controversial policy areas, classical regulatory tools have sometimes been reintroduced to ensure effective implementation. For example, in 1996, a covenant was signed between the Ministry for Agriculture, Nature Management and Fisheries and representatives of the agriculture sector to diminish the use of pesticides, reduce emission levels and limit the dependence on pesticides. This agreement, taking place in a very sensitive area and so remained limited both from the point of view of its scope (the agreement did not cover impact assessment) and from

243|

Box 10. "Auto-regulation" in the Netherlands

One interesting feature of the Dutch system is the fact that, through the covenant systems business has been forced to exercise self-discipline over itself in order to ensure application of the agreements The self-regulatory aspect is one of the main advantages of the covenant system for all involved parties.

Administrative advantages

- Covenants accelerate the legislative process. Due to the consensual nature of the Dutch legislative system, a considerable amount of time can pass until legislation is implemented. Covenants are increasingly used in those areas demanding more responsive policy action, especially environmental policy-making.

- Covenants enable a customised approach to environmental policy regulation. This allows a more direct identification of target groups and choice of policy instruments, thus saving administrative resources due to reduction of monitoring and hindering over-regulation.

- The self-regulatory nature of covenants reduces time-consuming and resource-consuming monitoring and enforcement procedures as the target groups are bound to goals to which they have consented, thus ensuring their co-operation.

Target group advantages

- The covenant system can provide industry with a greater influence on the government's environmental policy making, as the producers are directly involved in the formulation of environmental goals and their implementation.

- The customised nature of covenants, which is based on co-operation between public authorities and industry, does allow a certain degree of flexibility in the implementation of environmental policies. Companies can frequently combine cost efficiency with environmental issues. Individual time-spans, and inclusion of different requirements depending on the nature of the individual firm or sector can ease the structural adjustment of an industrial production base.

- The structural adjustment of industry towards environmentally friendlier production methods has stimulated technical innovation in the field of environmental technologies. Environmental policy-making has created a demand for cleaner production technologies, thus improving conditions for domestic and international competitiveness for Dutch companies.

Sources: (VNO-NCW 1999: 8-9; OECD 1999: 130-131; Jänicke/Jörgens 1998: 31-32).

the point of view of its effect on farmers, because of the absence of government sanctions combined with the absence of specific non-regulatory incentives for individual farmers to comply with these agreements. The total objective of reduced use of pesticides could only be reached through new regulations (*e.g.* on potatoes). Therefore, the new pesticide policy has been largely based on a traditional mix of government intervention: regulations, authorisations and tax benefits granted to farmers. One issue is also that the European Union does not accept an alternative to regulations when these alternatives do not function perfectly (although some regulations can prove not to be always fully effective in practice).

Public consultation

The co-operative nature of policy formulation, the use of "negotiated" alternatives to regulations, and a large scope for consultation are key features of the Dutch system of governance. One typical means of consultation is to meet regularly around the negotiating table, with a significant role granted to NGOs. These formal meetings are often backed up by more or less informal and ongoing consultation between the government and various groups. Most existing NGOs are involved in public policy formulation through these processes. This co-operative approach includes representation of NGOs in advisory committees (like the Sustainable Development Council and the Countryside Planning Council), public funding of most NGOs, as well as giving a voice to non-governmental actors in policy processes and trying to reach consensus with them.

Drawing on the government's awareness that sustainable development, or at least environmental management, requires long-term commitment from the industry, the public, and the government, there is now an established practice of citizen participation in many areas that are key to sustainable development. For example, the development of more sustainable transportation modes is an open planning process with the users of the traffic systems.

Most ministries subsidise NGOs. Governmental financial support takes place mostly on a project basis, at central, provincial and local levels. For example, VROM is supporting projects with environmental protection NGOs, the Women's Council, and the Youth Organisation. Financial support from the government is often considered as a good way to ensure involvement from the "silent majority". It is important to highlight that public financing is not perceived as a way to impose the government's agenda over NGOs or to generate conformity. Inclusion in consultation processes and public financing reaches out to organisations that are critical of government action. This limits the risk of collusion between government and NGOs. However, it does not totally prevent an internal risk of "bureaucratisation" within organisations.

The systematic use of consultation and participation mechanisms nevertheless raises a number of issues. It is not always clear whether its primary objective is to facilitate a more open debate or to gain public support on specific policies. For example, one of the alleged reasons for the failure of the initial consultation process carried out for the extension of the Schipol Airport was the sense that options for choice were not totally open to debate. A related issue to the risk of bypassing traditional mechanisms of representative democracy. For instance, the consultation mechanisms set up for reforming the transportation strategy of the city of Groningen illustrate the tension between the expectations of the population and the limitations to direct public influence in a representative democracy (see Annex V). In Groningen, the citizens expected to have real influence in decision-making process (deciding about transport policy), but found out in the end that the final decisions were under the responsibility of the elected politicians and that their role was limited to choosing more or less sustainable modes of transport. This means that before developing a participation process, a good consideration of the scope is crucial (OECD 2001c).

One problem, which arises when systematically including NGOs, is to know whether they have enough resources to actively participate in consultation and negotiation processes. Some NGOs, and in particular environmental protection organisations, even though they are subsidised, do not always have the financial or technical capacity to be fully credible counterparts compared to government or professional organisations.

There has not yet been any evaluation of the exact influence of stakeholders in the policy processes. However, following the "inclusive" tendencies of Dutch "corporatism", the current trend is to accelerate the integration of NGOs in the policy process. Improving the quality of consultation and participation has been one of the major goals of NEPP4, and sophisticated consultative processes were put in place for developing NEPP3 and NEPP4. NGOs participate regularly in consultation processes. They have been invited to be official members of the scientific advisory councils of most ministries. But all NGOs cannot of course participate, which is clearly an issue in terms of equity. This is balanced by the fact that, increasingly, NGOs dealing with environment and nature are co-ordinating their efforts to come up with a single NGO position.

To be perceived as meaningful, NGOs need to have sufficient credibility based on competence, policy capacity, and representation. One issue is to know when an NGO becomes "representative" enough and can be included in the policy process. Another concern is to ensure a fair representation of different societal forces: this is why, for example, the motor and car driver association (ANWB) is playing a central role when it comes to dealing with issues related to transport and planning, in addition to environmental organisations.

The extensive use of consultation has been questioned on the assumption that it could slow down policy process. Consultation with small groups focussing

---

Box 11. **The Consultation Side of Developing Environmental Policy Plans in VROM**

Main points

- The development of the environment policies started with a project group including people from other departments (for NEPP3 this took about two years). This involved continuous discussion at the level of policy-makers.
- Formal meetings with representatives of big companies and of civil society were then organised. Considering that an increasing part of the policy is formulated through *covenants*, the success of this consultation has been essential to prepare a framework for future agreements. Regular meetings have been set up at the level of Director General with NGOs (*e.g.* dealing with environmental protection but also with other like the Women's Council or Youth Organisation).
- Informal consultation was also used extensively.
- Information and communication technologies (ICTs) do not seem to have added value to the consultation process.

Main learnings

When developing current plans and strategies, it becomes difficult to talk about "the public" in general. In addition to traditional groups (employer associations, etc.), diverse "postmodernist groups" – that are often very active – interfere in the political debate, and government must develop capacities to cope with them.

---

on rather narrow objectives (car drivers, farmers) is, for example, more difficult than with big firms more aware of the global consequences of issues.

The relation between participation and civil society is therefore not self-evident. The case of traffic planning in the Dutch city of Groningen, for instance, provided an example of participatory decision-making that implied considerable participation of citizens and interest groups (Welles 1997). Evaluation from this case and from a similar case in the city of Deventer shows that taking people's feeling seriously can be more important than substantive outcome of the decision-making process. One could also argue that lengthy procedures are often due to internal management of institutions rather than consultation itself.

Turning talk into action

Two major factors have aimed to make environmentally sustainable policies effective: developing a consistent policy process within the VROM, and improving policy integration in government and more generally among various stakeholders.

247

Policy consistency was enhanced by the appointment of Target Group Managers (see Box 3), who are responsible for co-ordination in the Ministry of all work relating to the themes outlined in the NEPP and the chosen target groups. More information was needed for the new emphasis of the Ministry towards the long-term setting of objectives and influencing sources of pollution instead of short-term *ad hoc* reaction to issues and emergencies. The report "Concern for Tomorrow", published by the RIVM in 1988, provided the desired scientific basis for formulating precise quality objectives and emission reduction targets for the major economic sectors. Furthermore, the Ministry increased its co-operation with other government agencies working in the field of economic data collection, such as the Central Planning Bureau and the Central Bureau of Statistics. An internal restructuring of the Ministry took place which reflected the two main areas of environmental policy-making: quantity and quality effects, referring to policies directed at specific environmental detriments (*e.g.* noise, waste, toxins); and pollution sources, relating to pollution target groups. This intra-ministerial restructuring led to a spread of knowledge by pooling environmental expertise and so created a common understanding of problems and duties. Finally, the introduction of the Environment Management Act of 1993 enhanced previous numerous legislation on environmental protection and licensing (with the exception of the areas under the jurisprudence of the Surface Waters Pollution Act). This greatly facilitated the granting of licenses to industry.

The second factor – executive policy integration and stakeholder involvement – was attained via the formulation and implementation of the NEPPs. During the drafting of NEPP II and the subsequent plans, the sector ministries played a prominent role in preparing the goals and targeting the areas of activity. The formulation of environmental policy is the responsibility of the Ministry for Agriculture, Nature Protection and Fisheries, the Ministry for Economic Affairs, and the Ministry for Transport and Public Works. The Ministry for Housing, Spatial Planning and the Environment (VROM) is responsible for overall policy co-ordination and has the leading role in policy formulation. The NEPPs are also supplemented by sectoral policy plans, which formulate the provisions contained in the NEPPs specifically for their sectors of responsibility. Stakeholder involvement has been attained via covenants and other agreements between the government and private actors. There has also been some degree of voluntary action on the part of private enterprise, such as in the energy sector. The involvement of stakeholders in the formulation of policies and the adherence to long-term covenants stating time-spans, pollution reduction targets and clear responsibilities, have created a considerable amount of self-regulation and so partly relieved government agencies of continuously controlling and enforcing legislation.

Many public authorities contribute actively to enforcing laws. In addition to traditional law enforcement tools (police, public prosecutors), specific measures have been initiated to better manage the enforcement. In 1997, provinces, municipalities, waterboards, police, public prosecutors and inspectorates of each ministry established a general framework for agreement and established standards. Two indirect mechanisms are also critical for effective enforcement:

- **Environment Impact Assessment** (came into force in 1987). Can be initiated by government or a public body or the authority in charge of a proposed activity. Provides for the obligation to describe relevant activity, giving comparative analysis, participation of all interested parties. Intervention of an independent committee of experts which provides advice to the competent authority on the guidelines that have to be satisfied by the report (see Annex IV) (VROM 2000).

- **Lodging objections and appeal procedures** (provisions of the Environment Management Act, March 1993). Requires authorities to draft decision before the actual decision becomes legally binding, thus allowing individuals and organisations to formulate objections at an early stage. Sometimes authorities organise a public hearing if needed. This procedure is the basis for launching future appeal procedures in case of disagreements.

Key challenges for the future will be to improve green procurement and green budgeting. A study of procurement practices in the Netherlands identified seven barriers to green procurement in public authorities (Mielisch/Erdmenger 2001: p. 4-6). The first barrier is low awareness and motivation. Green purchasing practices suffer from a general lack of commitment, environmental awareness and motivation. This deficit in understanding is especially present in the areas of behavioural change towards more environmentally friendly conduct, the role of the public sector in setting standards for the private sector, assessment of environmental consequences, the knowledge of alternative environmentally friendly products and the will to tackle environmental problems. This green "ignorance" has even led to official discrimination against "greener products".

Second, the study identified economic barriers, which refer to the cost-benefit relation for "greener" products in relation to conventional products. Budgetary constraints have led to the perceived prejudice that the initial costs of purchasing green products and the subsequent costs for new operating procedures, as well as initiation of behaviour patterns and integration into new product environments, are higher than conventional purchases. A further economic barrier to green purchasing practices is the lack of budgetary consideration of social or environmental follow-up costs of environmentally harmful products.

Third, the lack of sufficient knowledge and information on green products and their assessment poses a further barrier to green procurement. This barrier includes a lack of information on overall environmental policy concepts, product contents, viable definitions of "green" products, credible environmental impact assessments of products, and product selection guidance systems in the form of "eco-labelling" of products. Especially, the last point shows that there is a lack of scientific knowledge, as currently there is no established methodology to implement an officially recognised environmental standard on products. This could also be the result of a lack of availability of practical experiences and networking between procurement officers from different countries, which could provide a valuable information exchange.

Further barriers are seen to exist in organisational, technical and legal areas. Legal barriers include discrimination against environmentally friendly goods through certain legal requirements and the lack of specification of environmental purchasing policies. Organisational deficits are seen to exist in the purchasing system itself which is generally decentralised, thus complicating the overview of purchasing practices

---

Box 12.   The Environment Inspectorate (VROM)

The role of the Environment Inspectorate is:
- To enforce the legislature under the competence of the minister.
- To make sure other levels of government also enforce laws and regulations.
- To signal and observe relevant developments.
- To detect and fight serious criminality in this area.

Concrete examples of the tasks of the Inspectorate are:
- Indirect supervision to guarantee that municipalities observe building legislation.
- Control of risks originating from materials hazardous to health and the environment such as asbestos, PCB and CFK.
- Control of international waste material transport according to requirements.
- Checking approved building plans to make sure proper energy saving methods are applied.

In addition, the Inspectorate judges whether regional and scheme plans of regional and local governments correspond to the national government's policy. It also issues judgements on urbanisation and the modernisation of cities. It supervises housing corporations to make sure they deliver the required services.

The government is aiming to increase international co-operation in law enforcement. The harmonisation of laws and regulations as well as the transfer of know-how with the current and future members of the European Union is especially important. Interpol will play an increased role in fighting international environmental criminality (Green Interpol).

Source: VROM Internet site (*www.minvrom.nl/minvrom/pagina.html?id=1&goto=3948*).

and the organisation of an authority's environmental purchasing policy, causing incoherence as well as insufficient co-ordination of green purchasing policies. New purchasing procedures will require increased training of all personnel. Technical barriers arise from the in adaptability of existing equipment to new environmentally friendly products and the insufficient offer and supply of green products.

Policy monitoring

More discretion also implied sophisticated methods for policy monitoring. A system of inspections has been developed to ensure that good implementation and policy monitoring takes place. This reveals the existence of rather strict top-down mechanisms for compliance, compared to the co-operative policy tools for example, in the field of environmental management, the Environment Inspectorate in VROM is checking the implementation of government policies (see Box 12). The unitary nature of the State and the good levels of acceptance of national policies ensure the efficiency of such controls. This is partly due to the country's homogeneity and to policy formulation methods.

D.   Learning from the Dutch experience

The degree of effective implementation of environmental policy, which is only one indicator of sustainable development, has been rather well evaluated. The situation regarding environmental policy in the Netherlands is characterised by an enormous number of studies devoted to its implementation. Results are reported in Table 2.

According to the Dutch Government, the following Lessons have been learned from the integration process and benefits have been the following (Royal Netherlands Embassy 2000):

- Integration is an evolutionary process which cannot be fully "planned" since it depends on the circumstances and attitudes of many actors and the end product cannot be known in advance. All parties must remain flexible and seek solutions jointly.

- New environmental responsibilities are not always welcomed by government ministries or economic sectors in society; until the interconnectedness of environmental problems is understood and accepted, there will be resistance to environment "overstepping its boundaries". There must also be a *quid pro quo*: development of environmental policy must take greater account of sector ministry concerns.

- Even within an environment ministry, integration can be taken to imply criticism of past work on sector policies. Highly expert officials who have developed successful measures to counter, for example, air pollution may be

251

Table 2. **Key Environmental Facts on Achievements**

	What has been done	Further steps
Environmental measures	From 1970 to 1980 organic pollution from industrial effluents fell by two-thirds following the introduction of charges (licences had little effects).	Policy instruments and in particular licensing should be further improved. There are complaints from companies about stringent norms, lack of flexibility and inconsistencies between target group policy and issuing of licences.
Efficiency gains	To make the system more efficient, general rules have been drawn up for specific sectors so that large numbers of companies no longer need to apply for individual licences. Attention has been given to avoiding dissipation of resources. National Environmental Policy Plans resulted in an intensification of policy efforts with specific attention to safeguarding efficiency and preventing dissipation of resources in the "booming sector".	Expenditure for the environment has been increasing dramatically. Attention needs to be sustained in order to make best use of these resources.
Improved governance	Efforts to integrate policy through a thematic approach based on issues (*e.g.* manure problem), geographic areas, material flows and target groups rather than traditional policy fields (like soil or water). Integration has resulted in concrete plans, laws and institutions at national, provincial and local level.	Efforts have been mainly focussing on integrating environmental concerns into transport policy, physical planning, agricultural policy, economic structure policy, water management, building regulations, energy policy, education policy. Progress is slow, partly due to the complexity of this goal. Efforts should be maintained and intensified. Right balance between legislation and enforcement on the one hand and consultation and self-regulation on the other. Risk of conflict between consultative processes and regulations if this process is not well managed.

Source: (Bressers/Plettenburg 1997: 126).

made newly aware of problems they helped to create in waste disposal. Integration must be presented in terms of a solution to environmental quality failures, not policy failures.

- Integration has allowed policy-makers to form an overall picture of environmental quality in which causes, effects and inter-relations are better understood.
- The strategic environmental management approach set out in the NEPP provides a context in which all policy proposals and implementing actions can be assessed: do they contribute to achieving measurable quality objectives?

- Setting of objectives and targets across environmental themes has promoted a major shift to longer planning timeframes in government and industry. Government has a practical method and scientific basis for developing preventive policies. Industry, given clear targets and tasks, is gaining the confidence to invest in integrated (process-based) solutions rather than short-term "fixes".

- Above all, the co-operation, co-ordination and transfer of responsibility that are required by integration are now well under way. Sector ministries and economic groups have produced their own environmental policies or action plans; some can already demonstrate significant environmental improvement as a result. The process is not complete, but there is no longer a debate over the legitimacy of the approach. In the Netherlands, all sectors of government and society have come to recognise their shared responsibility for achieving sustainable development.

Policy integration is paramount for the from environmentally unfriendly policies to environment-friendly ones. Within central government, the fact that agriculture, water and environment are integrated into "bigger" ministries dealing also with transport, land use, and housing can be identified as a positive factor for achieving sustainability goals. Yet, there is a sense that integration should go further. For example, the three different branches of the Ministry of Ho using, Spatial Planning and the Environment still develop separate plans and their legal framework is not always co-ordinated. This is why the Ministry recently engaged in re-examining its legal framework to improve the consistency and integration of environmental policy with other fields.

To be effective, integrative processes within each ministry should be supported by a central steering capacity. For example, in the agriculture sector, the mission of the Strategic Policy Division (BSB) is to be a "strategic policies catalyst in the interest of the Ministry's overall policy area". Although strategic policy-making will primarily remain with the staff of the different departments in the Ministry, BSB points out developments and stimulates the departments to launch a debate about strategic issues that are being discussed at central government level or to make further analyses. BSB also supports and facilitates the departments in the development of a long-term view.

The fact that environment-related tasks have been entrusted to other ministries than VROM and to other public sector entities calls for deepening integrative processes in the future, in particular in a context of more decentralisation of tasks. At a later stage, it could be envisaged to develop steering capacities at Cabinet level for monitoring cross-governmental integration.

Decentralisation is another trend that has proved to be rather positive for achieving policy goals. The local level showed examples of successful integration

253

of policies dealing with "all aspects of the physical and living" environment. Traditionally the management of main infrastructure projects – perhaps the major threat to sustainable development in the Dutch context – has taken place at the national level. In some cases this could lead to endless debates, such as for Schipol Airport or concerning the railway connections to the German border. There is sometimes a sense that, for some of these projects, managing conflicts locally would have resulted in more positive outcomes. Decentralisation of decision-making is expected to prevent negative effects of lengthy consultation procedures and avoid too much politicisation inherent to national debates.

However, the right balance should be struck, as further decentralisation could raise issues relative to more complex and fragmented decision-making. The impact of conflicting political agendas between the different entities concerned at regional and local level should also be considered. It is sometimes asserted that devolution of competencies to lower levels of government would imply building local capacities for:

- Better translating European legislation into local regulations.

- Developing the ability to support the implementation of environmental measures.

- Improving technical knowledge where it is too weak.

Moving to more decentralisation should be accompanied by specific attention to integration across levels of government. To support coherence of the new Dutch water policy, the Ministry of Transport, Public Works and Water Management has, for example, introduced an integrative process between central government, provinces, municipalities and water-boards (see Box 13).

In the Dutch context, consultation is often presented as a positive factor for reaching workable solutions. Some observers underlined that the cost of consultation remains quite limited compared to the social cost of not consulting stakeholders (see section on *public consultation*). However, some examples show that consultation processes can become difficult to manage when the issues relate to sustainable development. The project to expand the Schipol airport is a good illustration of such difficulties. In this case, a broad official group was set up including VROM, the administration of the Schipol airport, the Dutch airline company KLM, provincial and local authorities, and various NGOs. The integrative approach in this case has not delivered any tangible results to date. On the contrary, public consultation brought the conflict to the public view. One could argue that there is no alternative and that this will still be the most efficient way to reach agreement. That said, the main dilemma that rapidly emerged from this process is how to simultaneously involve stakeholders with conflicting agendas and still come up with a manageable consensus.

Box 13. **Water Management: Integrated Approach Towards
Dutch Water Policy**

In February 2001, central government, provinces, municipalities and water-boards signed an agreement on the start of joint implementation of the water policy for the 21st century. They shared the view that firm agreements need to be reached concerning the consequences of climate change, the rise in sea levels and land subsidence. Action needs to be taken now in anticipation of future situations. Intentions to that end will be laid down next year in a "National Water Administrative Agreement". The current agreement is a rapid response to the announcement by the government of a radically different approach towards water management in the Netherlands. This provides evidence of the jointly perceived urgency of the water issue. Apart from safety and water nuisance, the new policy also concerns the tackling of regional water shortages, measures to combat the drying out of sandy soils, and further improvements in water quality. A particularly radical measure is the intention to establish retention basins in low-lying areas for the temporary storage of river water so as to avoid flooding. Efforts will now be made to identify such areas along the rivers on the basis of "regional water visions". In the meantime, supplementary technical measures are to be worked out and introduced in the short term along the coast, rivers and Lake IJsselmeer.

Source: Ministry of Transport, Public Works and Water Management Internet site (*www.minvenw.nl/cend/dco/home/data/international/gb/brief.htm#rws*).

In a representative democracy, informal consultation arrangements could also be questioned. This would be particularly important if the "polder model" of co-operation between government and stakeholders is to be translated into other systems. If not carefully managed, extensive consultation and bargaining with "established" groups runs the risk of shifting responsibilities from elected officials, who are accountable to citizens, to unaccountable "groups". In a less open society, it would be highly risky to take decisions away from all open decision forums to more hidden power centres. Therefore only an open, transparent and inclusive consultation process can meet democratic criteria. One issue also relates to the level of internal democracy of the groups associated to the policy process.

One key challenge for the future is the ability to expand capacities for strategic thinking within government: in-house information is provided by various institutions. Units have been set up within most ministries to enhance more strategic vision. The size of these units is uneven. In some cases, they are rather "big" structures, such as in the Ministry of Housing, Spatial Planning and the Environment

255

Box 14. **Strengthening Strategic Policy in the Ministry of Agriculture, Nature Management and Fisheries**

In 1994, the Ministry of Agriculture, Nature Management and Fisheries established a small Strategic Policy Division (currently composed of 6 people) to help develop vision for the longer term. The role of this unit is to question "business as usual" in order to generate innovative thinking and to encourage various parts of the Ministry to deal with emerging issues such as sustainable development. Its role evolved. During the first five years the division was very much "process oriented", focussing on how to integrate new issues in to the policy process and helping management teams within various directorates (mainly through organising meetings) to develop scenarios and to better connect outside pressures with policy options. It is now entering a new phase, since staff from this unit is now considered to be sufficiently trained to analyse signals from outside. The focus is now more on substance, and the division is putting specific topics on the table where it feels that important developments are happening or that "taboo topics" require discussion. Directly connected to the top level, it has a key role for promoting new concepts. One recent example was on the sensitive food safety issues. The Division developed forward-looking arguments for co-managing food safety between the public and private sectors. The Strategic Policy Division is key to developing the future agenda of the Ministry of Agriculture, Nature Management and Fisheries.

Among the main issues that it identified:

• IT and governance.

• Consumer concerns.

• Food agenda for the future.

Innovation policy (government role in innovation).

Development of rural areas in the Netherlands and abroad (include co-operation with developing countries).

Crisis management (mainly how to read the signals of potential crisis).

---

and in the Ministry of Water and Transport. In other ministries, like the Ministry of Agriculture, Nature Management and Fisheries, these units remain very limited in staff and resources (which is also seen as an opportunity to remain very dynamic). These different units meet regularly and constitute a network of innovative thinking. They also actively interact with various stakeholders.

Policy evaluation is also a key challenge. Despite systematic legal evaluation as well as many studies from universities and private institutes, there is to date no systematic evaluation of policies done within government. In particular, there are no ex-post accountability mechanisms to check progress on the sustainable development agenda. For example, the General Accounting Office is not competent to evaluate progress on the greening of government. There is sometimes a feeling that an outside and impartial body to report on sustainable development would definitely add value, although this should be balanced with the cost of establishing a new institution.

But developing strategic thinking and evaluation also implies to broadening the basis of knowledge on which public choices can be made. Research remains uneven in the Netherlands as in most OECD countries. Sectors like agriculture where extensive research is done (see Box 15) can draw on wide information, but other sectors rely on information done in other countries.

In order to strengthen the knowledge basis of organisations, the National Initiative on Sustainable Development (NIDO) was launched at the end of 1999 and is one of the twelve initiatives taken by the Dutch government with the aim of investing in the Netherlands' knowledge infrastructure. NIDO has the objective to achieve leaps forward in sustainable development, meaning the creation of a link between prosperity and well being, a link between economic growth and improvement of the living environment. Sustainable development in the Netherlands needs a new impulse. Many actors have already contributed to sustainable development within the range of their own possibilities. In order to make further improvement, forces should be joined. The combination of experience and insights of people in business, the government, social institutions and science may help to bring the issues of sustainable development closer to a solution. This requires a collective effort in which several parties will co-operate. For this purpose, the Dutch government initiated NIDO. NIDO employs an integral approach in which various parties from a wide vision on sustainable development may find each other. NIDO is formally organised in a Foundation at an arm's length of government. In order to initiate leaps in sustainable development NIDO introduces a process based on three pillars:

- Co-operation: bringing together all relevant parties involved in a specific theme, to elicit discussion about what each actor can do (in line with the Dutch "Polder Model" – approach).

- Future-oriented: joining programs related to future societal trends that have an impact on sustainable development.

- Focus on societal needs: only carrying out projects with sufficient support.

A prominent organisation with a key role in producing integrated data for sustainable development is the National Institute of Public Health and Environmental Protection (RIVM). This government institution keeps records and makes predictions on environmental and health issues in order to promote public health. It works in co-operation with other institutes and publishes surveys to support national environmental policy planning. These entail both forecasts and policy alternatives. From 1995 onwards, the RIVM has published an annual environment report containing the latest environmental data as well as indicators of the expected effects of policy measures

257|

Box 15. **Research for Sustainable Development in the Ministry of Agriculture, Nature Management and Fisheries**

Research carried out by the **Wageningen Research Centre** (Wageningen UR) focuses on sustainable and competitive agriculture, forestry and fisheries and a sufficiently high quality of life in rural areas. Research is conducted in 12 sophisticated institutes and covers a wide range of subjects. Over 3 200 specialised men and women are working towards a high-quality and useful contribution to agriculture in the widest sense:

- The **Research Institute for Agrobiology and Soil Fertility** (AB) aims to advance soil quality, sustainable plant production systems and the quality of agricultural products. The institute carries out research on the functioning of soils, plants, crops, vegetation and agrosystems. A special characteristic of AB is the integration of knowledge of processes at soil, crop and agrosystem level.

- The **Agro Technological Research Institute** (ATO) deals with post-harvest processes in agricultural plants and plant products. The research focuses on food products, industrial products and fresh plant products and covers aspects such as storage, shelf life, safety and quality, processing, logistics and integrated chain control.

The **Centre for Plant Breeding and Reproduction Research** (CPRO) carries out research aimed to solve practical problems and to further develop plant breeding and plant reproduction to support growers, plant improvers and plant breeders, trade, the processing industry, consumers and the environment.

The **Institute for Forestry and Nature Research** (IBN) aims to maintain, restore and develop forests and nature. This includes land and water ecosystems in urban and rural areas. The research focuses on the identification of problems in forests and nature, and aims to suggest sustainable development to solve these problems.

The **Research Institute for Animal Husbandry and Animal Health** (ID) carries out research covering the entire animal production chain. This includes animal health and welfare, production safety and minimisation of the burden placed on the environment, as well as efficient production and high added value in the production of meat, milk and eggs.

The **Institute of Agricultural and Environmental Engineering** (IMAG) works on new techniques and technology, which contribute to the realisation of socially acceptable production methods in agriculture. In addition to qualified researchers specialised in many technical disciplines, there is much agricultural expertise available at the institute, both as regards the crop and the livestock sector.

The **Research Institute for Plant Protection** (IPO) bears a central responsibility for research on crop protection for agriculture, natural vegetation and public open spaces. The institute conducts strategic research to enhance the economically and socially responsible protection of plants against pests and diseases.

Box 15. **Research for Sustainable Development in the Ministry of Agriculture, Nature Management and Fisheries** (*cont.*)

The **Agricultural Economics Research Institute** (LEI) carries out research on the management of agricultural, horticultural and forestry holdings, and of fishery companies. Its research programme is mainly based on data collected by LEI in a national bookkeeping network that forms part of the EU Farm Accountancy Data Network.

The **Centre for Agricultural Publishing and Documentation** (PUDOC) is a service institute working closely with the library of Wageningen Agricultural University. Its expertise covers the building up of a collection of scientific journals and books and giving advice on initiation and management of data bases for bibliographic and other information.

The **State Institute for Quality Control of Agricultural Products** (RIKILT) conducts fundamental and applied research focused on the advancement of safe food production and food products. This is implemented in six research programmes, *e.g.* the risk assessment of additives, natural toxins and contaminants, the quality control of agricultural products, and the development of fast and reliable screening methods.

The **National Institute for Fisheries Research** (RIVO) carries out applied research focused on the contribution of biological, environmental, microbiological, biochemical, technical and technological solutions to problems in the exploitation and management of aquatic ecosystems in sea, coastal and inland waters.

The **Winand Staring Centre for Integrated Land, Soil and Water Research** (SC) conducts research on patterns and processes to solve problems encountered in the integration of the various uses of rural areas. The institute aims to contribute to a responsible management of the environment, water and landscape, and to achieve a balanced physical planning and land development.

Source: Royal Netherlands Ministry of Agriculture, Nature Management, and Fisheries Internet site *www.minlnv.nl/international/lnv/index07.shtml*

and medium-term forecasts; an environment survey covering a period of at least 10 years is published every four years.

One issue is to maintain government capacity to access knowledge that often becomes more and more technical, while citizens are more demanding. Information can be improved through research. Research bodies are an important tool for building support for developing sustainable development policies. The Advisory Council on Nature and Environment (RMNO,)) contributes to improving environmental knowledge through research programmes on the impact of economic development on the environment and the environmental "constraints" that need to be taken into consideration. In other areas knowledge is more sophisticated, and this could

---

become a constraint to policy-makers (although this could be alleviated by new modes of information circulating in networks). This is the case of nature and environment issues, where research is more widespread. An agenda for the future could be to develop work on the social aspects of sustainable development. The RMNO is launching a programme in 2001 directly connected to social aspects of sustainable development. One area of investigation is "social scientific behaviour of people about environment and nature" (*e.g.* one aspect will be traffic congestion).

Research is also complemented by sector councils for health, agriculture and development assistance. This provides a framework for dealing with sustainable development. There is a feeling in the Netherlands that in the context of a knowledge-driven society, the role of research should evolve from providing information to developing information networks, which would then imply better connections between universities, various government research centres and private research. Responding to the complex issues of sustainable development is making this need more challenging. It calls at the same time for strengthening connections between government and "knowledge production centres" (mainly universities) in order to bring both relevant and sensible advice to policy-makers, and for ensuring that knowledge centres enjoy sufficient autonomy to undertake their own research programmes rather than carry out research driven by government. The need for autonomy is reinforced by the changing knowledge structure, which is globalised, uses ICT, etc. It is essential to ensure sufficient creativity and flexibility and to broaden the knowledge basis of the society.

Selected promising initiatives

Several promising initiatives have been introduced in recent years. Two specific innovative strategies providing interesting examples of specific attention paid to policy integration and multi-stakeholder processes in order to achieve sustainable development goals are described below: new policy on managing substances, and restructuring the poultry and pig sectors.

New policy on managing substances

Increased concerns about the effectiveness of existing legislation to control the emission of hazardous substances, the increase in production of and increasing exposure to substances with unknown environmental consequences, and the presence of hazardous substances in remote rural areas, have prompted a review of existing legislation. It was found that the existing provisions were ineffective and thus inadequate to guarantee efficient risk management and respond to these growing public concerns. These findings were included in the third environmental policy plan (NEPP III, 1998). In line with the conditions stated in NEPP III, the Dutch government announced that it would keep Parliament informed of problems associated with hazardous substances, especially with persistent, bio-accumulating toxins, hormone-disruptive substances and non-assessed chemicals. These agents all have in common that little is known about their environmental effects. This knowledge deficit led the Dutch government to commence vigorous c onsultations during the period 1999-2000 with all relevant stakeholders in the debate called "Strategy on Management of Substances" (SOMS). The results of these discussions were incorporated into the "Strategy on Management of Substances Programme" which the Cabinet accepted on 16th March 2001 (Cabinet 2001).

This new policy on chemical substance management goes much further than existing legislation. Rather than only trying to address the *ex post* problems raised by the production and use of chemicals, it envisages an *ex ante* approach. The main aim of the policy is to close the knowledge gap that impeded successful policy-making in the area of chemical substance regulation and so allow sufficient risk management in this policy sector. This requires a holistic approach encompassing knowledge of possible environmental risks associated with the use of such substances in each stage of their respective life-cycles. The implementation of this strategy calls for close co-operation between industry, public authorities and civil society members, as a constant exchange of knowledge and monitoring are prerequisites for the success of the programme.

Box 16. **Main Elements of the Strategy on Management
of Substances Programme**

Facilitation of the implementation of precautionary principles through the development of new risk management instruments.

- Public availability of information on hazards and risks associated with certain substances.
- Collection and pooling of all possible information on potential risks at very short notice.
- Production quality improvements and increased production chain responsibility in the chemical industry.
- Suspending the use of chemicals that pose an unacceptable environmental risk.
- Prohibiting the use of carcinogenic, mutagenic, reprotoxic (CMR) substances and very persistent, bio-accumulating (PBT) substances in consumer products and open applications and restricting their industrial use.
- Complete abolishment of emissions of PBTs by 2020.

Source: (Cabinet 2001: 3).

261

Restructuring the poultry and pig sectors

In the 1980s the Netherlands was confronted with immense problems for managing stocks of pigs in a sustainable way (*e.g.* manure issue). In particular, it became apparent that it would be difficult to continue managing a poor strategic choice: unlike other countries (such as Denmark) that had made efforts since the 1960s to combine arable land and pigs, the Netherlands had continued to concentrate on intensive pig farming.

An initial failure occurred in 1984, when the first regulations were issued to limit the expansion of poultry and pig farms which were responsible for the increase of phosphor emissions. This was expected to be achieved through a decree initiating more restrictive licences. During the days preceding the enforcement of the new system, a significant number of pig producers requested licences in order to escape the new system. In one weekend, this provoked a significant augmentation of the pig stock from 12 million to 14 million.

This bad experience led to negotiation with both agricultural organisations and NGOs in order to find a solution. IT then required a re-definition of the traditional negotiation mechanisms – which had been based on the leadership of the Christian Democrats within government – which meant a close dialogue between the government and farmers' organisations. This consultation process was a preliminary step to a stricter programme of reduction of the use of phosphates, promoting alternatives to traditional fertilisation. But this initiative was strongly opposed by farmers' organisations and did not work mainly because of economic reasons: the new system was too expensive for farmers. One factor was that there was no strong incentive to encourage farmers to find alternative solutions.

In 1996, the government initiated a very big shift. For the first time, the Christian Democrats were left outside the government coalition and the Minister for Agriculture, Nature Management and Fisheries did not come from the agriculture sector nor the agro-food complex. The consequence was on the one hand more tensions with the farmers' organisations, but on the other hand radical and effective solutions for controlling emissions of phosphates. Among the most innovative measures initiated:

- The creation of a **Mineral Accounting System**. Farmers declare inputs and output of minerals in their farms, which forms the basis of a "mineral tax" similar to the income tax.

- Following the pig fever of 1997, and despite former unsuccessful attempts to reduce the number of pigs through voluntary agreements, the *Pig Restriction Act* was imposed on farmers. The Act entailed a reduction of 25 per cent of the number of pigs to be carried out in two stages. This was the first time that such a drastic measure was taken for environmental purposes. About 20 000 farmers were concerned, half of them relying only on pig production.

A major limit to the implementation of the new policy came from judicial cases initiated by the farmers' organisations, and the first reduction target of 10 per cent was not questioned. However, the next target of a 15 per cent reduction was successfully challenged by farmers on the basis of sufficient motivation, and this was a reason for the government to try to negotiate new compliance objectives for 2003.

A new system is being introduced to get equilibrium: a "manure disposal system". There is agreement with most farmers' organisations to achieve this equilibrium by 2002. The new system is based on a certain ratio between size of land and the number of pigs. Farmers and Parliament have agreed to this system. It must be validated by the European Commission.

One of the key lessons may be that passing the Pig Restriction Act was only possible because government was strongly supported by Parliament and by public opinion. The fact that the economy was growing played a significant role, because it gave good perspectives for redeployment. The pig policy went through three phases:

- Collusion.
- Constraint and *ex post* contestation and bargaining.
- Ex *ante* co-operation and negotiation.

In search of innovative decision-making

Some of the critical advantages of the Dutch system include:

- An attempt to generate politically and ideologically neutral research in the fields of science and economics.
- A commitment by the government to lengthy and complicated processes.
- A commitment to the consensual process that permitted diverse and often conflicting political and economic actors to work together towards systematic change.

According to some authors (De Jong 1996, p 10), the Dutch model, even though it is based on specific social, economic, environmental and cultural conditions contains elements that could be transferred to other countries, for example:

- Goal setting.
- Economic and environmental modelling.
- Scheduled progress reviews.
- Appropriate lead time for major change.

Other elements, could perhaps be less easily translated, such as the capacity to follow "regulatory reinvention", and the "consensus on objectives".

263

Dutch environmental policy reflects the structure adopted for dealing with environmental matters within the government. Dutch environmental policy is not compartmentalised according to affected elements such as air or water, but is formulated and implemented according to an integrated thematic approach which creates the ability for dealing with inter-related issues.

The evolution of policy tools from an "authority-based" policy style (licences and regulations) to a system of instruments involving the participation of society constitutes a major feature of environmental policy and is key to sustainable development. This evolution could be a major asset for moving to a more comprehensive sustainable development strategy after 2001. In the previous system, government decisions often gave rise to contestation and bargaining when entering the implementation phase. This situation had a negative impact on policy effectiveness and changed the relationship between government and target groups. Now that open negotiation is taking place at the stage of policy formulation, society is vested with more "ownership" over policies. This change in the governance style may also facilitate a more open attitude and mutual understanding between traditionally conflicting groups, like for example environmental groups and farmers'organisations. However, "convergence" is still limited when major economic interests conflict, and debates remain very lively in a number of sensitive areas. Strong government intervention is concentrating on these areas. In the case of the use of pesticides, for example, it seems impossible to reach a consensus between various stakeholders without active Governments involvement for defining rules on their use.

Co-operative mechanisms between business and government also call for a clear commitment from political decision-makers an the elaboration of a National Strategy for Sustainable Development (NSSD) may offer an opportunity in this respect. It is not possible to treat equally co-operative and non co-operative companies, therefore the licensing system should be used in a flexible way: for some companies, government should retain the option of issuing instructions; in other cases – *e.g.* when companies have developed efficient environmental management systems – more freedom could be granted. Desireable measures could include:

- Sophisticated data collection and modelling in some areas.

- Present the data in simple terms.

- Re-examine ministerial oversight. The key role played by VROM is to disseminate knowledge so that other parts of government understand. However, in a few sectors that are key to sustainable development, the available knowledge is instead in the hands of the Ministry of Agriculture, Nature Management and Fisheries (nitrates, energies, pesticides).

- Finding framework for discussing these issues with government companies and NGOs.

There are imbalances in the level and access to information between different non-governmental stakeholders. For example, Industries have been often much more equipped than environmental NGOs to fund research and bring evidence to decision-makers. Developing further capacities for independent research on sustainable development will be an issue of particular importance for the future.

Notes

1. The views expressed in this paper are those of the authors, and do not necessarily reflect those of the OECD, or those of its Public Management Service.
2. The number has gradually been reduced. The number of municipalities was, for example, 1015 in 1950, 913 in 1970 and 636 in 1994 (OECD 1997: *ibid.*).
3. See evaluation of the Netherlands court of Audit: *www.rekenkamer.nl/en/summary/integrationlanguage.htm.*
4. For example, the negative social consequences of moving to a more environmentally sustainable agriculture have been neglected, reflecting a rather strict interpretation of the "polluter pays" principle.

Annex I

Taxation and Sustainable Development in The Netherlands

The new tax system

From 1 January 2001, the Netherlands has a new tax system that involves substantial changes to income tax. The new system creates a robust taxation system with a broader base and lower rates, and addresses future developments. The objectives of this revision include the stimulation of employment opportunity, strengthening of the Dutch economic structure and international competitive edge, and the promotion of sustainable economic development ("greening").

In order to stimulate the economy and employment opportunity, the basic rates of taxation were lowered. Work is made more attractive by the introduction of an "employment rebate": those people in paid employment enjoy a tax advantage in the form of a fixed non-taxable deduction. The reduction in taxation on labour is financed by reductions in expenditure and by increases in indirect taxes, such as VAT and environmental levies.

By lowering the taxation on income from employment, together with a shift from direct to indirect taxation, the economic structure of the Netherlands and its international competitive edge will be strengthened. Greater emphasis on environmental levies will make a significant contribution towards achieving sustainable economic development.

Further general requirements

Persons liable to environmental taxes are required to keep accounts which give a true and fair view of all transactions, manufacturing processes, and movements on all products concerned (for fuel tax and regulatory energy tax), on all withdrawal and infiltration of groundwater (for the tax on groundwater) and of the sort, the quantity and the origin of the waste delivered to them (for the tax on waste). These accounts must be suitable for presentation to the tax authorities at any time.

Source: Dutch Ministry of Finance Internet site *www.minfin.nl.*

Environmental Taxes

Tax	Form	Revenue	Target groups	Exemptions
Fuel Tax	Levied on mineral oils, coal, natural gas, blast furnace gas, coke oven gas and coal gas. Mineral oils are petrol, diesel fuel, heating gas oil and heavy fuel oil.	Approximately NLG 1 381 million (€ 626.67 million) in 2001.	The fuel tax on mineral oils is levied together with excise duty on mineral oils. Fuel tax on the other fuels mentioned is levied on persons who extract, produce or import these fuels, and subsequently use them as fuels or transfer them to others for use as fuels. The number of taxable persons liable to fuel tax is restricted as the tax is levied primarily on the manufacturers and importers of fuel.	All usage other than as fuel is exempt.
Groundwater Tax	Levied on the extraction of fresh groundwater. This tax has been levied since 1 January 1995.	Approximately NLG 375 million (€ 170.17 million) for 2001.	The proprietors of the establishments extracting groundwater, for example: the manufacturers of drinking water, farmers, and industries that use groundwater.	Exemptions are applicable under certain conditions, for example in case of extraction of groundwater for draining a building site, as well as test extraction, extraction for use for sprinkling and irrigating land, and extraction needed to clean groundwater.
Tap Water Tax	Levied on the supply of tap water to a maximum of 300 cubic metres per year.	Approximately NLG 220 million (€ 99.83 million) for 2001.	Water utility companies.	
Tax on Waste	Levied on the disposal of waste to establishments operating dumps and incinerators.	Approximately NLG 527 million (€ 239.14 million) for 2001.	Waste disposal companies (*e.g.* landfill sites or incinerators)	Exemptions apply, for instance, to non-purifiable polluted dredging sludge and soil.
Regulatory Energy Tax	Levied on the consumption of natural gas, electricity and mineral oil products when used as substitutes for gas by domestic and commercial users.	Approximately NLG 5 474 million (€ 2 484 million) for 2001. The revenues are returned to domestic commercial users through other tax reductions.	Energy distribution companies and manufacturers and wholesalers of mineral oils. These companies pass on the tax to their customers.	All usage other than as fuel and for natural gas used to produce electricity.

Source: Dutch Ministry of Finance Internet site *www.minfin.nl.*

Annex II

The Dutch Budget for 2001

Thanks to the surplus, the budget for 2001 spending increased by 14.8 billion guilders in relation to 2000, taxes were lowered by 6.6 billion guilders and the national debt was reduced by 20.7 billion guilders.

In addition to the extra public spending of 7.1 billion guilders laid down in the coalition agreement, the government has found flexibility within the spending limits for an additional injection of 7.7 billion guilders in 2001. This will bring the total increase in spending in 2001 to 14.8 billion guilders, which will go mainly to care (3.3 billion guilders), education (2.8 billion), infrastructure (2.4 billion) and employment and incomes policy (2.1 billion). There is also extra money for safety and habitability (1.2 billion), nature and environment (0.8 billion), and international policy and defence (0.3 billion).

Table 1.   **Spending Increases in 2001 (in Billions of Guilders)**

Spending cluster	Coalition agreement	Extra	Total
Care (waiting lists, workload, absenteeism, medicines)	1.7	1.6	3.3
Education (reduction in class size, ICTs, teachers, early years education)	1.4	1.5	2.8
Infrastructure (southern high-speed line, Amsterdam N-S metro, *Randstad* rail, roads)	1.7	0.7	2.4
Nature and environment (pollution, sustainable energy, nature conservation areas)	0.3	0.5	0.8
Safety and habitability (police, judiciary, major cities)	0.6	0.6	1.2
International and defence (peace operations, clean development)	−0.3	0.6	0.3
Employment and incomes policy (labour participation)	1.3	0.8	2.1
Other	0.5	1.4	2.0
Total extra spending			

Table 2.   **Main Elements of 2001 Tax Plan (in Billions of Guilders)**

Tax	2001
Increase in general VAT rate from 17.5 per cent to 19 per cent	+4.8
Increase in eco-tax	+1.9
Changes to taxation of capital/income from capital	+2.6
Reduction in taxes on work	−15.5
Other tax and social insurance contribution reductions in 2001	+0.4
Total reduction in tax and social insurance contributions	**−6.6**

Source: Dutch Ministry of Finance Internet site (*http://www.minfin.nl*).

269

Annex III

The Advisory Council for Research on Nature and Environment (RMNO)

The Advisory Council for Research on Nature and Environment (RMNO) is a sectoral council established in 1981. Sectoral councils give advice to the government on research into problems in a specific sector of society. Environmental issues in the medium and long term, nature conservation and landscape conservation issues included.

The RMNO advises the government, either of its own accord or in response to requests from ministries, on the content and organisation of research concerning the environment, nature and landscape. This includes not only research in the natural sciences and technological research, but also research in the social and political sciences. Multidisciplinary and/or inter-disciplinary research is often needed to analyse environmental problems and their possible solutions.

Tasks

- *Drawing attention* to trends in society and science, which are relevant to both current and future problems involving nature and the environment, and doing research on these problems.

- *Determining knowledge gaps* and formulating research needs to find ways of solving future nature conservation and environmental problems.

- *Acting as an intermediary* between the parties involved in research on the environment, nature and landscape, for instance assisting social groups in formulating research needs and improving communication between people who need knowledge and researchers.

- *Stimulating* public debate on research on nature conservation and environmental problems in the medium and long term.

Target groups

- Ministries: Economic Affairs (EZ); Agriculture, Nature Management and Fisheries (LNV); Education, Culture and Science (OCW); Public Works and Water Management (V&W); and Housing, Spatial Planning and the Environment (VROM).

- Local authorities: provinces, municipal councils (metropolitan and urban) and district waterboards.

- Knowledge institutes.

- Large firms and branch organisations.

- Social organisations.

- The European Commission, the General Directorates of the European Union, the Organisation for Economic co-operation and Development (OECD) and other international organisations.

Composition of the RMNO

The RMNO is tripartite in its composition: its council members come from networks of researchers, policy-makers, and users of research (consultants, trade and industry and agencies using the research in their work). The RMNO secretariat has eight members of *staffuk3.htm* – staff.

Annex IV

Departmental Organisation of the Ministry for Agriculture, Nature Management and Fisheries

Department	Responsibilities and Aims	Tasks	Associated Agencies
Agriculture	Policy-Making in the agricultural sector, in particular primary production.	Overall economic and social affairs, environmental issues, structural questions, aids and incentives, R&D policy, education in the areas of animal and crop production. Multi-year Crop Protection Plan, national and international phytosanitary and pesticide policy. Farm and animal welfare; general agricultural management issues.	The National Reference Centre for Agriculture (IKC-L) supports policy development and implementation.
Dept. of Nature Management	Mainly policy formulation on national and international policy on nature, forests, landscape and wildlife, but also development and application of policy instruments.	Development and evaluation of policies for nature management, policy integration in overall government policymaking, development of standards and frameworks for implementing services.	The National Reference Centre for Nature aids the Department in the fulfilment of its duties; the Nature Assessment Bureau, is being developed to monitor and assess relevant policies.
Dept. of Trade and Industry	Promotion of Dutch agricultural industry, support of its international competitiveness, and liaison in government matters with agricultural industry.	Developing, influencing and structuring of national and international policy towards the agricultural industry; international promotion of Dutch agricultural industry; structuring and developing the agricultural industry (R&D, clustering, investment programmes).	
Fisheries	Promotion of responsible and balanced exploitation of fish stocks; promotion of the entire fishing industry as an economic activity; protection of Dutch fishing interests on EU and international level.	Fish stock management; development and implementation of the EU Common Fisheries Policy and other international fishing agreements; production, marketing, price-setting, quality and processing of fishery products; management of the Fisheries Development Fund.	

**Departmental Organisation of the Ministry for Agriculture,
Nature Management and Fisheries** (*cont.*)

Department	Responsibilities and Aims	Tasks	Associated Agencies
International Affairs	Development and propagation of the Dutch agricultural interests on international level.	Inter-ministerial and intra-governmental co-ordination and development of policies on international co-operation in the sphere of agricultural policies; government and ministerial liaison with international organisations and institutions on agricultural subjects; co-ordination of market and prices policy implementation to prevent EAGGF claims.	
Legal Affairs	Ensure conformity of ministerial actions with national and international law.	Contribute to choice of policy instruments in respect of national and international legal obligations; legal adaptation of policy.	
Rural Areas and Recreation	Responsible for enhancement of rural development with rural tourism.	Main policy tasks are strategic rural area development and management, rural tourism development.	
The Environment, Quality and Health	Responsible for the improvement of animal and plant health, development of ethical production guidelines, public health related issues of agricultural production.	Development and implementation of policies in the area of public health and agricultural production; risk management, analysis and communication; development of quality assurance systems regarding agricultural production (food safety, veterinary medicine guidelines and legislation, animal and plant production process).	Bureau for Food and Nutrition Education; National Nutrition Council; Council for Animal Matters; Side-effects of Veterinary Medicines Office; Registration of Veterinary Medicines Office.
Science and Knowledge Dissemination	Responsible for R&D and knowledge transfer in the agricultural sector to stimulate agricultural innovation.	Policy co-ordination with other government bodies; scientific information gathering on the agricultural sector for policy-making.	

Source: Dutch Ministry of Agriculture, Nature Management and Fisheries web site *http://www.minlnv.nl/international/lnv/ index07.shtml*

273|

Annex V

Participatory Process in the City of Groningen: An Open Process of Urban Transport

In the Dutch mid-size city of Groningen, an open planning process of urban transport was undertaken from November 1995 to May 1997. Several studies have documented this process (Woltjer, 1998; Koolen, 1997; Paf, 1997; Welles, 1997). One of the motives for the city to start a new planning process was the outcome of a referendum on the closure of a particular road. It appeared that many citizens opposed the closure because of their general discontent with Groningen traffic policy. Fearing that a new traffic plan would lack support, the city decided to update the traffic policy with broad participation by the population.

A three phase process

The planning process was subdivided into three phases. The first phase (November 1995-March 1996) was the exploration of problems and solutions. To gain insight into traffic and transport policy problems, a telephone survey among 600 respondents and a questionnaire through a local newspaper (5000 respondents) were undertaken. Two roundtable discussions were held in order to present the results of the surveys and initial conclusions on the main problems. All inhabitants of Groningen were invited to the roundtables. Eighteen working groups, with a total number of 300 participants, worked out the analyses of the problems and possible solutions.

The second process phase (March 1996-June 1996) was the elaboration of policy directions. The working groups of the first phase evolved into four workshops. Participants from the working groups formed these workshops together with traffic experts and representatives of pressure groups. In every workshop, different interests were represented and the workshops led to four policy directions or models:

- Pro-car ("full room for the car").
- Selective car use.
- Collective transport and priority for the bicycle.
- The real alternative: emphasis completely on public transport.

These four alternatives were assessed by experts for the effects on mobility, spatial planning, the economy, the environment, technical feasibility and costs. The calculated policy directions formed the basis for the municipal draftvision on traffic policy.

The third phase (June 1996-May 1997) was the decision-making phase. Final decisions had to be taken by the local politicians, but citizens were still actively involved in this phase. Citizens had the opportunity to react in writing to the ideas of a "concept-vision" of the city council. Furthermore, support for a concept-plan was measured through another questionnaire among the respondents of the first survey in November 1995. The survey and written reactions were used to distil main problems that were then discussed in two public debates in the autumn of 1996. The results from the debates and the survey were used to prepare a concept-traffic plan. In November 1997, the concept-traffic plan was presented for the formal legally required participation process (official public enquiry). In May 1997, the final plan was accepted by the city council.

During the entire process, general information was offered to the inhabitants of Groningen through a series of door-to-door information bulletins and through articles in the local newspaper.

The decision-making process resulted in a plan with proposals for a light rail system, car parks outside the city centre, and a cycle path system. The main policy conclusions from the process were that the commuters to the city needed to adopt more sustainable travel patterns. They were expected to use public transport and bikes to go to work. Economically important traffic (freight and business traffic) was allowed to use the roads, as well as people who want to shop by car.

Discussion

The purpose of participation in the Groningen traffic planning process case was to raise the legitimacy of decisions taken and to reduce the level concerning conflict on traffic policy. It offered the possibility of articulating the interests for all stakeholders and citizens. In practice, the participation process served these purposes in that it gave the government necessary information for decision-making, particularly in the identifying of problems and causes and in developing alternative solutions. Another outcome of the process was that the participants learned more about the environmental traffic problems that the city faces. In the Groningen case, citizens could put forward proposals but they did not have the authority to decide on policy. The scope of the participation process was the full range of traffic policy issues and not just sustainable modes. The decisions in the end were taken by means of representative democracy.

Throughout all planning phases, citizens were involved in remarkably large numbers. The municipality received nearly 10 000 suggestions on how to deal with the traffic problems from about 6 000 respondents. But even the citizens that were not directly involved were well informed about the process through the information bulletins.

Given the many opportunities citizens had to formulate their discontent about traffic policy, one would expect that a large part of the frustration about traffic policies among the inhabitants of Groningen would disappear. And it was expected that the participation process would raise support for the new policy. An indicator of this support is that the official public enquiry procedure was relatively short and no main adjustments were made. In addition, separate research after the process found that many participants were more or less satisfied with the final result (Paf, 1997). The research also showed that people had gained more insight into the traffic problems and their difficult solutions. Given the fact that the local council was also satisfied, one could call the Groningen process a success. Still there are two points of criticism on the process: first the representative capability of those involved in the process; second the impacts of participation.

The participation process was not representative of all transport system users, because while all the inhabitants from Groningen were consumers of the urban transport system not all consumers were citizens. About half of the working population in the city are commuters from outside the municipality. Furthermore, the city is an important regional shopping centre

275|

that attracts a lot of visitors. Only about 20 per cent of the participants in the open planning process were from out of town; thus, most of the commuters and visitors did not participate.

Despite the total number of participants, as a consequence of the organisation of the process only a small number of people were involved in the second phase. In addition, individual inhabitants accounted for only a small part of the participants in the workshop in the second phase: most participants were members from organised interest groups (40 per cent), experts (20 per cent) or members of political parties (20 per cent). The background of the participants showed a distinction between "active participants' (members of the workshops) and less-active participants. From the research (Paf, 1997), it appeared that both these participants were representative in terms of age. The group of less-active participants was also representative in terms of education. However, active participants with a higher education (University, professional education) were over-represented (62,7 per cent compared with a representation in the total population of 48%).

Several factors can be identified that could have led to this over-representation. In the first place, the entire process took 18 months; during this time, some people lost interest and dropped out of the participation process. Secondly there was a problem of information overload: The participants judged the quality of information as good, but felt the amount of information was sometimes too much. This could have discouraged participants during the process, especially less-educated participants.

The Groningen example illustrates the tension between participatory decision-making and representative democracy. This tension results from the expectations of the citizens that they will have real influence in decision-making. In the end many participants felt there was somehow a gap between the participation process and the process of "real" decision-making. However, the survey afterwards showed that most participants said they would enter new open planning processes in the future. A problem was that the open planning process preceded a formal legal procedure. In that second procedure, the local council was a key actor. This relates to the issue of institutionalisation of participatory decision-making in legislation. The other side of the coin is that an internal evaluation showed that civil servants and planners had their doubts about the process at the start. They were afraid that an open planning process would lead to an inferior and immature outcome.

In summary, the participation process in this case was a success since the new traffic plan for Groningen did use many of the ideas and contributions of participants and the results of public discussions. The case also shows some drawbacks to the use of a participatory approach. One of them is that highly educated people were over-represented in the group of active participants. Another drawback is that – perhaps due to the broad participation of citizens and interest groups – the plan is a compromise between many different interests. Apart from this, however, the main influence of participation on the decision-making process may well be the support for the proposals, especially amongst interest groups and government bodies.

Annex VI

E.IA.-Procedure in The Netherlands

1. Inception Memorandum	The proponent presents the notification of intent with a brief description of the proposed activity. The competent authority makes the memorandum public. The procedure begins.
2. Public Participation	In a public participation period of four weeks, the public and the advisers comment on the memorandum to the competent authority. This participation and advice aims at the guidelines for the contents of the EIS. Especially the advice of the EIA Commission is important.
3. Guidelines	Thirteen weeks after publication of the inception memorandum, the competent authority draws up the guidelines. The guidelines define the environmental effects and alternatives to be assessed in the Environmental Impact Statement.
4. Environmental Impact Statement (EIS)	The proponent is responsible for drawing up the EIS. There is no maximum time limit. In this phase, intensive interaction between the EIS process and the development of the project or plan is recommended. On completion, the EIS is sent with a permit request or draft plan to the competent authority.
5. Acceptation of the EIS	The competent authority checks the EIS on the basis of guidelines and legal requirements within six weeks.
6. Publication	The competent authority publishes the EIS within eight weeks after receiving it. The EIS is published simultaneously with the permit request or draft plan for public comment and advice.
7. Public Participation	The public and the advisers give their comments on the EIS and on the permit request or draft plan. The public participation period is at least four weeks. A public hearing is included.
8. Review	Within five weeks after the public participation period, the EIA Commission reviews the EIS both for completeness and scientific quality, taking into account the comments from the advisers and public participation.
9. Decision	The competent authority decides on the basis of the EIS and the received comments and advice. It includes in the decision how the EIS and comments were taken into account. The competent authority must also formulate an evaluation programme.
10. Evaluation	In co-operation with the proponent, the competent authority evaluates the environmental impact on the basis of the evaluation programme. If necessary, the competent authority may order extra mitigating measures to reduce the environmental effects.

Source: (VROM 2000, p. 11).

Bibliography

BRESSERS, Hans Th. A. and Loret A. PLETTENBURG, (1997),
"The Netherlands", in: Jänicke, Martin; Weidner, Helmut (eds.): National Environment Policies: A Comparative Study of Capacity-Building, Berlin; p. 110-131.

CABINET (2001),
Strategy on Management of Substances Accepted by the Cabinet on March 16 2001, The Hague.

DE JONGH, Paul E. (1996),
The Netherlands Approach to Environmental Policy Integration: Integrated Environmental Policy Planning as a Step towards Sustainable Development. Paper Prepared for Enterprise for the Environment at the Centre for Strategic and International Studies, Washington, DC.

DE KONING, M.E.L. (199"),
In dienst van het milieu. Enkele memoires van oud-directeur-generaal Milieubeheer prof. ir. WC. Reij, Alphen aan den Rijn.

GIJSWIJT, A.J. and M. VAN DER VLIET, (1993),
"Regering en parlement over mondiale milieuproblemen", Milieu 8,1.

GUTTELING, J.M and J.F. Caljé, (1993),
"De invloed van het milieurisico's in het nieuws: Mondiale risico's en risico's dichter bij huis", Milieu 8, 1, p. 14-19

JÄNICKE, Martin and Helge JÖRGENS, (1998),
"National Environmental Policy Planning in OECD Countries: Preliminary Lessons from Cross-National Comparisons", in: Environmental Politics vol. 7, No. 2, p. 27-54.

MIELISCH, Arndt and Christoph ERDMENGER, (2001),
Green Procurement at the Municipal Level – The Local and the European Dimension. 21/03/2001, Berlin, www.gruene-berlin.de/wirtschaft/papiere/Daseinsvor/Procurem.htm>.

Van MUIJEN, Marie-Louise (2000),
"The Netherlands: Ambitious on Goals – Ambivalent on Action", in:Lafferty, William M.; Meadowcroft, James (Eds.): Implementing Sustainable Development: Strategies and Initiatives in High Consumption Societies, Oxford Universty Press, Oxford; pp. 142-173.

OECD (2001a),
OECD Employment Outlook June 2001, Paris.

OECD (2001b),
Towards Sustainable Consumption, Policy Case Study Series: trend and issues in Participatory Decision-Making for Sustainable Consumption. OECD Paper, Paris.

OECD (2001c-forthcoming),
Synthesis Report of the 1999-2000 OECD Programme towards Sustainable Consumption, Paris.

OECD (1999),
Regulatory Reform in the Netherlands, Paris.

OECD (1997),
Managing across Levels of Government, Paris.

OCDE (1995),
OECD *Environmental Performance Reviews. The Netherlands*, Paris.

ROYAL NETHERLANDS EMBASSY (2001),
Environmental Policy in the Netherlands, Washington, D.C., *www.netherlands-embassy.org/ fie_hltenv.html*

ROYAL NETHERLANDS MINISTRY OF HOUSING, Spatial Planning and the Environment (VROM) (2000),
The Texts of the Regulations on Environmental Impact Assessment in the Netherlands, The Hague.

ROYAL NETHERLANDS MINISTRY OF TRANSPORT, Public Works and Water Management (2000),
Safety, Accessibility, Quality of Life and Innovation in a Dynamic Delta. Press Release 19/09/2000, The Hague, *www.minvenw.nl/cend/dvo/international/english/pressrelease/000919_5929e.html*

TE RIELE Harry, Martijn VAN ELBURG, and René KEMNA, (2001),
Dematerialisation: Less Clear Than it Seems. Thematic Exploration Written for the Dutch Ministry of VROM (Environment), The Hague, *www.vhk.nl/Download/Dematerialisation.pdf*

VNO-NCW (1999),
Environmental Agreements in the Netherlands, The Hague.

WELLES, H. (1997),
Kwaliteit van het planproces Groningen; conpet-tekst t.b.v brochure Platform Duurzaam Stadsverkeer, CROW, Ede; Francino 2994

Government Web Sites:

Royal Netherlands Ministry of Agriculture, Nature Management and Fisheries: *www.minlnv.nl*

Royal Netherlands Ministry of Finance: *www.minfin.nl*

Royal Netherlands Ministry of Housing, Spatial Planning and the Environment: *www.minvrom.nl*

Royal Netherlands Ministry of Transport, Public Works and Water Management: *www.minvenw.nl*

Royal Netherlands Ministry of Economic Affairs: *www.minez.nl*

Royal Netherlands Embassy: *www.netherlands-embassy.org*

United Kingdom

By
James Medhurst[1]
ECOTEC Research and Consulting Limited

Purpose

The study focuses on practices for improving institutions and decision making for sustainable development in the United Kingdom. It was prepared by James MEDHURST from ECOTEC Research and Consulting Limited and edited by Frédéric Bouder from the Public Management Service (PUMA) of the Organisation for Economic co-operation and Development (OECD). It does not intend to provide an exhaustive review of sustainable development governance in the United Kingdom but is rather highlighting current trends as well as selected promising developments that could help achieve sustainable development. The paper focuses on the strategies that have been formulated and implemented but an overall review of policies and programmes was left outside the scope of the study. Similarly the paper focuses primarily on developments at national level and therefore it does not intend to provide a detailed review of the multiplicity of local and private initiatives but rather selective illustrative examples.

General introduction

Given the international readership of this paper, it will be helpful to outline briefly the institutional structure for policy making in the UK and within which sustainable development policy is being developed. It will also be helpful to outline a number of current strands in UK public policy, which directly or indirectly, contribute to the current position in relation to defining and implementing sustainable development objectives.

Governance patterns

Public policy making in the UK is the responsibility of central and local government. Central government, under parliamentary scrutiny, formulates and publishes policy proposals for consultation and Parliamentary debate and approval. Ultimately all policy is subject to statutory powers, but only a minority of policy proposals require legislation and therefore only a minority of approved policy is published as Acts of Parliament. The normal mechanism for publishing new policy is White Papers whose contents and implementation may or may not require legislative change. Implementation of policy, often requiring considerable interpretation. Traditionally, it took primarily place through various public bodies, regulating agreed activity in line with the provisions of Acts of Parliament. But, considering the key objectives of this and previous administration to deregulate government activities there has been a tendency to develop more diversified implementation mechanisms. Local Government, which is itself governed by Acts of Parliament, also has a role in implementation of national policies, as well as having responsibilities for local policy making.

During the period of the current Government, major changes to the policy making structure have taken place, with the devolution of some policy making powers to new institutional bodies:

- The Northern Ireland Assembly.

- The Scottish Parliament.

- The Welsh Assembly.

- The Greater London Authority.

At the same time there is a growing debate about devolution of power to the English regions, in the wake of the new regional development agencies (RDAs) and regional chambers (comprising representatives from local authorities), to provide improved political accountability, and to invest regional level policy with more influence.

The focus of public policy is inevitably on issues; sustainable development is therefore an issue of major policy significance. However, sustainable development is still seen by some as synonymous with environmental protection and the broader concept of sustainable development – encompassing social and economic, as well as environmental, objectives – is not as readily or widely understood.[2] "This study is seeking to understand current and emerging policy debates in terms of their relevance and potential for sustainable development, even when sustainable development is not explicitly defined as the driving force.

At the current time in the UK, there are a number of policy related debates which are significant to sustainable development and which can make a positive contribution when dealing with the challenge posed by sustainable development. These debates, some of which are considered in more detail in the paper, include:

- Improved methods of public administration, both in the formulation and implementation of public policy. This debate has a number of aspects:

- Increased focus on the definition of objectives and subsequent policy review, with a strong emphasis on the use of indicators of policy effects to measure policy achievements.

- Increased concern to challenge existing boundaries between policy areas. The pursuit of so-called "joined-up thinking" finds expression in both central and local government.

• Greater involvement of customers/clients/users of public services, in the management of such services, seeking to improve effectiveness, transparency of decision making and the ownership of policy outcomes.

• Deregulation and outsourcing of former public sector activities.

• Some aspects of regional, urban and rural policy, tied to discussion of the balance between regional (especially economic) interests and national interests. This can be extended to include the issue of regeneration of urban areas, which finds expression in the context of regional economic and planning fora, and an appreciation that the regional level provides opportunity for improved regeneration policy.

• Growing appreciation that traditional methods of policy decision making are less suitable to a policy context which recognises more fully the uncertainty of surrounding policy choices and the desire for greater transparency (partly as a reaction to reduced levels of confidence in the quality and efficacy of decision making).

• A growing understanding that sustainable development needs to embrace social as well as economic and environmental policy goals, and that issues of poverty and equality of opportunity are integral to "sustainable" development. At the same time there is an emerging debate concerning the dilution of focus that a broader definition of sustainable development has for the environment; and a concern at a failure to recognise that the need for changes in patterns of consumption and production are not optional policy choices (*e.g.* needed in response to real and finite limits to the use of environmental resources).

A.   Main issues and tensions

The overview describes the main domestic challenges relating to sustainable development, the perception of the issues and public awareness and the state of the political agenda.

International context

The adoption of a sustainable development agenda in the UK has been promoted by the international debate. The 1992 Rio Earth Summit concluded that

283

sustainable development could only be achieved if social, economic and environmental goals were balanced in decision-making. The UK Government responded to the Earth Summit by publishing, in 1994, the UK Strategy for Sustainable development, following on from an earlier White Paper, This Common Inheritance. Since the publication of this Strategy, the definition and the institutional and policy implications have been constantly evolving. The nature of the current Strategy is discussed below.

The international pressure to develop a sustainable development agenda has also been articulated through the policy making of the European Commission. A key policy driver has been the Environmental Action Plans of the European Commission, combined with the related environmental Directives, which strengthened the environmental dimension of sustainable development. For a period in the 1990s, the debate largely ignored the social dimension of sustainable development. However, again aided by the development of social policy ideas by the European Commission, accompanied by a number of social Directives, the inclusion of a social dimension has been developing (see also Article 2 of the Amsterdam Treaty).

Domestic challenges

Current UK government policy for sustainable development is based on the strategy published in 1999: A *better quality of life – A strategy for sustainable development for the* UK. The key points of the Strategy are summarised in Annex I. The Strategy not only recognises the three main dimensions of sustainable development, it also recognises the need for new forms of dialogue and institutional responses, necessary to secure the increased participation of communities at different spatial scales. This emphasises the nature of the interaction between institutions and stakeholders, and the need to engage in partnerships in order to deliver policy through processes of active dialogue.

The Strategy provides a cornerstone for UK sustainable development policy making, by confirming the dimensions to sustainable development and providing the basis for policy development and appraisal in different policy areas and at different spatial levels. The Environmental Audit Committee, with the remit to assess the contribution of UK Government policies to environmental protection and sustainable development, has provided a response on the Strategy. Some key challenges emerged, including:

- The environment was seen as the most important consideration in the past. Now there is a paradigm shift towards making sure the economic and especially the social pillars are set on an equal footing. The risk is however that the environment now gets pushed down the agenda and that some decision makers will have an excuse to ignore it.

- Many of the targets relating to sustainable development (such as climate change) are national. This raises the potential problem of integration between the devolved administrations and central government. If there is a risk that national targets will not be met, central government may have to step in.

- In general the strategy was found to be weak in terms of methods for its implementation.

- While the Green Ministers are responsible for sustainable development in their respective departments, as yet there is no one responsible for the cross-cutting aspects of the sustainable development indicators.

- As well as introducing sustainable development indicators, to ensure effective measurement it will be important to set baselines.

Political agenda

A key challenge identified from consultations is the perennial issue of accounting for sustainable development. The use of indicators has been a major element of recent work, but their remains a strong interest in other approaches to environmental accounts (see Box 1). A second issue highlighted was the importance of developing more integrated decision making, and the tools to allow it. This is discussed further, in Section D.

A more thorough review of the range of currently important issues raised in relation to the sustainable development debate, has recently been published by the DETR, in the context of identifying research gaps and opportunities for sustainable development. The research study is available at *www.environment.detr.gov.uk/sustainable/research/gapsopps/index.htm*

The sustainable development agenda in the UK has found particular expression in the wider policies of regional, urban and rural development. The government has a vision of towns, cities and suburbs which offer a high quality of life and opportunity for everyone. The *Urban White Paper, "Our Towns and Cities: The Future – Delivering the Urban Renaissance"*, was published in November 2000. In terms of urban policy it sets the agenda for England – for the rest of the UK most of the issues addressed are matters for devolved administrations. The Urban White Paper set out the social, economic and environmental challenges and the key steps that need to be taken to achieve an urban renaissance. It takes forward a large number of the recommendations made by the Urban Task Force in their report "Towards an Urban Renaissance" published in June 1999 (see Annex II).

The work of the task force has been the subject of considerable debate, not least the amount of time that government has taken to respond to the recommendations, especially those proposing changes in the tax system to benefit regeneration.

285|

Box 1. **Environmental Accounts**

The UK environmental accounts (UKENA) show the pressures imposed by economic activity on the domestic environment. This approach is consistent with international environmental accounting practices. However, goods and services consumed in the UK frequently originate in other countries. To make a full assessment of whether the UK economy is sustainable, overseas impacts need to be considered. A funded research project was commissioned by DETR and DFID from the Royal Institute of International Affairs in 1999 to identify methodologies for assessing the UK's sustainable development footprint overseas. A report was produced in January 2000 "*Assessing the UK's Sustainable Development Impact Overseas – Methodological Approaches and Key Issues*" available at: *www.riia.org/ Research/eep/hwconf2.pdf*

There are a number of methodologies, developed by academics, to describe the environmental consequences of a territory's consumption.

Ecological footprint analysis converts all resources into the area of land required to meet the sustainable agricultural, energetic and material needs of a community (Wackernagel M and Rees W.E 1997). Typically these analyses show that imports by crowded OECD countries embody land from less crowded OECD and non-OECD countries. Land rather than monetary value is used as the numerate to compare resource flows.

The Wuppertal Institute has pioneered and participated in the development of a number of measures to describe material use by an economy. The Material Inputs Per unit Service (MIPS) methodology describes the mass of water and earth (both excavated and simply moved) used by the economy (Hinterberger *et al* 1997). This has been criticised for not distinguishing between relatively benign materials such as sand, and more hazardous materials like nuclear waste. The authors use the concept of material flows simply as an indicator of whether the economy is becoming more or less dematerialised. Wuppertal defines *total material requirement* (World Resource Institute 1997) as the mass of solid and gaseous material consumed or otherwise relocated – calculated for the Netherlands, Germany, USA and Japan.

Material Flow Analysis (MFA) tracks the movements of bulky commodities, including imports, through the economy. Rather than denominating these movements by their monetary value, MFA accounts record the physical quantity of material flows between industries. The results resemble an input-output table in all but units of mass. The German statistical office has performed this type of analysis (Radermacher and Stahmer, 1996) and suggests it used to give a macro-economic perspective to long term trends in material flows. Substances can be aggregated into material themes *e.g.*: agriculture, fish, fossil fuels, metals, non-metal minerals, water and wood. DETR commissioned a research project on *Sustainable Prosperity: Measuring Resource Efficiency* to the Universities of Edinburgh, Stirling and Glasgow to identify and describe relevant measures of resource use efficiency and assess the methods and evaluate their usefulness for policy making.

There is also concern that the task force, by focussing heavily on issues of physical design, failed to properly address the economic and social aspects of regeneration. These issues were addressed in the Urban White Paper (launched in November 2000) and the 2001 Budget, which announced a substantial wide-ranging package of fiscal measures aimed at bringing about an urban renaissance. The package includes:

- Complete exemption from stamp duty for all property transactions in the UK's most disadvantaged communities.
- A 5 per cent rate of VAT for the costs of residential to residential conversions and for the costs of renovating homes which have been empty for three years or more.
- Relief of VAT on the sale of renovated homes which have been empty for ten years or more.
- An immediate tax relief to property owners for the costs of converting redundant space over shops into flats.
- A 150 per cent accelerated payable tax credit for the costs incurred in the clean-up of contaminated land.

The whole package will be implemented as soon as possible after Royal Assent. These measures are aiming to:

- Help to bring empty property back into use.
- Encourage the recycling of brownfield land.
- Help the most disadvantaged communities.

The Budget measures are also complemented by local taxation measures included for consultation in the Local Government Finance Green Paper – including Town Improvement Schemes and a local tax reinvestment programme.

The development of urban policy increasingly recognises the requirement to secure the active contribution of citizens in policy making. This includes a growing need to identify the views and perceptions of citizens as a way of ordering public policy priorities. A major exercise to this end was undertaken across the EU (including UK cities) in 1999 (see Annex III).

The sustainable development agenda has to some extent focussed on policy goals, reflected in the discussion above. However, it also needs emphasising that the sustainable development debate is increasingly recognising that the policy goals require conflicts – in some cases major – to be resolved between policy objectives. As a result there is increasing consideration of the underlying values and judgements of public policy, and about how (and whose) values are determined and applied in decision making. This has led to a realisation that there is a fourth dimension to sustainable development, that of the issues of how society

287

structures itself to articulate values and to make decisions. This issue of "governance" is reflected upon in the discussion on decision making in Section C below.

B. Institutions and policies

Overview of the institutional structure at national level

The basic institutional structure can be characterised in terms of the policy cycle and the spatial focus. The policy cycle can be divided up into problem identification, policy formulation, policy implementation, monitoring, evaluation and policy reformulation, viewed as a continuing cycle. The responsibility for promoting sustainable development in the UK, or territorial sub-divisions, is determined by how the responsibilities of the different institutional bodies relate to the policy cycle (see Figure 1).

The development of policy and problem identification is driven both by international and domestic policy drivers. International drivers have probably been the most important influence on sustainable development policy in most countries concerned with its implementation, including the UK. It was at the "Earth Summit" in Rio de Janeiro that the nations present discussed how to achieve sustainable development. Since then a number of international conventions and legislation, including Agenda 21 and the Kyoto Protocol, have been very important in driving national policy. In the UK, EC legislation has had a strong influence on policy formulation, especially in terms of environmental, and latterly, social policies. There are also institutions at international level, which evaluate progress in sustainable development, such as the UN and the European Environment Agency (EEA), which also have some influence.

Domestic policy drivers change over time, but these too have major influences on both the institutional structure and policy making. A key driver in the recent past has been devolution and the re-introduction of a regional policy. New regional bodies, initially driven by a concern to boost regional economic development, are increasingly seen as an important part of a government process for delivering sustainable development.

The bodies which make up the institutional structure in the UK can be divided between those which have a UK focus and those with a sub-UK focus. Their responsibilities depend on their role in the policy cycle. The national (UK) responsibilities rest with central government departments and the related government and parliamentary committees. Government departments all have different roles and mechanisms for supporting sustainable development, depending on their policy focus, operating in the context of cabinet government.

The department central to promoting and supporting sustainable development is the Department for the Environment, Transport and the Regions (DETR).

Figure 1. **The UK Institutional Framework for Delivering Sustainable Development**

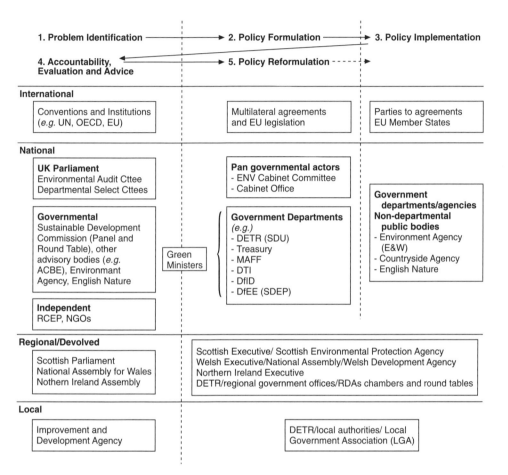

The Sustainable Development Unit (SDU) in DETR is responsible for ensuring that sustainable development issues are integrated in the main guidance and machinery of Government and for providing advice on sustainable development to DETR staff. It led the development of the revised strategy and indicators for sustainable development in the UK (A *better quality of life*). See Box 3 for a description of the terms of reference of the Sustainable Development Unit.

Other important departments include: the Treasury, which aims to incorporate sustainable development into its process for allocating public expenditure (*e.g.* Spending Review 2000); the Cabinet Office, which is developing an integrated policy-appraisal tool for sustainability as part of its Modernising Government initiative and will be co-sponsor, with DETR, of the advisory Sustainable Development Commission; DTI, which is consulting on its own departmental Sustainable Development Strategy; MAFF, which is producing its own sustainable agriculture indicators; and DfEE, which has set up the Sustainable Development Education Panel.

"Joining-up Government" and promoting the integration of policy necessary to support sustainable development is an inherent part of the policy-making process and a major focus for the sustainable development as "catalyst" for integration. Another initiative designed to foster policy integration is the "Green Ministers" initiative (see Annex IV), which attempts to ensure sustainable development is a cross-cutting theme across all the departments, allowing co-operation and the potential to learn from best practice.

Government departments are primarily concerned with policy formulation and reformulation and in the context of sustainable development, using the Sustainable Development Strategy as a framework for new policy. There are a number of bodies, also acting at the national level, involved in problem identification and evaluation of progress in sustainable development policy. Within Parliament, the Environmental Audit Committee (EAC) (see Box 2) is responsible for judging whether the Government is effectively integrating sustainable development into policy and decision making. It is able to call the Government to account on all aspects of its policy and programmes, but has no power to insist on actions or alterations. The Royal Commission on Environmental Pollution (RCEP) is a long-standing independent voice on environmental and – increasingly – sustainable development issues. In addition, the Government's Round Table on Sustainable Development and the British Government Panel on Sustainable Development (to be merged to form the Sustainable Development Commission) provide strategic advice on sustainable development issues.

There are 27 Non-Departmental Public Bodies (NDPBs) involved in advising on issues pertaining to sustainable development, *e.g.* the Advisory Committee on Business and the Environment (ACBE) and the Trades Union and Sustainable Development Advisory Committee. Non-governmental organisations in the wider policy community also play an important role in highlighting important aspects of the sustainable development agenda, as well as casting judgement on existing policy. Their role is also important at a sub-national level, participating in formal partnerships with Government (*e.g.* as set out in section 114 in the remit for the Welsh Assembly (see Annex X).

There are a number of bodies involved in policy implementation at a sub-UK level (England, Scotland, Wales and Northern Ireland) with similar responsibilities. For example, sustainable development is an important part of the remit for the Countryside Agency, the Environment Agency (having developed its own sustainable development guidance) and English Nature (the Government's biodiversity adviser). Many of these bodies are primarily concerned with environmental matters, although the integration of social and economic perspectives is increasing in importance as understanding matures about the limitations of end-of-pipe solutions.

There are limitations when attempting to describe the regional and local levels of the framework, given the large number of bodies, the variations in their roles and responsibilities and the fact that significant recent innovation has yet to bed down. At a sub-UK level, there are the devolved Welsh and Northern Ireland Assemblies and the Scottish Parliament, all of whom take responsibilities for supporting sustainable development. In England, there are nine Regional Development Agencies (RDAs), including the London Development Agency, which have sustainable development as a secondary duty after economic development. All these bodies, operating within overall government policy and policy guidance, have both policy formulation and implementation responsibilities contributing to sustainable development. In addition, there are chambers, round tables and regional sustainable development frameworks.

At the local level, local authorities (LAs) now have new powers to promote the economic, social and/or environmental wellbeing of their areas (Local Government Bill 2000). LAs were responsible for Local Agenda 21 action, with all LAs challenged by the Prime Minister to adopt Local Agenda 21 strategies by the end of 2000. The Government and the LA co-ordination body act together to provide guidance to LAs on developing effective Local Agenda 21 strategies, plans and examples of successful LA 21 case studies. According to the Department of the Environment, Transport and the Regions (DETR), the success rate is over 90 per cent, not counting those who have already proceeded to community planning.

A more detailed description of the institutional framework is provided in the following sections.

Legislative level

The Environment Act (1995) places a responsibility on Government to promote sustainable development, although it covers only a limited part of the sustainable development agenda and applies only to England and Wales. The lead Government department is DETR, in which the Sustainable Development Unit is located, charged with providing a policy framework within which sustainable development can be achieved in the UK. Further details of the sustainable development are given below.

The legal requirement to promote sustainable development is under constant development. The most recent enactment is in the Government of Wales Act

---

Box 2. **The Role of the Environmental Audit Committee**

The Environmental Audit Committee (EAC) is one of a large number of Parliamentary Select Committees which report on – amongst other matters – the expenditure, administration and policy of Government on behalf of the House. Select Committees are made up of between 11 and 16 Members of Parliament, supported by a small number of staff. They operate by taking written and oral evidence from various interests, usually to set against evidence from Ministers on the Government's approach. Select Committees present recommendations in reports to the Government which, by convention, responds within two months. These recommendations are advisory; Government is under no statutory obligation to act in line with the advice given.

The specific remit of the EAC is to assess the contribution of all and any UK Government activity – policies, programmes and operations – to environmental protection and sustainable development, and to audit performance against relevant targets. Unlike many Select Committees, the EAC has power to ask for evidence from any government department. This cross-departmental role is important. The EAC's remit does not extend to matters for which the devolved bodies have responsibility, but it does cover regional bodies (RDAs). The accountability of local government is to the local electorate. The EAC considers the impact of central government policy on the ability of local authorities to deliver local sustainable development. The Committee enjoys good informal relations with various quasi-governmental and other independent organisations, including those mentioned above.

The EAC reports on the environmental dimension of the tax and spending systems and departments' performance on policy appraisal, environmental reporting and green housekeeping, on an annual basis. The Committee also looks at individual policies on an *ad-hoc* basis, in response to particular issues and as case studies in the integration of environmental considerations. Details of work undertaken and other matters can be found on the Committee's Homepage: *www.parliament.uk/commons/selcom/eahome.htm*

(section 121), which places the National Assembly for Wales under a statutory obligation to ... *make a scheme setting out how it proposes, in the exercise of its functions, to promote sustainable development.*

The development and implementation of sustainable development policy is the formal responsibility of the Cabinet Environment (Env) Committee. The Environmental Audit Select Committee (see Box 2) is responsible for reviewing Government performance in promoting sustainable development and advising on future policy.

The legislative basis for sustainable development is strengthened further by the proposed new Local Government Act, which provides for a new responsibility of local authorities to promote sustainable development and engage in community planning.

There are also a number of statutory instruments that help to support the implementation of sustainable development. This includes the land-use planning system and the use of development plans, the requirement for environmental impact assessments of specified forms of development, and new legislation relating to the definition and treatment of environmental liabilities.

The setting up of a "Green Ministers" Committee (see Annex IV) is a promising measure to integrate environmental concerns and raise awareness of sustainable development in all government departments. In the words of the EAC, it "has started to make a difference" and "we [EAC] under-estimate its potential for achieving change" (para.17 EAC 6th report 98-99 "The Greening Government Initiative 1999"). The mechanism continues to operate.

Executive level

The main executive responsibility for promoting sustainable development is the Sustainable Development Unit, located in the DETR. The Sustainable Development Unit (see Box 3) has responsibilities both within the DETR and across Government for advising and encouraging policy directions which are supportive of sustainable development. To this end, the Sustainable Development Unit has been seeking to improve the quality of policy appraisal, by better linking existing methods to provide a more wide-ranging but integrated methodology. Advice for government departments on the use of this method is currently being drafted.

- Policy monitoring

In addition to improved policy appraisal, the Sustainable Development Unit is also actively promoting the better monitoring of policy. A key element in this monitoring is the publication of a set of 15 "headline" indicators with which to review progress on sustainable development. These indicators are supported by a further set of some 150 indicators. The scope for linking these sustainable development monitoring indicators to the wider department performance monitoring system is also under some discussion. This system is based on the use of "public service agreements" (PSAs), which are individual department targets, related to their policy responsibilities, agreed with the Treasury as the basis of funding decisions.

The development of the institutional framework at executive level has recently been the subject of a special report of the Performance and Innovation Unit (PIU) (see Annex VII). Whilst not explicitly addressing the issue of sustainable development, the report examined the necessary requirements to improve the

Box 3. **The Role of the Sustainable Development Unit**

The Sustainable Development Unit's remit comprises a number of objectives:

To increase the understanding and acceptance of sustainable development, at international, regional and local levels.

To include the promotion of policy on access to information, public participation in decision making and access to justice in environmental matters.

To provide a policy framework within which sustainable development can be achieved in the UK. This will involve influencing policy making within the DETR, in other Government departments and across the wider public sector.

To identify, refine and bring to bear the tools necessary to deliver sustainable development. This will include establishing: a system for annual reporting of progress towards sustainable development by the country as a whole; a new Sustainable Development Commission; and, systems through which Government will lead by example in integrating sustainable development into all its activities.

Specifically, each of the Sustainable Development Unit branches has responsibilities as follows:

SUSTAINABLE DEVELOPMENT UNIT 1 – Support for the Green Ministers Committee; relations with EAC; implications of sustainable development for policies of other departments; greening operations.

SUSTAINABLE DEVELOPMENT UNIT 2 – Sustainable development monitoring and reporting; sustainable development objectives and principles; environmental appraisal; implications of sustainable development for DETR policies and DETR executive agencies, NDPBs and non-ministerial government departments and other associate bodies.

SUSTAINABLE DEVELOPMENT UNIT 3 – Sustainable development at regional and local levels, the "Aarhus" Convention (UNECE Convention on access to information; public participation in decision making and access to justice in environmental matters and related regulations, EC directives and guidance.

SUSTAINABLE DEVELOPMENT UNIT 4 – Supporting sponsorship of the Royal Commission on Environmental Pollution, the Government Panel on Sustainable Development, the UK Round Table and the new Sustainable Development Commission.

strategic policy making of Government, by emphasising the need to understand policy links and to ensure an integration of policy initiatives. This work produced a series of recommendations (see Annex VIII) to improve "joined-up thinking", which is seen as an essential precursor to the integration of policy necessary for promoting sustainable development.

• Departmental responses

Government departments are responding to the imperative of recognising their individual contributions to sustainable development and attempting to reflect this in revised policy making. One example of a department that has integrated the sustainable development agenda is the Department for International Development (DFID). Sustainable development is on the international agenda and national organisations involved in overseas development often face the same challenge of promoting the status of the environment equitably with economic and social issues. The need to ensure local and national sustainable development policy within developed countries should be related to the efforts of developing countries, otherwise important elements of sustainable development in the international context may be overlooked, and the "act local – think global" slogan could become meaningless.

The UK Government's Department for International Development (DFID) offers some good examples of ways to address some of the above issues (see Annex V).

• Non-departmental bodies

The 27 NDPBs are also present at the executive level. They act either in an advisory capacity, such as the Sustainable Development Commission (see Annex VI), or as an instrument of policy development, such as the Environment Agency (see Box 4). The latter bodies receive budgets and are charged with implementing specified statutory duties.

Judicial level

The judicial level, compared to the other levels of government, is relatively less important to the pursuit of sustainable development. This reflects UK convention in the use of the discretionary approach to environmental policy rather than an essentially legalistic approach.

The major judicial issues relate to the operation of the planning system, through which environmental assessments are required, and which arbitrates, through planning inquiries, major development decisions. The role of the Planning Inspectorate and the codes of conduct governing inquiries therefore represent key aspects of the institutional management of sustainable development. However, given the detail involved, we have chosen to focus on other aspects of the institutional structure, namely the regional and local levels of government, where there is considerable policy and institutional change with important implications for the pursuit of sustainable development.

Sub-national level

The devolution of national policy objectives for sustainable development to the regions has occurred in the creation, by the present Government, of four new regional or sub-regional bodies:

- Northern Ireland Assembly.

- Wales Assembly.

- Scottish Parliament.

- Greater London Authority.

All four bodies have an explicit responsibility for supporting sustainable development.

In the remainder of the UK, the English regions do not have formal regional government. Rather, regional policy is developing organically in each region, with regional differences depending on local circumstances. This organic development is taking place around three bodies:

- Regional Government Offices, representing national government departments, with increasing co-ordination of national policies at regional level (GOs).

- Regional chambers, comprising local authority representation and, depending on the region, other non-government bodies.

- Regional Development Agencies (RDAs).

The exact roles of, and relationships between, these bodies is not formally defined. Only in the case of the RDAs is there a written duty to support sustainable development. However, in a number of regions it has been the GOs which have been responsible for drafting regional sustainability frameworks, or integrated regional strategies, which set out policy objectives for sustainable development. The statutory responsibility of the chambers is only to advise on and subsequently scrutinise, regional economic strategies. However, again depending on the region, chambers are beginning to consider a wider policy portfolio.

The role of regional Government Offices has been subject to significant review, driven by a concern over the level of co-ordination of national policies at regional and local levels, with no part of central government responsible for bringing its contribution together to assist local levels.

The response has been to propose a strengthening of Government Offices, covering all Government policies, with discretion on how to achieve results, which are clearly accountable for the delivery of cross-cutting outcomes. To support this, a Regional Co-ordinating Unit (RCU) has recently been set up, based within the DETR.

Box 4. **Environment Agency**

The Environment Agency is a Non-Departmental Public Body for England and Wales [there is a similar body for Scotland, the Scottish Environment Protection Agency (SEPA)] which is sponsored by the DETR and MAFF. It was formed in 1996 by a merging of waste, water and industrial process regulation organisations. As a result, the new Agency has a wide range of duties and functions often reliant on working with other organisations. Thus its corporate vision and aims include:

A better environment in England and Wales for present and future generations.

To achieve major and continuous improvements in the quality of air, land and water.

To encourage the conservation of natural resources, animals and plants.

- To make the most of pollution control and river basin management.
- To provide effective defence and warning systems to protect people and property against flooding from rivers and the sea.
- To reduce the amount of waste by encouraging people to re-use and recycle their waste.
- To improve standards of waste disposal.
- To manage water resources to achieve the proper balance between the country's needs and the environment.
- To work with other organisations to reclaim contaminated land.
- To improve and develop salmon and freshwater fisheries.
- To conserve and improve river navigation.
- To tell people about environmental issues by educating and informing.
- To set priorities and work out solutions that society can afford.

The Agency has *seven regional offices* in England and *one in Cardiff* representing *Environment Agency Wales*. These are split into a total of 26 area offices, which have external boundaries based on local authority areas and internal boundaries based on river catchments. Most of the 9,500 staff work in these area offices and support-ing depots. This allows the Agency to respond quickly to incidents and emergen-cies across England and Wales and to provide a local service. Each region has a general manager and each area has an area manager. They make decisions and manage the areas to make sure the needs of the local community are met. The Chief Executive and Directors are based in the head office in Bristol, with support-ing offices in London. They manage the overall business and put new laws into practice to benefit the environment.

Within the Head Office Environmental Directorate there is a Sustainability Unit, which seeks to issue specific guidance on a range of issues as well as apply-ing decision-making frameworks to the Agency's own activities and the work of its partners. There is an unresolved tension within the Agency between its specific focus (reflected in its structure and resources) on regulatory issues (such as legis-lative compliance within specific areas of the environment) and its broader vision but limited scope to become more proactive and to act strategically. In addition, the Agency has to be careful when it presents specialist advice that this is in line with its sponsor departments.

297|

National policy is also delivered regionally and locally through the actions of executive NDPBs (Non-Departmental Public Bodies). Many of these NDPBs, for example the Environment Agency (EA), which is largely responsible for implementing environmental policy, operate through regional and/or local units.

Local authorities are now represented nationally by the Local Government Association (LGA) which deals with legislation and policy issues, while the Improvement and Development Agency (IDEA) deals with guidance and support on practical implementation based on disseminating best practice between members. In the past, the Local Government Management Board had a dedicated team to support LA21 within local authorities. As a result of these changes, the dedicated support for LA21 has been substantially reduced. Critics argue that this reflects a reduced priority, while others believe it is the result of sustainability issues being mainstreamed into the wider local authority modernisation agenda. There is also a national LA21 steering group, consisting of a large range of organisations or stakeholders, which acts as an advisory body to the LGA and IDEA.

The history and future of LA21 in the UK

The Earth Summit in 1992 provided the initial catalyst for many local authorities to produce voluntary LA21 strategies. A few local authorities, such as Leicester, Lancashire, Sutton and Kirkless, were the pioneers of comprehensive economic, social, environmental and corporate strategies due to a combination of local political commitment, the right creative or lateral thinkers in positions of influence, and adequate resources.

Without an adequate "top-down driver" such as a central commitment to produce LA21, many local authorities would not have produced LA21 strategies. At the Earth Summit "Rio+5" in 1997, the Government made the commitment that all local authorities should produce LA21 strategies by the end of 2000. This put a new emphasis on the LA21 process within the UK and was accompanied by new guidance (see Box 5) to help those that had not started, and the others, to improve the coverage and quality of their strategies.

The future of LA21 is dependent on how it becomes mainstreamed within the local authority modernisation agenda driven by central government. For example, the new "best value" performance review system of local authority services has the production of an LA21 strategy as its first indicator for local authorities. This is replaced by the requirement to produce an overarching community strategy for the local authority area which carries forward LA21 work and mainstreams sustainable development policy.

Many practitioners believe that the "LA21 Label" has had its day, and that the principles are now being incorporated into the various changes occurring within local authorities. This may mean that the dedicated LA21 co-ordinators and expertise will

---

Box 5.   **Characteristics of a Sustainable Society –
Checklist for Local Authorities**

IDEA defines LA21 as "the process of building partnerships between local authorities and other sectors to develop and implement local policies for sustainable development". In a sustainable community:

- **Resources** are used efficiently and waste is minimised by closing cycles.
- **Pollution** is limited to levels with which natural systems can cope without damage.
- The **biodiversity** of nature is valued and protected.
- Where possible, **local needs** are met locally.
- Everyone has access to **basic needs**: good food, water, shelter and fuel at a reasonable cost.
- Everyone has the opportunity to undertake **satisfying work** in a diverse economy.
- People's good **health** is protected.
- **Access** to facilities, services, goods and other people is not achieved at the expense of the environment.
- People live without fear of personal violence from crime or persecution: they feel **safe**.
- Everyone has access to skills, **knowledge** and information.
- All sections of the community are **empowered** to participate in decision-making.
- Opportunities for culture, **leisure** and recreation are readily available to all.
- Diversity and local **distinctiveness** are valued and protected.

Source: LGMB Indicators of Sustainable Development Project.

---

disperse, with one group of practitioners moving into a more central role within their authorities to concentrate on process and integrated policy. This group could ultimately develop a sustainable development quality control function to ensure that Sustainability is properly considered throughout their authorities (as Equalities Officers currently do for equality issues). Another group will perhaps return to the more traditional environmental role, with a focus on environmental management systems and sectoral practices such as energy and waste. This potential separation of roles within the local authority would result in the corporate goal of sustainable development and the various environmental management functions led by different teams in different parts of the authority. Only time will tell if this approach will finally help sustainable development to be perceived as different from environmental management and mainstreamed.

Sustainable development frameworks

Sustainable development frameworks provide an example of attempts to develop high-level visions at regional level. Regional sustainable development frameworks have been conceived as high-level documents that set out a vision for sustainable development in each region, and for the region's contribution to sustainable development at national level. These are in addition to the existing or evolving strategies contained in regional planning guidance (RPG), and the sustainable development strategies being prepared by the regional development agencies. These frameworks should take a wide overview of regional activity and the regional impact of Government policy. It is clear that their success will depend on the commitment and support of local activities and other organisations in the region. In 2000, the Government issued guidance on the regional frameworks. In summary, the Government encouraged frameworks to:

- Define **a high-level vision** with wide-ranging support, for moving towards sustainable development in the region, considering the key social, economic, environmental, and resource issues and the inter-relationship between them.

- Define sustainable development **objectives** for the region, and set priorities with the help of regional **indicators** and **targets** – in doing this the aim should be for **all the headline indicators to be moving in the right direction** at regional level.

- Provide a point of reference for other regional activity, showing how all four objectives of the national sustainable development strategy – social, economic, environmental, and resource use – can be met.

- Identify gaps where a regional approach would add value and provide a regional vehicle for meeting the national target for increasing production of renewable energy.

- Identify significant challenges and conflicts faced within the region and look towards solutions.

- Map out the relationships between the various regional and national initiatives that can contribute to sustainable development in order to minimise duplication, highlight and promote good practice, and to help identify partnerships.

- Establish a process of monitoring and review, taking account of the role envisaged for the framework.

- Support and draw from existing work including Local Agenda 21 (LA21) strategies and initiatives.

- Be endorsed by the Regional Chamber.

Modernisation agenda and sustainable development

When the new government took power in May 1997, it promised sweeping reforms for local government. This has broadly been referred to as its agenda for "modernising local government". Policy and legislation have followed.

The centrepiece of the intended transformation for local government is the new duty to promote wellbeing. There have been various debates as the legislation has been drafted on the meaning of "wellbeing", which is now defined as a local authority duty to produce a community strategy to promote economic, social and environmental wellbeing of its area and contribute to the UK Sustainable Development Strategy. The other key aspects of the modernising agenda are described below, along with the potential links with sustainable development policy.

Best Value

In order to improve the economy, effectiveness and efficiency of service delivery by local authorities, the Government has decided to replace compulsory competitive tender (CCT – where cost was the only permitted consideration) by a duty of Best Value, which takes into account both the cost and quality of a service. The Government Office for London (GOL) has commissioned a piece of work to enable the publication of a guide to Lo ndon Boroughs to facilitate the inclusion of sustainable development in Best Value Reviews. A series of seminars with representatives from those boroughs has been held, and a report is due in April 2001. It is also envisaged that such a guide could be rolled out in all regions. The Local Government Competition and Quality (LGQ) Division in the DETR sponsored the setting up of a Best Value waste network in February 2001, to consider the sharing of good practice in all aspects of waste management.

Best Value also stresses the importance of continuous improvement in service delivery, via the setting of targets and reviewing performance under four headings: *challenge* why and how a service is being provided; *compare* performance against national indicators; *consult* with local communities in order to give them a say about the delivery of services; and a willingness to open services up to *competition* as a way of delivering continuous improvement. Best Value also stresses the need to understand the "cross-cutting" nature of problems, and to promote "joined-up" solutions, which relates well to the Sustainable Development Agenda (see Box 6). However, there is concern about how the long-term and quality elements of Sustainability will fare within the service framework.

Duty of community planning and wellbeing

As part of the modernising agenda, local authorities have a duty to promote the economic, social and environmental wellbeing of their area. As part of the process

301

Box 6. **Best Value and Sustainability Checklist**

The Society of Local Authority Chief Executives and Senior Managers (SOLACE), IDEA and the LGA have produced a Best Value Sustainability Checklist based on the economic, social and environmental criteria established in the UK Strategy. The Checklist is intended to be a straightforward way of testing the sustainability of individual Council services. It helps in assessing the potential impact of a service on the environment and will identify where the service is successful in meeting the principles of sustainability. Example areas within the checklist are:

- Building Sustainable Communities – does your service increase the cohesiveness and capacity of the local community by increasing the capacity of local communities to influence decisions that affect their lives and their capacity to manage resources and facilities?

- Buildings, Planning and Land Use – does your service make the best use of land and buildings by using brownfield sites or vacant buildings rather than greenfield sites?

- Managing the Environment and Resources – does your service ensure energy and resources are used wisely and that the broader environment is protected and enhanced by: being registered with or adhering to the principles of an environmental management system such as EMAS or ISO 14001?

- Health – does your service maximise health promotion by taking measures to reduce factors that contribute to ill health (poverty, diet, lifestyle, stress and pollution), especially for more vulnerable communities?

- A Sustainable Economy – does your service add to the local economy and the employment needs of people and businesses by reducing low pay and dependency on long working hours for in-house and external contracting teams?

- Housing – does your service promote decent housing and amenities by increasing the energy efficiency of housing (public and private sector) and the use of renewable energy?

- Social Equity and Opportunity – does your service encourage equity and opportunities for all by increased opportunities for lifelong learning for all?

- Transport – does your service improve its transport profile (meeting people's transport needs and protecting the environment) by improving conditions for pedestrians and cyclists and promoting public transport?

- Sending the Right Signals – does your service put sustainability into practice and encourage others by using fair-trade products such as tea, coffee, etc.?

The full checklist can be found at: *www.solace.org.uk*

Table 1. **LA21 Strategies, Community Plans and Regeneration Strategies: Similarities and Differences in Processes and Plan Content**

	LA21 Strategy	Community Plan	Regeneration
Impetus	Agenda 21/ sustainable development	Democratic renewal and community leadership	New Commitment to Regeneration
Process	Partnership	Partnership	Partnership
	Community involvement	Community consultation	Community consultation
	Outcome/issue oriented	Service/outcome oriented	Outcome oriented
	Global and local area focus	National sustainable development and local area focus	Local area focus
	Concern for present and future generations	Concern for present and future generations	Concern for present generation
	Often promoted by Environment Department	Corporately driven by LA	Multi-agency approach
Plan content	Vision	Vision	Vision Statement
	Environmental, social, economic integration	Economic, social and environmental wellbeing	Economic, social and environmental wellbeing
	Action Plan	Action Programmes	Strategy Statement
	Implementation	Implementation via other plans and strategies	Programmes
	Indicators, assessment and review	Indicators, benchmarking, audit and review	Benchmarking and baselines (socio-economic and environmental)

Source: Local Government Association 2000, DETR 2001.

for achieving this, Government has recommended that local authorities develop Community Strategies in consultation with local people. Community Strategies are encouraged to build on LA21 strategies. Table 1 illustrates that there are a number of similarities between these two processes and regeneration activities. Unlike LA21, community planning is more likely to be at the heart of the corporate workings of a local authority because of its statutory basis within the modernising agenda. This potentially means more resources, more action, and monitoring of programmes and implementation. This should result in greater impacts on sustainable development, as the emphasis of the duty is not just on local issues, but on demonstrating how activities contribute to the UK strategy. Local authorities will also be able to develop new powers (within the legislative framework) to respond more flexibly to the needs of their area when seeking to deliver the wellbeing objectives of their community strategy (*e.g.* a particular transport charging or congestion scheme).

Community leadership and democratic renewal

The Government is legislating for new political structures to help local authorities "engage with their local communities more effectively" (Modern local government:

303|

in touch with the people, DETR, 1999). Local authorities have been encouraged to move away from a narrowly defined service delivery role to a wider more pro-active community leadership role. This includes guidance and support for councils to develop their arrangements for participation and consultation. Sustainable development requires a reinvention of local democracy if it is to lead to fundamental change; this policy area is therefore of great potential interest to sustainable development practitioners. However, despite the growing experience of using different techniques to engage with local communities, at present there still appears to be a deficit of guidance on how to systematically engage with communities to regularly incorporate feedback into local authority decision making in a sustained way. Concrete efforts are, however, being made to improve this situation.

The role of the non-governmental sector

The UK has a very active NGO sector, which helps to form an important part of the institutional framework for the UK in developing and implementing sustainable development policy. The significance of NGOs in the UK in terms of their size (members and staff) and influence is considerable. A full review of the role of the Non-Governmental sector would be too ambitious for a report of this size, but two significant examples and approaches used by NGOs are presented below.

Friends of the Earth (FoE) is one of the leading environmental pressure groups in the UK and the largest international network of environmental groups in the world, represented in 61 countries. Largely funded by supporters, over 80 per cent of its income comes from individual donations, the rest from special fund-raising events, grants and trading.

Within the UK, it uses a unique network of local groups actively campaigning for a safer, cleaner local environment in 250 communities. These groups campaign on a wide range of local issues, as well as joining together on major national and international campaigns. They also use a wide range of campaigning tactics, ranging from political lobbying to public education through street stalls, and promoting citizen action. Many groups are also actively involved in injecting genuine policies and practices on sustainable development into their Local Agenda 21 process. FoE local groups network across their region, supported by a Regional Campaign Co-ordinator.

Friends of the Earth Trust is the research wing of FoE. It commissions detailed research and provides extensive information and educational materials. Over the years, it has provided influential research to help win campaigns with government and industry, achieving bans on ozone-destroying CFCs, reduced trade in rainforest timber, and increased support for cleaner energy technologies.

Forum for the Future was founded in 1996 as a small, focused, strategic "think tank" which would influence key decision makers and inspire sustainable solutions. The Forum is a small organisation, with around 50 core and project staff, and intends to remain so. It relies for the majority of its funding on corporate sponsorship or grants through its partnership programme. This programme involves partners from government, business, education, local authorities and other organisations who sign up to particular projects or activities that are of relevance. In return, they are provided with agreed tailored support from the Forum on particular sustainable development issues. Through this focused partnership programme, the Forum receives support and is a vital route to wield influence with key decision makers and opinion formers.

Forum for the Future channels its work through seven main activities, each aimed at accelerating the adoption of sustainable practices across key sectors in society. These sectors are:

- Education and Learning Programme: higher and further education sectors and scholarships.
- Sustainable Economy Programme: examining future economic growth models.
- Forum Business Programme: business sector.
- Local Government Programme: regional and local government sector.
- The Natural Step: science-based technique for measuring sustainability impacts.
- Forum Directory of Sustainability in Practice: good-practice guide.
- Green Futures: topical magazine of issues and good practice.

C.   Decision-making mechanisms

Considerable attention has been paid to decision-making methods in the UK. This includes work to better define the roles and responsibilities of government, and ways of improving the ability of government to consider policy in strategic terms, identifying important cross-cutting issues, and avoiding the risk of considering policy only in terms of individual government departmental interests. This enthusiasm for "joined-up" thinking has been expressed by setting up the Performance and Innovation Unit (PIU) within the Cabinet Office (see Annex VII). This Unit has been expressly charged with addressing strategic policy questions, including issues which have a major effect on sustainable development, through a non-departmental perspective, based on detailed analysis informed by extensive consultation with stakeholders. An early report of the Unit focussed explicitly on the issue of policy making in government (see Annex VIII).

The issue of decision making, as informed by policy appraisal, has featured strongly in recent national policy issues of major importance for sustainable development. Traditional policy appraisal is characterised by using the advice of scientific analysis and applying comparisons of costs and benefits, with social cost-benefit analysis playing a major role in policy decisions. For example, within the Cabinet Office, the Better Regulation Unit requires that new regulations and policies be subject to a full regulatory impact assessment, of which cost-benefit analysis constitutes the major part.

Scientific and economic analysis, important though it is, does not provide a complete methodology. There is an appreciation that this approach, as with all appraisals techniques, requires the explicit recognition both of uncertainty and the need for consultation, making transparency a key element in decision making. This is consistent with the evolution of the sustainable development agenda from "development that is environmental" into "economic and social as well as environmental". The sustainable development agenda has increasing implications in terms of decision-making mechanisms, good governance and equity.

For example, the assessment of the safety of genetically modified organisms, based on closed, scientific committees and technocratic approaches, has come under pressure from public concerns over the decisions being reached. Following this, a more open and consultative approach has been recently set up (see Annex X). More generally, this change in approach to informing major policy choices is illustrated by a more open and transparent approach to cost-benefit analysis.

Use of cost-benefit analysis as a basis for sustainable development

The main source of appraisal guidance in the UK for many years has been the HM Treasury's "Green Book", Appraisal and Evaluation in Central Government (*www.hm-treasury.gov.uk/pdf/2000/greenbook.pdf*). This high-level guidance to Departments is firmly based in cost-benefit analysis. A parallel development has resulted from the need to integrate the various, broader objectives which Government supports (such as sustainable development, equal treatment of minorities, human rights considerations, etc.) into the main appraisal framework. The PIU developed a Policy Makers' Checklist (*www.cabinet-office.gov.uk/regulation/1999/checklist/intro.htm*) as a toolkit to help analysts identify and incorporate all necessary impacts into appraisals. The latest (1997) version of the Green Book is currently being revised, and may include a broader interpretation of appraisal to address the distribution issues and handling of non-monetised effects which are not traditional strengths of the cost-benefit framework.

Discussion of sustainable development issues has been influenced by cost-benefit approaches in the UK. The DETR approach to policy appraisal makes this an important element of all new environmental policies. The weight being accorded to such approaches has been strengthened by the Cabinet Office Better Regulation Unit and its desire to ensure that all policies are subjected to a cost-benefit test. It seems clear to us that there are differing views in Government departments as to the weight that should be accorded to such approaches. Valuation of non-market goods, whilst it has rapidly become the "meat and drink" of all orthodox environmental economists, is viewed with more scepticism by those outside this epistemic community.

A number of reasons can be cited for this unease. The methodological limits of approaches such as contingent valuation, as well as the fact that scientific uncertainty is sometimes thought to be downplayed in the valuation of effects (although this is a problem with whatever appraisal methodology is applied), are but two possible reasons for this scepticism. Another which appears to present ethical dilemmas to some is the approach of attaching values to life, whether through the value of statistical life approach, or the value of life-years lost method (and the two may suggest different answers to specific problems). Proponents of valuation methods highlight the advantages of such methods. They allow impacts to be compared in the same unit, decrease the likelihood that non-marketed impacts are ignored, and reduce the potential for arbitrary or inconsistent judgements. The UK is thought to be leading the way in the use of valuation methods, and the Government is continuing to use them as part of its evidence-based policy-making agenda.[3]

Work in the Environment Agency's Sustainable Development Unit shows appreciation of the requirement for a more open and transparent approach to decision making, in which a plurality of approaches is carried forward. One consequence that may flow from this is that decisions will be less than clear-cut. The approach to dealing with this wealth of information and the opinions which flow from it becomes more political and more openly subjective. Furthermore, in an age in which mediated experience plays a major role, rather than suggesting a once-and-for-all solution to a problem, the "best solution" may itself change over time (just as people switch allegiance between political parties). The implied requirement for reversibility and change makes flexibility a desirable characteristic of any solution.

Public consultation and participation

The corollary of a well-functioning process of this nature is the requirement for education and mechanisms for dissemination of relevant information to enable citizens to engage in discussions in an informed manner. The recognition of the importance of engaging stakeholders in policy development has grown in all areas of public policy. Arrangements made for public consultation and participation, at different levels of government, will be described. Key issues will be the extent to which arrangements are formalised, and the extent to which arrangements are inclusive of the range of potential stakeholders. Issues of consultation/participation will also be considered by reference to particular policy initiatives (see below).

The consultative process is a critical element to the development of integrated policy. Methods of balancing competing interests and building ownership of policy are increasingly based on extended consultation, undertaken and reported with greater transparency than in traditional policy-making processes. An example of the importance, and nature, of the consultative process in promoting sustainable development is provided by the new Welsh Assembly.

A further example of the growing use of consultative processes is the development of a People's Panel, comprising a random selection of 5 000 people who can be consulted on various policy proposals. This is a resource available (at cost) to all policy makers.

During 1998, the Service First Unit (now the Modernising Public Services Group) in the Cabinet Office commissioned MORI, the market research company, and Birmingham University's School of Public Policy to set up a People's Panel. The Panel consists of 5 000 members of the public randomly selected from across the UK, and is designed to be a representative cross-section of the population (by gender, age, background, region, etc.). Panel members are being consulted about how public services are delivered and how that delivery can be improved from the point of view of the user, rather than the system.

Citizens' panels have been used in local government in the UK for many years, but the People's Panel is a world first at national level. There were extensive consultations with the private sector, academics and research organisations on how the People's Panel should be set up and the type of research for which it could best be used. A pilot survey was set up prior to launching the Panel in order to test its effectiveness.

A Panel is thought to have three major advantages over *ad hoc* research projects and other forms of consultation:

1. It enables organisations to measure how and why people's views are changing.

2. It provides a ready resource for consultation with both users and non-users of services.

3. It is an ideal vehicle for examining cross-cutting issues.

The Government is committed to publishing all results from the Panel. Summaries of findings are widely distributed and, along with the full topline results, are published on the website. Full data sets will also be available for secondary analysis, from MORI and the UK's Economic and Social Research Council.

The Panel has already been used for a range of both quantitative and qualitative research covering many public service issues. These have included transport, modernising government, local democracy, care in the community, and new technology in government.

Three waves of quantitative research are planned each year and results should be published at the end of May, October and January: the actual publication dates may vary depending on the type of research that is carried out. Because the People's Panel is a new approach for central government, it will be evaluated annually, for at least the first three years of its life.

Turning talk into action

The use of monitoring and reporting, as the basis for dialogue with stakeholders, has been taken to the heart of some business reporting (see Annex XII). There is some interest in seeking to apply the lessons from good practice sustainability reporting by businesses to government.

Examples are used to illustrate the process of implementation of international and national policy commitments (economic, environmental and social), requiring translation into the policies at lower spatial scales.

Overview

Overall responsibility for advising on the translation of policy across spatial boundaries rests with the Sustainable Development Unit, in so far as explicit sustainable development policies are concerned. However, policy implementation across spatial boundaries is a common issue in the translation of European Parliament policy into UK policy, relating to economic, environmental and social issues. Efforts to transpose international agreements and conventions into UK policy also regularly occur. Recent policy development includes the introduction of European Directives on social policy (e.g. in relation to working hours), and the transposition of the Kyoto Protocol. Examples are detailed below.

At sub-national level, there have been recent initiatives by the Government to strengthen regional policy, by introducing devolved government in Wales, Scotland and Northern Ireland, and a new Regional Co-ordinating Unit for regional government offices in the English regions. A new Local Government Act is also being introduced, featuring explicit responsibilities for sustainable development.

Transposition of international agreements

Probably the best example in the UK of an attempt to transpose an international Agreement into actions which deliver the objectives of the Agreement, is the response to the Kyoto Protocol.[4] Not only did the response deal directly with the Agreement; it did so by introducing new and appropriate policy instruments, themselves based on a consultative process, which has given rise to an integrated mix of fiscal and voluntary measures.

309

The UK, like other OECD countries, signed the Kyoto Protocol of the Climate Change Convention and has agreed to the international commitment to reduce greenhouse gas emissions by 12.5 per cent by the period 2008-2012 relative to 1990. In its first budget in July 1997, the Government published a "Statement of Intent" that signalled its commitment to introduce environmental taxes as long as they were effective and did not damage the UK's competitive position. In its first full Budget of 1998, it announced it would be asking Lord Marshall, then the Head of the Confederation of British Industry (and Chairman of British Airways), to investigate and consult on the use of economic instruments in industry, and in particular the use of a carbon or energy tax.

Lord Marshall produced a report in November 1998 (with Secretariat support provided jointly by the environment and the finance ministries) that argued that, under certain circumstances, energy taxes should be introduced, alongside tradeable permits and subsidies for investment in energy conservation.

In April 1999, citing Lord Marshall's recommendations, the Chancellor announced that a climate change levy (CCL) would be payable from 2001. This was a tax on energy use by business, the proceeds from the levy being returned to business in the form of a reduction of employer's payroll taxes. At the same time, the taxation authority (HMC&E, 1999) issued a consultative paper which spelt out in more detail the sectors to be covered by the CCL and the illustrative rate at which it would be levied.

This policy has been set out in more detail since implementing the CCL. Part of the policy encourages firms to enter into a negotiated agreement, which allows an 80 per cent reduction in the level of CCL, in exchange for a binding commitment to improve energy efficiency. Officials in these negotiations have focussed on extracting what they regard as *all cost-effective energy efficiency savings* from business. All countries have exhorted their industries to improve their energy efficiency, but the UK is unusual in linking the improvement in energy efficiency to a reduction in CCL, in order to leverage a strong commitment from industry to enhance energy efficiency. Only Denmark has anything equivalent, although France is also considering a similar policy.

The Government made it clear that industry should take forward the concept of tradeable permits. In response, the CBI and the Advisory Committee for Business and the Environment produced a paper outlining the case for an industry-led and designed domestic emissions trading scheme, which would be consistent with the international scheme.

The Government's climate change policy contains a number of interesting features. It has appointed senior business figures such as Lord Marshall to chair the design phase. Business has very much led the development of the domestic emissions trading. All stages of the policy design have been open to consultation. The

introduction of the CCL in particular was announced two years before the introduction of the tax allowing firms to modify their investment plans in light of the
tax. Though the Climate Change Levy is still unpopular with the business community, the modifications that have been made have greatly reduced the cost to the
energy-intensive industries, while still committing them to improvements in
energy efficiency. The policy has created a special funding mechanism for capital
investments in energy efficiency for small business. It also includes incentives to
use CHP and renewables.

The transposition of national policies, supportive of sustainable development,
into local policy is best exemplified by the introduction of the New Deal for Communities. In the context of a national strategy for neighbourhood renewal, this recent programme is seeking to implement regeneration policy in ways which are inclusive,
transparent, and which better integrate existing policy. The cornerstone of this policy
is the use of clear local frameworks and delivery plans for the agreed outcomes of local
partnerships, seeking to use mainstream programmes to better support community
renewal. Further details are given in the next section, on new policy initiatives.

D.   Learning from the United Kingdom experience

The study considers good-practice examples of recent policy measures
embodying ideas of integration and participation. In particular, attention is given
to good-practice examples of recent policy measures embodying ideas of integration and participation, *e.g.* National Strategy for Neighbourhood Renewal, Voluntary
Agreements and Regeneration Zones.

National Strategy for Neighbourhood Renewal

Through the emerging National Strategy for Neighbourhood Renewal, the
Government is seeking to narrow the gap between the most deprived areas and
the rest of the country. In the recent Spending Review targets have been set, for
the first time, to improve the outcomes in these areas that are achieved by core
spending programmes. For example, in relation to crime, the target is to reduce
domestic burglary by 25 per cent by 2005 (with no local authority area having a
rate more than three times the national average).

To help ensure that these targets are delivered, Government departments
will be reviewing funding allocation processes to ensure that sufficient funds reach
deprived areas. A new Neighbourhood Renewal Fund (NRF), with national
resources of £100 million in 2001-02, £300 million in 2002-03 and £400 million
in 2003-04, will be paid to local authorities in the most deprived areas of England.

The purpose of these additional non-ring fenced resources will be to help local
authorities in the most deprived areas focus their main programme expenditures in
order to deliver better outcomes for their most deprived communities. The Govern-

ment will expect to see evidence that funding from the Neighbourhood Renewal Fund is being used to improve the delivery of services to the most deprived wards and neighbourhoods within the eligible areas.

A consultation paper set out the Government's proposals on how the Fund will operate, on the authorities which will be eligible for the fund, on the indicative proposed allocations to these authorities for the three financial years from April 2001 to March 2004, and on the conditions upon which funding will depend.

Separate guidance has been issued setting out the role envisaged for Local Strategic Partnerships. The Government recognises that it takes time to develop effective partnerships and that, in doing so, local authorities are reliant on securing the co-operation and participation of a range of local partners for such partnerships to work. The Government believes that, in many of the most deprived areas of the country, substantial progress has already been made in developing strategic local partnership arrangements, not least through developments such as the Local Governments Association's New Commitment to Regeneration Initiative, Health Action Zones, Crime and Disorder Partnerships, and so forth.

Local neighbourhood renewal strategies will involve identifying deprived neighbourhoods, and setting in train action – agreed with the community – to improve them. They will be part of Community Strategies. Each year, local authorities will be expected to provide a short statement of usage of their NRF resources, showing how they support the local neighbourhood renewal strategy (or its general direction, if the strategy is still work in progress). The forthcoming Neighbourhood Renewal Action Plan (to be published later this Autumn) will give more detail on what these strategies might entail.

The Government wants the emergence of Local Strategic Partnerships to build on the best models that are already in place locally, not to set up separate and overlapping new partnership mechanisms. Continuation of support through the Neighbourhood Renewal Fund will be conditional on effective local strategic partnerships, which fully involve key local players, particularly voluntary groups and local communities, being in place.

Use of negotiated agreements

Voluntary Initiatives (VIs) in general, and Negotiated Environmental Agreements (NEA) in particular, could be valuable instruments in achieving sustainable changes. They could be of particular importance in helping reduce greenhouse gas emissions (GHGs) to achieve the Kyoto targets and beyond, and a number of such agreements have been concluded in the UK.

Many issues relating to sustainable development, including an effective climate change policy, require the involvement of the whole group of society stakeholders, allowing, for example, greenhouse gas emissions to be tackled from different perspectives (local, regional and central governments, business, NGOs and the public) and sectors. This crucial multi-stakeholder approach forms an integral part of a successful Voluntary Initiative, when designed and implemented efficiently.

Voluntary Initiatives represent a process of broadening the level of "shared responsibility" and indeed "shared liability" for addressing climate change throughout the sectors of the economy, and include a range of different instruments, reflecting the different country, cultural, legal, institutional and economic contexts in which they were launched. VIs include negotiated environmental agreements, public voluntary programmes, self-declarations or commitments, implementation of voluntary environmental management and audit schemes (EMS, EMAS), environmental labelling, voluntary reporting, and codes of conduct.

Each of these has particular values and limitations. Of these, NEAs offer a promising new instrument. They require the appropriate use of targets, transparency, monitoring and stakeholder involvement, and need to be integrated appropriately into the existing, and developing, policy instrument portfolio. They also need to be backed by continued political commitment to ensure that these agreements are subject to a process of improvement over time, to help meet policy targets.

Where NEAs offer to be a useful instrument, the key to their success lies not only in the appropriate design, but also in ensuring that there are appropriate "carrots" (incentives) and "sticks" (sanctions) for their update and implementation. Furthermore, it is essential that other instruments – regulation, taxation, technology support programmes, public reporting, EMS implementation, public awareness, self-declarations and codes of conduct – are also assessed, to see whether they would be appropriate complements in addressing the environmental issue concerned.

Regional Economic Strategies and Regeneration Zones

The concept of Regeneration Zones (RZs) originally emerged from the initial consultation workshops carried out to inform the drafting of the Regional Economic Strategy (RES) for the West Midlands in Summer 1999. Regeneration Zones were included in the draft RES and, following a generally positive response, the approach has been carried forward into the final West Midlands Regional Strategy (WMRS), published in March 2000.

The idea of Regeneration Zones did not have sustainability as the driving force behind its development; the concept was derived from a desire to target resources more efficiently. The RZ approach is intended to focus on a limited number of areas of investment opportunity that can be linked to immediately adjacent or nearby areas of need. In contrast to existing initiatives such as Single Regeneration Budget Funding, the RZs should include areas capable of generating significant private-sector investment. In rural areas, the RZs should offer opportunities to service the needs of relatively dispersed areas. Sustainability criteria

313|

have been built into the framework of the policy and this, along with the nature of the concept in linking opportunity with need, aims to ensure that sustainable development is reflected in the outcomes of RZs.

Preliminary work to identify the characteristics of RZs pointed towards two types of zone, one urban-focused and the other rural-based, with the different approaches reflecting the different ways that needs in urban (spatially concentrated) and rural (more dispersed) areas present themselves. Initial thinking suggested that the size of the RZs could vary substantially, depending on the issues that need to be tackled, and the life span of each zone would vary according to its specific characteristics and problems. An indicative time scale of between 5 and 15 years was identified as appropriate.

The implementation of RZs requires the development of primary criteria, for selecting appropriate geographic zones; and secondary criteria, for evaluating the potential effectiveness of proposed initiatives within the zone.

The primary criteria, aimed at identifying zones containing both opportunity and need, are as follows:

- **Opportunity** – all zones to include a significant level of development opportunities capable of realisation, based on an appropriate time scale and level of public-sector resources.

- **Need** – all zones to either:

  - Include or adjoin a number of the most *socially deprived* wards, as defined on the basis of the most recent Index of Local Deprivation or Local Conditions (1998).

  - Exhibit needs associated with one or more of the following:

    - Poor and degraded environment.

    - Economic vulnerability.

    - Limited economic opportunity.

These primary criteria include the index of deprivation, poor and degraded environment and economic vulnerability/opportunities, which relate directly to the three pillars of sustainable development namely social inclusion, environment and competitiveness.

The secondary criteria supplement the primary ones with a series of questions or considerations covering social, environmental and economic issues. When building the regeneration zones around a series of identified areas of opportunity and need, the supplementary criteria are capable of ensuring an explicit balance between the primary sustainable development objectives or pillars. Examples taken from the secondary criteria, divided up into the three pillars of sustainable development, include the following:

- Economic
- Capable of making a significant contribution to the development of the priority growth sectors.
- Capable of meeting the requirements of the inward investment and/or indigenous markets.
- Maximising links to the existing strategic transport networks.
- Social.
- Accessible or potentially readily accessible by public transport from surrounding socially deprived communities.
- Have the capacity to contribute to local employment needs, for example by providing jobs with a skill profile that can be met by local job seekers, and providing associated training opportunities.
- Environmental.
- Contributing towards more sustainable forms of development, *e.g.* by the use of existing transport, service and communications infrastructure; and
- Contributing to the development of the urban and rural environment by bringing about the (re)development of brownfield land.

The identification of well-defined spatial priorities in the more rural parts of the region has proved difficult in the context of the need for robust and transparent criteria. The very nature of the approach, in terms of linking opportunity and need, emphasises the need for establishing and developing effective partnerships in the Regeneration Zones.

E.   Concluding remarks

Sustainable development: implication for institutional change

Sustainable development remains a tenuous and often poorly understood concept. Ideas that sustainable development stands for the environment, and a recognition of environmental limits, are mixed with ideas that sustainable development is about balancing short term with long term, and the environmental with social and economic objectives. These are also linked to ideas that sustainable development policy can only be tackled by breaking down traditional ways of defining and appraising policy choices, and by encouraging a much wider range of interests to participate in decision making.

There is therefore a real sense of frustration. Labelling all policy development as "sustainable", and yet not really bringing in new policy perspectives or choices, means there is concern that apparent progress towards sustainability disguises a somewhat more limited rate of progress. Against this, a more pragmatic view might be that, because sustainable development raises a broad range of ideas, the directions to take in the name of sustainable development are inevitably uncertain. Consequently, policy making should be clearly iterative, learning the lessons of policy "making", and then applying them in the next cycle. This in turn means that explicit appraisal and evaluation systems have to be formalised, with the related process and results made as transparent as possible.

The review of institutional aspects presented in this report offers a mix of encouraging and less encouraging examples of policy making and new policy initiative. We summarise some of the lessons below.

Progress and direction

The institutional framework for sustainable development continues to evolve in the UK. A major part of this development is not explicitly driven by a focus on sustainable development, but has a significant, mainly positive bearing on the ability of policy to foster the objectives of sustainable development. Thus, the new regional policy agenda, and a new focus on the role of Local Authorities in supporting "wellbeing", provide a clear framework for "joined-up" policy making; whilst initiatives directed to community regeneration explicitly seek to do so by removing traditional barriers between policy fields.

At the same time, policy-making tools, which aid a more integrated approach to decision making, are being considered. The need to appraise public policy in a more comprehensive and less deterministic fashion is, with some reluctance, being considered. The opportunity to consider a wider range of criteria and perspectives, is being recognised.

At the same time as there is progress, there is also a recognition of the very real "cultural" inertia, which limits the pace of change and the ability to grasp new policy thinking. Of major concern is the failure to translate the need for longer-term perspectives into short-term policy making. Accompanied by a reluctance to devolve decision making, and to fully apply principles of sustainability, day-to-day policy making is still constrained by traditional paradigms. Arguably, the recent EU-wide protest at higher road fuel prices signifies a policy failure to communicate the rationales in terms of sustainable development for desired changes in transport behaviour, and to achieve a reduction in the social and economic dependence on the car. This provides a warning that real changes in support of sustainable development will require many years, and will face many difficult challenges from those with an interest in the status quo.

In terms of the developing roles of the different actors that make up the institutional fabric for sustainable development in the UK, a number of concluding remarks might be made in the light of the foregoing review:

- Central government has moved considerably to take on the challenge of changing traditional policy- and decision-making processes. The concepts of "joined-up" thinking and the removal of "silo" policy debate have taken hold, even if difficult to implement. The scope to introduce ideas and to challenge conventional wisdom of sustainable development has been fostered through the Environmental Audit Select Committee, the Performance and Innovation Unit and by the new Commission for Sustainable Development. The opportunities made available to "rock the (policy) boat" provide a good test of Government commitment to allow the necessary scope for the processes required by sustainable development to evolve.

- Regional government has still to develop in England, but the progress made in Wales and Scotland, and the early development of RDA strategies in England, provide a promising signal that the regional level can play the "transformer" role, in translating strategic policy ideas into practical policy proposals to be implemented at the local level.

- Local government has new responsibilities and opportunities to take on, through initiatives such as the New Deal for Communities, Best Value, and regional sustainable development frameworks. The challenge is to define and implement policy proposals and decision-making processes which are supportive of sustainable development.

- Non-Government Organisations (NGOs) have also played important roles in challenging conventional ideas, and promoting new thinking. Some of this activity has been through "green" protest, targeted at traditional decision-making processes. More recently, there has been a more active engagement in newer stakeholder-driven processes. These roles can be seen in the examples given in the report. This engagement carries risks, both to the process – NGOs can lead to an unbalanced representation of opinion – and to the NGOs – compromise and costs. However, as new decision-making processes evolve, the role of NGOs is likely to increase.

- The Social Partners (businesses and trades unions) have played different roles. The engagement of business interests in policy making has been sought, through for example the use of negotiated agreements. Again, this process carries risks: the use of environmental negotiated agreements has led to "regulatory capture", where the negotiated changes for businesses are less than might have been expected from more traditional environmental regulation. This risk can be reduced through rigorous adherence to transparent decision making. Some businesses, and business sectors, have

317|

played an active role in developing a recognition of and response to the need for change. UK Trade Union involvement in the sustainable development debate has been far less evident, retaining its focus on traditional areas of concern relating to the conditions of employment of members.

Developments in the UK institutional framework

The principal institutional change in the UK is the emergence of an explicit regional policy, and related bodies. This emergence provides a major opportunity for defining sustainable development policy. This is recognised by, for example, the drafting of "regional sustainability frameworks". The opportunity to open up a role as "transformer" of sustainable development policy, translating strategic policy directions into measures capable of implementation at the lowest levels of government, is one which is as yet poorly defined, but which will be explored and tested in the next few years.

There are also key changes in both central and local government. At the central level, the "increasing" attempts to break out of "policy silos" and to link performance to funding of departments, could lead to more integrated policy. At the local level, the new remit for local authorities to promote the wellbeing of communities should also lead to a more integrated approach.

There are a number of lessons for future developments in support of sustainable development. These include:

- The need to develop a more explicit set of tools and methodologies for *integrated* policy appraisal, and a greater use of review and evaluation of what policy measures work, and under what circumstances. The interest of both the Sustainable Development Unit and the Environment Agency in the development of integrated policy appraisal tools is to be welcomed.

- The need to engage stakeholders in the appraisal and evaluation process is widely acknowledged in principle, but suffers from the lack of a greater body of experience of the practical means to achieve this, and the transfer of that experience. Areas for development include building on the best practice in company-level integrated auditing and reporting, and the transfer of this corporate experience to government.

- The "culture" of government has still to fully evolve to one that is more sympathetic to integrated and participative approaches, with the corollary of greater transparency in decision processes. The reported democratic deficit in the English regions, contrasted with the approaches in Wales and Scotland, is evidence of the need for stronger political leadership in shaping the nature of the debate on how to take sustainable development forward. This leadership has, in turn, to address problems which result from maintaining "silo" thinking, from a reluctance to cede decision-making authority, and "short-termism".

- The need to transfer experience and apply more widely the approaches to increase stakeholder contributions to policy formulation. The report has shown contrasting UK experience between the implementation of policy responses to the Kyoto targets, with a strong element of social dialogue, and the somewhat technocratic approach to waste-management policy. At the local level, the New Deal for Communities Programme has adopted an integrated and participative approach. This programme has the challenge to ensure that the consultation process is linked effectively with the decision-making processes, so that it does not become an exercise in tokenism, but neither is it used as an excuse for deferring decisions when faced with sensitive trade-offs in policy choices.

- The development of sustainable development, both as a process of policy and decision making, and as a set of policy objectives, is recognised to require time and to be uncertain. This means that the institutional development has to allow for iteration and to ensure transparency in decision making. Current UK developments to this end are encouraging.

319|

Notes

1. The views expressed in this paper are those of the author, and do not necessarily reflect those of the OECD, or those of its Public Management Service.

2. In terms of defining sustainable development, Chapter 1 of A *better quality of life – A strategy for sustainable development for the* UK (May 1999) states that at the heart of the concept is the simple idea of ensuring "a better quality of life for everyone, now and for generations to come", and acknowledges that this is a simple idea – but a substantial task as it means meeting four objectives at the same time:

   • social progress which recognises the needs of everyone;

   • effective protection of the environment;

   • prudent use of natural resources; and

   • maintenance of high and stable levels of economic growth and employment".

3. For example, work is currently being developed within DETR on valuing the effects of air pollution on health, and ascribing a value to a tonne of carbon.

4. The Convention on Access to Information, Public Participation in Decision Making and Access to Justice in Environmental Matters (Aarhus Convention), which constitutes another key international agreement in this field, had not been ratified by the United Kingdom when this case study was prepared. It is therefore left out of the scope of the study.

Annex I

United Kingdom Sustainable Development Strategy:
A Better Quality of Life

Background and development of the strategy

A consultation document *"Opportunities for Change"*, which discussed issues for the strategy, was distributed. A series of regional consultation events were also organised. An Inter-Departmental Steering Group was established to develop the strategy, including representatives from the DETR and other Government Departments. The draft of the strategy was then approved at Cabinet level and by the Prime Minister before its publication was announced in Parliament.

Aims and objectives

The aim of the strategy is "ensuring a better quality of life for everyone, now and for generations to come". It encompasses four main objectives:

1. Social progress, which recognises the needs of everyone.
2. Effective protection of the environment.
3. Prudent use of natural resources.
4. Maintenance of high and stable levels of economic growth and employment.

The strategy outlines **10 *principles and approaches*** that reflect key themes from the Rio Declaration on Environment and Development, the 1994 strategy, and responses to the *"Opportunities for Change"* document:

1. Putting people at the centre.
2. Taking a long-term perspective.
3. Taking account of costs and benefits.
4. Creating an open and supportive economic system.
5. Combating poverty and social exclusion.
6. Respecting environmental limits.
7. The precautionary principle.
8. Using scientific knowledge.
9. Transparency, information, participation and access to justice.
10. Making the polluter pay.

Approach

The strategy includes three sections, which outline the government's plans and specific initiatives for a sustainable economy, building sustainable communities and managing the environment and resources. More generally, devolution is seen as an important aspect of sustainable development, in terms of the concept of "thinking globally, acting locally". The Government aims over time to reform the tax system in ways which deliver a more dynamic economy and a cleaner environment: shifting taxes from "goods", like employment, towards "bads", such as pollution, while subsidies and voluntary agreements are also seen as important. Research and advice are seen as important aspects of the strategy in terms of more support for sustainable development themes through the Research Councils and the importance of the advisory bodies in the institutional framework.

Measuring and advising progress

The Government revised in 1999 the national set of sustainable development indicators published in 1996 in "*Quality of Life Counts*". The new set of about 150 indicators reflects social issues to a larger extent and includes a subset of 15 key headline indicators. "*Regional Quality of Life Counts*" indicators and "*Local Quality of Life Counts*" indicators were also published in 2000. Following the commitment made in 1999 in "A Better Quality of Life, a Strategy for Sustainable Development for the UK" to review progress in the country as a whole towards sustainable development and to report annually from 2000, the Government launched its first annual report on sustainable development "*Achieving a Better Quality of Life – Review of Progress Towards Sustainable Development*" in January 2001. The report identifies key issues relating to quality of life and focuses on progress against each of the 15 headline indicators of sustainable development. It also discusses strategic developments, the principles and approaches that underpin sustainable development and action on priorities outlined in the Strategy. Having recognised the importance of continuous and regular monitoring, reporting and reviewing progress on sustainable development, the Government launched in parallel to the annual report a new website on sustainable development: *www.sustainable-development.gov.uk*

Annex II

Towards an Urban Renaissance:
The Report of the Urban Task Force (1999)

Aim

The aim of the Urban Task Force was to identify causes of urban decline in England, and recommend practical solutions to bring people back into cities, towns and urban neighbourhoods. It aimed to establish a new vision for urban regeneration, founded on the principles of design excellence, social wellbeing and environmental responsibility, within a viable economic and legislative framework.

Key themes and measures

The study highlighted a number of key themes and important measures associated with them. These themes are listed below:

Recycling land and buildings. To enable the Government to meet its 60 per cent target for accommodating new dwellings on previously developed land, better use must be made of derelict, vacant and under-used land and buildings before Greenfield sites are developed.

Improving the urban environment. Attractive urban neighbourhoods are important and can be achieved by improving the quality of design and movement, creating compact developments, with a mix of uses, better public transport and a density which supports local services and fosters a strong sense of community and public safety.

Achieving excellence in leadership, participation and management. Local authorities should lead the urban renaissance. They should be strengthened in powers, resources and democratic legitimacy to undertake this role, in partnership with the citizens and communities they represent. Urban areas should be managed more effectively and response to the special needs of council estates and other deprived neighbourhoods is important.

Delivering regeneration. Local authorities and their partners should be given more freedom to target long-term resources on areas in need of regeneration. Public investment should be used to lever larger amounts of institutional investment into the process of regenerating our towns and cities.

To achieve an urban renaissance, the report highlighted a number of important areas, along with a number of recommendations associated with each of these areas, some of which are included as examples below:

Designing the urban environment

- Introduce a national urban design framework, disseminating key design principles through planning and funding guidance, supported by a new series of best-practice guidelines.

- Introduce a mandatory double performance rating for houses, combining an environmental and a running cost rating, so house buyers know what level of building performance they are getting for their money.

Making the connections (transport infrastructure)

- Place Local Transport Plans on a statutory footing, with targets for reducing car journeys, and increasing year on year the proportion of trips made on foot, bicycle and public transport.

- Commit a minimum of 65 per cent of transport public expenditure to walking, cycling and public transport over the next ten years.

Managing the urban environment

- Assign a strategic role to local authorities in ensuring management of the whole urban environment, with powers to require other property owners to maintain their land and premises to an acceptable standard.

- Provide an above-inflation increase in central resources allocated to local authorities for managing and maintaining the urban environment in each of the next seven years.

Delivering urban regeneration

- Create designated Urban Priority Areas, enabling local authorities and their partners in regeneration, including local people, to apply for special packages (tax incentives for developers, investors, owners and tenants) of powers and incentives to assist neighbourhood renewal.

Investing in skills and innovation

- Establish joint working between professionals, institutions, education providers and employers to develop a plan of action for improving the skills base in urban development over the next five to seven years.

Planning for change

- Produce dedicated Planning Policy guidance to support the drive for an urban renaissance.

- Simplify local development plans with an emphasis on strategy to create a more flexible basis for planning. The plans should avoid including detailed site-level policies.

Managing the land supply

- Formally adopt a sequential approach to the release of land and buildings for housing, supported by a system of regional and sub-regional reconciliation of housing needs and demand.

Cleaning up the land

- Establish a national framework for identifying, managing and communicating the risks that arise throughout the assessment, treatment and after-care of contaminated and previously contaminated sites.

Recycling the buildings

- Give local authorities a statutory duty to maintain an empty property strategy that sets clear targets for reducing levels of vacant stock.
- Harmonise VAT rates at a zero rate in respect of new building and conversions and refurbishments. If harmonisation can only be achieved at a 5 per cent rate, then a significant part of the proceeds should be reinvested into urban regeneration.

Making the investment

- Establish national public-private investment funds that can attract an additional £1 billion in private investment for area regeneration projects over the next three years.

Sustaining the renaissance

In working towards an urban renaissance, the measurement of progress will be very important. One of the concluding proposals is that the Government should produce an annual "*State of the Towns and Cities*" report, detailing progress across a range of social, economic and environmental indicators. The report outlines a number of aims to be achieved by the year 2021, including the following examples:

- The main urban environmental indicators – air pollution, ground contamination, energy use, water recycling and waste disposal – will all show significant improvement.
- Urban depopulation will have given way to year-on-year growth in the number of people living in towns and cities. Movement will have taken place from the outskirts to inner areas and distinctions between market and social housing will have become blurred.

Criticism

The report has also been criticised on a number of points. These include the call for the reintroduction of the middle classes back into the city centres through a process of gentrification and modernisation. The claim is that if the Government were successful in gentrifying inner-city areas, it would lead to rises in property and land prices and the likely expulsion of the poor. Also, with the urban renaissance being delivered through regional development agencies and local government with specific remits to promote economic competitiveness and inward investment, how far can implementation meet the needs of deprived communities?

Annex III

Survey of the Quality of Life Perceptions of City Residents

Work was undertaken, as part of the Urban Audit of EU cities, to survey the perceptions of city residents as to the important factors affecting their quality of life. The surveys were carried out in a sample of 20 cities, using a combination of face-to-face interviews and focus groups. The objectives were:

- To investigate the use of indicators to identify discrepancies in the weight attached by citizens of different cities to the various quality-of-life factors.

- To identify whether there are differences between the perceptions of aspects of quality of life and actual scores on the indicators for which data is being gathered.

- And to assess variations in perceptions of quality of life between neighbourhoods within cities and between population age groups.

Respondents in the face-to-face interviews, undertaken in 12 cities, were asked to rate the importance of 18 factors potentially affecting their quality of life. All of these factors were considered important by at least one third of respondents, and all but three factors were important to over half the respondents. **Overall, the level of unemployment, quality of air and crime were considered the most important factors affecting quality of life.**

The focus groups were asked to identify additional important factors not included in the list of 18. A large number of additional factors were mentioned, some of which were considered as amongst the five most important factors. Some of the latter were qualitative and thus difficult to quantify (**for example, civility, urbanity, politeness, tolerance, respect for others, variety, diversity of cultural** "scene", **community participation, atmosphere, and distinctiveness** of the city). Many related to the quality of and access to public and private services (health, social services, urban planning, education, street cleaning, shopping and public spaces) and other factors included the cost of living and access to the countryside.

The findings of the face-to-face interviews indicate that residents in different cities attach different weights to the 18 factors. The differences were most marked for the factors: quality of housing and level of unemployment. The results of the focus groups pointed to less marked differences between cities, but highlighted differences in opinion between participants in the focus groups in their attitudes towards *"controversial"* factors. Overall, however, of the five "most important" factors mentioned in each city, **unemployment, air quality, and crime** occur in at least 9 of the 12 cities. Other factors, such as the quality of the transport system and amount of green space, have a particular significance for specific cities. These findings provide support for the continued development of a single set of comparable indicators across the EU cities, but also suggest the parallel need to assess systematically differences in the weight attached to particular factors in different cities.

At the city level, there appears to be a reasonably close correspondence between the perceptions of respondents as to quality-of-life factors and the objective, relative position of the cities.

Separate focus groups for different age groups were held in 12 cities. The young age group (18-24 years) most commonly cited "the level of crime", "employment opportunities" and "cultural opportunities (cinema, theatre, etc.)" among the five most important factors related to the quality of life. The middle age group (25-59 years) most often cited "the quality of housing", "the quality of the transport system", and "unemployment" among the five most important factors affecting the quality of life. The elderly age group (60 years and over) was most frequently concerned by "the level of crime", "the health of the population" and "unemployment".

Source: The European Urban Audit, ECOTEC Research and Consulting Ltd, EC (DG Regio), 2000.

327|

Annex IV

The Green Ministers Initiative

The 1990 White Paper *"This Common Inheritance"* and subsequent reports introduced several institutional reforms, including the appointment of Green Ministers. Each Government Department has a Green Minister. The aim of Green Ministers is to promote sustainable development and environmental matters in their own departments and collectively work to:

- Promote the integration of sustainable development across Government and the wider public sector.
- Encourage the use of environmental appraisals as part of policy making.
- And continue to improve the environmental performance of Departments in managing their buildings and facilities (otherwise known as "greening operations").

The Cabinet Committee on the Environment (ENV), chaired by the Deputy Prime Minister, plays a strategic role, and Green Ministers report to it twice a year to consider environmental policies and co-ordinate those on sustainable development. The Green Ministers Committee produced its first annual report in July 1999, and a second was produced in November 2000. These documents set out its achievements and future work programme. The achievements listed included the following examples (from 1999 report):

- The agreement of a Model Policy Statement for Greening Operations accompanied by a Model Improvement Programme (almost all Departments now have their own green housekeeping strategies).
- Set targets for energy efficiency and waste recovery, as well as green transport plans for Executive Agencies and Government Officers for the Regions.
- Provision of assistance to Departments on implementing Environmental Management Systems (EMSs), including issuing a guide, holding a major seminar, setting up a telephone helpdesk and establishing call-off contract for consultancy advice.
- Joint DETR and HMT guidance to clarify the opportunities for Departments to take into account the environmental impacts of purchasing decisions through their procurement policies.
- Advice to Departments on environmental appraisals of policies.
- A review, by Green Ministers, of the best way for sustainable development to be taken into account in the aims and objectives of Departments and their associate bodies.

The Parliamentary Environmental Audit Committee (EAC) monitors the work of Green Ministers through an annual inquiry. In a report in June 1998, the EAC concluded that the Green Ministers Committee (GMC) "could make a significant contribution to the Govern-

328

ment's pursuit of sustainable development". Their comments on the first annual report from the GMC include the following examples:

- The Green Ministers should set out a strategic assessment which maps the environmental impacts of each Department, to identify priority areas for environmental gains and, equally, for risks of adverse impacts.

- Leadership from the very top in Government, and in each Department, is crucial for the success of cross-cutting initiatives such as greening government and encouraging sustainable development.

- A firm target for the establishment of environmental management systems is required, along with a firm target for the accreditation of such systems.

- Only the DfEE is explicitly committed to the systematic publication of the results of screening and appraisal of all policy proposals for their environmental impacts. Other Departments should follow suit.

- The Government is blurring the distinction between a genuine "options appraisal" and "impact assessment" (which is likely to be much more about defending decisions) For example, the seven appraisals, from four Departments, given as examples of published environmental appraisals are, with the exception of countryside access, assessments of the impacts of preferred options, or already announced decisions.

- Transparency is required in publishing a full list of policies where environmental appraisals have been undertaken by Departments, whether fully published or not.

- While Departments are putting greening housekeeping policies and procedures into place, there are still gaps in Departments' data collection, and hence target setting and reporting of performance.

- While Departments have iterated their understanding that procurement policies can have major environmental impacts, there is no performance data or independent assurance that departmental procedures are being adhered to. There is particular concern over the development of the Public Finance Initiative (PFI) and Public Private Partnerships (PPP) initiatives and the extent to which environmental criteria are being built in to those processes.

- The lack of Government target setting suggests that the GMC is settling for a slow pace of progress.

Annex V

Good Practice in National Government: Department for International Development (DFID)

The new Government has taken the former Overseas Development Agency (ODA), which was part of the Foreign and Commonwealth Office, and created in 1997 a separate Government Department with its own Cabinet Minister. This has helped to raise the profile of international development. For example:

- DFID are taking the lead on encouraging other Government Departments to make policies on environment, trade, investment and agricultural policies more consistent with support for developing countries.

- DFID has successfully persuaded the Treasury of the need to increase the UK's overseas aid budget.

- DFID has also worked closely with the Treasury to promote debt reduction for heavily indebted poor countries (HIPC).

The new Department published, in 1997, a White Paper focusing on an outcome-orientated and more long-term approach to international development, focusing on seven international targets for sustainable development based on UN Conventions and Resolutions. The key target is to reduce the proportion of the people living in extreme poverty by half, from an estimated 25 per cent of the world's population in 1990 to 12.5 per cent by the year 2015. The other targets focus on universal primary education, gender equality, infant and child mortality, maternal mortality, reproductive health, and the environment. While all the targets collectively address sustainable development, the environmental target specifically states that there should be a current national strategy for sustainable development (nssustainable development) in the process of implementation in every country by 2005. DFID has recently produced a series of Target Strategy papers to address how each of these targets can be achieved.

DFID is taking steps to address the economic, social and environmental issues of sustainable development:

Economic issues have traditionally been at the forefront of DFID's efforts, but there is now a recognition that pro-poor growth is needed which specifically benefits the poor. The new White Paper on globalisation will address how the wealth generated by globalisation can help developing countries and the poor. Social issues are now central to DFID, helped by the recruitment of a large cadre of social development advisors. They have helped DFID focus on poverty as a multi-dimensional issue, which is more than just lack of income. DFID also places greater emphasis on participation and ownership, both at the country level and at the micro level. Environmental issues have traditionally not been negatively affected by DFID interventions, but opportunities to improve the environment have in some cases been missed. To address this and respond to the new focus on poverty reduction, DFID is now paying greater attention to environmental issues that affect the health, livelihoods and vulnerability of the poor.

One of the challenges of sustainable development is not just to address economic, social and environmental issues separately, but to take a more holistic and comprehensive approach to development that seeks to integrate these three pillars of sustainable development. This is now recognised internationally, both by developing countries and donors, who realise the need for a strategic framework for government and civil society to develop and implement, and to encourage greater donor co-ordination. To achieve this, the poorest countries are being encouraged to prepare poverty-reduction strategies (initially as a requirement for debt relief). Poverty-reduction strategies should be country driven, be developed transparently with broad participation of elected institutions, stakeholders, including civil society, key development agencies and regional development banks, and have a clear link with the international development targets. These principles are embedded in the Comprehensive Development Framework and are similar to the principles of strategies for sustainable development.

More holistic working is also being promoted within DFID itself. For example, most DFID interventions are now prepared jointly by multidisciplinary teams. There are also a number of multidisciplinary policy units, for example the Sustainable Development Unit created in 1998 to promote understanding of national strategies for sustainable development.

A second challenge of sustainable development is to recognise that it requires political will to address the very real political issues involved, such as whether wealthy elites will share more power and resources with the larger population. These issues are now easier to address, given the end of the Cold War. DFID, along with many others, now places a much greater emphasis on "governance", with a large group of governance advisors. Traditionally their focus was on public sector reform, but there is now engagement with a much broader range of political and institutional issues such as corruption, transparency, democratic reforms and civil society involvement in policy making.

Annex VI

The Sustainable Development Commission

As proposed in the White Paper "A *Better Quality of Life*", the Government has established the Sustainable Development Commission, subsuming the UK Round Table on Sustainable Development and the British Government Panel on Sustainable Development. It has done so jointly with the Scottish Executive, the Welsh Assembly and the Northern Ireland Executive. The Commission is chaired by Jonathon Porritt. There are 21 other members, drawn from a wide range of backgrounds and from all parts of the United Kingdom.

The Commission is sponsored, within the UK Government, by the Cabinet Office and reports to the Prime Minister, the First Minister in Scotland, the First Secretary in Wales and the First and Deputy First Ministers in Northern Ireland. Its work will be of interest to a wide range of sectors and organisations. The Commission will hold its first meeting in November 2001.

Mission statement

"To inspire sustainable development in government, the economy and society".

Strategic objectives

- To advocate a compelling vision of a sustainable economy and society.
- To review how far sustainable development is being achieved in the UK across all sectors.
- To identify the opportunities for, and obstacles to, step changes to sustainable development by government, business and the media.
- To promote mechanisms which will deliver a sustainable society.
- To advance innovative approaches to policy making and encourage wider participation.
- To help mainstream the principles and practices of sustainable development, and to support and encourage leadership and best practice, in all sectors of society.

Main focus

Following a process of consultation and a series of preparatory exercises, the Sustainable Development Commission has recently agreed its mission and strategic objectives and forward programme of work for 2001-2003. The Commission will initially be focussing its attention, and most of its resources, on five key themes. These are:

- **The economic paradigm:** does the relentless quest for ever-upward levels of economic growth translate into improvements in human welfare? How must we adapt our policies in pursuit of growth, and how we measure their success, in order to meet the imperative of sustainable development?

- **Climate change:** how well is the UK doing in reducing greenhouse gas emissions, at national, regional and local levels? How can we adapt in a way which does least harm to the environment, the economy and the least well off? In the long term, what is the best route to a low carbon economy?

- **Regeneration:** how can urban and rural policies best support each other, and promote environmental, economic and social goals together?

- **Sustainable food production:** the foot-and-mouth crisis has raised the profile of "sustainable agriculture". Can we have access to the food we need, whilst managing the land it is grown on (three-quarters of the UK landmass) in a sensitive and sustainable manner?

- **Communication:** the idea of sustainable development is absolutely crucial, but absolutely invisible to most people. What can we do about this? Can we communicate in an accessible way how the UK is performing on sustainable development?

In addition to this topic-based work, the Commission will be working with people in all sectors of society – business, devolved areas, regional organisations and local government – to develop strategies for sustainable development. We will also maintain some capacity to deal with relevant topical issues. For example, we plan to respond to the Government's current consultation exercise on the future of aviation, and to comment on the EU's emerging sustainable development strategy.

In all our work, the Commission will give a very high priority to bringing a wide range of interested people into what we are doing and keeping them involved as our work progresses. Over the coming weeks, our individual project teams will be starting to implement the specifications we have developed for each of these work streams. So, if you have views on what we are doing, or would like to contribute to it in a particular way, then please do get in touch. More detailed information about our plans for individual topics – plus a round-up of our recent activities – will shortly be published on the website.

Annex VII

The Performance and Innovation Unit

The PIU was created in July 1998, after an internal review of central government revealed there was not enough cross-cutting working and service delivery within and between Government Departments. Part of the role of the PIU is to improve the capacity of Government to address strategic, cross-cutting issues and promote innovation in the development of policy and in the delivery of the Government's objectives.

The Unit reports directly to the Prime Minister, through the head of the Civil Service, and acts as a resource for the whole of Government, tackling issues on a project basis, and focusing on long-term issues that cross public sector institutional boundaries. Although the Unit does not have a direct sustainable development remit, its very nature of promoting strategic and cross-cutting issues within central government make it an ideal method for promoting new ways of working required to help deliver sustainable development.

Influence of the unit

The Unit has a high level of influence because it is supported by high-ranking ministers and civil servants based within the Prime Minster's Office, Cabinet Office and the Treasury, and reports directly to the Prime Minister. However, the Unit is widely regarded as transparent and impartial in the way it operates because it has no role in policy delivery and is allowed to operate independently from other Departments.

The resulting project reports from the Unit are either public reports from Government with the status of Official Government Policy, or reports to Government with more restricted publication, as these are often more "think pieces" to help inform Government Policy.

The PIU relies on the strength of the analysis and recommendations within its reports to promote its role and reputation, as emphasis is laid on relevant ministers and implementing departments to launch the reports.

Selection and scoping of projects

Any projects proposed either within or outside Government are considered, if they fall within the cross-cutting, strategic remit of the Unit. For example, projects should usually:

- Involve more than one Government Department.
- Deal with long-term strategic issues.
- And could not be tackled by a more appropriate department.

The proposed project is then assessed by a steering board, consisting of senior representatives from the Prime Minister's Office, Cabinet Office, the Treasury, and other stakeholders with a good overview of Government and of the issues. If successful, the project then goes through an extended scoping period to ensure any work will not be "reinventing the wheel" and meet relevant needs. The scoped project will then need approval again by the steering board before a team is assembled which will report to an advisory group chaired by a sponsor minister who has no direct stake in the research. Work on the projects is carried out by small teams assembled both from inside and outside Government to ensure new thinking and a wide range of experience are brought to bear on the issues.

Transparency, consensus, and implementation processes

The multidisciplinarity and different organisational backgrounds of the project teams are co-ordinated and supported by the independent PIU, which encourages freedom of thought and hard-hitting analysis. This also enables the project to engage directly with important stakeholders that traditional Government Departments would find difficult. As thinking and initial results begin to emerge, they are passed on to the key stakeholders to enable them to provide valuable feedback.

As the initial results and recommendations from the project are formulated, a detailed implementation plan is drawn up for a large range of actions within Government to help address the identified issues. The draft actions are set out in such a way as to ensure that a hierarchy is established, with one or two ministers reporting on progress directly to the Prime Minister. It is the sponsor minister's role, from the initial draft actions through to the submission of the report, to negotiate agreements between identified ministers, with any unresolved issues, such as views which conflict with the analysis, being dealt with by the Prime Minister's Office. The Prime Minister then signs off the report and identified ministers report implementation progress back to him. The report is launched by the appropriate minister. The project teams are reassembled annually to help assess progress or changes that may affect their initial analysis.

Examples of reports and work

- Reaching Out: The Role of Central Government at Regional and Local Level (February 2000).
- Leadership in the Public Sector (Ongoing).
- Social, Health, Environment and Trade Objectives on the Global Stage: Developing a Common Set of Criteria and Principles to Help Deliver Government Objectives (Ongoing).
- Strategic Challenges: The Future and How to Think About It (Ongoing).
- Rural Economies (December 1999).
- Wiring it Up: Accountability and Incentives for Joined-Up Government (January 2000, see Box 4.2).

For more information go to: *www.cabinet-office.gov.uk/innovation*

Annex VIII

"Wiring It Up" – Accountability and Incentives for Joined-up Government

The Modernising Government White Paper sets out the Government's agenda for modernising the institutional framework. "Joining up Government" is an important aspect of this modernisation process and this report, carried out by the Performance and Innovation Unit (part of the Cabinet Office), was commissioned to look at how Government could better deal with cross-cutting issues, and what could be done to remove some of the barriers that stand in the way of "joining up". It is recognised that tackling issues such as sustainable development requires effective joined-up Government, as classical departmental decision-making structures tend to be poor at addressing such cross-cutting issues.

The report identifies a number of both positive and negative examples of joined-up Government, with the intention of learning from best practice. It also sets out a package of measures to improve and modernise the way the Government handles cross-cutting issues.

It includes the following aspects of the current governmental structure, which inhibit the tackling of problems and issues which cross-departmental boundaries:

- There is a tendency to take a provider-centred perspective rather than that of the service user.
- There is little incentive or reward for organisations or individuals that contribute to corporate goals or those of another department or organisation.
- The skills and capacity to develop and deliver cross-cutting solutions are often absent.
- Budgets and organisational structures are arranged around vertical, functional lines (education, health, defence, etc.) rather than horizontal, cross-cutting problems and issues (social exclusion, sustainable development, etc.).
- Systems of accountability (*e.g.* audit) and the way risk is handled can militate against innovative cross-cutting working.
- And the centre is not always effective at giving clear strategic direction, and mechanisms for resolving conflicts between departments can be weak, leaving local service providers to wrestle with the consequences.

This report recommends action in the following six key areas to improve the formulation and management of cross-cutting policies and services. Examples from each of these sectors are given below.

Effective leadership for cross-cutting policies and services

- Cross-cutting activity should be more visibly valued and rewarded.
- Ministers and senior civil servants should act as "champions" for cross-cutting policies and services and so help to create a culture conducive to cross-cutting working.

336

- And departmental loyalties should be progressively replaced by corporate and cross-cutting ties to the Government's overall aims and objectives.

Improving cross-cutting policy making

- There should be more effective channels for Government to receive views from service users and those delivering programmes about areas where more cross-cutting working is needed.

- And better use should be made of the knowledge and experience of outside experts and practitioners who are not constrained by departmental boundaries. They should be brought more fully into the policy-development process.

Skills for cross-cutting policies and services

- There should be more movement and interchange of staff within and outside the Civil Service to encourage the acquisition of necessary skills.

More flexibility in the funding of cross-cutting policies

- Further changes should be made to the Treasury's budgetary rules to make it easier for Departments to move money between years, organisations and budgets to promote cross-cutting working.

Audit and external scrutiny of cross-cutting policies and services

- Any barriers or disincentives to cross-cutting working due to audit and inspection systems should be minimised.

- And changes in Parliamentary procedures which promote the scrutiny of policies that cross departmental boundaries should be encouraged, including for example the creation of more cross-cutting Select Committees in both Houses of Parliament.

Getting the role of the centre right

- Articulating corporate goals and cross-cutting objectives, and securing buy-in to them from Departments and deliverers.

- Identifying where important cross-cutting links are not being made, or best practice is not being spread, and challenging those shortcomings.

- And sorting out conflicts of priorities where these threaten delivery of corporate goals and cross-cutting objectives.

The central message of the report is that simply removing barriers to cross-cutting working is not enough: more needs to be done if cross-cutting policy initiatives are to hold their own against purely departmental objectives.

Annex IX

Decision Making for Waste Management

Best Practical Environmental Options (BPEO) is defined as; "the outcome of a systematic consultative and decision-making procedure which emphasises the protection and conservation of the environment across land, air and water. The BPEO procedure establishes, for a given set of objectives, the option that provides the most benefit or least damage to the environment as a whole, at an acceptable cost, in the long term as well as the short term".

According to this definition, the BPEO could be whatever one wishes it to be since the procedure is established "for a given set of objectives". Indeed, some representatives of the waste management industry are quite candid in expressing the view that the BPEO for municipal waste can be whatever one wants it to be. This can be seen as one reason why the UK has continued to landfill so much waste even though the Waste Framework Directive, and the whole thrust of European waste policy, is to move waste management away from disposal to landfill, and to maximise recovery of materials through composting and recycling. Where this is not possible, recovery of energy is recommended.

In some respects, the BPEO principle appeared to be a way of enabling local authorities to arrive at their own judgements concerning municipal waste. That the conclusion that most of them reached was that they would continue landfilling might have given cause for concern. That it did not, can be seen as a consequence of the lack of resources put into waste management, since landfill is cheap. The financing of waste management occurs partly through locally raised taxes and partly through central government grants made on a formulaic basis. These together are intended to cover the costs of a range of activities undertaken by Local Authorities, of which waste management is only one. The lack of priority accorded to sustainability concerns in Local Government (at least until very recently) has led to the emphasis being placed on minimising the costs of waste management, a process which was given further impetus by the introduction of Compulsory Competitive Tendering (CCT) for Local Authority contracts. CCT has now been superseded by a new framework, that of Best Value, in which the lowest cost tender is not necessarily accepted as the best. Furthermore, under Best Value, Local Authorities are advised to set challenging targets for continuous improvement within contract terms.

In the mid-1990s, what is now the Environment Agency chose to embark upon a major programme in Life-Cycle Assessment (LCA). The ultimate aim was to produce a software tool which could be used by Local Authorities in designing strategies for waste management. This tool, WISARD, was launched late in 1999 by the Agency after a peer review process, which was extremely critical of the tool (the results of the review have not been published), and a number of trials by Local Authorities.

The tool presents information for different, user-specified waste management systems on the associated burdens, "direct" and "avoided" (through displacement of other processes).

The Agency has also been investigating combining this information with environmental valuation data, presumably so as to produce an externality assessment of waste management options. Note the implied cost-benefit aspect of the BPEO definition, towards which this type of approach would appear to be moving.

The danger here is that one of the other aspects of the BPEO definition – the need for systematic consultation – appears to be slipping by the wayside. The tool does not (and arguably cannot) lead unequivocally towards the making of a decision. It leaves the user to trade off dioxin emissions from incinerators against car journeys made to recycling banks which may or may not be made specifically for that purpose. In addition, it captures only flows of pollution rather than intangibles, such as loss of amenity, visual intrusion, etc., which would appear to be significant. It also takes no account of employment effects. To the extent, therefore, that the tool is used by decision makers, it can be used either as part of an open consultation process, in which the other aspects of waste management are considered in making decisions, or it can be used as a means through which experts/decision makers make judgements as to which approach is the best one. Almost by implication, the time and resources spent on developing the tool, and the absence of time and resources spent on other approaches, suggest that the more open consultative process will be the exception rather than the norm.

WISARD is still being used by Local Authorities in the development of their strategies. The implicit rationale for WISARD now stands challenged by the implementation of statutory targets for recycling and minimisation, and indeed, the Agency official responsible for WISARD has been critical of the statutory targets for "not being the BPEO" even though, as discussed above, the BPEO is ill defined. The suggestion is that the Agency, despite its remit to promote sustainable development in its broader sense, perceived its duties rather narrowly. Its interpretation of how the BPEO could be determined has been overly technical, with an over-dependence upon information from life-cycle inventories.

Annex X

New GM Commission

The Agriculture and Environment Biotechnology Commission (AEBC), set up in June 2000, will advise the Government on any Genetic Modification issues that have an impact on agriculture and the environment. It will also look at the ethical and acceptability issues surrounding GM technology. The members of the Commission will come from a wide range of backgrounds, with experience of consumer and environmental issues, as well as farming, science, ethics and the biotechnology industry.

The remit of the Commission is to:

- Offer strategic advice to Government on biotechnology issues which impact on agriculture and the environment.
- Liaise closely with, but not duplicate the work of, the other two bodies which, together with the AEBC, form a new strategic advisory framework. They are: the Human Genetics Commission (HGC), which will advise on genetic technologies and their impact on humans; and the Food Standards Agency (FSA), which will include within its responsibilities all aspects of the safety and use of genetically modified food and animal feed.
- Keep under review current and possible future developments in biotechnology with actual or potential implications for agriculture and the environment.
- Advise Government on the ethical and social implications arising from these developments and their public acceptability.
- And consider and advise on any specific issues relating to relevant aspects of biotechnology, as requested by the Government.

As part of this process, the Commission is expected to:

- Identify any gaps in the regulatory and advisory framework.
- Consider the wider implications of the lessons to be learned from individual cases requiring regulatory decision.
- Advise on any changes that should be made to Government guidelines which regulatory bodies are required to follow.
- Make recommendations as to changes in the current structure of regulatory and advisory bodies.
- Co-ordinate and exchange information with the relevant regulatory and advisory bodies.
- Seek to involve and consult stakeholders and the public on a regular basis on the issues which it is considering.
- Operate in accordance with best practice for public bodies, with regard to openness, transparency, accessibility, timeliness and exchange of information.

The Commission will:

- In carrying out its work, take into account European and global developments.
- Nationally, adopt a UK perspective taking appropriate account of legal and other differences between England, Scotland, Wales and Northern Ireland.
- And draw up a work programme.

Annex XI

Good Practice in Sustainability Reporting –
The Co-operative Bank Report

In 1997, the Co-operative Bank declared its intention to produce an independently verified ethical and ecological health check of the bank's performance, "warts and all". The first two Partnership Reports were positively received: the first winning a total of seven commendations in 1999; and the second hoping to receive similar recognition in 2000. Of the 61 targets set in the last report, 39 were achieved fully, considerable progress was made on a further 15, but the bank failed to achieve 7.

Social responsibility is increasing in importance, and the Co-operative Bank has undertaken a number of initiatives over the last two years. The bank's parent, the Co-operative Wholesale Society (CWS), is committed to honest labelling policies and fair trade. The Institute of Social and Ethical Accountability launched a global ethical reporting standard, AA1000, and the Co-operative Bank became the first company in the world to adopt this standard. The Co-operative Bank is one of a small group of companies taking the UK Government's "SIGMA Project" forward, which aims to develop and test a new British standard in social and environmental management. The UK adoption of social accounting has been slow. As a result, the Co-operative Bank is calling on the UK Government, and the Company Law Review, to strongly consider the case for mandatory ethical and environmental reporting. Also, because of the generally poor standard of the independently audited ethical and environmental reports, it is also calling on the Institute of Social and Ethical Accountability to launch a standard for auditor's statements as a matter of urgency.

The bank highlighted seven groups, or partners in the report, upon whom its continued success is dependent: shareholders, customers, staff and their families, suppliers, local communities, national and international society, and past and future generations of co-operators.

Three key areas of assessment are set out, with a number of indicators associated to each. There were 61 in total in the second report and there are 67 in the third. The first key area is *delivering value*. Examples of the indicators include the following: profit before taxation; personal customer satisfaction with quality; staff satisfaction with salary and benefits package; and degree of partnership with suppliers. The second key area is *social responsibility*, which has an Ethical Policy as well as indicators, *e.g.*: ethical policy implementation; ethical policy development and customer participation; health and safety; and community involvement. The third key area is *ecological sustainability*, which has an Ecological Mission Statement as well as indicators, *e.g.*: environmental management systems; phase-out of CFCs/HCFCs/HFCs from air-conditioning systems; minimising the impact of transport on the environment; and provision of ecological financial products and services.

Targets are set against almost all of the indicators, and in the reports each of the indicators is examined in detail to assess any progress made and whether the target has been met. There is also a commentary against each indicator, explaining progress and drawing comparisons with other countries in the UK, and abroad.

The Co-operative Bank also runs a number of "special projects" for a particular financial year. This has included concepts such as the global "Rip it up, write it off" campaign to cancel "Third World" debt, and a project to enhance community involvement. The reports include sections on each of the projects written or audited by the independent auditor.

The reports contain statements from the independent auditor and from three others, one for each of the key areas outlining the fairness of the reports, the progress for the year and where improvements could be made.

Annex XII

Consultative Processes Used by the Welsh Assembly for Sustainable Development

Under section 121 of the Government of Wales Act, the National Assembly for Wales has a unique statutory obligation to… *make a scheme setting out how it proposes, in the exercise of its functions, to promote sustainable development.* An important aspect of this is the consensual government approach, which differs from that of the central UK Government.

The small-scale nature of government in Wales makes an inclusive approach far easier to attain. Many of the consultative and co-operative procedures between Government Departments, and also to a certain extent with interest groups, do not need to be conducted solely on a formal basis because of the limited numbers of individuals involved. This offers opportunities for a high degree of collaboration on most issues, especially those pertaining to sustainable development.

The inclusion of local interest groups is also an important aspect for the Welsh Assembly. Section 114 lays out the Assembly's duty to promote the interests of the voluntary sector through a formal partnership agreement. The voluntary sector, represented by the Wales Council for Voluntary Action (WCVA), is more unified than its colleagues in the UK as a whole, and this consensus has helped the consultative process in Wales. Formal partnership is also required with local government, and the Welsh Assembly must consult with business.

Evaluation of the sustainable development process at present is not externalised in Wales in the same way as in England, and some view this as a deficit. The Welsh Assembly is both an executive and a legislature (albeit with secondary legislative powers only), with a single legal identity. In principle, the Welsh Assembly has the responsibility for both policy formulation and evaluation and monitoring. In terms of relevant committees, the Agriculture and Rural Development Committee remit embraces sustainable development, along with agriculture and the development of rural economy. The Environmental Planning and Transport Committee scrutinises the Welsh Assembly's environmental performance. The Welsh Assembly is developing sustainable indicators (see below), but it is not yet clear whether there will be a statutory obligation associated with them. The Assembly does not have to report to the Environmental Audit Committee, and is hence no longer involved in the Green Ministers process. However, it is committed to seeking an external input to its statutory reports, and will be requesting the new Commission on Sustainable Development to give an overview of its policy and progress, and provide advice where appropriate. The Assembly has a legal obligation to keep its scheme under review, to report each year on its implementation, and assess its effectiveness every four years to the Welsh public. Aside from this, the Assembly does not have to report on its progress in sustainable development to an institutional body.

The sustainable development institutional framework in Wales is comparatively simple compared with the UK as a whole. Many of the roles, in terms of problem identification, policy formulation and implementation, and evaluation, merge together because of the factors concerning size outlined above and the limited number of bodies involved. The framework can be expressed spatially with the Welsh Assembly sitting above bodies such as the Welsh Development Agency (WDA), The Countryside Council for Wales (CCW) and the Environment Agency Wales (EAW). There are four Regional Committees of the Assembly, but these have no decision-making powers. Unitary local authorities (Agenda 21) form the basis of local government.

In January 2000, the Welsh Assembly released its consultation document on a sustainable development scheme for Wales, "A Sustainable Wales – Learning to Live Differently". A number of interested stakeholders (academics, representatives of key government agencies, the WCVA, the business community – although its representation was limited – and environmental bodies) formed the informal Glamorgan Building Group to help put the consultation document together. 2 000 copies of this document were sent out, as well as being posted on the Internet, and there were a total of 161 replies. The Assembly's Regional Committees held open meetings where interested organisations were invited to give presentations on the important aspects of sustainable development, and what role they thought their organisation might be able to play in the area. A consultancy has analysed the data in a two-phase approach. Phase one was to amalgamate all the comments relevant to the scheme. The resulting document is being put before the subject committees for comment, before a plenary debate in September 2000 gives the Assembly members an opportunity to specify the important aspects to be included in the scheme. Phase two is a compendium of "bright ideas" taken from the consultation process, for possible implementation under the scheme. At present, the Welsh Assembly is also preparing a consultation document for a set of sustainability indicators for Wales, building on the work done primarily by the UK central government. The consultation process will be simpler, as the scope for responses is smaller. The final scheme for sustainable development in Wales should be completed to be approved by the Assembly by November 2000. This highlights one of the big differences between the UK as a whole and Wales. The UK-wide Sustainable Development Strategy is the policy of Her Majesty's Government, and acceptance by Parliament is only required in regard to the legislative proposals to which it may give rise, while the Welsh sustainable development scheme is the property of the Assembly as a whole and therefore its approval is required.

In parallel with this exercise, the Assembly has consulted upon and finalised a strategic action plan document (*www.betterwales.com*). This indicates ways in which a wide range of policy initiatives should contribute towards sustainable development. The monitoring and reporting system put in place for this plan should help the Assembly to discharge its statutory annual sustainable development reporting obligation.

The WDA has undertaken its own consultation process on a Sustainable Development Strategy. This involved many of the same procedures as the Welsh Assembly's version outlined above. However, the process highlighted one of the problems associated with public consultation in sustainable development. Because consultation, in terms of sustainable development, tends to focus on the processes, the vast majority of the responses come from interest groups as opposed to the general public, as the public is interested only in the results of truly sustainable decision making. This illustrates the importance of the breadth of consultation across interest groups, to ensure that public opinion can be properly represented. The consultation document received a good deal of praise and the final strategy will be published after the Welsh Assembly's scheme to ensure consensus.

345

Both the Welsh Assembly and the WDA had a number of comments concerning their approaches to public consultation and important lessons to be learnt for the future. As outlined earlier, breadth of consultation is very important, and the WDA tackled this by organising face-to-face meetings with a number of the important interest groups to make sure of their contribution and to clear up any possible misunderstandings. The Welsh Assembly noted the importance of an independent domain name for a consultation document, along with associated publicity. The Welsh Assembly also indicated its initial intention, not eventually realised, to work with the WCVA on developing group working seminars which aimed to identify questions, as well as providing answers. The aim was to provide training for those involved to carry out the same process at a local level. Guidance for consultation does exist in the Assembly's declared values and in the partnership agreement with the voluntary sector. The guidance itself is quite general, mainly citing important issues to remember and highlighting the importance of time in the process.

Bibliography

DEPARTMENT OF THE ENVIRONMENT, TRANSPORT AND THE REGIONS (1999),
A Better Quality of Life: A Strategy for Sustainable Development for the United Kingdom, Cm 4345, ISBN 0 10 14352 9.

DEPARTMENT OF THE ENVIRONMENT, TRANSPORT AND THE REGIONS (1990),
This common inheritance: Britain's environmental strategy, Cm. 1200, ISBN 0 10 112002 8, HMSO.

Environmental Audit Committee Response to the UK Sustainable Development Strategy, 16 March 2000,
HC 175-i, ISBN 0 10 219600 1.

Environmental Accounts Paper: References contained in this paper:

HINTERBERGER F., F. LUKS and F. SCHMIDT-BLEEK (1997),
Ecological Economics, vol. 23, No. 1, pp. 1-14, "Material flows vs. natural capital: what makes an economy sustainable?"

RADERMACHER W. and C. STAHMER (1996),
"Material and energy flow analysis in Germany: accounting framework, information system, applications". Papers of international symposium on integrated environmental and economic accounting in heory and practice, Tokyo.

WACKERNAGEL M. and W. E. REES (1997),
"Perceptual and Structural Barriers to Investing in Natural Capital: Economics from an Ecological Footprint Perspective", Ecological Economics, Vol. 20, No. 1, pp. 3-24.

WORLD RESOURCES INSTITUTE (1997),
"Resource Flows: The Material Basis of Industrial Economies", 1709 New York Avenue, NW, Washington, DC 20006.

ECOTEC for the Department of the Environment, Transport and the Regions (2000),
Sustainable Development Research: Gaps and Opportunities.

The Urban Task Force (1999),
Towards an Urban Renaissance. Final Report of the Urban Task Force, ISBN 185112165X, Department of the Environment and Department of Transport Library.

ECOTEC for DG Regio (2000),
The European Urban Audit: Survey of the Quality of Life Perceptions of City Residents.

ENVIRONMENT AGENCY (1996),
Introductory Guidance on the Agency's Contribution to Sustainable Development, SD1.

Performance and Innovation Unit Special Report (p. 14, Annex VII).

347

CABINET OFFICE PERFORMANCE AND INNOVATION UNIT (2000),
Wiring it up: Whitehall's management of cross-cutting policies and services, ISBN 0 11 430160 3, Stationery Office.

LGMB Indicators of Sustainable Development Project, Statutory Instruments – Local Government, England, Local Government, Wales – The Local Government (Best Value) Performance Indicators Order 2000.

THE SOCIETY OF LOCAL AUTHORITY CHIEF EXECUTIVES AND SENIOR MANAGERS (SOLACE),
IDEA and the LGA have produced a Best Value Sustainability Checklist: *www.solace.org.uk*

DEPARTMENT OF THE ENVIRONMENT, TRANSPORT AND THE REGIONS (1999),
Modern local government: in touch with the people, ISBN 0 10 140142 6, Stationery Office.

DEPARTMENT OF THE ENVIRONMENT, TRANSPORT AND THE REGIONS (2000),
Waste strategy 2000 for England and Wales, Parts 1 and 2, Cm. 4693-I ISBN 0 10 146932 2 and Cm. 4693-II ISBN 0 10 146933 0, Stationery Office.

LORD MARSHALL'S REPORT on Economic Instruments and the Business Use of Energy (1998).

FINAL WEST MIDLANDS REGIONAL STRATEGY (WMRS) published in March 2000, Advantage West Midlands.

DEPARTMENT OF THE ENVIRONMENT, TRANSPORT AND THE REGIONS (1998),
Sustainable Development: "Opportunities for Change". A Consultation Paper on a Revised UK Strategy, Stationery Office.

ENVIRONMENT AUDIT COMMITTEE (1998),
Second Report on the Greening Government Initiative, HC 517-I, ISBN 0 10 554126 5, Stationery Office.

DEPARTMENT FOR INTERNATIONAL DEVELOPMENT (1997),
Eliminating world poverty: a challenge for the 21st century. White Paper on international development, Cm. 3789 ISBN 0101378920, Stationery Office.

DfID,
Strategies for Achieving the International Development Targets, *www.dfid.gov.uk/public/what/strategy_papers/target_strategy.html*

THE CABINET OFFICE (1999),
Modernising Government, Cm 4310, Stationery Office.

THE CO-OPERATIVE BANK (1999),
Partnership Report: Ethical/Ecological Report and Financial Statement. *www.co-operative-bank.co.uk/1999/index.html*

NATIONAL ASSEMBLY FOR WALES (2000),
"A Sustainable Wales – Learning to Live Differently": A Consultation Document.

OECD PUBLICATIONS, 2, rue André-Pascal, 75775 PARIS CEDEX 16
PRINTED IN FRANCE
(42 2002 05 1 P) ISBN 92-64-18747-2 – No. 51995 2002